Progress in
Applied Social Psychology

Volume 2

Progress in
Applied Social Psychology

Volume 2

Edited by
G. M. Stephenson
University of Kent at Canterbury
and
J. H. Davis
*University of Illinois
at Urbana-Champaign*

JOHN WILEY & SONS
Chichester · New York · Brisbane · Toronto · Singapore

Copyright © 1984 by John Wiley & Sons Ltd.

Library of Congress Catalog Card Number 83–641069
ISSN 0740–297X

British Library Cataloguing in Publication Data

Progress in applied social psychology.—Vol. 2
 1. Social psychology—Periodicals
 302'.05   HM251
ISBN 0 471 90361 2

Typeset by Inforum Ltd, Portsmouth
Printed in Great Britain by St. Edmundsbury Press, Suffolk

List of Contributors

BERNDT BREHMER — *University of Uppsala, Box 227, S-751 04, Uppsala, Sweden*

DAVID FRYER — *MRC Social & Applied Psychology Unit, University of Sheffield, Sheffield, S10*

JEAN F. HARTLEY — *Industrial Relations Research Unit, University of Warwick, Coventry, CV4 7AL*

CHARLES A. KIESLER — *Department of Psychology, Carnegie-Mellon University, Schenley Park, Pittsburgh, PA 15213, USA*

J. KLOFAS — *School of Criminal Justice, State University of New York at Albany, 135 Western Av., Albany NY 12222, USA*

SAMUEL KOMORITA — *Department of Psychology, University of Illinois at Urbana-Champaign, 603 East Daniel, Champaign, Illinois 61820, USA*

ALLAN E. LIND — *Department of Psychology, University of Illinois at Urbana-Champaign, 603 East Daniel, Champaign, Illinois 61820, USA*

SALLY LLOYD-BOSTOCK — *SSRC Centre for Socio-Legal Studies, Wolfson College, Oxford, OX2 6UD*

AUGUSTO PALMONARI — *Instituto di Scienze Dell'Educazione, Via Zamboni 34, 40126 Bologna*

M. L. POMBENI — *Instituto di Scienze Dell'Educazione, Via Zamboni 34, 40126 Bologna*

JACOB RABBIE — *Instituut voor Sociale Psychologie, Rijksuniversiteit Utrecht, St. Jacobsstraat 14, Utrecht, Netherlands*

PETER ROBINSON — *School of Education, University of Bristol, Helen Wodenhouse Building, 35 Berkeley Square, Bristol*

A. E. SIBULKIN — *Department of Psychology, Carnegie-Melton University, Schenley Park, Pittsburgh, Pennsylvania 15213, USA*

H. TOCH — *School of Criminal Justice, State University of New York at Albany, 135 Western Av., Albany NY 12222, USA*

Jos van Oostrum   *Institut voor Sociale Psychologie, Rijksuniversiteit Utrecht, St. Jacobstraat 14, Utrecht, Netherlands*

Laurens Walker   *University of Virginia, School of Law, Charlottesville, Virginia, USA*

Contents

Preface   ix

SECTION A – INSTITUTIONS, PROFESSIONS, AND ORGANIZATIONS

1. **The Psychology of Unemployment: A Critical Appraisal**   3
   J. Hartley and D. Fryer

2. **Episodic Length of Hospital Stay for Mental Disorders**   31
   C. A. Kiesler and A. E. Sibulkin

3. **Psychologists vs Psychologists: an Outlook on a Professional Orientation**   63
   A. Palmonari and M. L. Pombeni

4. **Social Psychology in Classrooms**   93
   W. P. Robinson

5. **Pluralistic Ignorance, Revisited**   129
   H. Toch and J. Klofas

SECTION B – GROUP DECISION-MAKING

6. **The Role of Judgment in Small-group Conflict and Decision-making**   163
   B. Brehmer

7. **The Role of Justice and Power in Reward Allocation**   185
   S. S. Komorita

8. **Environmental Uncertainty, Power, and Effectiveness in Laboratory Organizations**   207
   J. M. Rabbie and J. van Oostrum

vii

SECTION C – PSYCHOLOGY AND LAW

9.   **Legal Literature, Dialogue with Lawyers, and Research on
     Practical Legal Questions: Some Gains and Pitfalls for
     Psychology**   265
     S. M. A. Lloyd-Bostock

10. **Psychological Studies of Procedural Models**   293
     L. Walker and A. Lind

Author Index   315

Subject Index   323

Preface

The international flavour of Volume 1 is again reflected in this second volume of *Progress in Applied Social Psychology*. The chapters are grouped this time by topic area. The grouping was retrospective, and was not a guiding principle in our choice of authors. We sought out those whose work advances theoretical understanding of the issues, and we aimed to illustrate a variety of methodological approaches in different fields of application.

The five chapters in our first section illustrate this strategy. A truly international audience will be attuned to the theme of the opening chapter by Hartley and Fryer, on the psychology of unemployment. Despite the pioneering study of Jahoda and Lazarsfeld havin been conducted as long ago as 1930, the authors find that 'our understanding of psychological aspects of unemployment is still both insubstantial and narrow'. The assumption that unemployment means psychological deprivation has dominated thinking in this area; as a consequence, research has lacked analytic rigour and discovered little of practical value. They suggest a number of ways forward.

'Efficient teaching' is another universally compelling topic, and it is perhaps sad to find Robinson admitting that 'the most educationally useful results obtaind so far seem to have been constructed out of ideas that derive more from classroom folk wisdom than from theory in social psychology'. As in the study of unemployment, so for teaching, social psychologists have been too content merely to establish correlations, and too little concerned with providing explanations for the associations they discover. Interestingly, it is not that the necessary theoretical perspectives are unavailable; the problem lies rather in the failure to develop appropriate methodologies for their implementation.

Kiesler has in previous work documented the 'self-perpetuating' effect of hospitalization, and his present work with Sibulkin is designed to evaluate the successfulness or otherwise of the 'de-institutionalization' programme in the US. Perhaps alarmingly, we discover that 'the number of people hospitalized has increased sharply over the last twenty years, but that the total days of inpatient care per person have decreased'. The fact that a national policy of de-institutionalization should lead to more people being hospitalized raises social psychological questions that should challenge the applied social psychologist to further study.

Psychology students loom large in experimental investigations, but professional psychologists as a group have largely escaped scrutiny. In Italy the profession is still establishing itself, and Palmonari and Pombeni have provided a fascinating insight into the social dynamics of what is happening. Despite sharing 'social representations' in common, University and Social Services psychologists are busily differentiating themselves, and the interesting suggestion is made that only if the University psychologists' research broaches the practical concerns of their colleagues in the front line will the process be halted. How to change professional orientations is also the subject of Toch and Klofas's resurrection of social psychological interest in an institutional phenomenon first documented by F.H. Allport in the 1930s – that of *pluralistic ignorance*. Pluralistic ignorance describes a state of affairs in which members of an institution privately reject group norms in ignorance of the fact that a majority shares their deviant attitude. Several variants of this phenomenon are established in the context of a study of prison officers' 'alienation', and suggestions are made for attitude change programmes which have application beyond the particular institutional framework studied by the authors.

The study of cognitive biases in decision-making is of growing concern, and Brehmer's chapter is a welcome account of the cumulative contribution of Hammond and his associates to our understanding of the role of cognitive conflict in group decision-making. Laboratory and field studies suggest that the 'rational actor paradigm' must be replaced by the 'judgement paradigm' whose important implication is that new methods of communication between parties in dispute must be developed: evaluation of these new techniques is an urgent priority. Komorita provides a model for research in applied social psychology in which policy evaluation is given a key mediating role between theoretically based laboratory research and decision-making in the real world. A review of the mainly laboratory literature on bargaining argues for the importance of both equity norms and the distribution of power, and Komorita suggests a number of hypotheses that may be tested in studies of real-life collective bargaining. By way of contrast, Rabbie and von Osstrum report a programme of research which was designed to test organizational theories in small laboratory groups. In the past decade or so 'contingency' theories have predominated in the study of organizational behaviour. Naturalistic evidence for anything but the broadest propositions of contingency theory is not strong, and Rabbie and Oostrum's work is a bold attempt to assess the validity of detailed hypotheses regarding the fit between environmental uncertainty and organizational structure.

The application of psychology to law is well represented in journals covering all branches of psychology. The first of our contributions on law and psychology in this volume considers rather the usefulness of law to psychologists. In a variety of ways law is a *resource* for psychologists, social psychologists in particular. It may well be said that law has in the past been exploited by experimental social psychologists seeking a quick route to relevance. Lloyd-Bostock suggests that a different strategy – one that takes seriously the study of legal literature and establishes a dialogue, if not negotiation, with lawyers – will prove more worthwhile. Lawyer and psychologist in collaboration are represented in the final chapter of the volume, by Walker and Lind. This provides a welcome review of the advanced state of the art in the study of 'procedural justice' using the techniques of experimental social psychology. Reading both chapters, it becomes clear, nevertheless, that the potential for collaboration between lawyer and psychologist in the study of procedural justice has not yet been fully exploited. A detailed study of existing forms, their justification and use by the parties, is urgently required. This is why, in the Preface to Volume 1, we asserted that the applied approach to social psychology will produce better theories, and why we suggested that social psychology should be regarded essentially as an applied discipline. Social psychology shares with other social science disciplines the fact that its conclusions are subject to the judgement of those whose behaviour it investigates.

Social psychology will be judged, however, by the extent to which it provides a theoretically *distinctive* contribution to our understanding of social life and institutions: we cannot pretend to provide all the answers. The recent rapid growth in applied social psychology may be regarded as providing a pragmatic resolution to the so-called 'crisis' in social psychology. As is evident from the contributions to this second volume, those from the 'laboratory' end of the spectrum more directly address issues of social and practical consequence, and those employing social psychological techniques in the study of social problems feel better able to contribute to theoretical debate. Social psychologists need to become more immersed in the critical concerns of law, industrial relations, education and other fields of application in order to ensure that theories are both better informed and more useful. The problem is how to do this whilst maintaining the integrity and distinctiveness of its own field and viewpoint. We expect future volumes to provide some of the answers.

Geoffrey Stephenson
James Davis

SECTION A

Institutions, Professions, and Organizations

Progress in Applied Social Psychology, Volume 2
Edited by G.M. Stephenson and J.H. Davis
© 1984 John Wiley & Sons Ltd

1

The Psychology of Unemployment: A Critical Appraisal

JEAN HARTLEY
University of Warwick
and
DAVID FRYER
University of Sheffield

INTRODUCTION

In this chapter we critically appraise psychological research on adult unemployment. We start with the literature providing an indication of the state of the art. We go on to offer some criticisms of the literature in terms of its content, methodology, theoretical paucity, value orientation, and narrow psychologistic focus. However, research should not be evaluated only by what it says, those issues on which it is silent are also revealing, so we conclude constructively by indicating a range of topics at present under-researched, whose investigation would greatly extend our understanding of the field.

Our review of the literature is intentionally brief and selective. We concern ourselves here primarily with adult unemployment rather than the joblessness of school-leavers. Some similarity in the consequences of the two might reasonably be expected at an appropriate level of analysis, given that they both involve non-employment. However, adult unemployment generally involves leaving the labour market and problems of maintaining financial viability whilst school-leaver joblessness involves failing to join the labour market and problems of achieving financial independence. Also there are great differences in potential sources of social interaction, personal identity, and esteem. For all these reasons adult and youth unemployment merit separate consideration. Besides, there is a burgeoning literature on youth unemployment, reflecting current governmental concerns, to which we refer the interested reader (Gurney, 1981; Carroll, 1979; Stafford *et al.*, 1980; Roberts *et al.*, 1981, 1982). Actually we do not even attempt a detailed and exhaustive survey of studies of adult unemployment since others have written literature reviews (Jahoda and Rush, 1980; Eisenberg and Lazarsfeld, 1938; Mackay and Haines, 1982; Liem and Rayman, 1982).

Nevertheless, our literature review does include the most substantial and influential studies in the field. We restrict the detail of our survey to allow space to concentrate upon what we believe are a number of cogent criticisms. Whilst we are not alone in criticizing a number of studies (e.g. Gurney and Taylor 1981) we do have some original points to make.

The main burden of this chapter is that our understanding of the field does not constitute such an advanced state of knowledge as is sometimes rather optimisitically claimed. It is often suggested, for example, that the psychology of unemployment has been extensively, even exhaustively researched, resulting in the uncontroversial establishment of the main consequences. Hill (1977), for example, describing the results of some research, claims that 'broader based research is unlikely to modify these findings greatly'. We feel, on the contrary, that even six years later our understanding of psychological aspects of unemployment is still both insubstantial and narrow. To support this claim we now proceed to a brief summary of the research literature before embarking on its critical appraisal.

THE LITERATURE ON UNEMPLOYMENT

Fundamentally, the literature is concerned with what the effects of unemployment are, rather than, for example, the causes of the effects. Reports of effects are the result of a range of studies using a range of methodologies and techniques such as interviews (Marsden and Duff, 1975; Gould and Kenyon, 1972; Fagin, 1981; Seabrook 1982); other qualitative methods (Zawadski and Lazarsfeld, 1935; Beales and Lambert, 1934); sociographic method (Jahoda *et al*, 1933/1972); quantified psychological (Warr, 1978; Hartley, 1978); quantified psychiatric (Hepworth, 1980; Shanthamani, 1973); physiological (Cobb and Kasl, 1977); and community aggregate (Brenner, 1973; Catalano *et al.*, 1981). Often evidence from a range of approaches is cited indiscriminately in favour of a particular hypothesis, a practice which is worrying, given that often the studies are addressing rather different questions (Dooley and Catalano, 1982). Whilst still concerned with effects an increased level of sophistication is to suggest that families of effects are grouped together for example in time (according to stage accounts, e.g. Eisenberg and Lazarsfeld, 1938; Kaufman, 1982; Swinburne, 1981) or in subgroups of the unemployed population, according to moderating variables (Hepworth, 1980; Warr *et al.*, 1983).

Psychopathological Effects

It has become common to begin assessments of the psychological impact of unemployment with evidence of its overtly pathological effect, on the basis that if such damage can be observed in some, there is likely to be less overt but still considerable psychological trauma in others. Most popular in the marshalling of this evidence have been Brenner and his associates (Brenner 1967, 1971, 1973, 1977). Brenner attempts to correlate community indicators of economic performance with indicators of pathological stress, for example, suicide levels, psychiatric hospital admissions and deaths due to certain illnesses such as cardiovascular dysfunction. The investigation of association involves certain assumptions about the economic and psychopathological indicators and the time lag between the two. First conducted in the USA, attempts have been made in other countries to replicate the findings. Results are controversial but indicate at least tentative support for an association between psychopathology and negative economic indicators.

Some individual level research has focused on investigating physical health symptoms in unemployed samples. The most notable and important study is that of Cobb and Kasl (1977). In a number of papers, they report on their study of 100 manual workers from two US manufacturing plants. The study, conducted over two years, followed the all-male sample from the announcement of job termination through unemployment and, for some, re-employment. A range of health indicators were recorded, including the recording of physical ailments and the taking of blood and urine samples for biochemical analysis. Importantly, there was a control group of matched men in stable employment, from whom identical measures were taken. Physical indicators of stress were higher for the unemployed group during all phases, including for many, the immediate period of re-employment, but the association was relatively weak.

Psychological Effects

It is often asserted that, given the values attached to occupation in western societies, unemployment is damaging to mental health (e.g. Tausky and Piedmont, 1967; Hayes and Nutman, 1981). The evidence for this assertion has been documented in general terms with measures of psychological well-being or broad psychiatric vulnerability, and with more specific psychological indicators of distress.

A number of studies have suggested that unemployment has a major impact on general psychological well-being. This is asserted in a wide variety of impressionistic accounts of unemployment (e.g. Marsden and Duff, 1975; Gould and Kenyon, 1972; Seabrook, 1982) but also in studies utilizing psychometric measures. The study by Warr (1978) of 1655 steel-workers six months after plant closure found a significant decrease in present life satisfaction with a strong correlation between age and dissatisfaction. Hepworth (1980) also indicated a decrease in present life satisfaction among a group of 78 unemployed men. A decrease in general well-being was also noted for the studies conducted during the 1930s, reviewed by Eisenberg and Lazarsfeld (1938) and touched on by Jahoda (1982). Warr (1983a) details much of the recent UK research on global measures of well-being during unemployment.

The reverse perpsective on well-being involves examining psychiatric vulnerability. A number of studies using a self-report instrument indicating minor psychiatric morbidity, the General Health Questionnaire (Goldberg, 1972), have suggested that certain groups of unemployed people are more likely to experience psychological problems, particularly associated with anxiety and depression, than members of the general population (Payne et al., 1983; Hepworth, 1980). This instrument has also been used in youth studies (e.g. Stafford et al., 1980). Liem and Liem (1979) in a study of 80 unemployed men matched with 80 employed men from a variety of occupations, found that being unemployed was strongly associated with higher levels of psychiatric symptoms than the controls, based on interviews. Fagin (1981) also uses case-study material, again interview-based, to document in some considerable detail the increased vulnerability to psychiatric impairment. Other interview-based studies have also reported a general decrement in well-being (see, e.g. Hill, 1977; Shepherd, 1981; Stokes, 1981; Tiffany et al., 1970).

Of self-reported complaints about the effects of unemployment, the investigation of self-esteem has been the central focus. Although this is a complex concept (Hartley, 1980b), a number of studies have attempted to investigate both it and related concepts such as identity, lack of self-confidence, lack of self-worth and so forth (see e.g. Komarovsky, 1940; Tausky and Piedmont, 1967; Hill, 1978; Bakke, 1933; Eisenberg and Lazarsfeld, 1938; Jahoda et al., 1971; Swinburne, 1981; Beales and Lambert, 1973). Generally a link between unemployment and falling self-esteem is asserted. Where quantitative techniques have been used, the data are more equivocal or complex (Hartley, 1980; Kasl et al., 1975; Tiffany et al., 1970; Kingsley, 1976), that is, self-esteem falling in some cases and increasing in others with unemployment. However, a number of texts on unemployment or coping with unemployment continue to emphasize a decrease in self-esteem (Kinn, 1973; Powell, 1973) and it is also mentioned frequently in labour economic or sociological studies of redundancy and unemployment (e.g. Daniel, 1972; Wedderburn, 1965).

The social isolation of the unemployed was commented on in the studies of the 1930s (e.g. Komarovsky, 1940; Jahoda et al., 1972) and is a recurrent theme in studies in the last decade. Komarovsky (1940) noted that: 'the social isolation of the family is truly striking. The typical family in our group . . . for months at a time does not have social contacts with anyone outside the family'. Social isolation is reported to increase with length of unemployment with the long-term unemployed cut off from community and friendship networks, occasioned partly by financial deprivation and partly by a sense of shame about being unemployed (Komarovsky, 1940; Hill, 1978; Harrison, 1976; Bakke, 1933).

The use of time was examined by Jahoda *et al.*, (1972) in their study of an unemployed community in Austria. Subjects were encouraged to record their activities in diaries and were timed by observers as they moved between locations. It was reported that the sense of time atrophied or disintegrated, with punctuality for the few remaining arrangements disappearing and days only crudely divided into mornings and afternoons. Boredom is also reported as a major problem for many unemployed people (Hepworth, 1980; Hill, 1978; Marsden and Duff, 1975). Depression, apathy, resignation, lowered expectations and blunted ambition are also frequently reported (Eisenberg and Lazarsfeld, 1938; Hill, 1978) and more behavioural studies have confirmed that activities may become restricted even where facilities do not require financial expenditure. In the sociographic study of Marienthal (Jahoda *et al.*, 1972) the use of community clubs declined and library-book borrowing declined even though loan charges were abolished. A sharp decline in self-reported activities costing money has been found (Warr and Payne, 1983; Morley-Bunker, 1982).

The effects of unemployment on the family have been discussed since the early pioneering studies and commentaries of the 1930s (Komarovsky, 1940; Cavan and Ranke, 1938; Eisenberg and Lazarsfeld, 1938). A number of studies have reported increased friction and stress within the family (Fagin, 1981; Liem and Liem, 1979; Tausky and Piedmont, 1967), attributing this to unemployment, although it is important to note that Komarovsky found that the quality of family relationships depended crucially on family interaction patterns prior to unemployment.

STAGES OF UNEMPLOYMENT

A refinement on simply reporting effects of unemployment is to suggest that those effects occur in a set order in time or in set patterns across the population. A large number of writers agree that the impact of unemployment changes over time and with it the reactions of the individual. The attitudes and feelings of someone who is long-term unemployed are likely to be different from those of someone who has only been out of work a month or two. It is frequently suggested that these changes occur in stages, with recognizable psychological characteristics associated with each stage. The stage model described by Eisenberg and Lazarsfeld (1938) has become most famous. In reviewing a number of studies they suggested a common thread in the descriptions. There is first shock, followed by an active hunt for a job, during which time the individual is still optimistic and unresigned. Thirdly, as efforts fail, the individual becomes resigned and adapts to a new state by limiting demands and expectations. Hill (1977) talks of stages of 'initial response', 'intermediate phase' and 'settling down to unemployment' commenting on the similarity with the 1930s studies Harrison (1976) claims that most groups 'still go through the shock-optimisim-pessimism-fatalism sequence when they experience prolonged unemployment for the first time'.

Other phase-progression models have been put forward to describe changes in unemployment although they do not describe the same pattern of response. The model by Fink (1967), developed to describe reactions to a crisis, has been applied to job loss and unemployment (e.g. Kingsley, 1976). Not all accounts agree on the stages, or even numbers of stages through which people allegedly pass. Briar (1977) distinguishes two phases: optimism and 'joblessness as a way of life'; Beales and Lambert (1973, first published 1934) distinguish optimism, pessimism, and fatalism, and Zawadski and Lazarfeld (1935) settle for a seven-stage model. Kaufman (1982) goes for four portmanteau stages: shock, relief, and relaxation; concerted effort; vacillation, self-doubt, and anger; resignation and withdrawal.

Moderator Variables

It has been increasingly emphasized, as research has progressed, that there is not a single effect of unemployment which occurs in all unemployed people but a range of experiences depending on a range of factors known as moderating variables: age, sex, social class, occupational status, financial position, and more individual factors such as length of unemployment, degree of social support, and employment commitment have been mooted in the literature.

Length of unemployment has frequently been cited as a variable negatively affecting the experience of unemployment (Hill 1977; Harrison, 1976; Marsden and Duff, 1975; Hepworth, 1980) but there are many contradictory findings (Kasl, 1979; Goodchild and Smith 1963; Feather and Davenport, 1981). Recent thinking suggests that moderating variables may sometimes be interactive. For example, it seems that length of unemployment and decreased well-being are associated but only in middle-aged people; in younger and older people measures of psychological distress and length of unemployment and distress are generally associated for men but not for women overall.

The work of Gore (1978) stands out for the excellence of her investigation of the family and social-support network of unemployed men, finding that greater social support ameliorated distress. Although reference is frequently made to financial position (Harrison, 1976; Jahoda, 1982), little has so far been done to investigate it systematically or to find ways of disentangling the effects of unemployment from those of poverty.

Occupational status has been widely discussed as a moderator but conclusions are difficult to draw as more skilled employees have greater financial resources, greater psychological resources, and a better position in the labour market (Slater, 1975; Hartley, 1978; Jahoda, 1982). Moreover, results have generally been depicted dichotomously with an over-simplified distinction being made between managerial/professional and other occupations. Employment commitment, earlier called 'work involvement', was first investigated by Warr (see Warr, 1982, for summary) although it has been used in other studies of adults (Hepworth, 1980) and school-leavers (Stafford *et al.*, 1980). It has generally been found that those with a strong motivation to be employed are distressed psychologically by being unable to find work.

Discovery and precise description of the variety of effects of unemployment on a range of people are of vital importance in understanding the psychology of unemployment but are not, in themselves, that understanding. Fully to explain a phenomenon we need to know not only what occurs but how and why it occurs, that is, what causes the effects we document. Unfortunately, the literature is less than forthcoming about the reasons why the reported deleterious psychological consequences of unemployment occur, that is, theories of the psychology of unemployment.

The nearest we come to a theory of the psychology of unemployment is not so much explicitly stated as implicit in the literature: that the essential psychological problem of unemployment is that of employment deprivation. We are not here talking about financial deprivation, which in our society is unfortunately manifest, but of the alleged psychological deprivation which accompanies unemployment.

The psychological deprivation approach maintains that a person's manifest intention in becoming employed, that is to earn money, also brings about, perhaps even enforces, other (latent) functions, which though unintended are of great value to the employee. Latent functions of employment suggested up to now (Jahoda, 1979; Sofer, 1970) include: imposition of a time structure on day and week; shared contact and experience outside the home; linking with values and projects outside oneself: enforcement of activity; achievement and opportunities for testing and affirming competence. Upon becoming unemployed, these latent consequences are lost and sorely missed, with deleterious psychological effect.

The deprivation approach has been a regular theme in unemployment research, underlying most of the literature since the 1930s, and is still central today in the work of Warr (1982), Jahoda (1979), Kelvin (1980), Hill (1978) and others. Work is argued to be psychologically advantageous, or even psychologically necessary (Hill, 1977), for mental health and well-being; being deprived of such opportunities therefore causes a variety of deleterious psychological effects. These writers often give extended descriptions of the psychological benefits of work, and these assertions are now being picked up and reiterated in the secondary literature (e.g. Hayes and Nutman, 1981).

PROBLEMS WITH THE RESEARCH FINDINGS

In spite of assertions that the psychology of unemployment has been extensively, even exhaustively researched we feel that current understanding of
psychological aspects of unemployment is both insubstantial and narrow.
There are a number of major problems with the literature.

The Empirical Base

It is often suggested that psychological studies of unemployment are numerous.
For example, Hayes and Nutman (1981) indicate that they studied over 200
articles on unemployment in order to write their book. It is sometimes noted
that the influential Eisenberg and Lazarsfeld (1938) paper contains 112 references. However, on close examination, one finds that although the number of
commentaries on unemployment is large, the number of empirically-based
studies is, in sharp contrast, disturbingly small. A lot of the claims about
unemployment are based on the small number of influential studies of the
1930s but leaving those aside for the moment, at the time of going to press we
were able to find less than 40 empirically based studies of post-1930s adult
unemployment (as opposed to redundancy studies) from a predominantly
psychological perspective (even this is a generous estimate since we include
studies such as those by Marsden and Duff which are not, in intellectual origin,
psychological).

   While accepting that our trawl may not have been exhaustive (it only
includes British and American studies in any case) it is still more extensive than
many other citations. For example, imposing our own criteria on the biblio-
graphy of Jahoda and Rush (1980) produces an empirical base of 6 studies.
Hayes and Nutman (1981) make reference to 11 post-1930s empirical studies
of unemployment. On the basis of these small numbers of actual projects
(articles and papers are of course more extensive since a project can produce a
number of articles) it certainly seems premature to be certain that we can
describe, much less understand, the psychological effects of unemployment.

   Although 40 projects may sound substantial, we argue below that some of
these are far from satisfactory on methodological, theoretical, and other
grounds. Additionally, given that the experience of unemployment can vary in
objective terms according to financial position, labour market experience,
duration of worklessness and so forth, the studies cannot possibly cover the
range of experiences and effects adequately. The main point, however, is that
once commentaries and secondary literatures have been set aside the evidence
for psychological effects is sometimes less than is claimed.

Use of 1930s Material

It is striking, and somewhat disturbing, that the most widely quoted accounts and descriptions of the psychological impact of unemployment derive from studies done in the 1930s and commentaries on such research: for example, Jahoda *et al*. (1972); Eisenberg and Lazarsfeld (1938); Bakke (1933; 1940); Pilgrim Trust (1938); Beales and Lambert (1973). It may be that the psychological effects of unemployment described in the 1930s are equally true of today's unemployed. However, that equivalence needs to be demonstrated, instead of being merely assumed.

There are a number of reasons for questioning the extent of the relevance of these classics to the contemporary employment situation. As has been pointed out (Jahoda, 1979, 1982; Fraser, 1981; Gurney and Taylor, 1981) there have been changes both in financial provision and in moral climate surrounding employment and unemployment in the last 50 years. The 1930s studies were set in a particular historical and social context, and it remains an empirical question as to how far results located in one historico-cultural niche are generalizable to another. It cannot be assumed that the psychological effects remain constant, or even similar, though the 1930s research may be classics and as such can be fertile sources for suggesting further lines of investigation.

To take just one example, Fryer and Payne (1984) looked at level of unemployment and public-library use in the South Yorkshire region over the years 1975–81 in an attempt to replicate the decrease in such use reported in the Marienthal study. In contrast to 1930s Austria, in the late 1970s in the UK public-library use was found overall to increase, albeit slowly, with increased unemployment.

Methodological Considerations

The function of a good research design is to examine a situation in such a way that possible alternative interpretations of results can be excluded. This is especially important when there are many variables to consider. Unfortunately this ideal is seldom realizable with psychological research on unemployment. Of course, in dealing with a complex human situation such as unemployment it is not always possible to use the rigorous scientific procedures of the experimental laboratory, even if one had confidence in other respects in such procedures. Nevertheless, there are aspects of research design to which careful attention could and should be paid. Firstly, the majority of studies of the unemployed have been cross-sectional. Although there are exceptions (Cobb and Kasl, 1977; Goodchild and Smith, 1963), a number of studies have consisted of interviews or questionnaire completion at one point in time. There is nothing wrong with cross-sectional studies *per se*; they can often be extremely revealing of subgroup differences. The problem arises when causation is inferred from a cross-sectional design. Two forms of inappropriate inference about causation are prevalent in the literature. One involves using a research design with people having been unemployed for different lengths of time and from that inferring the psychological stages or processes of unemployment. Hill (1977) for example used single interviews to substantiate his view of stages, with different people illustrating each stage. There is no comment in the text about the difficulties of cross-sectional inference to a phase-progression model. Swinburne (1981) discusses the stages model in her study of unemployed managers although the evidence she presents cannot actually be used either to substantiate or reject the model. In contrast, Kingsley (1976) does acknowledge this kind of methodological problem in her study, using Fink's (1967) model, although the problems cannot be overcome with her design.

Another form of inappropriate causal inference is where a research design involves interviewing people after they have become unemployed and then inferring that changes have taken place which are due to unemployment. For example, a popular assertion is that unemployment causes a breakdown in family relations, or that unemployment causes loss of self-esteem, yet generally there is no evidence as to what family relations or self-esteem were like prior to unemployment. Often only circumstantial or uncorroborated evidence is available, for example the person reports a change. Until more longitudinal research is carried out genuine understanding of the psychology of unemployment will be severely circumscribed.

A second major problem of research design concerns the lack of adequate control groups, or even at times control groups at all. Clearly there are practical problems associated with the use of control groups but selective and cautious use could be enlightening about the degree of the effects of unemployment. In some cases this could be achieved by using individuals as their own controls, as in before/after job loss or in unemployment/re-employment studies, or by selecting a group of employed people matched on a number of variables (e.g. demographic characteristics) with whom to compare the unemployed on a number of specific variables. That control groups can provide valuable additional material is demonstrated by a number of studies (e.g. Warr, 1978; Stafford et al., 1980; and Hartley 1980b), where indication is given of the prevalence or strength of a variable amongst the employed.

A third major design problem concerns ambiguities in the collection of data. In part this stems from a clear bias in the field for linguistic rather than behavioural data. It is clear that what people say, what people think and what people do may not always be strongly related. Even with the least biased methods of elicitation, the most we can hope to find out is what people are able and willing to say in public about what they think the researcher wants to know. This is made even more difficult, in studying unemployment, by the guilt and shame generally attached to being unemployed. A number of studies have not addressed themselves to such problems of image presentation and rationalization, instead taking at face value the verbal information given by the unemployed person. Psychologists could pay more attention to verbal accounts of those close to the unemployed. Additionally, they could make considerably more use of *behavioural* data. For example, we know many unemployed complain of being lonely or bored but little evidence has yet accumulated on how time is spent or what activities people become engaged in. The Marienthal study (Jahoda *et al.*, 1972) was exemplary in using a variety of observation and interview techniques in combination; this methodological variety has only been approached subsequently by Cobb and Kasl (1977).

Fourthly, many studies have inadequately conceptualized the variables they discuss. A favourite method of many researchers has been to conduct 'semi-structured', or 'open-ended' interviews with the unemployed. Frequently no indication is provided as to how concepts were operationally defined and how data were analysed. It is then impossible to tell whether what one researcher describes as 'loss of confidence' has anything to do with that to which another researcher refers when using the term. Frequently there is no means for resolving this uncertainty. One consequence is that studies cannot be replicated (or whatever the nearest applied research equivalent is) and hence also cannot easily be invalidated. A cluster of terms develop which may, or may not, refer to the same psychological phenomenon. For example, when researchers talk of loss of self-esteem, loss of self-confidence, loss of self-worth, feeling inferior, or loss of morale, we do not know whether these terms refer to the same phenomenon. While there are numerous cogent criticisms of quantitative research it has at least the merit of forcing the researcher to articulate and operationalize key variables in a way which other researchers can understand and employ themselves.

In addition to these over-arching methodological problems, specific research techniques may raise their own issues of interpretation. The aggregate level approach (for example Brenner, 1967, 1971, 1973, 1977) seeks to establish whether aggregate economic indicators (for example unemployment) are statistically associated, after an appropriate time lag, with community-level indices of pathology (for example psychiatric hospitalizations). Controversy surrounds both the statistics and the indicators. How far do official figures of unemployment embrace the social psychologically people at risk? How far does psychiatric hospitalization reflect the true level of mental illness? Controversy also surrounds the lagging period. How should its length be determined? There is a disquieting tendency to adopt different lagging periods for different countries. The issue is crucial since the adoption of different lagging periods may suggest pathology is associated with economic boom rather than slump. Additionally, aggregate suicide increase following unemployment rate increase cannot establish that the unemployed person is any more likely to commit suicide than anyone else in the community.

The failure to consider or discuss the concept of unemployment itself has serious methodological consequences in terms of identifying and choosing samples of the unemployed for research. In studying unemployment, psychologists are essentially interested in it as a social psychological phenomenon, yet generally the official government definition of unemployment is implicitly used, which means that samples are chosen from the official register of the unemployed. As well as leading to a bias towards male unemployed samples (since more men register than women) this fails to take into account the subjective definitions of unemployment which could be important in understanding worklessness and unemployment in our society.

Theoretical Considerations

Theoretical under-pinnings of the research on the psychology of unemployment have been deficient in a number of ways. Firstly, a number of studies lack any clear or articulated theoretical framework at all and instead merely give an account of 'what it feels like to be unemployed'. To the extent that it does this the psychological literature is fundamentally descriptive and lacking in analytical insight. Description is, of course, a necessary starting point for any form of scientific or systematic enquiry and so this is not in itself a criticism. However, it is arguable that the present state of psychological knowledge concerning unemployment is barely more insightful than a lay person's understanding, being essentially a redescription using the specialized jargon of social science. There is an urgent need to go beyond this.

The lack of theoretical development is in part due to a lack of elementary conceptual analysis of the concepts of unemployment and employment. We will briefly explore these in turn. The concept of unemployment is rarely discussed. It would appear to have several components, which are each important in its definition. Official definitions vary not only between countries (Sorrentino, 1981) but in the same country at different times. In the UK employment is recorded where the person registers with the Department of Employment as unemployed. In late 1982, registration was made non-compulsory for those who sought financial aid from the state and it had the effect of taking a considerable number of people out of the official statistics. Even before this change, it was recognized that official statistics systematically under-recorded the number of unemployed, particularly of women. In order to be officially recorded as unemployed an individual has to be of working age (i.e. between 16 and 65, or 60 for women) and to be seeking employment or self-employment. In other words, the individual must be seeking to re-enter the labour force. For macroeconomic purposes these two components (of working age, seeking to re-enter the labour force) are sufficient but social-psychological analysis might wish to recognize that the category of the unemployed has more blurred boundaries than that. 'Discouraged workers' are those who cease to look for work perhaps because they recognize that it will be difficult to obtain.

Unregistered, these people often include a large number of women and those nearing retirement. They may have very similar experiences and life-styles to those who are registered unemployed. What are the features distinguishing discouraged workers from the unemployed? Financial need is likely to be one variable, but some research also suggests that self-definition is significant in the case of women for example. (Martin and Roberts, 1984; Cragg and Dawson, 1983). If social psychological analysis is about the effects of being without employment then the fuzzy boundaries of the category are important for analysis. There may be not a single, obvious category of 'the unemployed' (however attractive the use of an official definition is) but rather a set of states.

Understanding the concept of unemployment can be also considered by examining what can be contrasted with it. For psychologists, the concepts of work and employment are valuable here. Although the two terms are used interchangeably in everyday speech, there is considerable value in avoiding their conflation. This point has been discussed elsewhere (Hartley, 1980; Pym, 1974, 1979; Gowler and Legge, 1976) but bears repetition. Employment can be defined as essentially the relationship between the employee and the employer, a relationship based on the exchange of economic reward for labour (Taylor, 1968). Work, on the other hand, is an activity which can be performed either inside or outside the employment relationship. Housework, voluntary work, and educational study can all be considered to be work, in that they involve activity to achieve a purpose, although they do not involve an employment relationship.

Although work can take place outside employment, employment itself involves both work and economic reward. Strictly speaking unemployment is the lack of an exchange relationship, although it usually involves the loss of the particular activity. However, the conceptual distinction between work and employment is important. It means that unemployment may be a double blow to the individual; losing a source of income and losing the psychological rewards of engaging in an activity. But the distinction between work and employment also means that reactions might not be simple: for example, a person may regret the loss of the weekly pay packet but be overjoyed to get away from a dirty, monotonous, alienating work activity. Alternatively, one can imagine situations where a person does not miss the economic remuneration but wants to continue the work, as in some jobs with a vocational calling. The distinction between work and employment thus allows for the possibility that an individual may have ambivalent feelings about becoming unemployed, and allows for a more complex view of human experience. The distinction, however, is rarely recognized in the literature, with the consequence that more simplistic reactions by the unemployed are described. The distinction could be valuable in developing psychological theories about unemployment.

The most influential framework for understanding unemployment is that of the deprivation approach described earlier. We consider this in some detail, given its predominant place in explaining the effects of unemployment. There are a number of serious problems with the deprivation approach. This is not to suggest that it is a framework without value. However, its limitations need to be discussed if a better framework for understanding unemployment is to emerge. The first point to note is its vagueness. The latent functions of employment are ambiguous, and hence difficult to operationalize in a research setting. What does it mean to say that employment 'compels contacts and shared experiences with others outside the nuclear family' or that it 'demonstrates there are goals and purposes which are beyond the individual but require a collectivity' (Jahoda and Rush, 1980)?

Secondly, we should note that these latent functions of employment are not theoretically derived or theoretically coherent. They consist of a set of assertions about the value of employment without explaining why these particular functions are important. Of course, *ad hoc* assertions are adequate as a starting point if they are then tested against empirical data. The third point about the deprivation approach, however, is that it is unfalsifiable. If a person suffers psychologically as a result of being out of work then this demonstrates that he/she lacks the benefits of the latent functions of employment but if an unemployed person does not suffer then this is explained by him/her having found these latent functions outside employment. The vagueness of the concepts themselves aids their unfalsifiability. Moreover, inadequate arguments are used to demonstrate the value of the latent functions. For example: 'That the intensity of a sense of deprivation, financially and psychologically, is greater in unemployment is already indicated by the fact that the overwhelming majority of the unemployed want a job' (Jahoda, 1982, p.48). Certainly the unemployed want something but it does not inevitably point to the latent functions of employment.

Fourthly, the deprivation approach is to some extent incompatible with known research on employment and unemployment. It implies a starker contrast between employment and unemployment than may actually exist. The deprivation approach ignores the fact that employment can be psychologically harmful or that unemployment, in certain circumstances, may be psychologically liberating. There is already an extensive literature on the negative aspects of employment, much of which is low-skilled, low-paid, dirty, dangerous, and alienating. In considering unskilled jobs in engineering or vehicle manufacturing, for example, the ideas of the positive functions of employment, so eloquently expressed by some, sound hollow.

Even for more highly skilled and rewarded employees, employment is not always as positive as it is sometimes made out to be by certain psychologists. In a study of unemployed managers Hartley (1978) came across a number who had found their previous work stressful and dissatisfying. The question can be raised also, as to why so many people positively seek redundancy. There is also evidence that a number of people about to lose their jobs have been aware of their declining job security and likely eventual job loss and therefore are not so much shocked by the news as relieved (Hartley, 1978; Fineman, 1979; Fagin 1981).

There are, moreover, even beneficial effects of unemployment for some people, a factor which has not been acknowledged by the deprivation approach. People may see opportunities in unemployment: doors opened as well as doors closed. Unemployment, especially initially, may provide opportunities for improved health and relaxation and a chance to get more involved in domestic and family interests, according to some studies, admittedly predominantly concerned with managerial and professional unemployed (Hartley, 1978; Fineman, 1979; Huzynski, 1978; Slater, 1975; Fryer and Payne, 1983). This is not of course to say that all individuals enjoy unemployment or that unemployment is not generally a bad thing. Even a cursory glance at the position of the unemployed in society should negate the view that it is generally a pleasurable experience. The deprivation approach is based on a simplistic analysis of work, employment, and unemployment and hence leads to simplistic predictions about reactions and feelings connected with these states. Importantly the 'psychological value of work' thesis conflates the two concepts of work and employment. Additionally we may also note here that the deprivation approach has a value basis which essentially supports the *status quo* in society, where employment is seen to be positive and unemployment negative.

Fifthly, the deprivation approach is based on assumptions about people's nature as being essentially passive and reactive. According to it, people are reliant on the conditions of employment to sustain, support, and motivate them. They socialize, for example, because they are forced into contact in the course of their job. The very words used – compels, enforces, imposes (Jahoda and Rush, 1980) – reinforces this notion of passivity in human nature. It implies that if the external structure of employment is taken away then people are isolated, purposeless, and temporarily adrift.

Consequently, it discourages, for example, attempts to understand the unemployed as active, indeed pro-active, resourceful people, changing their perceptions as their circumstances change and developing adaptive strategies to deal with the new situation and its new problems. Of course, the new strategies may involve behaviour which is quite different from that necessitated by previous employment strategies. It may even be possible and useful to conceptualize certain (though not all) unemployment problems as ones we actually construct for ourselves rather than as subtractions we passively suffer.

The unemployment as deprivation perspective, then, which underpins so much research, is not only a negative, diminishing view of people, not only identifies psychology with the industrial-political *status quo*, but also throws into darkness and distorts the theoretical framework potentially available to researchers in the field.

Problems of Inference

The predominant concern in the literature has been to provide a description of the psychological effects of unemployment. There has been a corresponding lack of interest in the processes of unemployment (although recent research using moderator variables has been somewhat encouraging in this respect) and very little adequate discussion of the causes of these psychological effects.

The problems of inferring causation because of inadequate research design have already been alluded to, but there are inferential problems in addition, due to an excessive psychologism in the literature. This refers to the process whereby psychological explanations of cause and effect are proposed where other levels of explanation are, or might be, more appropriate. In a number of research fields, psychologists have been accused of failing to take account of more social and economic variables (e.g. Pepitone, 1976) and the field of unemployment is no exception in this respect.

The causes of psychological distress are generally attributed to loss of the psychological benefits of work, as we have outlined in the deprivation framework. The concomitants of unemployment are less frequently discussed. The point that loss of employment involves a loss of economic reward is an important one. Fraser (1981) has rightly taken psychologists to task for ignoring the financial aspects of unemployment. There is a grave danger that the interest in the psychological consequences of unemployment overshadows recognition of the fact that there is still a major link between unemployment and poverty (Walker, 1981; Piachaud, 1981; Sinfield, 1970). While some groups, such as professionals, may be better provided for materially in the first months of unemployment, the consequence of unemployment for all groups is a large drop in income: 50 per cent on average according to Brittain (1981, quoted in Jahoda, 1982; see also Payne *et al*, 1983). In considering the vexed question of causation, researchers need to bear in mind that in many cases the health and psychological changes often documented among the unemployed may be more related to financial deprivation than social or psychological losses. Much more work needs to be done in this area. To begin to disentangle some of these issues, psychologists could examine the psychological consequences for those in employment but living below the poverty line, and those who, while unemployed, are financially relatively well-cushioned.

The lack of interest in financial matters is only one aspect of an overly narrow psychological approach. Psychologists have sometimes failed to recognize the variations, in objective terms, of the experience of unemployment. Without considering contextual factors, the experience of unemployment is seen to be invariable and essentially similar for whoever undergoes the process. Thus, generalizations develop, and are maintained, about how 'the individual' reacts to unemployment. Without examination of contextual factors, disaggregation is unlikely to occur, and an understanding of how psychological influences interact with structural factors is obstructed.

The influence of social structure and the economy could potentially be considered by psychologists as influences upon the subjective experience of the individual. For example, if one accepts that occupational skills and education place one in a different labour market, as a number of writers have suggested (Doeringer and Piore, 1975; Blackburn and Mann, 1979) then the psychological experience may be dependent on one's occupational experience, one's previous experience of unemployment (Sinfield, 1981), or how one arrived in the unemployed pool (Wood and Cohen, 1978).

An indication of the lack of interest in contextual factors by psychologists is given in the treatment of stages. There is seen to be an inexorable progression from one stage to the next: a progression only halted by the person escaping from the situation by getting a job. The progression is not closely tied to financial, social, or family events. In other words, the process occurs in a vacuum. The length of time in each stage, by implication, is due to personal characteristics: for example if the individual is persistent in job-seeking he will stay in the optimism stage (using the Eisenberg and Lazarsfeld model). Personal fortitude, rather than the number or availability of jobs at that particular occupational level is seen to be the key.

The interest in moderator variables is important, but although such variables are being researched, and they may represent first steps in theory development, their precise role in mediating unemployment effects has not been investigated or discussed to any extent. The dangers of failing to be aware of contextual, labour market factors can be illustrated in a comment by Hill (1978): 'It seems as if those who are most likely to become unemployed are those who have the weakest psychological grip on their employment'.

It is not clear whether moderator variables, if they are indeed influential, reflect variation in the objective circumstances of unemployment or whether they influence social psychological factors operating at the individual level, and this is not discussed to any great extent. For example, age could be a sociological shorthand, signalling variation in the objective opportunities existing in the labour market (an older worker is less attractive to employers) or else age may represent a psychological dimension of mental flexibility, risk-taking propensity, domestic involvement and so forth. This is true for many of the so-called mediating variables. Their exploration could present opportunities for psychologists to engage in interdisciplinary analyses, of benefit to psychologists, sociologists and economists alike.

Values of the Researchers

Psychologists have often been accused of accepting the *status quo* in society (e.g. Heather, 1976; Buss, 1979; Gergen, 1973) and the understanding of the impact of unemployment is an area of enquiry which is at least as susceptible to unarticulated values as any other area. A number of researchers clearly not only accept the values about the place of work and employment in western society but treat those values as though they were universal in time and place. Sociologists have described the dominant values of employment, discussing the Protestant ethic, and noting that employment is seen to be the moral duty of all able-bodied adults (with the exception of certain alternative roles such as child-care). Within such a value system the state of being employed is seen as 'normal' and is highly valued (often regardless of the actual job) while being unemployed is seen as abnormal, deviant or morally deficient, as a number of writers have pointed out (Berger, 1964; Wood, 1975; Marsden and Duff, 1975). 'Normal' of course, in this context carries the connotation of 'acceptable' as well as 'average'.

These dominant values are reflected in a number of psychological studies about unemployment, for example, in the particular interest in job-seeking as an activity of the unemployed (attempts to become 'normal' again) and the almost complete lack of interest by psychologists of the problems of re-entering employment after unemployment. The dominant moral values are also evident in the deprivation model, where the view is implicitly offered that employment is essentially a positive experience for all who submit to it, while unemployment is viewed as negative – a dreadful, even disastrous, psychological loss. To identify the working conditions of the twentieth-century industrialized West with the necessary conditions for psychological health must be dubious, when one considers that the greater proportion of the human population for most of its history has not inhabited a world whose parameters are clocking on and off, assembly lines, and employment cards given and received. It would surely be too coincidental if the conditions suitable for maximum profits in western capitalist economies were just those not only ideal but also necessary for mental health. The view of unemployment as essentially and wholly negative may partly be due to the frame of reference created by the middle-class positions of researchers in society, which perhaps makes them less able to perceive that other people's attachment to the labour market may be different from their own.

BIASES OF CONTENT

Work on the psychological impact of unemployment suffers from certain biases of content: the bias towards affective consequences, towards the individual, and towards treating a spell of unemployment as an isolated event.

Feelings and Emotions

It is clear from our overview that the majority of unemployment studies have looked largely at its affective consequences. There has been much less interest in the behaviour of the unemployed – what they actually *do* (although this is being rectified to some extent) and little interest in the cognitive functioning of the unemployed. This latter could be an interesting area to explore since some unemployed people comment that they are 'slowing down' or 'getting rusty'. More specific complaints are of failing concentration, mental agility, and memory. There are relevant literatures in the stress and clinical fields which could be pertinent in understanding changes in cognitive functioning. Such studies would have a number of methodological difficulties but are, perhaps, worth pursuing (Fryer and Warr, 1984).

The Individual

In many studies, the focus has been entirely on the individual. Yet investigations could profitably be widened to examine the interaction of the individual and the labour market, especially in the areas of job loss and job gain. As Harrison (1976) writes: 'Those least attractive to employers' are most likely to get stranded as the economic tide washes out', that is, to lose their jobs. This vital phrase 'to employers' is, however, frequently omitted conceptually by psychologists. On the contrary, the issue of job loss is usually framed in terms of 'the attitude to work', 'need for achievement', or 'work motivation'. Armchair theorizing is also rife: without recourse to data, one commentary suggests that, among managers 'we would expect very few really able people to be involved [in job loss]. . . . They influence organisations rather than letting organisations influence them' (Williams and Sneath, 1973), clearly implying that only the less able allow themselves to be exposed to redundancy. These approaches fail to take account of specifically organizational factors involved in job loss. Awareness of such factors frequently requires the rephrasing of the research question from 'why did this person become unemployed?' to 'why did this organization make this person unemployed?' (Hartley, 1980a). The latter question allows for personal, organizational, and structural factors to interact. Interest in organizational factors also entails a concern with personnel department policy, and the perceptions by employers of their employees and of job applicants. That employer attitudes may influence job loss was tentatively suggested in research (Hartley, 1980a) where a group of unemployed managers appeared to possess certain characteristics traditionally admired in managers although in excess of organizational requirements at that time. Such information may tell us as much about organizations as about job losers. Similarly, organizational aspects of re-employment could be examined. The job-search experiences of the unemployed may be as informative about the selection procedures, perceptions, and values of the employers as about the psychological attributes or employment motivation of the job-seeker.

Unemployment as an Isolated Event

Psychologists could and should also be exhorted to extend their horizon of interest even beyond longitudinal research into periods of unemployment, seeking to discover what goes on after re-employment. Although much effort has been applied to examining job-seeking behaviour, little has been directed to the problems of adjusting to and keeping the new job. This may partly be due to dominant societal values which imply that re-employment is the end of the problem, yet the limited evidence there is suggests that re-employment may be associated with a number of problems: adjustment to the new job may itself be stressful (Cobb and Kasl, 1977) and the re-employed person may have to make personal adjustments in order literally to 'make the best of a bad job' (Hartley, 1981), since the new job may be of lower intrinsic and extrinsic quality. Moreover, in terms of the operation of the labour market, those who have previously been unemployed are more likely to re-experience it again later in their careers, a phenomenon described as 'accelerating' or 'galloping' redundancy (Daniel, 1972; Thomas and Madigan, 1974; Norris, 1978). Research on employment careers would draw attention away from unemployment as an isolated and abnormal event and rather examine it as part of the process of organizational experience. This would be in line with the recommendation (Norris, 1978) that social scientists should examine *job insecurity* rather than worklessness. Furthermore, and importantly, the importation of the concept of job insecurity, or even subemployment, into the language of psychologists would link the worlds of employment and unemployment via a continuum of states intermediate between full-time employment and total unemployment. The knock-on effects of unemployment: inappropriate employment niche, insecure temporary employment, and underemployment are important psychological topics in their own right. 'It became clear to me that under-employment among the highly educated is an even greater problem than unemployment' (Kaufman, 1982).

RECENT DEVELOPMENTS

While we have been firmly critical in our assessment of the contemporary literature on unemployment, there has been much good work in the field which has been innovative and keenly inquiring and has provided much-needed additions to the field. We should like to devote some attention now to these developments in the field. Essentially, such research is methodologically more rigorous, is becoming more concerned with the explanation of processes rather than effects, and is gradually documenting the range of variation in reactions to unemployment.

First, there has been some development of psychometric measures of the impact of unemployment, which allows interstudy comparison and replication to occur. The work of Cobb and Kasl (1977) is a significant development, systematically examining physiological and psychological indicators of stress. Other studies have attempted to develop empirical measures of other alleged psychological effects of unemployment, particularly of self-esteem (e.g. Fineman, 1979; Hartley, 1980b) and vulnerability to psychiatric symptoms (Hepworth, 1980; Stafford et al., 1980). Effort is being devoted systematically to develop objective measures of personal characteristics which may moderate the effects of unemployment (Payne et al., 1983). Also Warr (1983b) Stafford et al. (1980) and others are amassing useful comparative data on the extent to which groups of people are motivated to be employed for its own sake and how these motivations correlate over time with experiences of employment and unemployment. This is not to suggest that only quantitative, psychometric data are acceptable in developing understanding of the processes and effects of unemployment. The detailed case-studies, using qualitative interview material, are still very important and valuable, where the study has been adequately conceptualized.

Secondly, there has been an increased interest in moderator variables, which is encouraging. Although there are problems in explaining their influence (which have already been discussed), interest in them represents a change from the simple documentation of effects of unemployment towards a greater interest in the explanation of processes. For example, in the search to explain psychological consequences of unemployment there has been a greater interest in the pre-unemployment state of the individual. This has been suggested through the distinction between work and employment, since these may represent, for example, contradictory values for the individual, with consequent ambivalent feelings about job loss. It has also been suggested by some of the research on the importance of employment involvement as a mediating variable. This interest could lead to a more adequate conceptualization of the processes accompanying unemployment than the deprivation approach currently allows for.

Thirdly, the recent research provides evidence that unemployment is a more complex social and personal process than much of the previous literature would have us believe. Unemployment itself is not a homogenous event – relatively uniform for everyone except in terms of its length. We must reject the notion that the differential effects of unemployment must be entirely due to individual psychological characteristics, remarking instead on the complexity of the phenomenon of unemployment itself. Important changes may occur concurrently with the loss of a job, but not be due to unemployment *per se* (Slater, 1975), that is the changes may occur independently as a result of the enforced changed routine and resources.

In the light of this it is not surprising that recent research suggests a *variety* of reactions to unemployment. For example, although there has been a tendency to characterize reactions to job loss in terms of one of the popular stages models, with shock and then passivity being dominant reactions, some research documents alternative reactions.

Some studies have discovered groups of managers who had felt stressed and dissatisfied in employment and who subsequently saw unemployment as providing them with the opportunity, and at times a retrospectively valued nudge, to make occupational changes they otherwise would have hesitated to make (Little, 1976; Hartley, 1978; Fineman, 1979; Huczynski, 1978; Hepworth, 1980). The reasons for this broad occupational difference are unclear (Slater, 1975). Similarly, anger has been described as a reaction to job loss in a number of studies (Fagin, 1981; Hartley, 1978; Little, 1976) again predominantly, but not entirely, of the unemployed from higher occupational levels.

Any model of the psychological processes associated with unemployment needs to take account not only of the predominant reactions, but also those of the minority. It is not adequate to describe these reactions as atypical, for example Harrison (1976) of the well-off, those who find the unemployed role legitimate and those with low aspirations. As psychologists, we have to accept this complexity and variety of reaction and seek to explain it rather than to stigmatize and ignore it. The reactions of 'atypical' individuals, however much a minority group, are nevertheless vitally important in understanding 'typical' reactions. Some research of this kind is currently in progress (Fryer and Payne, 1983).

Historically, the development of our psychological knowledge about unemployment seems to have proceeded by the establishment (almost by fiat rather than observation) of a generalization about the impact of unemployment, which succeeding series of researchers and commentators have sought to affirm. In this way, a stereotype has built up and has seldom been challenged. However, more recently the research evidence, combined with critical commentaries (Gurney and Taylor, 1981; Hartley, 1980c; Fraser, 1981), has begun to break down such generalizations.

THE FUTURE

Clearly this is still much research to be undertaken. In understanding the impact of unemployment, we need to document more fully the variety of reactions to unemployment, exploring differences in coping styles, impact on social and family behaviour and use of time for example. In trying to examine effects, we need to be able to disentangle, where possible, the effects of lack of a job from its financial concomitants. There are a number of ways this could be investigated. Research could investigate the effects of financial insecurity as opposed to unemployment by looking at individuals with highly fluctuating wages (see, for example, Aiken et al., 1968). Income-maintenance studies could be conducted, for example examining those unemployed for whom legislation provides an income at or near their previous wage for an extended period. Unemployed people who are relatively well-supported financially (for example, managerial and professional groups), perhaps contrasted with those employed whose income is at or below the poverty level (defined in terms of social security benefit level) could be extremely valuable here.

Moving beyond the investigation of impact, more attention could be paid to analysing the processes whereby unemployment, for many, leads to psychological distress. More concern to the processes would be more than repaid in terms of theory development, which could be insightful for understanding employment as well as unemployment.

The study of unemployment could, we also argue, be profitably extended beyond a single spell of unemployment to examining unemployment careers and the individual's attachment to the labour market. Beyond that, exploring the social meanings of unemployment within society could be valuable. Some research on this has already been initiated and the matter discussed (e.g. Kelvin, 1980; Furnham, 1982) but more work remains to be done.

Almost daily, newspapers refer to the physical and psychological damage created by our present high level of unemployment, and reference is also often made to such effects in the narrower sphere of the academic world. It is evident, according to these sources, that unemployment is clearly and ubiquitously associated with certain psychological changes in the individual. These claims have been repeated in a number of specifically psychological publications and our view is that the literature on the psychological impact of unemployment is virtually unanimous. This is an extremely unusual characteristic for an issue subjected to social scientific inquiry. The degree of consistency of views is such that we feel justified in describing it as a current orthodoxy.

We have made it clear that we do not think the claims that constitute the orthodoxy to be in themselves wholly untrue – rather that they are not the whole truth. In particular, we feel they are insecurely based on a small number of studies of often dubious methodological quality and that the conclusions drawn are over-extended in scope and simplistic in nature.

The consensus is reached, we fear, at the cost of ignoring exceptions to the rule: indeed probably one of the major problems of orthodoxy is the way it discourages the recognition of counter-examples and the development of alternative assumptions and approaches. It is disturbing how research findings have been streamlined and trimmed to fit the orthodox pattern by successive commentaries: actual research reports frequently reveal a far greater range of responses to unemployment and use a far greater range of techniques of investigation than is later acknowledged. For example, as Stern put it (personal communication): 'The consensus view of the near universal and identical impact of unemployment on people in the 1930s appears to be a post-1939 construct'.

We wished in this paper to raise a number of questions about the validity and generalizability of much of the evidence, in a way which is strongly provocative for the development of new research in this area. Perhaps, however, one of the most intriguing questions prompted by our look at the psychological research on unemployment is not empirical nor even really theoretical – but a meta-theoretical one. Why has the orthodox account of unemployment, given that it is so narrowly and insecurely based, become so accepted, widespread, and entrenched? It may be that the most illuminating way to phrase the question is not to ask what it is about the orthodoxy that makes it so plausible but rather what it is about us that makes us so ready to accept it?

REFERENCES

Aiken, M., Ferman, L.A., and Sheppard, H.L. (1968). *Economic Failure, Alienation and Extremism*, Ann Arbor: University of Michigan Press.
Bakke, E.W. (1933). *The Unemployed Man*, London: Nisbet.
Bakke, E.W. (1940). *Citizens without Work*, New Haven: Yale University Press.
Beales, H.L. and Lambert, R.S. (1973). *Memoirs of the Unemployed*, Wakefield: EP Publishing.
Berger, P.L. (1964). *The Human Shape of Work*, New York: Macmillan.
Blackburn, R. and Mann, M. (1979). *The Working Class in the Labour Market*, London: Macmillan.
Brenner, M.H. (1967). Economic changes and mental hospitalisation, *Social Psychiatry*, **2**, 180–188.
Brenner, M.H. (1971). Economic changes and heart disease mortality. *American Journal of Public Health*, **61**, 606–611.
Brenner, M.H. (1973). *Mental Illness and the Economy*, Cambridge, Mass: Harvard University Press.
Brenner, M.H. (1977). Personal stability and economic security, *Social Policy*, **8**, 2–4.
Brenner, M.H. (1979). Mortality and the national economy, *The Lancet*, 15 September, 568–573.
Briar, K.H. (1977). The effect of long-term unemployment on workers and their families, *Dissertation Abstracts International* (March), **37** (9–A) 6062. Doctoral Dissertation, University of California.
Buss, A.R. (1979). *Psychology in Social Context*, New York: Irvington.
Carroll, P. (1979). The Social and Psychological Effects of Unemployment upon Young People – a review of the literature. *Unpublished paper*, Department of Employment.
Catalano, R., Dooley, D., and Jackson, R. (1981). Economic predictions of admissions to mental health facilities in a non-metropolitan community, *Journal of Health and Social Behaviour*, **22**, 284–297.
Cavan, R.S. and Ranke, K.H. (1938). *The Family and the Depression*, Chicago: University of Chicago Press.
Cobb, S. and Kasl, S.V. (1977). *Termination: The Consequences of Job Loss*, Cincinatti, Ohio: US Department of Health, Education and Welfare.
Cragg, A. and Dawson, T. (1983). Unemployed women: a study of attitudes and experiences. *Department of Employment Research Paper*.
Daniel, W.W. (1972). *Whatever happened to the Workers in Woolwich?* London: Political and Economic Planning.
Doeringer, P.B. and Piore, M.J. (1975). Unemployment and the 'Dual Labour Market', *The Public Interest*, **38**, Winter, 67–79.

Dooley, D. and Catalano, R. (1982). Does Economic Change Increase Psychological Symptoms and Help Seeking? A Synthesis of Recent Research. *Unpublished paper*. Program in Social Ecology and Public Policy Research Organization. University of California, Irvine.

Eisenberg, P. and Lazarsfeld, P.F. (1938). The Psychological Effects of Unemployment, *Psychological Bulletin*, **35**, 358–390.

Fagin, L. (1981). *Unemployment and Health in Families*, DHSS Publication, ISBN 0 902650 23 8.

Feather, N.T. and Davenport, P.R. (1981). Unemployment and depressive affect: A motivational and attributional analysis, *Journal of Personality and Social Psychology*, **41**, 422–436.

Fineman, S. (1979). A psychological model of stress and its application to managerial unemployment, *Human Relations*, **32**, 323–345.

Fink, S.L. (1967). Crisis and motivation: a theoretical model, *Archives of Physical Medicine and Rehabilitation*, **43**, 952–957.

Fraser, C. (1981). The social psychology of unemployment in Jeaves, M. (ed.), *Psychology Survey No. 3*, London: Allen and Unwin.

Fryer, D. and Payne, R. (1984). Book Borrowing and Unemployment. *Library Review* in press.

Fryer, D. and Payne, R. (1983). Towards understanding proactivity in unemployment. *Unpublished paper*, MRC/SSRC Social and Applied Psychology Unit, Sheffield, Memo 540.

Fryer, D. and Warr, P.B. (1984). Unemployment and cognitive difficulties. *British Journal of Clinical Psychology* (in press).

Furnham, A. (1982). The Protestant work ethic and attitudes towards unemployment, *Journal of Occupational Psychology*, **55**, 277–286.

Gergen, K. (1973). Social psychology as history, *Journal of Personality and Social Psychology*, **26**, 309–320.

Goldberg, D.P. (1972). *The Detection of Psychiatric Illness by Questionnaire*, Oxford: Oxford University Press.

Goodchild, J.D. and Smith, E.E. (1963). The effects of unemployment as mediated by social status, *Sociometry*, **26**, 289–290.

Gore, S. (1978). The effect of social support in moderating the health consequences of unemployment, *Journal of Health and Social Behaviour*, **19**, 157–165.

Gould, T. and Kenyon, J. (1972). *Stories from the Dole Queue*, London, Routledge.

Gowler, D. and Legge, K. (1976). Working conditions and terms of employment *Unpublished paper*, MRC/SSRC Social and Applied Psychology Unit, Sheffield, Memo 135.

Gurney, R.M. (1981). Leaving school, facing unemployment, and making attributions about the causes of unemployment, *Journal of Vocational Behaviour*, **18**, 79–91.

Gurney, R.M. and Taylor, K. (1981). Research on unemployment: defects, neglect and prospects, *Bulletin of the British Psychological Society*, **34**, 349–352.

Harrison, R. (1976). The demoralising experience of prolonged unemployment, *Department of Employment Gazette*, April, 339–348.

Hartley, J.F. (1978). *An Investigation of Psychological Aspects of Managerial Unemployment*. Unpublished Ph.D. thesis, University of Manchester.

Hartley, J.F. (1980a). The personality of unemployed managers: myths and measurement, *Pesonnel Review*, **9**, 12–18.

Hartley, J.F. (1980b). The impact of unemployment upon the self esteem of managers, *Journal of Occupational Psychology*, **53**, 147–155.

Hartley, J.F. (1980c). Psychological approaches to unemployment, *Bulletin of The British Psychological Society*, **33**, 412–414.

Hartley, J.F. (1981). Career Transition among Managers over 40, in Cooper, C. and Torrington, D. (eds), *After 40: the Time for Achievement* Chichester: Wiley.

Hayes, J. and Nutman, P. (1981). *Understanding the Unemployed*, London: Tavistock.

Heather, N. (1976). *Radical Perspectives in Psychology*, London: Methuen.

Hepworth, S.J. (1980). Moderating factors of the psychological impact of unemployment, *Journal of Occupational Psychology*, **53**, 139–146.

Hill, J.M. (1977). *The Social and Psychological Impact of Unemployment: A Pilot Study*, London: Tavistock Institute of Human Relations.

Hill, J.M. (1978). The psychological impact of unemployment, *New Society*, **43**, 118–120.

Huczynski, A. (1978). Unemployed managers – a homogeneous group? *Management Education and Development*, **9**, 21–25.

Jahoda, M. (1979). The impact of unemployment in the 1930s and the 1970s, *Bulletin of the British Psychological Society*, **32**, 309–314.

Jahoda, M. (1982). *Employment and Unemployment*, Cambridge: Cambridge University Press.

Jahoda, M., Lazarsfeld, P.F., and Zeisel, H. (1972). *Marienthal: The Sociography of an Unemployed Community*, London; Tavistock.

Jahoda, M. and Rush, H. (1980). Work, Employment and Unemployment. *Occasional Paper Series*, No. 12, Science Policy Research Unit, Sussex University.

Kasl, S.V. (1979). Changes in mental health status associated with job loss and retirement, in J. Barrett *et al.* (eds) *Stress and Mental Disorder*, New York: Raven Press.

Kasl, S.V., Gore S., and Cobb, S. (1975). The experience of losing a job: reported changes in health, symptoms and illness behaviour, *Psychosomatic Medicine*, **37**, 106–122.

Kaufman, H.G. (1982). *Professionals in Search of Work: Coping with the Stress of Job Loss and Unemployment*, New York: Wiley.

Kelvin, P. (1980). Social psychology 2001: The social psychological bases and implications of structural unemployment, in Gilmour, R. and Duck, S. (eds). *The Development of Social Psychology*, London: Academic Press.

Kingsley, S. (1976). *An Investigation of Personal Constructs Concerning Unemployed Older Managers*, M.Sc. Thesis, UWIST.

Kinn, J.M. (1973). Unemployment and mid-career change. A blue-print for today and tomorrow, *Industrial Gerontology*, **17**, 47–49.

Komarovsky, M. (1940). *The Unemployed Man and his Family*, New York: Dryden.

Liem, R. and Liem, J. (1979). Social support and stress: some general issues and their application to the problem of unemployment, in Ferman, L. and Gordus, J. (eds), *Mental Health and the Economy*, Kalamazoo, Michigan: Upjohn Institute.

Liem, R. and Rayman, P. (1982). Health and social costs of unemployment: research and policy considerations, *American Psychologist*, **37**, 1116–1123.

Little, C. (1976). Technical-professional unemployment: middle class adaptability to personal crisis, *Sociological Quarterly*, **17**, 262–274.

Mackay, K. and Haines, H. (1982). The psychological effects of unemployment: a review of the literature, *New Zealand Journal of Industrial Relations*, **7**, 123–135.

Marsden, D. and Duff, E. (1975). *Workless*, Harmondsworth: Penguin.

Martin, J. and Roberts, C. (1984). *Women and Employment: A Lifetime Perspective*, London: HMSO.

Morley-Bunker, N. (1982). *Perceptions of Unemployment*. Paper to the BPS Annual Occupational Psychology Conference, Brighton.

Norris, G. (1978). Unemployment, subemployment and personal characteristics, *Sociological Review*, **26** (a) 89–108; (b) 327–347.

Payne, R., Warr, P.B., and Hartley, J.F. (1983). Social class and psychological ill-health in unemployment. *Unpublished paper*, MRC/SSRC Social and Applied Psychology Unit, University of Sheffield. No. 549.

Pepitone, A. (1976). Toward a normative and comparative biocultural social psychology, *Journal of Personality and Social Psychology*, **34**, 641–653.

Piachaud, D. (1981). The Dole. *Discussion paper* no. 89, Centre for Labour Economics, London School of Economics.

Pilgrim Trust (1938). *Men Without Work*, Cambridge: Cambridge University Press.

Powell, D.H. (1973). The effects of job strategy seminars upon unemployed engineers and scientists, *Journal of Social Psychology*, **91**, 165–166.

Pym, D. (1974). In quest of post-industrial man, in Armistead, N. (ed.), *Reconstructing Social Psychology*, Harmondsworth: Penguin.

Pym, D. (1979). Work is good, employment is bad, *Employee Review*, **1**, 16–18.

Roberts, K., Duggan, J., and Noble, M. (1981). Unregistered Youth Unemployment. *Research Paper, 31*, London: Department of Employment.

Roberts, K., Duggan, J., and Noble, M. (1982). Outreach Careers Work. *Research Paper 32*, London: Department of Employment.

Seabrook, J. (1982). *Unemployment*; London: Quartet.

Shanthamani, V.S. (1973). Unemployment and neuroticism, *Indian Journal of Social Work*, **34**, 43–45.

Shepherd, G. (1981). Psychological Disorder and Unemployment. *Bulletin of the British Psychological Society*, **34**, 345–348.

Sinfield, A. (1970). Poor and out-of-work in Shields, in P. Townsend (ed.), *The Concept of Poverty*, London: Heinemann.

Sinfield, A. (1981). *What Unemployment Means*, Oxford: Martin Robertson.

Slater, R.S. (1975). The Psychological Concomitants of Unemployment: A Study of Professional and Executive Employees. *Unpublished paper*, UWIST.

Sofer, C. (1970). *Men in Mid Career*, Cambridge: Cambridge University Press.

Sorrentino, C. (1981). Unemployment in international perspective in Showler, B. and Sinfield, A. (eds), *The Workless State*, Oxford: Martin Robertson.

Stafford, E.M., Jackson, P.R., and Banks, M.H. (1980). Employment, work involvement and mental health in less qualified young people, *Journal of Occupational Psychology*, **53**, 291–304.

Stern, J. (1981). *Personal Communication*, Centre for Labour Economics, London School of Economics.

Stokes, G. (1981). Unemployment among school leavers. *Unpublished paper*, University of Birmingham.

Swinburne, P. (1981). The psychological impact of unemployment on managers and professional staff, *Journal of Occupational Psychology*, **54**, 47–64.

Tausky, C. and Piedmont, E.B. (1967). The Meaning of Work and Unemployment, *International Journal of Social Psychiatry*, **14**, 44–49.

Taylor, L. (1968). *Occupational Sociology*, New York: Oxford University Press.

Thomas, B. and Madigan, C. (1974). Strategy and job choice after redundancy – a case study in the aircraft industry, *Sociological Review*, **22**, 83–102.

Tiffany, D.W., Cowan, J.R., and Tiffany, P.M. (1970). *The Unemployed: a Social-Psychological Portrait*, Englewood Cliffs, NJ: Prentice-Hall.

Walker, A. (1981). The economic and social impact of unemployment: A case study in South Yorkshire, *Political Quarterly*, **52**, 74–87.

Warr, P.B. (1978). A study of psychological well-being, *British Journal of Psychology*, **69**, 111–121.

Warr, P.B. (1982), Psychological Aspects of Employment and Unemployment. *Psychological Medicine*, **12**, 7–11.

Warr, P.B. (1983a). Work and unemployment in Drenth, P.J.D., Thierry, H., Willens, P.J., and De Wolff, C.J. (eds), *Handbook of Work and Organizational Psychology*, Chichester: Wiley.

Warr, P.B. (1983b). Job, loss, unemployment and psychological well-being, in van de Vliert, E. and Allen, V. (eds), *Role Transitions*, New York: Plenum Press.

Warr, P., Jackson, P.R., and Banks, M. (1983). Duration of unemployment and psychological well being in young men and women, *Current Psychological Research* (in press).

Warr, P. and Payne, R. (1982). Social Class and Reported Changes in Behavior after Job Loss. *Journal of Applied Social Psychology*, **13**, 206–222.

Wedderburn, D. (1965). *Redundancy and the Railwaymen*, Cambridge: Cambridge University Press.

Williams, R. and Sneath, F. (1973). A Suitable Case for Treatment – the Redundant Executive, *Personnel Review*, **2**, 52–61.

Wood, S. (1975). Redundancy and stress, in Gowler, D. and Legge, K. (eds), *Managerial Stress*, Farnborough, Hants: Gower Press.

Wood, S. and Cohen, J. (1978). Approaches to the study of redundancy, *Industrial Relations Journal*, **8**, 19–27.

Zawadski, B. and Lazarsfeld, P.F. (1935). The psychological consequences of unemployment, *Journal of Social Psychology*, **6**, 224–251.

Progress in Applied Social Psychology, Volume 2
Edited by G.M. Stephenson and J.H. Davis
© 1984 John Wiley & Sons Ltd

2

Episodic Length of Hospital Stay for Mental Disorders

C.A. KIESLER AND A.E. SIBULKIN
Carnegie-Mellon University

Kiesler (1980a) has distinguished between *de facto* and *de jure* national mental health policy. The *de jure* policy refers to that which we intend to implement through legislation and other public mechanisms. The *de facto* system is that which occurs whether intended or not. We focus here on the interplay between these two policies: specifically, the evaluation of one aspect of our *de jure* policy of de-institutionalization.

The two cornerstones of our *de jure* national mental health policy are de-institutionalization and the development of out-patient care, particularly through the Community Mental Health Center System. Bachrach (1976) emphasizes: '. . . two components of the de-institutionalization process: the removal of persons who have already been hospitalized from their institutional environments and then transferred into the community; and the prevention of hospitalization of those persons who might be considered potential candidates for institutionalization' (p.2).

How may we ascertain whether the policy of de-institutionalization has been effective? One method is to inspect national statistics for changes consistent with the national policy. There are three potential outcomes for the evaluation of the process of de-institutionalization that especially interest us. First, we could ascertain whether we have indeed developed alternative care mechanisms that could effectively keep people out of hospitals if used. Second, we could evaluate whether indeed we have reduced the rate of hospitalization. Third, we can inspect whether, once hospitalized, the length of stay there has decreased over the last few years.

The last, length of stay in a mental hospital, is an important datum for evaluation of our policy of de-institutionalization. The policy implies we are

31

keeping people in mental hospitals for shorter treatment periods. One pre-liminary question asks whether this is true. If so, a second level question asks whether it is uniformly true across all sites where people are hospitalized for mental disorders. A third level of inquiry deals with the patterns of (poten-tially) changing lengths of hospital stay across sites, over years.

Evaluation of such specific aspects of our national policy is an important ingredient to feedback loops between policy and implementation. In its ideal form, such evaluation research is value-free. It asks, given the current public policy, what are its implications and have they been successfully implemented?

In previous research we have focused on two other aspects of public policy and de-institutionalization: alternative care mechanisms and national episodic rate of hospitalization. Regarding the first of these, Kiesler (1982) assessed the effectiveness of currently available alternative care strategies, through a secondary analysis of existing studies in which patients with serious mental disorders were randomly assigned to a mental hospital or some alternative care. Across the ten studies, in no case was hospital care more effective than alternative care on such dependent measures as psychiatric evaluation, employment, development of close relationships, and the like. Further, across the ten studies, Kiesler calculated a highly significant effect of the self-perpetuation of mental hospitalization. Patients randomly assigned to a mental hospital were more likely, after discharge, to be readmitted than were those randomly assigned to alternative care ever to be admitted to a hospital. Kiesler concluded that alternative care methods exist such that the majority of mental patients now hospitalized could more effectively and less expensively be treated through alternative care mechanisms. Of course, the mechanisms for alternative care are not in place nationally, and there are extraordinarily complex barriers to implementing such a dramatic policy alternative.

Kiesler and Sibulkin (1983) investigated the number of hospitalizations by critically reviewing the results of national surveys. In their evaluation, they found that no national data source exhaustively reviewed all of the sites where people are hospitalized for mental disorders, nor all the hospitals within each category of site. Using a multiple-source method of estimation of national statistics, they juxtaposed estimations of hospital episodes from different sources. Looking closely at the details of the survey method employed by each source of data, they were able to select the more reliable sources for each aspect of the decomposed aggregate data. Using this method, they found that the rate of hospitalization for mental disorders has been increasing in excess of the population increase. As opposed to the NIMH estimate of 1.7 million in-patient hospital episodes, Kiesler and Sibulkin were able to uncover, more reliably, over 3 million such episodes (3.8 million if one includes nursing homes.)

Kiesler and Sibulkin did find that the site of mental hospitalization had changed dramatically in the last twenty years. Hospital episodes in state and county hospitals have decreased substantially, as widely publicized. However, the most popular site for mental hospitalization is now a general hospital without a psychiatric unit, and (extrapolating from trends of the most recently available data) the second most popular site is the general hospital with a psychiatric unit. The two traditional sites which the public is most likely to associate with mental hospitalization – private mental hospitals and state and county mental hospitals – accounted for only about 25 per cent of the total national episodes of mental hospitalization.[1]

Two core goals of the de-institutionalization policy are to reduce the number of people in mental hospitals *and* to keep them there for a shorter period of time. This latter aspect, the length of stay (LoS) is the focus of the present chapter. We ask, when hospitalized for mental disorders, has the length of hospital stay been decreasing? If so, is it true of all hospital sites? Kiesler and Sibulkin showed that the number of clinical episodes has decreased only for state and county mental hospitals, not for any other site of hospitalization. Could this be true of length of stay as well? What is the pattern of changes regarding length of stay over sites and across years?

DEFINITIONAL ISSUES

Before inspecting the data and sources, let us define the terms we are about to use. Some of the confusion in this area stems from imprecise use of technical terms. For example, it has been frequently asserted that the number of residents and their average length of stay in public mental hospitals has fallen dramatically over the last twenty years or so (cf. Vischi *et al.*, 1980). This statment is accurate but misleading, and some clarification of terms is necessary.

The term, public mental hospitals, refers to state and county mental hospitals, not all hospitals where mental patients are treated. State and county mental hospitals have been the prime focus of de-institutionalization efforts, but our intent here is to look across all sites of hospitalization. In this chapter, we survey state and county mental hospitals, those of the Veterans Administration (VA), private mental hospitals, Community Mental Health Centres (CMHCs), and public and private general hospitals with or without separate psychiatric units. As mentioned, state and county mental hospitals represent only a small proportion of total episodes of mental hospitalization. We focus here on a more complete and reliable national estimate.

The term, number of residents, refers to the people who are in a hospital at a given time, usually the beginning or end of a reporting period. It is not necessarily related to the number of people hospitalized during a given year. Episode refers to the total clinical occurrence of a mental disorder. An in-patient episode begins when a person is hospitalized and ends when he/she is discharged. In national epidemiological data, the number of episodes usually refers to the number of patients resident on the first day of the reporting year (1 January in NIMH data), plus all admissions that take place during the year. One can see that there could be some duplication of people in the number of episodes, to the extent that residents (or the new admissions) are discharged and readmitted during the year.

The precise definition of the length of stay refers to a specific episode. The length of stay should refer to the time actually spent in a hospital from the admission to the discharge. It should be calculated on the basis of each individual patient and then aggregated over patients and sites. As we shall see, length of stay for national aggregate data is seldom defined in this way, which can lead to rather systematic errors in that statistic. There are very few data nationally on true length of hospital stay for mental disorders. This turns out to be a very complex problem, but we can at least point out the sources of error, their likely direction (over-estimate or under-estimate), and ways to attempt to correct for the error. This issue will be discussed later.

Going back to our original example, it is true that the number of residents has decreased in state and county mental hospitals. For example, from 1965 to 1975, the number of *residents* at the end of the year fell from 475,000 to 191,000 (cf. Kiesler and Sibulkin, 1983). At the same time, the number of *admissions* rose from 317,000 to 376,000. Adding these together to find episodes, the number of *episodes* fell during this time from 792,000 to 567,000.[2] We note parenthetically that during this period the total number of in-patient episodes across all hospital sites rose rather sharply. Each statistic is only part of a complicated picture and must be interpreted with great care. Although it is technically true that the 'number of residents in public mental hospitals has decreased considerably', it is also misleading to take that statement to represent in any overall sense what the nation has been doing in recent years regarding in-patient treatment of mental disorders. Given Kiesler and Sibulkin's surprising findings regarding an overall increase in episodes, it seemed quite possible that a careful analysis of data on length of stay would be quite informative. We now turn to these data.

SOURCES OF DATA

The National Institute of Mental Health (NIMH) is the most widely cited source of data regarding mental health, but the Veterans Administration (VA), the National Center for Health Statistics (NCHS), and the American Hospital Association (AHA) also conduct national surveys. However, for purposes of obtaining length of stay data, we were limited to the surveys which either published or had readily accessible true average or median length of stay. The following is a description of the various ways length of stay is reported, which provided the rationale for selecting the figures presented here.

A method often used to calculate LoS, particularly for general medical care, is in-patient days (the total days people spend in the hospital during the year) divided by either admissions or discharges. However, the numerator includes all days spent in the hospital by people who are still there at the end of the year, but does not include the days those admitted will spend in the next year. It also does not include days spent by discharges during the previous year(s). In other words, in-patient days during a reporting period do not correspond to the actual admissions or discharges that contributed to these in-patient days. Therefore, dividing in-patient days by admissions or discharges does not result in a true average length of stay. If the true length of stay is constant over years and the number of admissions/discharges is also constant, the ratio would be arithmetically equal to true length of stay. However, since hospital admissions for mental disorders have been increasing (Kiesler and Sibulkin, 1983) and our de-institutionalization policy stresses shorter hospital stays, neither assumption is defensible.

In order to calculate a true average length of stay, the actual number of days spent in the hospital accumulated by a group of discharges is needed. Discharges must be used because it is not until people are discharged that the total number of days they were in the hospital is known. However, the number of days accumulated by the discharges must include any days spent during the previous year(s). These days are called 'total days', 'discharge days', and 'days of care' by various surveys. They should not be confused with 'in-patient days', which is used only to mean total days spent *during* a specific year. Discharge days can only be obtained from inspection of actual discharge records and not from aggregate national statistics within any given year.

Surprisingly, national statistics for length of stay are rare. Statistics kept fairly routinely by a hospital include: admissions, discharges, residents, average daily census (ADC), which is the average number of in-patients per day during the year, episodes (residents plus admissions), and total in-patient days (ADC × 365). Although average length of stay based on in-patient days divided by admissions is often reported for general medical care, discharges, discharge days, and true length of stay are rarely published for psychiatric care. The following is a description of the national data sources and the length of stay data they provide.

The Survey and Reports Branch, Division of Biometry and Epidemiology of the NIMH, operates a national reporting programme, and the results are reported in their Statistical Notes and Report Series on Mental Health Statistics. Their inventories of mental health facilities vary as to how frequently they occur and which facilities and characteristics are covered. We focus here on the length of stay for in-patient care, and hence concentrate on the NIMH surveys covering state and county mental hospitals, private mental hospitals, general hospitals with a psychiatric unit (NIMH does not cover general hospitals without a psychiatric unit), and the community mental health centres (CMHCs). Most of the data NIMH collects are aggregate figures of admissions, discharges, and in-patient days, which do not provide true average length of stay figures. However, we will see that sample surveys of patient records provide a few figures for median length of stay.

The American Hospital Association (AHA) conducts an Annual Survey of Hospitals and publishes these results in its *Hospital Statistics* series. Prior to 1971 the results appeared in the journal of the AHA, *Hospitals*. AHA does request discharges and discharge days from its hospitals but only publishes admissions and in-patient days, which is used to calculate average length of stay for non-psychiatric hospitals. Therefore, our source of psychiatric hospital data was NCHS, described below.

The National Center for Health Statistics (NCHS) conducts several surveys of health care facilities and publishes the results in its Vital and Health Statistics Series.[3] Its National Master Facility Inventory, NMFI (formerly the Master Facility Inventory) is a survey of all nursing homes and health facilities that are not hospitals. In addition, NCHS obtains AHA's data tape on hospitals and publishes these hospital data as part of its NMFI. Therefore, NMFI hospital data are essentially AHA data. However, NCHS psychiatric hospital data do not include hospitals for alcoholism or mental retardation, whereas AHA published figures for psychiatric hospitals do include them. NCHS also adds some other hospitals from which AHA had not requested information. Discharges and discharge days were published for two years and we obtained previously unpublished figures for seven additional years directly from NCHS. Therefore, our major source of the average length of stay for psychiatric hospitals was NCHS' National Master Facility Inventory, rather than AHA.

For general hospitals, length of stay data cannot be derived from the AHA or NCHS surveys, because the hospital is the unit of analysis in those surveys. Since only a fraction of general hospital admissions or discharges are for mental disorders, any total utilization figures for general hospitals would include all health problems, not just mental health. Therefore, another NCHS survey, the National Hospital Discharge Survey, NHDS (formerly the Hospital Discharge Survey), was used for general hospital data.[4] In the NHDS, discharge records from a probability sample of short-stay hospitals listed in the NMFI are systematically selected, based on the terminal digits of their medical record numbers. Since individual records are inspected, the number of discharges, discharge days, and true average length of stay just for mental disorders can be obtained.

The VA maintains two information systems. One collects aggregate data on the utilization of VA facilities and is not designed to provide length of stay data. A separate information system, the Patient Treatment File, provides true length of stay data based on discharge records.

To summarize our major data sources, the VA's Patient Treatment File was used for all VA hospitals, the NCHS National Master Facility Inventory was used for state, county, and private mental hospitals, and the NCHS National

Hospital Discharge Survey was used for general hospitals. Since NIMH is the only data source for CMHCs, we inferred what trends in length of stay probably exist, given that true length of stay data were first collected in 1980 and are not yet published.

METHOD

Our general approach employs a multiple-source method of estimation of national statistics. Regarding source of information, we inspect closely the circumstances under which information is gathered, whether it is a complete survey or a probability sample, what the sources of possible error are in extrapolating to national generalizations, and the like. As Kiesler and Sibulkin detail, this method reveals quite substantial differences among data sources, even concerning the number of hospitals surveyed within categories. Further, the surveys can include rather different primary data; one data source may gather information about discharges but not admissions, while another may do the reverse. This often makes it difficult to extrapolate across data sources, particularly when their summary conclusions are statistically quite different.

In this chapter we pull together and present what is known about true length of in-patient stay in the sites in which people are most frequently hospitalized for mental disorders: the VA (both psychiatric and general hospitals), general hospitals (both with and without psychiatric units), private mental hospitals (both for-profit and not-for-profit), and community mental health centres. We suggest such data are partly an evaluation of our *de jure* policy of de-institutionalization, as well as an elucidation of our *de facto* policy of mental hospitalization (Kiesler, 1980a).

NATIONAL DATA ON LENGTH OF STAY IN MENTAL HOSPITALS

Veterans Administration

The Veterans Administration conducts an annual survey of discharges from all VA hospitals, which classifies patients on the basis of their primary diagnosis at the time of discharge. Since all individual discharge records are examined, the actual number of days from the date of admission to the date of discharge can be recorded, thus allowing a true average length of stay to be calculated. The statistics reported from this Patient Treatment File can differ from other statistics on mental disorders accumulated by the Veterans Administration in two ways. One, the discharge survey does not distinguish between mental disorders treated in psychiatric hospitals and those treated in other hospitals. We will present evidence that the stays for mental disorders in psychiatric hospitals are substantially longer than those in general hospitals. Overall statistics ignoring this distinction may mask the size of the differences.

Table 1.   Discharges, Total Days, Average and Median Length of Stay in all VA
Hospitals, by Patient Type, from Surveys by the VA, 1954–82

	Psychotic [a,b]				Other psychiatric [a,b]			
	Dis-charges	Total [c] days	Mean	Median	Dis-charges	Total [c] days	Mean	Median
1982	79,403	6,847,655	86.3	21.7	126,374	3,954,226	31.3	14.9
1981	78,538	6,944,803	88.4	21.7	129,853	3,927,811	30.3	14.1
1980	75,851	6,995,015	92.2	21.9	136,016	4,169,622	30.7	13.5
1979	78,524	7,777,489	99.1	22.0	134,032	4,390,282	32.8	13.5
1978	77,663	8,144,859	104.9	23.8	136,421	4,728,135	34.7	13.8
1977	75,149	9,231,886	122.9	24.9	139,983	4,824,591	34.5	13.8
1976	73,398	10,112,005	137.8	26.1	147,171	5,155,643	35.0	13.7
1975	73,026	11,614,048	159.0	27.6	145,752	5,269,606	36.2	14.0
1974	70,770	12,640,657	178.6	29.8	137,687	5,298,094	38.5	14.4
1973	66,838	13,610,474	203.6	35.2	128,252	5,179,094	40.4	15.7
1972	64,799	18,402,550	284.0	39.7	114,425	5,069,391	44.3	16.8
1971	66,603	29,801,010	447.4	48.4	100,186	5,732,808	57.2	20.0
1970	58,197	27,539,916	473.2	49.6	89,223	5,233,806	58.7	20.3
1969	57,851	26,986,958	466.5	48.4	87,100	8,008,886	92.0	22.7
1968	54,928	27,918,755	508.3	53.8	75,742	6,850,165	90.4	25.2
1967	—	—	—	—	—	—	—	—
1966	—	—	—	—	—	—	—	—
1965	—	—	—	—	—	—	—	—
1964	—	—	—	—	—	—	—	—
1963	—	—	—	—	—	—	—	—
1962	34,253	—	633.1	81.0	35,795	—	53.5	26.4
1961	31,152	—	662.8	85.8	34,582	—	55.7	25.5
1960	28,910	—	647.3	87.0	30,790	—	60.6	26.7
1959	25,100	—	643.5	90.0	30,775	—	52.1	25.2
1958	25,020	—	671.9	99.0	29,155	—	51.9	25.7
1957	23,630	—	583.8	96.3	30,605	—	46.4	24.2
1956	22,520	—	526.0	82.5	31,852	—	42.8	22.5
1955	24,004 [d]	—	453.0	70.5	32,328 [d]	—	41.8	21.8
1954	22,896 [d]	—	445.0	66.0	29,568 [d]	—	42.8	22.7

Notes:
1. The figures from 1954 to 1962 are based on random samples of varying sizes.
2. After 1969 the reporting period is for a fiscal rather than a calandar year.

[a]   The 'psychotic' and 'other psychiatric' patient type classification results from a recoding of the
      discharges with a principal diagnosis of mental disorder into these two groups. In condensing
      the several subcategories of mental disorder, as well as those in the other major diagnostic cate-
      gories, into fewer patient types, the sum of the psychotic and other psychiatric discharges does
      not always equal the total discharges with a principal diagnosis of mental disorder.
[b]   The VA defines 'principal diagnosis' as the diagnosis 'responsible for the major portion of the
      patient's length of stay as judged by the attending physician'. This is different from the National
      Center for Health Statistics' criterion of the condition resulting in the admission.
[c]   Total days equal the total number of days spent in the hospital by the discharges during the year.
      Unlike in-patient days, total days include days prior to the beginning of the reporting period.
      Total days are equivalent to NCHS' terms 'discharge days' (National Master Facility Inventory)
      and 'days of care' (National Hospital Discharge Survey).
[d]   Include discharges of veterans from VA and non-VA hospitals.

The second issue related to mental disorders is the classification of patients in this survey. People are categorized on the basis of their primary diagnosis at the time of discharge, based on inspection of their record. However, other statistics accumulated by the VA regarding admissions, in-patient days, and the like come from another information system which collects aggregate utilization data at each medical facility. The two types of data accumulation should be very similar, but not identical. That is, most admissions to the psychiatric sections of VA psychiatric and general hospitals presumably result in discharges with a principal diagnosis of mental disorder. However, one will find that the data on discharges shown here do not exactly match those reported by Kiesler and Sibulkin (1983) on clinical episodes.

The data reported by the Veterans Administration are presented in Table 1 for most of the years from 1954 to 1982. When available, we report the number of discharges in a given year, the total of days in the hospital accumulated by the discharges, and the mean and median lengths of stay of the patients discharged. The VA also separates data for mental disorder, differentiating between 'psychotic' and 'other psychiatric' diagnoses. (We will use the term 'non-psychotic' synonymously with VA's 'other psychiatric'.) Since the two distributions are substantially different, we present them separately here.

For both the psychotic and other psychiatric distributions, the means and medians are quite different. There are problems with both the mean and the median in looking at statistics of this nature. The degree to which the mean is the best measure of some central tendency depends upon the degree to which the distribution of length of stay is skewed. When the distribution is highly skewed the median is probably a better measure of central tendency. The mean, on the other hand, allows one to calculate the total number of days spent in the hospital by the patients. The combination of the two statistics is illuminating. For example, if the mean and the median are substantially different, as they are in most cases in in-patient treatment for mental disorders, one can look at the differences between them as one measure of changing patterns of treatment over years. If the mean is decreasing rapidly, while the median remains constant, one might suggest that institutions are pushing out long-term patients without substantially changing patterns of treatment. If all treatments were simply improved or intensified, one might expect all patients to get out more quickly, affecting both the median and the mean. The best approach in summary statistics would be to report the mean, the median, variance, and frequency distributions. No source of data currently does that, however.

Sources of VA data: Figures from 1970–82 are from the Veterans Administration Annual Report for that year, published by the Government Printing Office in the following year. Figures from 1954–69 appear in the next year's Annual Report. The medians for 1970–73 are unpublished figures calculated from the frequency distributions. The means for 1968–69 are unpublished figures calculated by dividing the total days by the discharges.

For the non-psychotic in-patients, one can see that the median length of stay remained relatively constant from 1954 through 1968. At that time it began to drop gradually from 25 days to 14 days in 1974 and has remained fairly constant to the present day. This suggests that a fairly substantial difference in the pattern of care at the VA occurred during those years. The mean of this distribution has a somewhat different array. The mean length of stay actually increased from the early 1950s through the late 1960s, and has subsequently decreased. Overall, the median length of stay for non-psychotics in VA hospitals has decreased from 23 days in 1954 to 15 days in 1982. The mean length of stay has changed from 43 days down to 31. Over the 29 years we see about a one-third decrease in the length of stay reflected in both the mean and median.

For psychotics the pattern of treatment is changing much more dramatically. In 1954 the median length of stay was 66 days, and rose to as high as 99 during the late 1950s and early 1960s. We see the same abrupt change in the length of stay for 1968 to 1974 and a gradual continued decrease since that time. The changes in the mean length of stay are more dramatic. In 1954 the average psychotic patient at the VA stayed 445 days, increasing to almost two years in the early 1960s, and decreasing fairly sharply since then. Overall, the average length of stay for a psychotic patient is 86 days, with a median of 22. The median length of stay for psychotics has decreased by two-thirds (and the mean by three-quarters) since the early 1950s.

Overall, the Veterans Administration shows the predicted pattern of decreased length of stay, reflected both for psychotics and non-psychotics (but more dramatically for the former). The decrease in the median length of stay suggests a changing pattern of treatment, and the change in the means suggests that an emptying out of long-term cases has also occurred.

In these data, the changes in LoS cannot be traced to the site of hospitalization, as previously noted. However, on direct request the VA did provide us with five years of previously unpublished data, sorting the data described in Table 1 by site of hospitalization. Before 1979 the VA distinguished between general hospitals and psychiatric hospitals. Beginning in 1979 all hospitals were called medical centres. Therefore, data by type of hospital are only available to 1978. We calculated the means from the overall data provided.

Table 2 shows a sharp difference between sites in average length of stay for both psychotic and other psychiatric patients. As can be seen, the LoS in general hospitals was stable 1974–78 for both psychotic (approximately 75–80 days) and other psychiatric patients (28–29 days).

The data for psychiatric hospitals are much different. Average LoS for both psychotic and non-psychotic treatment dropped during the five-year period. Yet startlingly, the LoS at the end of the period still was twice as long for psychiatric hospitals than for general hospitals for both categories of patients.

The differences between sites and the recent stability of LoS in general VA hospitals suggest a possibly serious qualification of our overall summary for the VA. We know from Table 2 that the decrease in average length of stay for 1974–78 reported in Table 1 is contained totally within psychiatric hospitals. The figures for treatment in general hospitals remained stable over that period.

Table 2. Discharges, Total Days, and Average Length of Stay in all VA Hospitals, by Patient Type and Type of Hospital, from Surveys by the VA, 1974–78

| | General Hospitals | | | | | |
| | Psychotic [a,b] | | | Other psychiatric [a,b] | | |
Year	Discharges	Total days [c]	Mean	Discharges	Total days [c]	Mean
1978	50,143	3,712,898	74.1	100,003	2,804,482	28.0
1977	52,201	4,293,029	82.2	110,359	3,169,582	28.7
1976	50,486	4,133,492	81.9	117,078	3,389,781	29.0
1975	47,587	3,445,097	72.4	114,635	3,315,370	28.9
1974	42,290	3,395,432	80.3	103,417	3,056,358	29.6

| | Psychiatric Hospitals | | | | | |
| | Psychotic | | | Other psychiatric | | |
Year	Discharges	Total days	Mean	Discharges	Total days	Mean
1978	27,407	4,402,610	160.6	36,279	1,917,182	52.9
1977	22,815	4,923,858	215.8	29,461	1,649,066	56.0
1976	22,912	5,978,513	260.9	30,093	1,765,862	58.7
1975	25,439	8,168,951	321.1	31,117	1,954,236	62.8
1974	28,480	9,245,225	324.6	34,270	2,241,736	65.4

Note: The sums of the two subgroups of psychotic discharges (and total days) and those for the two subgroups of other psychiatric discharges (and total days) do not equal the totals shown in Table 1 for 1977 and 1978. This results from a change in procedures regarding missing data. The Annual Report figures shown in Table 1 for 1977–78 include missing cases for which partial data were available. In previous years, cases with any missing data were left out. The figures in Table 2 for all years exclude cases for which any data relevant to the breakdown are missing.

[a] The 'psychotic' and 'other psychiatric' patient type classification results from a recoding of the discharges with a principal diagnosis of mental disorder into these two groups. In condensing the several subcategories of mental disorder, as well as those in the other major diagnostic categories, into fewer patient types, the sum of the psychotic and other psychiatric discharges does not always equal the total discharges with a principal diagnosis of mental disorder.

[b] The VA defines 'principal diagnosis' as the diagnosis 'responsible for the major portion of the patient's length of stay as judged by the attending physician'. This is different from the National Center for Health Statistics' criterion of the condition resulting in the admission.

[c] Total days equal the total number of days spent in the hospital by the discharges during the year. Unlike in-patient days, total days include days prior to the beginning of the reporting period. Total days are equivalent to NCHS' terms 'discharge days' (National Master Facility Inventory) and 'days of care' (National Hospital Discharge Survey).

Source: Discharges by patient type are published in the VA Annual Reports for those years. The breakdown of patient type by type of hospital shown here was obtained from the VA. We calculated the means by dividing the total days by number of discharges

The extent to which changes observed in other years are specific to site is unknown, but surely substantial.

The overall trends must be qualified by existing differences in average length of stay by site. Further, the overall figures are partly determined by variation in the proportion of total patients in each site. We know from admissions data (Kiesler and Sibulkin, 1983) that the proportion of total psychiatric cases admitted to the VA general hospitals (rather than psychiatric hospitals) has been rising. In 1970, less than half of the total of psychiatric patients were treated in general hospitals, whereas by the end of the decade over 75 per cent were. When the LoS for general hospitals is much less than that of psychiatric hospitals, the overall mean is partly determined by the proportion of the former. In this case, at least some of the decrease in overall LoS in prior years is due to an increase in the proportion of patients treated in general hospitals (and hence who stayed a shorter time).

Non-Federal Short-term General Hospitals

As previously mentioned, the major source of data on true length of stay is the National Hospital Discharge Survey (NHDS), conducted by the National Center for Health Statistics (NCHS). Approximately 220,000 discharge records are systematically selected (on the basis of their terminal digit numbers) from a probability sample of hospitals in the National Master Facility Inventory, and the discharge data are inflated to represent the universe of discharges. A true length of stay is obtained, since the date of admission and date of discharge are recorded for each discharge during the year. In 1978 the NMFI listed 6,263 non-federal short-stay hospitals, defined as those with an average length of stay of less than 30 days.[5] Of these, 94 per cent were general as opposed to specialty hospitals and 2 per cent were psychiatric hospitals (Health US, 1980). Also, the vast majority of general hospitals are short-stay and non-federal. Therefore, we use the term 'general' hospital to mean non-federal, short-stay, general and specialty hospitals.

Table 3 presents the mean length of stay from the National Hospital Discharge Survey for the years 1965 through 1981 and the medians for 1973–1981. One can see that the number of discharges has continued to rise over the years (678,000 in 1965 to 1,747,000 in 1981). The mean length of stay has remained remarkably stable over those years. Length of stay in the mid-1960s was slightly over 12 days and has fluctuated somewhere around 11 days ever since. One can see that in recent years, the median LoS was very stable as well.

These data do not fit neatly with some from NIMH. It is important to note that the NHDS includes all general hospitals, not just those with a psychiatric unit. This difference in universe plus NIMH's hospital-based type of survey account for the discrepancy between NHDS and NIMH figures. NIMH covers only non-federal general hospitals (short- and long-stay) with a separate psychiatric unit, which account for approximately one-third of the total psychiatric in-patient episodes in general hospitals (Kiesler and Sibulkin, 1983). However, most of NIMH data for these units is based on its Inventory of Mental Health Facilities survey of aggregate admissions, discharges, and

Table 3.   Discharges with First-listed Diagnosis of Mental Disorder, Days of Care, Average, and Median Length of Stay in Non-federal Short Stay Hospitals from NCHS Surveys, 1965–81

Year	Discharges [a]	Days of care [b]	Average LoS	Median
1981	1,747,000	20,898,000	12.0	7.1
1980	1,692,000	19,578,000	11.6	6.9
1979	1,723,000	18,983,000	11.0	6.7
1978	1,730,000	19,435,000	11.2	6.7
1977	1,625,000	17,606,000	10.8	6.7
1976	1,485,000	15,604,000	10.5	6.5
1975	1,494,000	16,496,000	11.0	6.7
1974	1,352,000	15,248,000	11.3	—
1973	1,227,000	14,176,000	11.6	6.8
1972	1,176,000	13,666,000	11.6	—
1971	1,050,000	12,341,000	11.8	—
1970	604,000	10,940,000	18.1	—
1969	—	—	—	—
1968	799,000	9,760,000	12.2	—
1967	753,000	9,329,000	12.4	—
1966	759,000	9,655,000	12.7	—
1965	678,000	c	12.6 [c]	—

Note: Non-federal short-stay hospitals are those having six or more beds and an average length of stay of less than 30 days. Although the universe includes short-stay specialty hospitals, 94 per cent of the non-federal short-stay hospitals were general ones in 1978 (*Health United States 1980*, 1981).

[a]   The first listed diagnosis is intended to equal the principal diagnosis, which is 'the condition established after study to be chiefly responsible for occasioning the admission of the patient to the hospital for care'. In the absence of other information, the diagnosis listed first on the medical record is assumed to be the principal diagnosis (Haupt, 1980).

[b]   Days of care are the total number of days accumulated at the time of discharge by all discharges during the year. Unlike in-patient days, days of care include days spent in the hospital prior to the beginning of the reporting period. They are equivalent to the National Master Facility Inventory's term 'discharge days'.

[c]   The unpublished days of care figure is 9,038,000. Dividing days of care by the 678,000 discharges equals a 13.3 average length of stay. However, the published average length of stay equals 12.6 days. Apparently, an error occurred in 1965 data.

Sources of NCHS data (Full citations appear under the authors' names in the References): **Discharges and Average Length of Stay:** 1966–67, 1970: unpublished data from the National Hospital Discharge Survey. We calculate the average length of stay by dividing the days of care (see below) by the number of discharges. 1965, 1968, 1971–80: Series 13, Nos. 6, 12, 16, 20, 25, 26, 31, 37, 41, 46, 60, 64. 1981: Unpublished data from the National Hospital Discharge Survey. **Days of Care:** 1974–76: *Nation's Use of Health Resources*, 1979. 1973: *Nation's Use of Health Resources, 1976 Edition*. All other years are unpublished data from the National Hospital Discharge Survey. **Medians:** Calculated from unpublished frequency distributions.

inpatient days. As discussed, we need the total number of days that discharges spent in the hospital, including those prior to the reporting period, in order to calculate an average number of days per discharge. These NIMH surveys do not allow calculation of a true LoS.

In 1971 and 1975 NIMH did conduct a sample survey of discharges from non-federal general hospital psychiatric units.[6] Discharge records from one month[7] were systematically selected from a probability sample of hospitals,[8] thus allowing for a calculation of true length of stay from the date of admission to the date of discharge, as well as the median length of stay. In 1975 the average length of stay was 17 days (Statistical Note No. 133), 6 days longer than the average for all general hospitals, with or without a psychiatric unit. Little is known about the differences in type of patient served and treatment between general hospitals providing psychiatric care in a psychiatric unit versus the general medical ward.

NIMH does not appear to have published an overall mean or days of care for 1971, preventing an observation of a possible trend in average length of stay in psychiatric units. However, the medians show little change between 1971 and 1975. In 1971 the median lengths of stay were 6.9 and 13.6 days, for psychiatric units in public and private non-federal general hospitals, respectively (Statistical Note No. 70). The medians were 8.1 and 13.6 days in 1975 (Statistical Note No. 133, Mental Health National Statistics Series CN, No. 2). One can see that the median lengths of stay in psychiatric units in public hospitals are similar to those found in general hospitals without psychiatric units. Rather longer median stays are found in private general hospitals with psychiatric units.

Short-term general hospitals are the site at which people are most frequently hospitalized for mental disorders, accounting now for over 50 per cent of the total in-patient episodes nationally (Kiesler and Sibulkin, 1983). In spite of the increasing use of these hospitals as places in which to treat mental disorders, the mean length of treatment has remained remarkably stable over a 17-year period. About two-thirds of these episodes take place in general hospitals without psychiatric units. The details of these cases, the methods of treatment, and the like are not well known.

Two points are worth emphasizing about treatment in general hospitals. The length of stay in these sites has remained stable over the years for which data are available. Further, the length of stay is also very short compared to other places of treatment.

State and County Mental Hospitals

State and county mental hospitals are one of the sites in which length of stay is not often calculated. The hospitals are surveyed consistently by both NIMH and the American Hospital Association, although the surveys are somewhat different. The AHA almost always shows a higher count of state hospitals, partly because they include hospitals treating primarily alcoholism and mental retardation. AHA surveys almost 7000 total hospitals each year, with a response rate average of approximately 90 per cent. Missing data are filled in either by using the previous year's data for a hospital or by using an estimate based on hospitals with similar characteristics. NIMH, on the other hand, compiles its list of state hospitals from the state mental health authorities and over 90 per cent of the hospitals submitted inventories in 1977 and 1978. Follow-up efforts are made to obtain missing data. Information that is still missing is estimated by using the previous year's figures or the average of the hospitals in the same geographical region (Statistical Notes Nos 153, 156). The number of hospitals in question has fluctuated over the years, but has remained around 300 for the last 25 years. According to both surveys, the number of residents in these hospitals has decreased about 75 per cent over the 25-year period, although admissions have approximately doubled during that same time period.

The data presented in Table 4 are from the National Master Facility Inventory. As previously described, these are essentially AHA data. However, psychiatric hospitals in the NMFI do not include hospitals for alcoholism or mental retardation, as they do in AHA publications. Data for 1971 and 1973 were previously published and NCHS provided us with previously unpublished data for 1969, 1972, and 1974 through 1978. In 1969, the average length of stay in a state or county mental hospital was 421 days or approximately 14 months. In 1971 this had been reduced to approximately a year, and the average length of stay continued to fall to 189 days in 1978.

NIMH conducted surveys of length of stay in state and county mental hospitals in 1969, 1971, and 1975 (Statistical Notes Nos. 57, 74; Mental Health National Statistics Series CN, No. 2). The 1969 survey, which is much less frequently cited than the more recent ones, sampled 'discontinuations' from state and county mental hospitals during one month.[9] The estimated total discontinuations were 376,105, and we calculated the median length of stay (from the frequency distribution) to be 47 days. Since the distribution is cut off at 721 days, we cannot calculate the mean, barring a comparison with NCHS data. However, the NIMH median of 47 is essentially equal to the VA median for psychotics of 48 days in 1969. In order to continue the comparison of NIMH medians with the VA data for psychotics, we turn to the 1971 and 1975 sample surveys.

The 1971 and 1975 surveys differ from that of the 1969 one and the NMFI in several respects. NIMH sampled records of state and county mental hospitals in 1971 and 1975. However, an important difference is that new admissions during one month rather than discharges were sampled.[10] These admissions were followed through their treatment and NIMH reports a median length of stay based on each case's length of stay from admission to discharge. Unfortunately,

46   PROGRESS IN APPLIED SOCIAL PSYCHOLOGY

Table 4.   Discharges, Discharge Days, and Average Length of Stay in State and
County Psychiatric Hospitals from NCHS Surveys, 1969–78

Year	Discharges	Discharge days [a]	Average length of stay
1978	392,121	74,164,396	189
1977	429,564	90,030,464	210
1976	443,874	114,544,086	258
1975	453,676	122,504,438	270
1974	457,721	119,715,721	262
1973	466,269	145,305,702	312
1972	480,010	167,161,427	348
1971	500,973	183,798,798	367
1969	436,695	183,818,098	421

[a] Discharge days are the total number of days accumulated at the time of discharge by all
discharges during the year. Unlike in-patient days, discharge days include days spent in the
hospital prior to the beginning of the reporting period. They are equivalent to the National
Hospital Discharge Survey's term 'days of care'.

Sources of NCHS data (Full citations appear under the authors' names in the References): 1973:
Series 14, No. 16. 1971: Series 14, No. 12. All other years: unpublished data from AHA/
NCHS (National Master Facility Inventory). We calculated the average length of stay by divid-
ing the discharge days by the number of discharges.

NIMH cut off its counting period at 6 months in 1971 and 3 months in 1975.
Therefore, medians for both years can be calculated, but a mean cannot
be calculated in either case because the cut-off of the counting period prohibits
calculation of the total number of discharge days. In addition, by taking only
new admissions, no potential effect on the overall data base from cases held
over from the previous years can be observed. In 1971 NIMH reported from
this survey that the median length of treatment in state and county mental
hospitals was 44 days, and that it had declined to 26 days in 1975.

In 1969 the NCHS reported an average stay of 421 days and 258 days in
1976, based on discharge days. Looking at the comparable years for the VA
treatment of psychotics, it is possible that the NCHS and the NIMH figures do
not conflict. The closest we have come to this comparison is that in 1969 for
psychotics the VA reported the median of 48 days which had fallen by 1975 to
28 days. In 1971 the VA reported the mean of 447 days which by 1975 had
fallen to 159. The data from the NMFI are more thorough, but report only
means. Despite the greater limitations of the NIMH data, their reporting of the
medians is not necessarily inconsistent with the NMFI data.

Overall, across the nine reporting dates for which data are available, the
average length of stay in state and county mental hospitals has fallen
dramatically from 421 days to 189 days over a 9-year period. The trend of
de-institutionalization efforts is clear, but we note the still remaining large
average length of stay of about 6 months (189 days).

Private Mental Hospitals

The only data on true length of stay for private mental hospitals are the 9 years previously described (7 of them unpublished) and obtained from the National Master Facility Inventory. These data are presented in Table 5, distinguishing between those hospitals run for profit and those not-for-profit.

Table 5.   Discharges, Discharge Days, and Average Length of Stay in Private Psychiatric Hospitals from Surveys by NCHS, 1969–78

	For-profit hospitals			Not-for-profit hospitals		
Year	Discharges	Discharge days [a]	Average LoS	Discharges	Discharge days [a]	Average LoS
1978	85,431	2,699,885	32	63,138	2,671,134	42
1977	76,436	2,527,421	33	62,901	2,701,822	43
1976	74,353	2,444,673	33	65,905	3,704,254	56
1975	76,021	2,361,208	31	63,679	3,025,789	48
1974	68,119	2,338,145	34	57,912	2,903,094	50
1973	63,932	2,259,160	35	51,696	2,252,881	44
1972	51,003	1,792,316	35	50,556	2,405,201	48
1971	54,864	1,938,132	35	50,254	3,270,442	65
1969	48,726	2,705,956	56	53,944	3,999,046	74

[a] Discharge days are the total number of days accumulated at the time of discharge by all discharges during the year. Unlike in-patient days, discharge days include days spent in the hospital prior to the beginning of the reporting period. They are equivalent to the National Hospital Discharge Survey's term 'days of care'.

Sources of NCHS data (Full citations appear under the author's names in the References): 1973: Series 14, No. 16. 1971: Series 14, No. 12. All other years: unpublished data from AHA/NCHS (National Master Facility Inventory). We calculated the average length of stay by dividing the discharge days by the number of discharges.

For private mental hospitals run for profit, the average length of stay was 56 days in 1969, falling to 35 days in 1971 and remaining stable through 1978. For private mental hospitals in the non-profit category, these data are much more variable. Over the 9-year period the average length of stay decreased from 74 days in 1969 to 44 days in 1973. It then fluctuated and reached a high of 56 days in 1976 before decreasing to 42 days in 1978, the lowest according to our most recent data. It is possible those fluctuations correspond to increases and decreases in the supply of beds. This hypothesis is indirectly supported by data showing a decrease of available beds from 1971 to 1973 and a corresponding increase from 1973 to 1976 (Vital and Health Statistics Series 14, Nos. 12, 16, 23 and unpublished data). The number of beds may have been increased to accommodate the press of patients or increased beds may have led to pressures to fill them. However, the length of stay began to drop again after 1976 while beds continued to rise (Vital and Health Statistics Series 14, No. 24 and unpublished data). It is quite possible the bed supply and length of stay follow each other, with time lags of varying degrees; however, these data do not afford definite conclusions.

Similar to its survey of state mental hospitals, NIMH followed a cohort of admissions during one month in 1970 and in 1975, thus providing median lengths of stay of admissions, but not the average lengths of stay for discharges.[11] In contrast to the means from NCHS data, the medians hardly changed from 22 days in 1970 to 20 days in 1975 (Statistical Note No. 75; Mental Health National Statistics Series CN, No. 2). This suggests that treatment may not have changed; rather that long-term care cases may have been released earlier.

Overall, the data for average length of stay in private mental hospitals show somewhat of a drop, although stable in recent years. We note that the average length of stay for private, for-profit mental hospitals looks fairly similar to that found for non-psychotics in the Veterans Administration. Perhaps the hospitals run for profit are more likely to take only patients that they feel they can treat more effectively, avoiding, perhaps, the more serious cases in the VA psychotic category.

Community Mental Health Centres

Only the National Institute of Mental Health gathers data from community mental health centres. Data were gathered yearly on the universe through 1976 and on an approximately 25 per cent sample since then. Although NIMH has reported average length of stay as decreased (Vishci et al., 1980), they do not calculate true length of stay. They do calculate the number of in-patient days within a given year per episode treated. As we have suggested, this number is a distortion of true length of stay, if the number of admissions, discharges or true length of stay actually vary across years. Basic data that NIMH has accumulated on in-patient care in community mental health centres is presented in Table 6.

As Table 6 shows, the number of in-patient episodes treated in community mental health centres has risen rather consistently, since the beginning of the system in the late 1960s. (Although 1980 may show the beginning of a decline.) The statistic, average number of in-patient days per episode, is also recorded in Table 6, as calculated by NIMH.[12] That number has fluctuated from around 13 to 18 days over the 10 years reported. As we have mentioned before, the number of in-patient days is the total number of days beds were occupied in the centres during the year; the number of episodes equals the number of admissions during that year plus the residents who are already in-patients at the beginning of the reporting period. This statistic will equal the true length of stay if, and only if, the number of admissions and discharges is invariant across the years and the true length of stay, itself, is invariant. The number of episodes has continued to rise, therefore the statistic is an under-estimate of true length of

Table 6.   In-patient Episodes, In-patient Days, and Number of Days per Episode in Community Mental Health Centres from NIMH Surveys, 1970–80

Year	In-patient episodes	In-patient days	In-patient days/episode
1980	254,288	3,609,000	14.2
1978	298,897	4,063,176	13.6
1977	268,966	3,818,497	14.2
1976	270,944	3,951,001	14.6
1975	246,891	3,948,466	16.0
1974	211,027	3,836,452	18.2
1973	191,946	3,275,630	17.1
1972	144,601	2,561,633	17.7
1971	130,088	2,225,396	17.1
1970	110,622	1,923,720	17.4

Sources of NIMH data: **Episodes and In-patient days:** 1980: unpublished data from NIMH. All other years: Provisional data on federally funded community mental health centers, 1978–79. **In-patient days per episode:** 1971 and 1975: Statistical Note No. 95 (based on responses from 194 of the 295 CMHCs in 1971); Vischi, *et al.*, 1980. We calculated the length of stay for all other years.

stay, particularly in later years. This under-estimate results because the numerator of in-patient days does not include the days the increased number of admissions will generate in the next year. Although there is not a great deal of variance across years in the number of in-patient days per episode, there is surely even less variance in the true length of stay, given the direction of the error underlying the reported statistic. One would suggest, therefore, that the true length of stay in CMHS has been rather stable across the 10 years for which data are available.

SUMMARY OF TRENDS IN LENGTHS OF STAY

We have presented all the available data on length of stay for in-patient treatment of mental disorders in the United States. Many of these data have been published in various federal sources, but a substantial proportion have not been published elsewhere. We have discussed trends across years within each site. In this section we try to present an overall summary of more recent trends in in-patient treatment. Table 7 presents a summary of the trends that we were able to detect during the decade of the 1970s. Table 7 summarizes our data by the site of hospitalization, our representation of the trend in the last decade or so, and the actual latest figures in the year obtained. In addition, we contrast these trends with changes in the site of hospitalization. Kiesler and Sibulkin (1983) used a multiple-source method of estimating the number of hospitalizations in various in-patient sites. The last column on Table 7 shows their data for the number of episodes in each of the sites, as well as the latest year for which data were available.

Table 7. Summary of Trends in Length of Hospital Stay for Mental Disorders and Current Number of Episodes by Site

Site	Trend of LoS during 1970s	Latest figures		Year of latest LoS	No. of[a] episodes (latest year)
		Mean	Median		
VA Gen. Hosp.					
Psychotic	Stable	74.1		1978	135,562(1978)[b]
Non-psychotic	Stable	28.0		1978	
VA Psychiatric Hosp.					
Psychotic	Very sharp decrease	160.6		1978	
non-psychotic	Slight decrease	52.9		1978	65,305(1978)[b]
Gen. Hosp.[c]	Stable	12.0	7.1	1981	1,804,000(1981)
State/county Hosp.	Very sharp decrease	189.1	25.5[d]	1978	527,000(1979)
Private (for-profit)	Stable	31.6		1978	
Private (not-for-profit)	Fluctuating	42.3	20.2[e]	1978	151,000(1979)
CMHCs	Stable	14.2[f]	N/A	1980	254,000(1980)

[a] The total of 2,936,867 differs from the 3,012,500 shown previously in Kiesler and Sibulkin (1983) due to the exclusion here of residential treatment centres for emotionally disturbed children, the use of somewhat different VA data [see note b below], and more recent figures for general hospitals, state and private hospitals, and CMHCs.

[b] The 135,562 episodes result from adding 121,186 admissions to psychiatric bed sections of general hospitals plus 14,376 average daily census. The 65,305 episodes equal 50,208 admissions to psychiatric hospitals plus 15,097 average daily census (Kiesler and Sibulkin, in press, Table 2 and unpublished VA data). This calculation of episodes does not include intra- and inter-hospital transfers.

[c] Includes hospitals both with and without psychiatric units.

[d] From NIMH's 1975 survey of admissions (Mental Health National Statistics Series CN No. 2).

[e] From NIMH's 1975 survey of admissions (Mental Health National Statistics Series CN No. 2).

[f] Approximate, see text.

As one can see from Table 7, the largest change in trends of length of stay has occurred in the VA's treatment of psychotic patients in psychiatric hospitals and in the state and county mental hospitals. Both of these sites show very sharp decreases in length of stay over the decades. At the same time, however, both still represent substantially the longest lengths of stay of any in-patient site. While state and county mental hospitals have demonstrated sharp decreases in the average length of stay, the most recent data available indicate a still lengthy stay of 189 days on the average, over 6 months. In the VA, the average length of stay for psychotics in psychiatric hospitals has also decreased substantially, but still represents 5 months of in-patient care on the average.

We emphasize that all the data in Table 7 represent episodes and not people.

To the extent that people are discharged and readmitted during a given year's reporting period, the figures presented in Table 7 represent an under-estimate of average length of total *treatment*.

The only other changes in length of stay represented in Table 7 are the VA's treatment of non-psychotic patients in psychiatric hospitals only, with a slight decrease of both mean and median in the 1970s, and the rather fluctuating data from private not-for-profit mental hospitals. All the other sites of mental hospitalization show rather stable average lengths of treatment during the past decade or so.

We can summarize Table 7 as indicating that for the seven sites of mental hospitalization we surveyed over the last decade or so, four have had fairly stable lengths of stay, one has fluctuated, and two have shown sharp decreases. Those represent the sites of hospitalization. We can change that question a bit to ask: 'What is the probability when a patient is hospitalized that the length of treatment would be less in 1980 than in 1970?' This question involves looking at the number of episodes in each site rather than just the sites. Unfortunately we do not have the number of patients *per se*.

The last column of Table 7 represents the most recent data on the number of episodes in each site. The numbers of episodes in private for-profit and not-for-profit hospitals are approximately equal over the years, although they fluctuate from year to year. For the purposes of our argument, let us assume that they are equal.

The outcome of this line of thought is as follows. The best estimate of the total number of episodes in these sites is 2,936,867 (but see Table 7, footnotes *a* and *b*). Of these episodes, 2,269,062 or 77 per cent occurred at in-patient sites where the average length of stay has been stable over the last decade or so. Three per cent occurred in sites whose length of stay has fluctuated, and 20 per cent of the total number of episodes reported have occurred at sites where there has been a sharp decrease in average length of stay over the last decade or so. In short, although there is some evidence that the average length of stay for mental disorders has decreased significantly at some psychiatric hospital sites, only increasingly small numbers of episodes nationally take place in those sites. In that sense, if one were to be hospitalized in 1980, one can probabilistically expect to be hospitalized in a place where the average length of stay has not changed over the last decade.

DISCUSSION

As we have discussed, the cornerstone of national *de jure* mental health policy is de-institutionalization. As Bachrach (1976), in a now classic paper, has described it, the two main components of this process are to get people out of hospitals who are already there and to prevent others from being hospitalized who might otherwise be. The evidence regarding the success of this venture is rather mixed.

Kiesler and Sibulkin (1983) outline in great detail the data on the number of episodes of hospitalization for mental disorders. They found that the episodic rate has been increasing, well beyond the increase in the population. Their most recent figures indicate 3,000,000 episodes of mental hospitalization a year. If the success of the de-institutionalization effort is to be predicated on a decreasing rate of hospitalization for mental disorders, then these data are certainly quite contrary to that intent. This is, however, merely one piece in a very complicated puzzle.

If the de-institutionalization effort is taken to mean getting people out of mental hospitals more quickly than before, then that picture is also very complicated. Many people see the de-institutionalization movement as specifically oriented towards state and county mental hospitals. To the extent that this is true, it has been a resounding success thus far. The average (or median) stay at a state or county mental hospital for a mental disorder is a fraction of what it was in the 1950s and 1960s. There is no question that such hospitals were the prime focus of de-institutionalization and that they represent the snakepits in film and literature. On the other hand, the average length of stay in a state or county hospital, in the most recent data available, was 6 months. It would seem, even given the sharp decrease in the average length of stay over the previous 20 years, that continued efforts must be made to shorten the stay. One must infer that the state and county mental hospitals have not lost their custodial role in mental health treatment in the United States. The degree to which such a custodial role is needed (assuming one of high quality could be played) probably would be open to sharp debate among knowledgeable professionals. Further, others have argued that as a result of the de-institutionalization movement, there has been a transfer of the elderly from state and county mental hospitals to nursing homes (Statistical Note No. 107). The number of patients in nursing homes with a diagnosis of mental disorder has increased through the same time period, but the national data are still difficult to disentangle (Vital and Health Statistics Series 12, Nos. 8, 22). Nursing homes may, but certainly do not necessarily, represent an advance in the treatment of the elderly who might otherwise in former times have been interred in a state mental hospital. If the custodial care of those mental disorders has only been transferred to nursing homes, then the nation's purpose of de-institutionalization may not have been well served.

The state mental hospital may still be attempting to serve patients who are commonly regarded as incurable and whom, perhaps, other sites would not accept. There certainly is some validity to that statement. On the other hand, the other site whose length of stay has sharply decreased is that of the VA psychiatric hospitals, particularly for psychotics. Average length of stay for such patients has decreased as sharply as for those in the state/county mental hospital, but the mean length of stay for psychotics in VA psychiatric hospitals is still 5 months.

The type of analysis that we have undertaken here ignores demographic and diagnostic differences among the populations of patients in the different hospital sites. It must be surely true, for example, that patients in private mental hospitals are quite different than those in, say, state and county mental hospitals on such variables as diagnosis, income, education, family background, and the like. Some data are available on demographic and diagnostic categories for different hospital sites. However, to adequately tease out what the relevant variables are would demand that these variables be related to the true length of stay of a given patient. Since data are so sparse for several sites on true length of stay, it would be impossible to disentangle completely the intricacies at a national level. A detailed analysis of national aggregate data is clearly needed. It would be expensive, laborious, and well beyond the scope of this paper.

The increasing popularity of general hospitals as a place to treat mental disorders is a relatively recent phenomenon. NIMH does track general hospitals which have a psychiatric unit. Those hospitals account for only one-third of the episodes reported in Table 3. Exactly what sorts of patients are involved in these general hospital sites, and the treatments they receive there, are relatively unknown. The two types of general hospitals, those with and without psychiatric units, deserve extensive and detailed analysis of the cases they treat for mental disorders.

Three-quarters of in-patient episodes of treatment for mental disorder occur in hospital sites whose average length of stay has been stable over the last decade or so. We note that these sites, whose average length of stay has been stable, are also those which tend to have the shortest average length of stay. We note further that even though particular sites have stable lengths of stay over years, they are nonetheless reliably different from other sites which are also stable. For example, the original length of stay for mental disorders in a general hospital has hovered around 11 days for the past decade or so. The average length of stay in CMHSs has also been stable, but about 3 or more days than that in the general hospital. More interestingly, the private, for-profit mental hospital, while stable, has a length of stay approximately three times that which occurs at a general hospital. Both stability of length of stay in these sites and continuing reliable differences among them are fruitful areas for future research.

PEOPLE AND TOTAL LENGTH OF IN-PATIENT TREATMENT

All of the data presented here pertain to the length of stay *per episode* for in-patient care. The number of people involved is unknown and can be only roughly estimated. This prohibits clear discussion of several important policy issues.

In our work (Kiesler and Sibulkin, 1983), the national data on in-patient episodes proved difficult to disentangle. Different data sources had different data bases, different sampling proportions of sites and patients, and the like. However, no attempt is made nationally to track people rather than episodes.

For years, the best evidence on the revolving-door phenomenon was a 1965 study by Bahn *et al.*, on the first-year data from the Maryland (State) Psychiatric register. Such registers track all psychiatric contacts within their geographical boundaries and are well suited to provide evidence regarding an individual's use of psychiatric facilities. In that study covering one year, they found that the average in-patient accounted for 1.2 episodes. Hence, one could multiply episodes by 0.83 to derive actual number of people involved. Until very recently, that was the best evidence on translating episodes to people. We note that the statistic is almost 20-years-old, covers one geographical area, and is for one year only. That is, the experience of the people as in-patients before and after that year is unknown.

A recent paper by Goldberg and Allen (1981) covers several years experience with the Monroe County (NY) psychiatric case register. In a 5-year period of the 1970s studied intensively, Goldberg and Allen found an average of 1.35 episodes per person, leading to a correction factor of 0.74. There is a slightly higher readmission rate in the Monroe County data than found for Maryland 15 years previously. Whether the difference reflects a change in national practice or some alternative mechanism based on other differences between the two regions is unknown.

It is possible the difference in readmission rates between the two studies is real and reflects the so-called revolving-door phenomenon. If so, several things should be noted. The Goldberg and Allen data show a readmission rate 12 per cent higher (for the mid-1970s) than Bahn *et al.* found for the early 1960s. We note that the average length of stay decreased much more than 12 per cent during this time.

The general conclusion behind the revolving door is that we have been placing the same number of people (or fewer) into mental hospitals over time, but more often and for a shorter period of time. The data discussed above would not support such a neat conceptual package. Keep in mind that our data on episodes and length of stay are national in scope and reliable. The data on readmission rate are local and therefore much less reliable. However, assuming their reliability and representativeness, our overall conclusion should be: we have doubled the number of people hospitalized, each slightly more often (12 per cent) but for many fewer days.

This suggests total treatment has changed considerably: even though the readmission rate has risen slightly, it is less than the concurrent drop in average length of stay, and hence total in-patient days per person have dropped. There are two major conceptual problems with this analysis (aside from the reliability issue with the readmission rate). First, the number of people hospitalized with mental disorders has risen so sharply that the population of hospitalized people surely changed also. That is, we apparently are hospitalizing people who would not have been hospitalized earlier in our history. If these are less serious cases, then their stay should be shorter and their addition to national statistics would both reduce average length of stay and retard or otherwise mask an increase in readmission rates. Second, in both the Maryland and Monroe County data, the rates computed are within one year only. Any readmission across years cannot be ascertained.

The problem of readmission in other years is important. An NIMH study (1976) of 10 years in Monroe County illustrates this point. In that study, people hospitalized during the first year spent an average of 86 in-patient days. Over the 10 years, however, the same patients accumulated a total of 332 days. Unfortunately this study did not track episodes, but it does illustrate the limitations of counting episodes per person only within years.

The lack of national data on people rather than episodes interferes with clear discussion of national policy alternatives in mental health policy. It seems very reasonable to conclude from the above data that the number of people hospitalized has increased sharply over the last 20 years, but that the total days of in-patient care per person have decreased. However, a more precise analysis cannot be undertaken, given the current state of the national data base.

BUT IS IT SOCIAL PSYCHOLOGY?

One can best describe the type of research we have outlined here as problem-oriented and policy-relevant. Although applied social psychology is growing rapidly, there is still a need to emphasize that one must put the problem first and the theory and method of one's field second (cf. Bickman, 1980; Kiesler, 1981a, 1981b).

The general problem we are interested in is what the nation does in the name of mental health, with what effect, and at what cost. The policy issues concern what we think we now do and what decision or policy alternatives are both effective and feasible. This chapter represents a relatively early point in a sequence of investigation.

Our previous reports might best be described as a top-down approach to policy research. Kiesler (1980a) describes our mental health policy, both *de facto* and *de jure*, and some of the major research questions that need to be answered. When described in this way, various questions regarding mental hospitalization loom large.

Mental hospitalization is clearly a critical ingredient of our national mental health policy. Historically, it has been the treatment of choice for 150 years (Mechanic, 1980), and some historians feel that our reliance on mental hospitalization has impeded our search for alternative, effective forms of treatment (e.g. Grob, 1973). Economists estimate that 6–10 billion dollars are spent a year on mental hospitalization (Rubin, 1978).

Viewed in the light of general policy issues, questions related to mental hospitalization are intriguing. The next step was to pull together and reanalyse experimental studies of the effectiveness of mental hospitalization (Kiesler, 1982). Kiesler concluded that the vast majority of patients now being hospitalized could be more effectively treated through alternative care mechanisms and urged a policy of *non*-hospitalization. On the other hand, the national policy of de-institutionalization implies that the rate of hospitalization should be decreasing and that hospital stays should be shorter. Kiesler and Sibulkin (1983) investigated the former and showed that the number of hospitalizations was increasing although the sites of hospitalization have changed considerably. The current chapter investigates the other part of the picture – the length of stay. As you have seen, that picture is complex. Although lengths of hospital stay have generally decreased over the years, they have been fairly stable over the last decade or so, with the rather dramatic exceptions of VA psychiatric hospitals and state mental hospitals.

As you can see, our interest is in the problem first. We have allowed the problem and relevant policy issues to dictate both specific projects and our approach to them. The top-down approach necessitates that. Our methods have been logical and analytical, with only elementary statistics involved.

There is not much social psychological theory or method in this series of studies. We would argue that more social psychology could have been a hindrance rather than a help, thus far at least. That is not to say that there are not important issues involved that are more central to social psychology. For example, hospitalization implies complex issues of professional judgement and decision-making. Being hospitalized involves self-fulfilling prophecies and normative influences of other patients. There are serious questions whether the various sites of hospitalization are qualitatively different environments or, rather, all are total institutions to varying degrees (Goffman, 1961). The challenge of these data to current practice also involves issues of effective knowledge use and utilization (Kiesler, 1981b).

The generally negative attitudes of the public towards mental illness, community placement of patients, and non-hospital alternative care strategies need intensive investigation. The fact that there are millions of people involved, each with a dramatic, potentially life-changing event, should alone intrigue social psychologists. These issues have been discussed in more detail elsewhere (e.g. Kiesler, 1980b, 1981a).

The question of whether this chapter is applied social psychology or not is moot, and the answer depends as much on intellectual taste as anything. We find these questions intriguing and share them in the hopes that the reader might do so as well. The style of the research and its problem orientation is something we would like to see more social psychologists adopt but, alas, that also is a matter of intellectual taste.

SUMMARY

The question of the average length of stay for patients hospitalized for mental disorders was investigated as part of the evaluation of the national policy of de-institutionalization. Using a multiple-source method of estimation and uncovering previously unpublished data, average length of hospital stay was ascertained for seven sites of hospitalization: state and county mental hospitals; community mental health centres; general hospitals, with and without a psychiatric ward; VA general hospitals; VA psychiatric hospitals; private, for-profit mental hospitals; and private, not-for-profit mental hospitals.

Over the years the site of hospitalization has changed. State/county and private mental hospitals now account for only 25 per cent of hospital episodes for mental disorders. Over a 30-year period, the average length of hospital stay for mental disorders has generally decreased. More recently, however, lengths of stay have been fairly stable, with two exceptions. Average lengths of stay in state/county mental hospitals and VA psychiatric hospitals continue to decrease sharply. However, the most recent data still indicate an average hospital stay of 6 and 5 months respectively.

NOTES

1. Kiesler and Sibulkin were able to calculate only clinical episodes, not the actual number of people hospitalized. Data are surprisingly sparse regarding unduplicated counts of people hospitalized. Anecdotal clinical evidence of the revolving-door phenomenon is probably valid, but precise national data on its degree are lacking.
2. We use these episode figures only to illustrate how a decrease in episodes has resulted from a decrease in residents despite an increase in admissions. These are not the episode figures published by NIMH and shown in Kiesler and Sibulkin. NIMH calculates episodes by adding residents at the *beginning* of the year plus *additions*, which include returns from long-term leave.
3. We are grateful to Alvin Sirrocco of the National Center for Health Statistics for providing us with extensive information and data regarding the National Master Facility Inventory.
4. We appreciate the assistance of Barbara Haupt of the National Center for Health Statistics in providing us with extensive information and data regarding the National Hospital Discharge Survey.
5. NCHS publications on the National Hospital Discharge Survey show a current universe of over 8000. This larger sampling frame results from the periodic addition of new hospitals. However, hospitals that have closed or are no longer eligible are retained, thus giving the appearance of a larger universe. The discharges, however, are adjusted in accordance with existing hospitals.
6. The AHA actually conducted the surveys under contract with NIMH.
7. In 1975, 4228 records were sampled (unpublished data from NIMH).
8. In 1971, 259 hospitals were selected to represent the 804 general hospitals with separate psychiatric units, of which 724 were non-federal and 80 were VA-operated, according to NIMH's universe (Bachrach, 1973). The 653 hospitals reported in Kiesler and Sibulkin (1983) existed in January 1972, the time of the NIMH Inventory of Mental Health Facilities Survey (Mental Health Statistics Series

B. No. 5). In 1975, figures are based on a sample of 227 out of the 742 non-federal general hospital psychiatric units known to exist at the time of the survey (Statistical Note No. 133; Mental Health National Statistics Series CN, No. 2). The 791 hospitals reported in Kiesler and Sibulkin (1983) existed in January 1976, the time of the NIMH Inventory of Mental Health Facilities Survey (Statistical Note No. 139).

9. Discontinuations include patients who were discharged, placed on leave, or transferred from the reporting hospitals. The number of reporting hospitals or the number of discontinuations is not stated.

10. The 1975 survey was based on 4636 cases (unpublished data from NIMH).

11. For 1970 all 6917 admissions during November to 141 private mental hospitals were followed for 6 months. At the time of this survey, 160 private hospitals were known (Statistical Note No. 75), a different count from the Inventory figure for that year (Mental Health Statistics Series A, No. 18). In 1975 a sample of 7864 admissions during May were followed for 3 months (unpublished data from NIMH).

12. NIMH published the 1971 and 1975 figures, and we calculated the others in the same way.

REFERENCES

American Hospital Association (1949–71). *Hospitals* (surveys appear in Volumes **23** to **45**).

American Hospital Association (1972–80). *Hospital Statistics 1971 to Hospital Statistics 1980 Edition*, Chicago: American Hospital Association.

Bachrach, L.L. (1973). Marital status of discharges from psychiatric in-patient units of general hospitals, United States 1970–71: II. Analysis by referral source, length of stay and primary diagnosis (Statistical Note No. 83). Rockville, MD: National Institute of Mental Health.

Bachrach, L.L. (1976). De-institutionalization: An analytical review and sociological perspective (Mental Health Statistics Series D, No. 4). DHEW No. (ADM) 79-351. Washington, DC: US Government Printing Office.

Bahn, A.K., Gorwitz, K., Klee, G.D., Kramer, M., and Tuerk, I. (1965). Services received by Maryland residents in facilities directed by a psychiatrist, *Public Health Reports*, **80**, 405–416.

Bickman, L. (ed.) (1980). *Applied Social Psychology Annual*, Vol. 1, Beverly Hills, CA: Sage Publications.

Faden, V.B. and Taube, C.A. (1977). Length of stay of discharges from non-federal general hospital psychiatric inpatient units, United States, 1975 (Statistical Note No. 133). Rockville, MD: National Institute of Mental Health.

Goffman, E. (1961). *Essays on the Social Situation of Mental Patients and Other Inmates*, Garden City, NJ: Doubleday.

Goldberg, I.D. and Allen, G. (1981). Unduplicated counts of persons receiving care in psychiatric facilities in Monroe County, New York (Statistical Note No. 158). Rockville MD: National Institute of Mental Health.

Gray, E.A. (1970). In-patient utilization of short-stay hospitals by diagnosis, United States, 1965 (Vital and Health Statistics Series 13, No. 6). Rockville, MD: National Center for Health Statistics.

Grob, G.N. (1973). *Mental Institutions in America: Social Policy to 1875*, New York: Free Press.

Haupt, B.J. (1979). Utilization of short-stay hospitals. Annual summary of the United States, 1977 (Vital and Health Statistics Series 13, No. 41). DHEW No. (PHS) 79–1557. Rockville, MD: National Center for Health Statistics.

Haupt, B.J. (1980). Utilization of short-stay hospitals. Annual Summary of the United States, 1978 (Vital and Health Statistics Series 13, No. 46). DHEW No. (PHS) 80–1797. Rockville, MD: National Center for Health Statistics.

Haupt, B.J. (1981). Utilization of short-stay hospitals. Annual Summary for the United States, 1979 (Vital and Health Statistics Series 13, No. 60). DHHS No. (PHS) 82–1721. Hyattsville, MD: National Center for Health Statistics.

Haupt, B.J. (1982). Utilization of short-stay hospitals. Annual Summary for the United States, 1980 (Vital and Health Statistics Series 13, No. 64). DHHS No. (PHS) 82–1725. Hyattsville, MD: National Center for Health Statistics.

Health United States 1980. (1981). DHHS No. (PHS) 81–1232. Hyattsville, MD: Office of Health Research, Statistics and Technology.

Kiesler, C.A. (1980a). Mental health policy as a field of inquiry for psychology, American Psychologist, 35, 1066–1080.

Kiesler, C.A. (1980b). Psychology and public policy, in L. Bickman (ed.), Applied Social Psychology Annual (Vol. 1), Beverly Hills, CA: Sage.

Kiesler, C.A. (1981a). Mental health policy: Research site for social psychology, in L. Wheeler (ed.), Review of Personality and Social Psychology (Vol. 2), Beverly Hills, CA: Sage.

Kiesler, C.A. (1981b). Barriers to effective knowledge use in national mental health policy, Health Policy Quarterly, 1, 201–215.

Kiesler, C.A. (1982). Mental hospitals and alternative care: Non-institutionalization as potential public policy for mental patients, American Psychologist, 37, 349–360.

Kiesler, C.A. and Sibulkin, A.E. (1983). People, clinical episodes, and mental hospitalization: A multiple-source method of estimation, in R.F. Kidd and M.J. Saks (eds), Advances in Applied Social Psychology (Vol. 2), Hillsdale NJ: Erlbaum.

Mechanic, D. (1980). Mental Health and Social Policy, Englewood Cliffs, NJ: Prentice-Hall.

Meyer, N.G. and Taube, C.A. (1973). Length of stay of admissions to state and county mental hospitals United States 1971 (Statistical Note No. 74). Rockville, MD: National Institute of Mental Health.

Moien, M. (1975). In-patient utilization of short-stay hospitals by diagnosis, United States, 1972 (Vital and Health Statistics Series 13, No. 20). DHEW No. (HRA) 76–1771. Rockville MD: National Center for Health Statistics.

Moien, M. (1976). In-patient utilization of short-stay hospitals by diagnosis, United States, 1973 (Vital and Health Statistics Series 13, No. 25). DHEW No. (HRA) 77–1776. Rockville, MD: National Center for Health Statistics.

National Center for Health Statistics (n.d.). The Nation's Use of Health Resources 1976 Edition, Washington, DC: US Government Printing Office.

National Center for Health Statistics (1980). The Nation's Use of Health Resources 1979, Washington, DC: US Government Printing Office.

National Institute of Mental Health (1976). The financing, utilization, and quality of mental health care in the United States (Draft report). Rockville, MD: Author.

National Institute of Mental Health (1981). Provisional data on federally funded community mental health centers, 1978–1979. Rockville, MD: National Institute of Mental Health.

Nelson, A.B. (1967). Prevalence of chronic conditions and impairments among residents of nursing and personal care homes, United States – May–June 1964 (Vital and Health Statistics Series 12, No. 8). PHS No. 1000. Washington, DC: Public Health Service.

Ranofsky, A.L. (1973a). In-patient utilization of short-stay hospitals by diagnosis United States – 1971 (Vital and Health Statistics Series 13, No. 16). DHEW No. (HRA) 75–1767. Rockville, MD: National Center for Health Statistics.

Ranofsky, A.L. (1973b). In-patient utilization of short-stay hospitals by diagnosis United States – 1968 (Vital and Health Statistics Series 13, No. 12). DHEW No. (HSM) 73–1763. Rockville, MD: National Center for Health Statistics.

Ranofsky, A. (1976). Utilization of short-stay hospitals. Annual summary for the United States, 1974 (Vital and Health Statistics Series 13, No. 26). DHEW No. (HRA) 76–1777. Rockville, MD: National Center for Health Statistics.

Ranofsky, A. (1977). Utilization of short-stay hospitals. Annual summary for the United States, 1975 (Vital and Health Statistics Series 13, No. 31). DHEW No. (HRA) 77–1782. Rockville, MD: National Center for Health Statistics.

Ranofsky, A. (1978). Utilization of short-stay hospitals. Annual summary for the United States, 1976 (Vital and Health Statistics Series 13, No. 37). DHEW No. (PHS) 78–1788. Rockville, MD: National Center for Health Statistics.

Redick, R.W. (1971). Referral of discontinuations from in-patient services of state and county mental hospitals, United States, 1969 (Statistical Note No. 57). Rockville, MD: National Institute of Mental Health.

Redick, R.W. (1974). Patterns in use of nursing homes by the aged mentally ill (Statistical Note No. 107). Rockville, MD: National Institute of Mental Health.

Rosenstein, M.J. and Milazzo-Sayre, L.J. (1981). Characteristics of admissions to selected mental health facilites, 1975: An annotated book of charts and tables (Mental Health National Statistics Series CN, No. 2). DHEW No. (ADM) 81–1005. Washington, DC: US Government Printing Office.

Rubin, J. (1978). Economics, Mental Health, and the Law, Lexington, MA: D.C. Heath.

Sirrocco, A. (1973). Chronic conditions and impairments of nursing home residents: United States – 1969 (Vital and Health Statistics Series 12, No. 22). DHEW No. (HRA) 74–1707. Rockville, MD: National Center for Health Statistics.

Sirrocco, A. (1974). In-patient health facilities as reported from the 1971 MFI survey (Vital and Health Statistics Series 14, No. 12). DHEW No. (HRA) 74–1807. Rockville, MD: National Center for Health Statistics.

Sirrocco, A. (1976). In-patient health facilities as reported from the 1973 MFI survey (Vital and Health Statistics Series 14, No. 16). DHEW No. (HRA) 76–1811. Rockville, MD: National Center for Health Statistics.

Strahan, G.W. (1981). In-patient health facilities statistics United States, 1978 (Vital and Health Statistics Series 14, No. 24). DHHS No. (PHS) 81–1819. Hyattsville, MD: National Center for Health Statistics.

Sutton, J.F. and Sirrocco, A. (1980). In-patient health facilities as reported from the 1976 MFI survey (Vital and Health Statistics Series 14, No. 23). DHEW No. (PHS) 80–1818. Hyattsville, MD: National Center for Health Statistics.

Taube, C.A. (1973a). Length of stay of discharges from general hospital psychiatric units, United States 1970–1971 (Statistical Note No. 70). Rockville, MD: National Institute of Mental Health.

Taube, C.A. (1973b). Admissions to private mental hospitals 1970 (Statistical Note No. 75). Rockville, MD: National Institute of Mental Health.

Taube, C.A. (1973c). Utilization of mental health facilities 1971 (Mental Health Statistics Series B, No. 5). DHEW No. NIH-74-657. Washington, DC: US Government Printing Office.

Taube, C.A. and Redick, R.W. (1977). Provisional data on patient care episodes in mental health facilities (Statistical Note No. 139). Rockville, MD: National Institute of Mental Health.

Veterans Administration (1955–83). Annual Report (Years 1954 to 1982) Washington, DC: US Government Printing Office.

Vischi, T.R., Jones, K.R., Shank, E.L., and Lima, L.H. (1980). The Alcohol, Drug Abuse, and Mental Health National Data Book. DHHS No. (ADM) 80–938. Washington, DC: US Department of Health, Education and Welfare.

Witkin, M.J. (1977). Private psychiatric hospitals 1974–75 (Mental Health Statistics Series A, No. 18). DHEW No. (ADM) 77–380. Washington, DC: US Government Printing Office.
Witkin, M.J. (1980). Provisional patient movement and selective administrative data, state and county mental hospitals, inpatient services by state: United States 1976 (Statistical Note No. 153). Rockville, MD: National Institute of Mental Health.
Witkin, M.J. (1981). Provisional patient movement and selective administrative data, state and county mental hospitals by state: United States, 1977 (Statistical Note No. 156). Rockville, MD: National Institute of Mental Health.
Witkin, M. and Bass, R.D. (1973). In-patient treatment in federally funded community mental health centers-1971 (Statistical Note No. 95). Rockville, MD: National Institute of Mental Health.

Progress in Applied Social Psychology, Volume 2
Edited by G.M. Stephenson and J.H. Davis
© 1984 John Wiley & Sons Ltd

3

Psychologists vs Psychologists: an Outlook on a Professional Orientation

A. Palmonari and M. L. Pombeni
Bologna University

With this chapter, we aim to demonstrate the way in which the fact of belonging to a particular professional category (i.e. psychologists in social and medical services vs university psychologists) contributes to define the social image of self and of ingroup and outgroup of every individual.

The reference context on the basis of which this study has been developed was given to us by the results of a more extensive survey on the work of the psychologist in Italy.

In this chapter, we shall make some essential references to the results of this survey, with particular regard to the varying social representations of the psychologist's work, and to the image which psychologists working in various professional areas present of one another. We shall then present the experimental plan of our research; and finally we shall analyse separately the results which emerge in the two groups we considered (psychologists who work in social services, and university psychologists).

A SURVEY ON THE WORK OF PSYCHOLOGISTS IN ITALY

It was only in 1971 that two Italian universities, Rome and Padua, began offering regular graduate psychology courses. Before then, one could become a psychologist only after post-graduate studies (specialist courses) open to just a few medical, philosophy and education graduates. This late start, added to the fact that in Italy the number of students that can register for a course is unrestricted, has created a disproportionate number of psychology students and graduates. There are at present at least 8000 psychology graduates and more than 5000 students registered for the psychology courses at the two universities. All these psychology graduates and students are increasing intellectual unemployment and will continue to do so. At the same time, however, the demand for psychological answers to individual and social needs has grown considerably. Private psychotherapist studios have greatly increased in number; university psychologists have nearly doubled; and the figure of the psychologist has been included as a full-time worker in the various sectors of the social and health services created under the law reform governing this field. This sudden expansion of the use of psychology has given rise to much enthusiasm and great expectations but also to disappointments and a great deal of confusion.

In 1979, therefore, the CNR commissioned our team to conduct a survey to identify the essential aspects of the process of professionalization that was taking place. (The results of this survey were published in the book *Psicologi*, edited by A. Palmonari, 1981).

Emerging Models of Psychologists

The image the psychologists interviewed[1] gave of themselves and their profession appears quite complex and varied. In fact four different ways of understanding and representing the psychologist's work and socio-professional identity emerge. In these different organizations of knowledge, each of which appeared to be shared by some of the persons interviewed, we recognized (several) social representations.

Ideally, these varying representations can be arranged on a continuum: at one extreme the psychologist sees himself as a 'social worker', mainly referring to his role as a political activist, while at the other extreme he considers himself exclusively as a 'psychotherapist'. In the first case, any identification in a technical role is rejected as dangerous, since it justifies the power that professional know-how allows psychologists to wield over others. Working as a psychologist is mainly considered a political choice. In the other case the definition is very precise: they prefer to define themselves as 'psychotherapists' rather than psychologists because they consider that the field of intervention implied by the latter definition is too extensive and too vague. The work carried out is based only partially on specific skills: the basic instrument of work is the therapist's personality. The profession is not seen just as a job in the strict sense, but as something wider which completely involves the person and for whose achievement the psychotherapist must have the greatest individual freedom.

Between the image of the psychologist as a 'political activist' and that of a 'professional psychotherapist' there are two further representations. On the one hand ('the interdisciplinary expert') the psychologist is a person who makes a specific professional contribution to the understanding of society and elaborates proposals for social intervention. In this case we see an attempt not to limit the definition of a psychologist either to someone who practises only psychotherapy and defines his own professional nature in exclusively clinical terms, or to someone who stresses only the political side and defines his profession in general and non-specific terms. The psychologist's work consists of promotional and preventive work and of surveys and theoretical analysis.

On the other hand ('the clincial expert') we have a figure of the psychologist whose definition is based on professional know-how and on the technical skills he has acquired. By this logic he has to defend and guarantee his professional identity as a psychologist, namely to differentiate himself from his 'social worker' colleagues. A fundamental element in specifying such a differentiation is therapeutic skill. Thus once more the reference model is the *clinical* one; it is felt that it is not easy, although it is necessary, to work in public structures because of the difficulty of reconstructing in the public field the working conditions typical of the private.

These social representations are shared by psychologists from various Italian towns and cities and from various professional contexts (Palmonari, 1981, 1982): only private practitioners define their work explicitly, excluding any reference to political programmes or extensive social renewal plans.

The Work of the Psychologist in Various Professional Contexts

The social representations which have emerged refer to the ideological attitude, cultural background, and working experience of the persons interviewed. However, the interviews, also brought out other information concerning the concrete and organizational aspects of psychologists' work according to *professional context* (social services, university, private profession). In this regard, it appeared that the psychologists from one particular professional context tended to regard themselves as a group separate and different from other groups of psychologists.

A remark of this kind seems at first glance to contrast the social representations expressed by the interviewees themselves. We decided to clear up this point by examining more thoroughly the Bologna psychologists who were working at the University and in social services. In fact, these two groups of psychologists share the four social representations indicated. Before presenting our study, however, we should like to give some basic information regarding the insitutional and organizational framework within which these psychologists work.

Psychologists in the Social Services

In the 1970s a number of reform laws (national and regional) progressively defined the form and establishment of local social and medical services. This, based on a global plan of an innovatory social policy, has offered psychologists new working possibilities. The new work of the psychologist entails a widening of the roles in which he has traditionally been recognized: from a relationship with the individual client (usually a person who needs help) to one with small groups of people, and to initiatives directed at the general public and institutions (Palmonari and Zani, 1982).

After a few years of great enthusiasm for the work in the area, during which a flourishing of advanced enterprise and bold experimental work was observed – with Bologna taking the lead in this policy of innovation – a period of difficulties began in which it became necessary to make the general plans more concrete, and develop the underlying areas for renewal into working plans for the services. Because of the difficulties encountered in developing work in these services to consistent and productive ends, there is a risk of psychologists falling back on a definition of their professional nature in exclusively individual curative terms. Both the psychologists' basic training and the fall in cultural and political commitment of politicians to the accomplishment of local services have contributed to this.

What concrete action are psychologists taking in this situation? The interviews carried out in our survey show that the main aims of the work of psychologists in the public services are the prevention of every sort of maladjustment and an increase in participation. But it is stressed that there is a lack of the necessary conditions, above all of an organizational nature, to carry out these tasks.

Concretely, the main initiatives are of a *clinical and rehabilitational* nature and among these there are various theapeutic activities. Psychologists are aware that they very seldom carry out programming and planning of the services: usually, besides their clinical work they must devote themselves mainly to the detailed organization of their working day. Therefore it is not possible for them to carry out research (even in the form of action-research).

The growing lack of faith in any possibility of carrying out preventive work in order to bring about some changes in community life increases the tendency of these psychologists to develop their work in such a way as to resemble a clinical model. In conclusion, the work on individual maladjustment allows the psychologist to give a more precise definition of his professional role and gives him an opportunity to see more immediate results from his work.

Psychologists in Universities

The 1970s have also been difficult for those working in Italian universities. After the opening up of university admission in 1969 and the increasing phenomenon of youth unemployment, the number of university students increased considerably. The cultural establishment on which the courses are based and the physical and organizational structures in which they are carried out, which were planned for an élite student population, were greatly affected by these changes. The traditional teaching staff, which is now too limited to meet the demands of this large influx of students, has been added to by the introduction of new teaching positions, which, however, do not have a defined institutional position. The new demands of the students, the uneasiness which has spread throughout the teaching staff (most of whom do not have a guaranteed job and are badly paid) has increased the difficulties of the universities.

Some other signs of problems were also found during this survey. It was noted that the university psychologists interviewed at the time worked in the faculties of medicine, political science, philosophy, education, and sociology: not one in the faculty of psychology. In describing their daily work, all the teachers interviewed said that they did not consider it their most important task. In fact, all teachers, above all the ones belonging to the lowest categories, regarded teaching as the heaviest and least satisfying component of their work load.

In some cases this work load is used as a justification for the little time and effort dedicated to scientific research. This is the professional work to which most importance is given, even though a series of concrete difficulties (lack of funds, inadequate structures and instruments, lack of time) impede its being carried out.

From the information which was obtained it is difficult to separate the information which specifically concerns university work from that of other parallel professional work. It has been proved that academic work leaves room for other types of work, and this is justified by economic needs (supplementing the low wages) and by interests in more professional work. University psychologists who also practise their profession elsewhere, usually do so in the psychotherapeutic field.

Most of those interviewed defined themselves as 'psychologists': however, they stated that this term was mainly linked to the professional work they did outside the university. As far as the academic work itself is concerned, psychologists working in the university see themselves mainly as 'research workers'. In fact *research* is the professional work which qualifies them on an institutional level and which differentiates them as psychologists from those who work outside the university.

Service Psychologists and University Psychologists: Mutual Perception

What then is the perception that the two groups interviewed have of each other? When they were asked to suggest criteria that might be useful to distinguish different kinds of psychologists, there were few replies. At times, however, the attitude that emerged was one of criticism for colleagues working in fields different from their own. The members of one group of psychologists very summarily define members of the other group in disparaging terms. (This happens even when the interviewer's question does not require a comparison to be made.)

> In my opinion, only a psychologist working in the field (in social services) can be called a true psychologist; others are all abstract theorists selling idle talk. (a service psychologist)

and an opposing viewpoint:

> In my view, psychologists should stay inside the University and carry out research and educational work; social workers should no longer exist because really they are only bureaucrats without either dignity or professionalism, stripped of all dignity and professionalism, and have become nothing but puppets. (a university psychologist)

It should be stressed that they have practically no direct contact with each other, even if the new social services plan explicitly for extensive collaboration with the University.

SOCIAL IDENTITIES COMPARED: A STUDY OF RECIPROCAL PERCEPTIONS

Thus, thanks to our previous survey, we have at hand some concrete data of particular interest. That is to say, our psychologists do not have a clear-cut overall image at their disposal by which to define their social and professional identity, the content of their work, the essential factors for the right training, and so on.

However, as the practicalities of their work force them to take sides, they adopt widely differing social representations which are based on different points of view (concerning the social function of science, and psychology regarded as a science). These social representations are expressed and shared by psychologists working in different professional spheres. In spite of this, when the psychologists working in a particular professional sphere compare themselves with psychologists working in another sphere, they express opinions which tend to be in favour of their own ingroup but to discriminate against the outgroup.

In what way, then, do various factors – namely the social representations and also the fact of belonging to a particular professional category – affect the process of the formation of social identity of psychologists belonging to professional groups which are very closely related, but different from the institutional point of view? This is the question we wanted to examine.

Theoretical Frame of Reference

In this study, we refer to the concept of *social representations*. According to Moscovici (1981, 1982), 'social representations' should be understood as a means for the individual to acquire knowledge, and to pass on knowledge already acquired. This concept of representation has been borrowed from Durkheim; but the point of view adopted in its study differs from that of classical sociology. Whereas collective representations, for Durkheim, are a term which defines a general class of knowledge and beliefs, for Moscovici they represent phenomena which can be described and explained, and which appear to be fundamental for the understanding of the mechanism of social knowledge and awareness.

Social representations are always produced within the context of the life of a social group, and there are basically two processes by which they are formed. The first of these – *anchorage* – allows something unknown to be incorporated into available cognitive schemes, in relation to already known points of reference. The second process, on the other hand, works by *objectifying* the knowledge: that is to say, it transforms something abstract into something more concrete. This process of *objectification* links concept with the group's own reality, transforming it in turn to something real. Each knowledge acquires a different degree of objectification, corresponding to a different level of reality. Social representations assume dynamic forms which are capable of influencing social relationships and behaviour; hence they do not have an independent existence but are created and kept alive by social groups.

The other theoretical line of thought we shall refer to is that which studies the relationship between social identity and intergroup relationships. Tajfel (1972a) emphasizes that the process of categorization plays its part in structuring even social interaction, creating groupings of individuals and differentiating between the social objects. The categorization of the perceived social reality influences the judgment given on the value of various groupings, and the attitude taken towards them. To clarify these ideas, Doise (1976) developed the concept of category differentiation.

A series of experimental studies, now famous (e.g. Tajfel *et al.*, 1971; Billig and Tajfel, 1973; Doise and Weinberger, 1972–3; Doise *et al.*, 1978), show that, even in cases where one's belonging to a group is based on artificial and uncertain grounds, the persons involved assume behavioural strategies which allow them to fix differentiations in favour of their group. The definition coined by Tajfel for this phenomenon is 'minimal group paradigm'.

It is Tajfel again (1972) who, in putting forward a more 'social' version of Festinger's comparison theory (1954), tries to evaluate the results. Social comparison – as Festinger sees it – basically concerns the comparison between individuals within a group, and implies a certain pressure towards uniformity. Self-evaluation is attained through comparison between similar individuals. In Tajfel's view, on the basis of one's self-evaluation, one finds a social identity, conceived as follows: 'social identity of individuals is linked to their awareness of being members of one (or more) groups and evaluative significance of that membership'. A group can only offer or preserve its positive contribution to the social identity of its members if, when compared with other groups, the evaluation of this membership appears significant for the persons concerned.

Tajfel's minimal group paradigm has undergone critical examination on the part of other studies which have been carried out. One of these in particular, Turner (1975), claims that, whereas it is possible to demonstrate empirically that social categorization under certain conditions is in itself sufficient cause for intergroup discrimination, there is however no automatic connection between this variable and intergroup discrimination. Taking into account the fact that the tendency to favour one's own group in preference to other groups is usually a characteristic of laboratory situations, he puts forward the idea that intergroup behaviour is linked (or owes itself) to the fact that the state of belonging to one of the two experimental groups appears to be the only reference category through which the persons can express, in the specific situation, their desire for positive self-evaluation. In Turner's opinion, it is the tendency to establish a positive distinction between others and oneself which is subject to the processes of social categorization: category differentiation is one way, but not the only way, to satisfy this need. Also, favouritism towards other members of the ingroup is an instance of social competition between groups, in which individuals act in terms of an intergroup categorization as a means to arrive at a positive evaluation inside the experimental situation. Identification with one's own group is a necessary condition for discriminating behaviour in favour of the group; but the intensity (or consistency) of this feeling of identification depends on numerous factors.

On the basis of these considerations, other studies have dealt with the problem of identification with one's membership-group (Deschamps, 1979; Brown and Deschamps, 1980; Deschamps and Lorenzi-Cioldi, 1981), confirming (vs Turner) that when the intergroup comparison is particularly significant for the definition of the social identity of the individuals concerned in the comparison, intragroup identification does not always appear strong and unanimous. Deschamps (1982) suggests that social tensions and contradictions, to be met with at various levels, are interlinked, and that it is possible – on the level of relationships between oneself and others belonging to the ingroup – to rediscover a tension parallel to that which is encountered in relations between groups, a tension which manifests itself in terms of intergroup fusion/-individualization.

Intergroup relations, then, are no longer studied only (or mainly) in terms of INGROUP–OUTGROUP comparison, but also in terms of SELF–INGROUP and SELF–OUTGROUP comparison. From this point of view, both the definition of SELF that the individual presents and the definition of his own INGROUP will figure in the definition of his social identity. Moreover, many studies carried out along these lines demonstrate the usefulness of a comparison between the SELF of each individual and the social groups (in- and outgroups) which are significant to him at a given moment, in so far as the SELF – in each individual's cognitive field

– is an object among significant others (Codol, 1982). By SELF, in this case, we mean that aspect of SELF focused by means of an anticipating scheme (Neisser, 1976), activated by the individual in the actual situation in which he has to relate himself to other social objects.

Aims and Hypotheses of the Research

In operational terms, the aims of the survey are as follows. First, to analyse the similarity/differentiation strategies adopted in the definition of self, of the ingroup and outgroups given by the psychologists working in social services and by the university psychologists when asked to define the peculiarity of their own group with regard to the other group and to the group of private practitioners. If being a member of a group working in a particular professional sphere implies a feeling of belonging to a different social category from that of the other group with which the comparison has been made, we should expect an over-estimation of intergroup differences and intragroup similarities. This result is to be expected, as we have several facts to support the view that the social service psychologists belong to a professional group whose duties are not yet clearly defined: it is not easy for them to form a satisfactory social identity by virtue of this membership. This difficulty is increased when they compare their own group with other groups of psychologists whose social prestige seems higher (for example, they have a high social status and a well-established role, and enjoy higher social esteem). The university psychologists, on the other hand, are able to form a more clearly defined, satisfactory social identity for themselves from their group membership, even if their salary is not sufficiently rewarding. This aspect makes the comparison with the group of private practitioners ambivalent: these psychologists are regarded as highly paid. However, the university psychologists seem to feel threatened by the fact of the increased importance (both social and professional) which psychologists in the social services have acquired. This threat – at times exaggerated on the part of the university psychologists – tends to make less certain the sense of superiority and prestige they traditionally enjoy.

The second aim is to establish to what extent Tajfel's theoretical model regarding intergroup relationships is valid – in a complex organizational situation – also with regard to intragroup similarities. This point, which has been confirmed by Turner and Brown, has been questioned following the results of some surveys (Deschamps, 1979), according to which a tension (effort of differentiation) similar to that occurring in intergroup relationships develops between SELF and the members of the same group. This effort of differentiation among members of the group does not affect the course of intergroup differentiation. The psychologists we are studying should express social identities that are different for the two groups (owing to the intergroup effect that the comparison triggers off), yet problematic also, on account of the features characteristic of the context in which they are expressed. Thus, following Brown and Deschamps (1980), we can expect the individual's identification with his own group (category) to be neither strong nor homogeneous on the part of group members. The reason for this is that intergroup comparison is of particular relevance for a definition of social identity of each individual involved in the comparison (for a similar problem, cf. Deschamps and Lorenzi-Cioldi, 1981).

The third aim is to explore the way in which the intergroup effect – where it is evident – and the influence of social representations start to interact in the defining of the individual's social identity. Also, to identify the crucial points on the basis of which the similarity/differentiation between groups is defined.

With these aims in mind, we have worked out the following hypotheses:

(1) in the reciprocal comparison between the categories of psychologists working in social services and university psychologists, and in comparing these two groups with the private practitioners, an intergroup effect emerges through a clear-cut differentation of the social identity of psychologists belonging to different categories;
(2) the identification of the individuals studied with their own professional group is not homogeneous; in fact a pressure towards individualization (rather than fusion) appears within the group;
(3) the pressure towards intragroup individualization can be accounted for on the basis of varying social representations shared by only some of the members of each group. In this way, intragroup differences can be traced back to two fundamental points of view (orientations) regarding the social function of the psychologists.

Methodology

The first group we examined was made up of 28 social service psychologists working in the province of Bologna. At the time of our research, there were 39 psychologists employed in that area. The second group – 35 subjects – consisted of a number of teachers working in various faculties of the University of Bologna where psychology is taught; the standard group included people from various academic levels: professors, lecturers, researchers.

Each of the subjects was asked to fill in a questionnaire. This required the making of five comparisons between the following social subjects:

For the persons interviewed who are members of the group Social Service Psychologists	*For the persons interviewed who are members of the group University Psychologists*
(1) Self-ingroup (group they belong to)	(1) Self-ingroup (group they belong to)

(2) Self-group₁ (group of university teaching psychologists)

(3) Self-group₂ (group of private practitioners)

(4) Ingroup–outgroup₁

(5) Ingroup–outgroup₂

(2) Self-outgroup₁ (group of social service psychologists)

(3) Self-outgroup₂ (group of private practitioners)

(4) Ingroup–outgroup₁

(5) Ingroup–outgroup₂

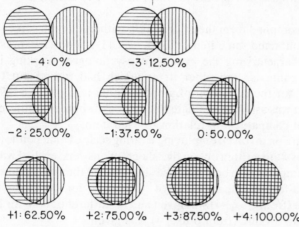

−4: 0%   −3: 12.50%

−2: 25.00%   −1: 37.50%   0: 50.00%

+1: 62.50%   +2: 75.00%   +3: 87.50%   +4: 100.00%

Figure 1. Response scale

For every situation, the instruction given was always the same and only the objects of comparison changed: 'The left circle represents . . . (1st element), the right circle represents . . . (2nd element); the intersection, if any, (i.e. the portion common to both circles) represents what . . . (1st element) and . . . (2nd elements) have in common' (see Figure 1).

Every comparison was made on a list of 14 items (always the same) covering various aspects of the psychologist's work. These items were derived from the in-depth interviews with the psychologist sample and concerned the most common topics of the interviews.

The list of items is as follows:

(1) To carry on an activity within institutions.
(2) To establish ways of safeguarding the professional category.
(3) To carry on a private activity.
(4) To devote themselves to working in the real world.
(5) To commit themselves entirely to increasing their own professionalism outside the institutional context.
(6) To carry on theoretical work on the problems tackled.
(7) To work within specific professionalities.

  (8) To commit themselves to vouch for the quality of professional work.
  (9) To privilege promotional and research activities.
(10) To take part in institutional training programmes.
(11) To work with other professional people.
(12) To seek personal training opportunities.
(13) To privilege therapeutic work.
(14) To employ their professionalism in socially significant work.

This list was compiled from the information gathered in the survey mentioned above, and contained some items (1,4,5,7,10,11,14) which expressed aspects objectively characterizing the groups of psychologists working in different professional contexts, and other items which had turned out to be more 'problematic' for the definition of a professional image (2,3,6,8,9,12,13).

The subject was asked to evaluate the degree of similarity/difference among the objects of comparison in relation to each item.

The comparison involved employing a rating scale of nine points (from +4 to −4); the items were written out on five sheets of answers, each of which showed the type of comparison to be made. We shall discuss the data, following current literature (Tajfel, 1978), speaking of 'similarity' for the items to which a positive value (from 0 to +4) was given and of 'differentiation' for the items to which a negative value (from 0 to −4) was given.

In the second part of the questionnaire, the subject was asked, as a psychologist belonging to a specific professional field,[2] to assign a score of importance to every item used for the previous comparison, on a rating scale of seven points.

RESULTS: SOCIAL SERVICE PSYCHOLOGISTS

Attribution of Importance

We went through the second part of the questionnaire (Table 1) first in order to obtain information about the importance ascribed to the various contents involved in the differentiation process.

Items 8 ('to commit themselves to vouch for the quality of professional work') and 6 ('to carry on theoretical work on the problems tackled') obtained the highest score on the rating scale. Then came a group of items with fairly high average values (from 5.46 to 4.75), either equal or very close to each other. Their contents, however, were often quite different, as, for example, with items 7 ('to work within particular professions') and 11 ('to work with other professional people'). This group of items made it difficult to identify an actual hierarchy of importance. On the other hand, only a very few items presented markedly low average values.

Table 1. Social Services Psychologists: Attribution of Importance

Order	$\bar{x}$														Subjects															
		1	2	3	4	5	6	7	8	9	10	11	12	13	14	15	16	17	18	19	20	21	22	23	24	25	26	27	28
1st	8	6.39	7	6	6	7	5	6	6	7	5	5	7	7	5	7	7	6	7	7	7	7	7	7	7	7	6	7	6	7
2nd	6	6.10	6	6	6	6	6	7	7	7	5	3	7	7	4	7	7	4	7	7	6	7	5	5	7	7	7	6	6	7
3rd	10	5.46	4	7	4	6	6	7	7	7	3	1	7	6	6	6	5	3	7	7	6	6	7	7	5	5	5	7	4	4
4th	1	5.32	7	7	5	5	5	6	7	5	6	4	6	7	7	5	3	5	5	5	5	7	7	5	3	5	5	7	5	4
5th	5	5.07	5	5	6	4	4	5	5	4	4	5	6	7	7	6	5	6	5	5	6	6	7	7	5	4	5	7	3	4
6th	4	5.07	6	6	5	4	6	6	3	4	4	3	5	5	6	5	5	5	6	3	4	3	2	5	3	3	4	5	7	4
7th	7	5.00	5	3	4	6	5	6	6	5	6	1	7	7	5	7	3	3	5	6	6	2	5	5	7	5	5	7	2	6
8th	12	5.00	6	3	5	5	4	6	7	6	1	5	4	6	3	5	4	4	7	5	7	3	1	6	4	5	5	6	4	7
9th	13	4.92	4	4	6	5	6	5	3	5	4	4	5	6	6	5	5	4	2	2	5	5	3	7	4	4	6	7	3	6
10th	2	4.75	4	5	7	5	5	7	1	4	1	5	6	7	4	7	7	6	4	4	6	7	5	7	6	7	7	7	1	4
11th	11	4.75	4	6	4	6	4	4	6	6	2	5	4	4	1	6	6	2	5	6	5	1	1	5	6	6	2	5	6	5
12th	14	4.75	6	7	4	5	4	5	7	5	5	3	6	6	6	6	3	5	6	6	6	5	1	2	3	5	4	6	7	3
13th	9	4.32	5	7	4	4	4	5	4	4	5	1	4	4	2	6	1	4	6	6	6	5	5	2	4	4	2	2	4	1
14th	3	2.82	4	1	3	3	4	4	2	3	2	3	3	3	2	1	1	4	4	4	4	3	1	2	1	1	2	2	2	7

A precise analysis of the rough scores of individual items indicates that the average values of the items with the highest scores on the scale (8 and 6) are the result of homogeneous scores (7 or 6 points). The average values of the central group items, on the other hand, derive from scores which vary greatly from one subject to another. For example, item 4 has some very high scores (7 or 6) and other much lower ones (3 or 2) and, in the case of items 7, 13, and 2, the values are even more strongly contrasted (7 or 6 on the one hand, 1 or 2 on the other).

Intergroup Differentiation Strategies

In comparisons between INGROUP-(psychologists in the social services) OUT-GROUP₁ (university psychologists) and INGROUP-OUTGROUP₂ (private practitioners), the persons interviewed made an obvious effort to differentiate their own group from the other two groups (Table 2).

In comparison with the group of university psychologists, the few items indicative of similarity mainly concerned objective characteristics of both working activities (for example, item 1), or very general aspects of the profession (for example, item 8). Most items, however (11 items out of 14), showed some tendency to differentiation, even if the values of this differentiation were not – except in a few cases (item 11) – very high (Table 2).

In the INGROUP-OUTGROUP₂ comparison, the differentiation was marked by more accentuated values (items 1 and 11). However, these items presented some contents that differentiated the two groups 'objectively'. Other items, however (14,9,4,7), given lower *negative* values than the previous ones, revealed the qualitative differences between the two groups more clearly.

Among those items expressing differentiation of the INGROUP from the two OUTGROUPS, there were some items (2,3,4,13, for example) that, even if they had a negative average value that was not high (between 0 and −1), indicated a rather remarkable difference in individual positions (cf. Table 2). This means that within the group of social service psychologists very different attitudes emerged as regards a number of items. These differences have been 'levelled' in calculating the *average* values.

There were very few items indicating similarity: 1,2, and 8 in the comparison with the university psychologists; 8 and 12 in the comparison with private practitioners.

We can state briefly that the data examined so far corroborate evidence of a differentiation process in a situation of explicit intergroup comparison. However, the remarkable degree of variation seems to indicate the presence of a strong tendency towards individualization within the ingroup rather than towards ingroup homogeneity. The variety of individual attitudes mainly concerns a group of items which regard more problematic aspects of the psychologist's professional process and to which have been assigned a very different degree of importance. In fact, some of the subjects assign a great deal of

Table 2. Social Service Psychologists: $\bar{x}$ and σ^2 in the Five Comparisons

Items	Self-ingroup		Self-outgroup$_1$		Self-outgroup$_2$		Ingroup-Outgroup$_1$		Ingroup-Outgroup$_2$	
	$\bar{x}$	σ^2	$\bar{x}$	σ^2	$\bar{x}$	σ^2	$\bar{x}$	σ^2	$\bar{x}$	σ^2
1	2.39	2.17	0.32	2.86	-3.25	1.46	0.54	2.66	-3.43	0.69
2	0.11	2.42	-0.79	2.32	-0.61	2.78	0.36	2.20	-0.14	2.38
3	-1.07	1.70	-1.57	2.20	-2.18	2.28	-1.14	2.07	-1.32	2.21
4	1.18	2.20	-1.71	2.48	-1.54	2.55	-1.46	2.27	-1.32	2.29
5	0.86	1.77	-1.07	2.39	-0.50	2.15	-0.46	2.15	-0.21	1.99
6	0.96	2.03	-0.36	2.13	-0.46	2.22	-0.11	2.22	-0.54	1.62
7	0.00	1.56	-0.96	2.25	0.54	2.10	0.64	2.06	0.18	2.06
8	1.64	1.87	0.96	2.25	0.54	2.10	0.64	2.06	0.18	2.06
9	-0.75	2.08	-1.11	2.22	-2.11	2.11	-0.61	2.49	-2.39	1.47
10	1.93	2.21	-0.36	2.00	-2.25	1.82	-0.32	2.33	-2.29	1.68
11	1.14	2.10	-1.89	2.06	-2.82	1.49	-2.04	1.88	-3.25	1.11
12	0.32	2.13	-0.14	2.29	0.43	2.17	0.64	2.11	0.68	1.98
13	-0.25	1.86	-1.46	1.93	-0.89	1.83	-1.11	2.20	-0.54	2.25
14	-0.32	2.25	-1.29	2.58	-2.71	1.46	-1.00	2.33	-2.50	1.45

importance to some of the items and little importance to the remainder, whereas the other subjects assign importance to the latter items and no importance to the former ones.

In the SELF-INGROUP comparison, items expressing differentiation (only four items as against ten indicating similarity) concern the topic of work in a public or private field (item 3) and the question of the contents of the psychologist's professional activity (9,14,13). In relation to the same items, high degrees of individual variation are shown.

In the SELF-OUTGROUP2 comparison (private practitioners), the differentiation is more clear-cut than in the SELF-OUTGROUP1 comparison (university psychologists) and the average value of those items is associated with a rather high variation index. In fact, we find the same differentiation strategy as before, some items showing considerable distance with average values towards the negative end of the scale (−4) and with lower variation (1,11,14), and other items showing shorter distance, but higher variation (2,4,6).

Social Identity and Group Membership

In the *differentiation* process carried on various comparisons, we have noticed the constant utilization of a particular group of items. To find out whether these items represent the characteristic features on which the group of social service psychologists bases its professional identity, we related the differentiation strategy to the assignation of value. We calculated the correlation index (Pearson's) between the scores assigned to each item in the scale of importance and in each of the similarity/difference scales used for the five comparisons made (Table 3). The significant correlations concern all the items which had previously been noted as crucial (2,3,4,5,13,14) in our discussion on the mechanisms of intergroup differentiation between psychologists working in the social service and the psychologists belonging to other groups. Our remarks on these correlations have stressed the necessity of examining whether the set of meanings the items expressed can relate to some fundamental aspects used to define more significantly the social identity of social service psychologists. The data relating to the SELF-INGROUP comparison have therefore been examined by factor analysis in main components, since this kind of statistical procedure is suitable for showing the possible presence of one or more 'typical structures'[3] employed in the differentiation.

In our case, two of these typical structures expressed by two 'clusters' of items appear. The first includes items 8,10,6, and 11, the second items 5,3,2,13,12, and 7 (Figure 2). Considered together, the items contained in these two clusters express those contents identified as crucial in the differentiation process related to various comparisons. These two typical structures show the very different trends in the psychologists identity: in one they indicate a tendency centred on the individual and based only on specific professional

Table 3. Social Service Psychologists: Correlations A, B, C, D, E

Items	Self-ingroup	Self-outgroup$_1$	Self-outgroup$_2$	Ingroup-Outgroup$_1$	Ingroup-Outgroup$_2$
1	0.29	-0.10	-0.26	-0.36 (0.064)	-0.09
2	0.64 (0.0001)	0.15	0.56 (0.002)	0.53 (0.004)	0.40 (0.036)
3	0.01	0.31	0.34 (0.08)	0.02	-0.08
4	0.34 (0.07)	0.20	-0.02	0.35 (0.07)	0.14
5	-0.05	0.50 (0.007)	0.40 (0.034)	0.05	0.36 (0.059)
6	0.23	0.06	0.23	0.21	0.20
7	0.32	0.07	0.09	-0.02	0.04
8	0.12	0.25	-0.08	0.24	-0.19
9	-0.09	0.56 (0.002)	-0.64 (0.0001)	0.27	-0.24
10	0.77 (0.0001)	0.15	-0.36 (0.059)	0.08	-0.11
11	0.26	-0.21	-0.38 (0.045)	0.08	-0.56 (0.002)
12	-0.39 (0.04)	0.32 (0.09)	0.38	-0.01	0.26
13	0.31 (0.11)	0.17	0.40 (0.035)	-0.50 (0.007)	0.45 (0.016)
14	0.30 (0.12)	-0.06	0.14	-0.10	0.25

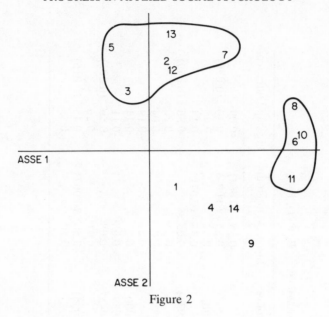

Figure 2

competence; in the other, they indicate a tendency in favour of promotional and preventive measures aimed at the social background, carried out together with other professional people. Those subjects using mainly the items of one of the two 'typcial structures' just marginally use the items expressed by the other 'typical structure'.

After separately identifying the two groups of items employed in the SELF-INGROUP comparison, it was hypothesized that it was possible to identify two groups of social service psychologists defining their social identity in a different way, assigning to their group characteristics different from those assigned to the other group.

We have verified the hypothesis that there are two 'identities', or at least two trends in defining the identity of the social service psychologist group in a different way, relating the contents in each of the typical structures to the attribution of importance to these contents. With this aim in view, a factor analysis (PA1) has been carried out regarding the importance scale expressed by the subjects in relation to the items.

At the positive pole of the first factor a group of psychologists (16 subjects) was placed, attributing more importance to items 6,8,9,10, and 11. These items were the same (item 8 has been added) as those forming the 'clusters' of one of the typical structures employed in the differentiation process.

At the negative pole of the same factor was the other group of subjects (10 psychologists).[4] In this case, the items to which more importance is attributed were items 2,5,3,12, and 13. It is this group of items (without item 7) which constitutes the second of the two typical structures at issue.

The items included in the two typical structures are therefore given a different degree of importance: the subjects attributing a great deal of importance to items included in one structure attribute little importance to items in the other structure.

RESULTS: UNIVERSITY TEACHING PSYCHOLOGISTS

Attribution of Importance

Let us first examine the data concerning the importance attributed to the various items. Items 6 ('to carry on theoretical work on the problems tackled') and 8 ('to commit oneself to vouch for the quality of professional work') have had the highest scores on the scale and the importance attributed to them varies little (variation index–Table 4). Items 9 ('to privilege promotional and research work') and 1 ('to carry on activity inside institutions') follow with an average value higher than 5 points; however, the persons interviewed agreed on these contents to a decreasing degree. A further group of items (5,10,4,14,11,12, and 7) presents average values that are rather high and very close to each other (between 4.88 and 4.40): they indicate different attitudes towards some important problems (items 5 and 10, and 11 and 7, for example). Items 13 ('to support therapeutic work'), 2 ('to establish ways of safeguarding the professional category'), and 3 ('to carry on activity in private') are given the lowest scores on the scale of importance.

Table 4. University Psychologists: Attribution of Importance

Order	Items	$\bar{x}$	σ^2
1st	1	6.25	1.55
2nd	8	6.05	1.40
3rd	9	5.51	2.43
4th	1	5.02	2.20
5th	5	4.88	2.86
6th	10	4.85	2.77
7th	4	4.80	2.98
8th	14	4.77	3.41
9th	11	4.57	2.66
10th	12	4.48	2.31
11th	7	4.40	3.48
12th	13	3.48	2.37
13th	2	3.42	2.78
14th	3	2.85	3.00

Intergroup Differentiation Strategies

In the INGROUP–OUTGROUP$_1$ (social service psychologists) comparison, 8 out of 14 items (4,5,6,9,10,11,13,14) show differentiation (between their own group and the group of social service psychologists). Items 13 ('to privilege therapeutic work') and 9 ('to privilege promotional and research work') show the largest differentiation. All the items with negative signs (i.e. showing differentation) also have a high value of individual variance. As for contents, the differentiation takes place on particular aspects of professional activity (therapeutic work, promotional and research activity, theoretical work), and actual working of both groups (working with other professional people).

On the other hand, the items showing similarity with the social service psychologists group concern both contents already defined as objective and without emotional importance for both groups (item 1), and contents more problematical for the definition of a professional pattern (items 7,2,3) as well.

However, even the elements of similarity noticed between the groups do not derive from a homogenous evaluation of those interviewed: in particular, items 1 and 3 show the highest degree of individual variance (Table 5).

In the INGROUP–OUTGROUP comparison the effort of differentiation from the private practitioners' psychologist group appears even clearer. In fact, not only do 11 items out of 14 have negative signs, but the average scores of each item are remarkably closer to the negative end of the scale. The biggest distance is that of item 1, on whose content individual attitudes vary to a very large extent ($\sigma^2 = 4.3$). At a qualitative level, another group of items (9,11,2,13) shows the most significant differences. In the SELF–INGROUP comparison, only two items (1 and 9) show similarity with positive scores higher than 1 (table 5).

Item 1 stresses an objective condition of all those belonging to the university psychologist group ('to carry on working inside institutions'), while item 9 deals with the topic of professional contents focusing on research activity). The other items with positive signs but lower values (between 0 and +1) deal with the topics of theoretical work, the quality of professional work, and training. There was some disagreement, however, among those interviewed about their opinion on similarity (Table 5). This leads us to believe that for some subjects these contents represent identification points with their own group more than the average values show, while for other subjects, they represent differentiation elements. Items 13 ('to privilege therapeutic work'), 3 ('to carry on activity in private') and 14 ('to employ their professionality in work of social significance') show the largest distance between SELF and INGROUP. Once again, opinions relating to the items considered more problematical, particularly the problems of working in a public or private context, the contents of professional activity and actual working methods, vary remarkably.

Table 5. University Psychologists: $\bar{x}$ and σ^2 in the Five Comparisons

Items	Self-ingroup		Self-outgroup$_1$		Self-outgroup$_2$		Ingroup-Outgroup$_1$		Ingroup-Outgroup$_2$	
	$\bar{x}$	σ^2	$\bar{x}$	σ^2	$\bar{x}$	σ^2	$\bar{x}$	σ^2	$\bar{x}$	σ^2
1	1.1	6.3	0.9	7.2	-2.8	4.3	0.9	5.8	-2.3	4.3
2	-0.7	5.7	-1.3	3.5	-1.9	5.3	0.2	4.1	-1.0	5.4
3	-1.4	6.7	-1.6	4.6	-2.5	5.6	0.2	5.9	-0.6	7.2
4	-0.6	3.8	0.0	5.8	-1.7	5.8	-0.3	5.3	-0.7	3.9
5	-0.1	4.7	-0.1	3.8	-1.0	4.8	-0.1	3.6	0.1	3.4
6	0.7	4.9	-1.6	5.5	-0.7	4.0	-0.6	4.7	-0.7	5.1
7	0.1	5.9	-0.7	4.7	-0.5	5.7	0.5	3.1	-0.1	5.0
8	0.7	4.8	0.0	5.4	0.5	4.9	0.5	4.1	0.7	4.0
9	1.0	4.4	-1.6	4.0	-2.3	4.5	-1.1	3.7	-1.9	2.8
10	0.6	4.1	0.1	4.6	-1.5	4.7	-0.1	3.3	-0.3	4.4
11	-0.7	4.8	-0.3	4.9	-2.4	4.1	-0.7	3.7	-1.5	5.0
12	0.4	4.8	0.7	4.9	0.6	4.7	0.6	3.1	0.1	4.9
13	-1.7	4.0	-1.7	5.0	-2.1	4.9	-1.1	4.1	-0.8	5.2
14	-1.2	3.7	0.5	5.8	-1.5	5.3	-0.1	4.4	-0.1	5.3

When SELF is compared to both OUTGROUPS the differentiation process increases. The biggest distance is felt towards the professional psychologist group; in fact, in this comparison all the items except two have negative signs.

As for contents, in the comparisons between SELF and both OUTGROUPS the differentiation mechanism takes place with regard to the items already defined as problematical (3,9,13, and 2). On the other hand, there are more elements of similarity (items 1,12,4, and 8) in the comparison with social service psychologists; in this case, however, item 1, whose content shows an objective peculiarity to both groups, presents the highest degree of variance of all the comparisons made ($\sigma^2 = 7.2$).

Social Identity and Group Membership

It remains for us to consider in this case what are the contents on which university psychologists base the psychological distinctiveness of their own group. In comparisons showing differentiation (SELF–INGROUP–OUTGROUPS) we have noticed that some items are constantly utilized: 3,9, and 13 with higher values and 14, 2, and 11 with lower values.

To make sure of the direction (attribution of these peculiarities to themselves – attribution to the others) to which the differentiation tends, we related the similaritiy-difference scales used for the first comparisons to the importance scale. With this aim in view, we calculated Pearson's correlation index among the scores assigned to each of the items for each pair of scales. In comparison with social service psychologists, the statistically significant correlations were fewer (Table 6).

In the comparisons among SELF–OUTGROUP,2 INGROUP–OUTGROUP1 and INGROUP–OUTGROUP2 on item 1, the significant negative correlation indicates that university psychologists feel it positive to carry on their own profession within a public institution and as regards this attitude they do not feel themselves similar either to social service psychologists or to private practitioners.

Item 4 also has a negative coefficient in two correlation groups, (A) and (C), showing that at a personal level, the subjects do not feel very similar either to members of their own group or to groups of private practitioners as far as devoting themselves to working in the outside world is concerned, a peculiarity considered quite important by university psychologists, even though individual variance is remarkable.

Finally, item 6 has a positive coefficient in the correlations where the SELF–OUTGROUP1 and INGROUP–OUTGROUP2 comparisons are made: as regards the theoretical work, those interviewed consider the SELF more similar to social service psychologists, while they consider the INGROUP (i.e. the university psychologist group as a whole) closer to professional psychologists. It should be remembered, however, that whereas there is not any disagreement among the

Table 6. University Psychologists: Correlations A, B, C, D, E

Items	A	B	C	D	E
1	-0.0007	-0.1174	-0.5283 (0.001)	-0.2869 (0.047)	-0.5322 (0.001)
2	-0.1131	-0.1218	0.1291	-0.0906	0.1592
3	-0.1437	-0.0226	0.1555	-0.1659	0.1067
4	-0.3666 (0.015)	0.1833	-0.2229 (0.099)	-0.0895	-0.1376
5	0.1166	0.0059	-0.0633	-0.0668	-0.0168
6	0.0437	0.2349 (0.087)	0.2118	0.2178	0.3279 (0.027)
7	0.0997	0.1231	0.0501	-0.0160	-0.0537
8	0.1747	0.0646	-0.2130	0.1953	0.0579
9	0.0494	0.0121	0.0876	0.2127	0.1056
10	0.0521	0.0752	-0.4004 (0.009)	-0.2195	-0.0700
11	0.0336	0.0235	0.1250	0.0363	0.0717
12	0.0691	-0.0276	0.0476	0.0253	-0.1221
13	-0.2329 (0.089)	0.1458	0.1973	0.1365	0.0460
14	0.0673	0.3285 (0.027)	-0.4080 (0.007)	0.1676	0.0128

subjects about the score of value assigned to this item, the degree of individual variance is always high in every similarity–difference scale.

In this instance, we thought it right to verify whether the single elements of the SELF–INGROUP comparison could be grouped around some fundamental aspects, by examining the data by factor analysis (PA1). This factor (Table 7), made up solely of positive values, explains 27.1 per cent of the total variance. Some items, (5,6,9,10) with values very close to each other and a score higher than 0.60, fill up the factor at the positive pole. Their contents mainly show those peculiarities identified as the most important for the group both in scale of importance and in similarity–difference scales, that is to say, in theoretical work, the quality of professional work, research, and continuous training activity. The lack of items at the negative pole of the factor shows that there is no contrast of contents in relation to the aspect identified by the factor. The perception of elements concurring to define what is central for the group is clearly outlined by the configuration of the first factor. The professional model, articulating but not differentiating a comparison between themselves and their membership group, finds a specificity of its own mainly in theoretical work and research.

Table 7.   University Psychologists: Factor Analysis Self-group

Factor	Eigenvalue	Variation %	Cumulative %
1	3.80116	25.3	25.3
2	2.12748	14.2	39.5
3	1.50957	10.1	49.6
4	1.44653	9.6	59.2

	Factor 1	Factor 2	Factor 3	Factor 4
V_1	−0.09407	0.02415	0.22348	0.63448
V_2	0.48219	−0.28282	0.33622	0.60054
V_3	0.67387	−0.00292	−0.00870	−0.10843
V_4	0.49995	−0.70392	−0.08381	−0.07173
V_T	0.70061	0.29530	−0.16767	−0.06519
V_6	0.64791	0.28453	−0.16889	−0.30132
V_7	0.62329	−0.13913	0.03823	−0.30381
V_8	0.42862	0.08973	−0.29031	0.41321
V_9	0.63212	0.00689	−0.08692	0.25994
V_{10}	0.61486	0.05246	0.61420	−0.00576
V_{11}	0.43336	0.09018	0.61644	−0.14695
V_{12}	0.25764	0.61054	−0.13193	0.05348
V_{13}	0.16559	0.68496	0.09728	−0.17470
V_{14}	0.28114	−0.70919	−0.12628	−0.31955
V_{15}	0.48438	0.00520	−0.62410	0.28922

DISCUSSION

Comparison and Social Differentiation: Two Different Strategies

The data we have presented show that there is an intergroup differentiation mechanism at work between the two groups of psychologists studied and between each of these and private-practitioner psychologists. The elements for the differentiation concern both objective data, associated with the different professional context in which the groups work, and 'critical' items for the definition of the meaning which the professionalization of the psychologists may imply. However, the two groups studied do not adopt the same differentiation strategy.

The social service psychologists differentiate the SELF and the INGROUP from the OUTGROUPS in a practically equivalent manner, while university psychologists differentiate the SELF to a greater degree than the INGROUP from the two OUTGROUPS. The above-mentioned modes are also evident in these two different strategies: when differentiation occurs with regard to 'objective' terms, individual variability is limited, while when differentiation occurs with regard to 'critical' terms, individual variability is very high.

As we have predicted, and in terms of the intergroup theory, we can therefore state that institutional membership of various professional groupings induces the psychologists studied to regard themselves and their group as different from other colleagues. There is therefore a force at work which increases the perception of intergroup differences and which can create the basis for negative value judgments in regard to the others (Tajfel, 1969; Ehrlich, 1973).

The two strategies employed to accentuate these differentiations further delineate the intergroup process at work. Social service psychologists appear to want above all to reassert the legitimacy of their professional group, and of themselves as psychologists, by showing that their difference from others lies mainly in concrete aspects of the work to be done (and not only objective aspects, but also aspects involving meaning).

University psychologists, on the other hand, bring out more the difference between themselves as professional people covering a certain social position, and other psychologists: they appear less eager to differentiate the group to which they belong from other groups. This fact questions the existence of a more marked perception of intergroup similarity of members.

In this perspective, a further element is provided by the dynamics between similarity and differentiation, in the two groups, between SELF and INGROUP. In both of the groups studied, the perception of similarity is markedly unmistakable only in regard to objective items, as working with others and in institutional contexts. For the university people, however, similarity emerges also with regard to central items such as those concerning research and theory. On the other hand, the perception of difference regarding items defined as 'critical' is much stronger among the university psychologists than among the social service psychologists.

An increase in the perception of intergroup differences does not therefore correspond to an equally high perception of intergroup similarity. Are these results a confirmation that the intergroup theory does not function in complex organizational situations? This question cannot be answered until a few other elements have been considered.

Social Identity and Intergroup Relations

The data we have at our disposal appear to tend in many directions: the Pearson correlations between similarity–difference scales and importance scales sometimes appear to indicate clearly discriminative elements for the definition of a social identity or group distinctiveness. The values of the scales on which the correlation is made are nevertheless the result of the variability of the opinions expressed. When it came to reading the data, this tended to give rise to the doubt whether the elements at our disposal were indicative mainly of individual, idiosyncratic attitudes rather than of the social identity of the psychologists studied. However, the factor analysis on the data related to the SELF–INGROUP comparison of the two groups studied, provided an explanatory reading line.

In the case of social service psychologists, two clusters of items were identified which led us to search for two groupings of subjects, each of which, in the differentiation process, adopts one of the two clusters of items and excludes the other. The two 'typical structures' brought to light by this analysis express two distinct tendencies with regard to the identity of psychologists, one centred on social context conditions in which the psychologist works to conduct research and prevent the causes of discomfort, and the other clearly centred on the psychologist's clinical intervention towards the individual person. These basic tendencies can be linked with the fundamental ones of the social representations expressed and shared by the psychologists interviewed during the initial stage of our previous survey.

This research was not carried out in such a way as to distinguish the differences between types A and B in the first trend and types C and D in the second. The data available, however, do offer the possibility of explaining the effort of intragroup differentiation, by referring to the social representations shared by the two subgroups which make up the largest group of social service psychologists.

The data are less enlightening when it comes to the university psychologists. In fact, the factor analysis brought to light only one cluster of items constituting a common element in the social identity of the subjects. This meant that we did not search for any grouping of subjects within the group. The social identity of the university psychologists seems therefore to be based entirely on items such as theory and the importance of research. Does this mean that unlike the social service psychologists, the social representations of the university psychologists do not influence their social identity?

The data would appear to support this hypothesis, but it can be supposed that different tendencies, corresponding to the shared social representations, would emerge if the members of the group were asked to indicate the objects of research, the methods to be used, the theories to refer to, and the actual significance of psychology as a science. In other words, it can be said that, unlike social service psychologists, the university psychologists base their social identity on a few widely shared themes (we could speak of 'ethics of research'). This appears to obscure the different fundamental options which previously emerged, on work in public or private practice centred either on the individual or on the social commitment. However, as we have said, the hypothesis can be put forward that these options will re-emerge when the subjects have to specify the meaning they attribute to research or to choose the fields within which to do research.

CONCLUSION

Finally, we should like to make a few points regarding the intergroup theory and the practical relevance of these data. Tajfel's theoretical concepts proved very important in identifying the dynamics underlying apparently contradictory phenomena. An institutional division in different working contexts of individuals who have the same professional training seems to influence their reciprocal perception, bringing out the intergroup differences. This occurs not only for the perception of sectors of work defined as institutional, but above all with regard to qualifying 'knots' ('critical' items) of a profession that is still in the process of being defined. The recognition of intergroup difference, however, does not appear to coincide with increasing intragroup similarity. It would seem rather that there are influences at work leading to an intragroup differentiation which can be traced back to the different representations shared by the member subjects of all groups.

There are, however, still a lot of data in our study to be investigated more thoroughly, if we want to understand whether this is merely incidental, or whether, on the other hand, it should be a key to interpreting the relationship which exists between social representations and intergroup dynamics. If this should indeed be the case, then the many contradictions the study has brought to light for and against ingroup identification could be explained in view of the different social representations regarding relevant objects present in the group. Thus a fascinating prospect for research is outlined: and perhaps this is the way in which the intergroup theory could be used successfully to examine complex social situations.

After this series of questions to stimulate research to clear up very important theoretical points and to develop social psychology itself, there is a practical consideration. The data collected demonstrate that, because of different institutional membership, there are obstacles in the way of collaboration between the social service psychologist group and the university psychologist group, even though their social representations have many points in common. In his discussion on intergroup conflicts, Sherif (e.g. 1967) maintained that collaboration between different groups can be induced by centring them on superordinate aims.

How can such superordinate tasks be found to induce collaboration between social service and university psychologists? We have an opinion on this which we think deserves to be experimented on and verified. Collaboration can only be put into practice if university psychologists agree to conduct their applied research into problems which social workers feel to be crucial. This does not mean cultural subordination or renunciation of clarity. In fact, the first contribution of university psychologists should be discussed with their social worker colleagues in order to single out the various aspects of the problem to be tackled and arrive at an operational definition of these aspects. Collaboration should then continue through all the stages and at all levels of research, including joint suggestions of criteria to verify and apply the knowledge acquired.

NOTES

1. This survey was carried out in four Italian cities (Arezzo, Bologna, Trento, and Salerno) and altogether it involved 140 psychologists engaged in different working situations: 46 psychologists in the social services, 39 in university teaching, 28 professional psychologists and 27 psychologists belonging to other public and private institutions (cf. Palmonari, 1981).
2. The instruction given was the following: In your experience as a psychologist belonging to . . . [whatever professional field he belongs to] to what extent are each of the aspects mentioned below important for you? To answer, just write a score from 1 (no importance) to 7 (maximum importance) in the square.
3. By 'typical structure' we mean a cluster of items used at the same time and in the same direction, that is, to show either similarity or differentiation. These items show specific contents the subjects use to compare themselves with members of their own group.
4. The two subjects completing the sample (28) are placed at the beginning of the axes.

REFERENCES

Billig, M. and Tajfel, H. (1973). Social categorization and similarity in intergroup behaviour, *European Journal of Social Psychology*, **3**, 27–52.
Brown, R. (1978). Divided we fall: An analysis of relation between sections of a factory workforce, in H. Tajfel (ed.), *Differentiation Between Social Groups*, London Academic Press.
Brown, R. and Deschamps, J.C. (1980). Discriminations entre individus et entre groupes, *Bulletin de Psychologie*, **34**, 185–195.

Codol, J.C. (1982). Differentiating and non-differentiating behaviour. A cognitive approach to the sense of identity, in Codol-Leyens (ed.), *Cognitive Analysis of Social Behaviour*.

Deschamps, J.C. (1979). Différentiation categorielle et différenciation de soi par rapport à autri, *Recherches de psychologie sociale*, **1**, 29–38.

Deschamps, J.C. (1982). Différentiatons entre soiet autrui et entre groupes, in Codol-Leyens (ed.), *Cognitive Analysis of Soviet Behaviour*, The Hague: Nijhoff.

Deschamps, J.C. and Lorenzi-Cioldi, F. (1981) Egocentrisme et sociocentrisme dans les relations entre groupes: recherches experimentales, *Revue Suisse de Psychologie pure et Appliquée*, **5**, 127–29.

Doise, W. (1976), *L'articulation psychosociologique et les relations entre groups*, Bruxelles: De Boeck.

Doise, W. (1979), *Experiences entre Groupes*, Paris: Mouton.

Doise, W. and Weinberger, M. (1973). *Representations masculines dans diffirentes situations de rencon tres mixtes*, Bulletin de Psychologie, **26**, 649–657.

Doise, W., Deschamps, J.C., and Meyer, J. (1978). The accentuations of intracategory similarities, in H. Tajfel (ed.), *Differentiation between Social Groups*. London: Academic Press, pp. 159–168.

Ehrlich, H.J. (1973). *The Social Psychology of Prejudice*, New York: Wiley.

Festinger, L. (1954), A theory of Social Comparison Processes, *Human Relations*, **2**, 71–282.

Gilly, M. (1980). *Maître-élève: roles institutionnels et représentations*, Paris: PUF.

Morley, I.E. (1982). Henril Tajfel, Human groups and social categories, *British Journal of Social Psychology*, **21**, 189–201.

Moscovici, S. (1961). *La psychanalyse, son image et son public*, Paris: PUF.

Moscovici, S. (1981). On social representations, in J.P. Forgas (ed.), *Social Cognition: Perspectives in Everiday Understanding*, London: Academic Press.

Moscovici, S. (1982). The coming era of representation in Codol-Leyens (ed.), *Cognitive Analaysis of Social Behaviour*, The Hague: Nijhoff.

Neisser, U. (1976). *Cognition and Reality*. S. Francisco: Freeman.

Palmonari, A. (ed.). (1981). *Psicologi*, Bologna: Il Mulino.

Palmonari, A. (1982). On becoming a psychologist: A field-study in Italy, in Codol-Leyens (ed.), *Cognitive Analysis of Social Behaviour*, The Hague: Nijhoff.

Palmonari, A. and Zani, B. (1982). Towards a community psychology in Italy, in P. Stringer (ed.), *Confronting Social Issues*, London: Academic Press.

Sherif, M. (1967). *Group Conflict and Cooperation*, London: Routledge and Kegan Paul.

Tajfel, H. (1969). Cognitive aspects of prejudice, *Journal of Social Issues*, **25**, 79–97.

Tajfel, H. (1970). Experiments in intergroup discrimination, *Scientific American*, **223**, 96–102.

Tajfel, H., Flament, C., Billig, M. and Bundy, R. (1971). Social categorization and intergroup behaviour, *European Journal of Social Psychology*, **1**, 149–177.

Tajfel, H. (1972a). Experiments in a Vacuum, in J. Israel and H. Tajfel (eds), *The Context of Social Psychology*, London: Academic Press.

Tajfel, H. (1972b). Some developments in European social psychology, *European Journal of Social Psychology*, **2**, 307–322.

Tajfel, H. (1974). Social identity and intergroup behavior, *Social Science Information*, **13**, 65–93.

Tajfel, H. (1978). *Differentiation between Social Groups*, London: Academic Press.

Tajfel, H. (1981). *Social Group and Human Categories*, Cambridge University Press.

Turner, J. (1975). Social comparison and social identity: some prospects for intergroup behaviour, *European Journal of Social Psychology*, **5**, 5–34.

Turner, J. (1978). Social comparison, similarity and ingroup favouritism, in H. Tajfel (ed.), *Differentiation between Social Groups*, London: Academic Press.
Zavalloni, M. (1973). L'identité psychosociale, un concept à la recherche d'un science, in S. Moscovici (ed.), *Introduction à la psychologie sociale*, Paris: Larousse.

Progress in Applied Social Psychology, Volume 2
Edited by G.M. Stephenson and J.H. Davis
© 1984 John Wiley & Sons Ltd

4

Social Psychology in Classrooms

W. P. ROBINSON
University of Bristol

INTRODUCTION

This critical review concentrates upon what has been discovered and claimed about the triadic relations between teachers, pupils, and learning. This limitation excludes much of social psychological interest. No mention will be made of teachers playing roles vis-à-vis parents, colleagues, headteachers or representatives of educational authorities. No mention will be made of issues in pre-service or in-service training. Matters of curriculum are not raised. Sociological perspectives are reduced to a minimum, as are the contributions from experimental and personality psychology to psychological processes central to and relevant to learning.

The fields to be covered fall into two broad categories: the first is efficient teaching, and the second is the associations between the behaviour of teachers and individual and socially-based differences in the educational achievements of children. Within the second category, the general analysis is used to illustrate the conditions under which 'self-fulfilling prophecies' may operate to yield unnecessary outcomes, and this issue is then exemplified through a brief consideration of the relationships between low socio-economic status of pupils and academic failure.

The evidence and opinions to be cited for the analysis of effective teaching and the self-fulfilling prophecy have to be based heavily upon American sources, because most of the work has been conducted in the United States. The subsidiary examination of teaching in relation to socio-economic status (SES) differences in academic achievement is presented from a heavily British perspective as a matter of preference. SES differences have been found in all countries that have conducted relevant investigations, in the East as well as the West and in the South as well as the North (see for example, Husen, 1972). The

93

extent of differences may vary from society to society, and presumably the reasons for the variability will doubtless be in part peculiar to each society and to the subcultures within those societies. However, the general principles governing the differentials may have much in common (Bourdieu and Passeron, 1970). I concentrate upon the British situation simply because that is the society with which I am least unfamiliar. While I may be deluded about the extent of my capacities to empathize with the *Weltanschauung* of British male 15-year-old semi-illiterates, I cannot even begin to make any claim to share the world view of their Harlem or Haarlem peers.

These issues will be treated via a critical examination of a number of generalizations (GI–G12) originally formulated to provide a helpful frame of reference for students to try to find out what the 'self-fulfilling prophecy' (sfp) meant (Thomas, 1928; Merton, 1957) and how it might be relevant to activities in classrooms. Available accounts of the relevance of sfp ('if men define situations as real, they are real in their consequences') to the classroom were disastrously over-simplified (Brophy and Good, 1974; Nash, 1976), resting on presuppositions of unspecified character and linkages that were not made explicit. Coming to social psychology of education, it was a shock to find so few attempts to explain such phenomena and an even greater shock to find that the explanations put forward were so weak.

The account offered here does not pretend to the status of a theory. It is no more than an attempt to bring some order into the descriptions of alleged associations between the conceptions of pupils held by teachers and the academic achievements of those pupils. Some possible mediating behaviours are specified. Some explanations are suggested. Throughout, worries are expressed about methods and methodology, and it is perhaps desirable to say why.

Methodological Worries

One reason why the explanations offered here cannot be integrated to construct a theory is that the data collected so far are too insecure a foundation on which to erect systematically ordered explanatory propositions. The apparently forceful adverse criticisms which can be made of many of the empirical studies to be cited point to the need for more careful collection of much more evidence, preferably guided by stronger conceptual analyses. Had theoretical concerns informed more of the empirical investigations, we might not have found ourselves in the sad position exemplified in the extensive reviews of teacher effectiveness made by Dunkin and Biddle (1974) and Rosenshine and Furst (1971). Their balance sheets based on hundreds of studies of classroom interaction yield evidence associating some marginal differences in pupil achievement to downwards of a dozen or so teacher variables. It might appear that variations in teacher behaviour make little difference to pupil learning. If we step outside the frame of reference defined by the studies conducted we can immediately see how absurdly misleading such ideas really are. While cultures may provide many learning opportunities outside the formal system of education for many learning problems, within the system we can readily conceive of a variety of circumstances in which 'teaching' would result in little or no learning. In logical extremes no teaching at all about a topic would ensure no learning about that topic. There are many ways of failing to teach. If we pose questions at the other extreme about ideal teaching, we might expect to be able to state certain necessary conditions, but to move forward to statements about universally valid sufficient conditions might best be viewed as a chimerical aspiration. While it may be reasonable to expect to find that certain variables need to reach certain values for any teaching to be effective, the relevance of many will necessarily depend upon the relational characteristics of the teacher, the learner, and the particular task. Efficient teaching of elementary reading skills to middle SES 5-year-olds in Britain in 1980 is unlikely to be mediated by many of the same procedures as would be found to be efficient for teaching university graduates the essentials of Kant's moral philosophy. Efficient teaching about agricultural issues to small farmers in Brazil may need to rely upon importantly different techniques from those efficacious for enabling Australian 15-year-olds to understand the concept of 'soil erosion'. These points appear to be so obvious that it is difficult to understand why social psychologists should have spent so much time and counting and rating bits and pieces of behaviour in a search for the secrets of the Philosopher's Stone of teaching.

One would have expected research workers examining relationships between *process* and *product* variables in classrooms to have been much more worried about their investigations. Which explanatory concepts and propositions of which theories of learning and instruction were underpinning the expectations of the investigation? Which precise theoretical statements linked the putative process-product relationships, and how well grounded were these? Did the teacher, child, and/or task variables reflect adequately the underlying theory? Were the measurements reliable and valid? Were these the appropriate variables to examine? Did the sampling of teachers, child and/or tasks provide sufficient variation in scores for significant covariation between processes and products to occur? These are not the only questions which need to be posed, but suffice it to say that even these have not been invariably posed. Had they been so, there might have been fewer inconclusive results of the kind reported by Dunkin and Biddle (1974) and Rosenshine and Furst (1971).

Had the aspirations of investigators been less grand, more substantial conclusions might have emerged. The effective application of general scientific principles to particular and specific contexts of action in the real world necessarily requires a prior knowledge of the initial values of the possibly relevant variables in that situation before predictions can be tested about the likely differential efficaciousness of various manipulations. Teaching is no exception. And this means that some theory must precede (as well as succeed) data collection. While Popper's (1968) precise formulation of the conjecture-refutation sequence of scientific activity may not command universal accept-ance as a necessary or an ideal procedure, it is difficult to see how what is called blind empiricism can make progress. All observations made have to be in terms of categories imposed by the observer. Changes in the divisions and groupings or levels of abstraction of these might be expected to be made when the initial categories fail to work. By 'fail to work' I mean that they cannot be entered into true propositions that describe and/or explain the data. We have to *invent* both the concepts and the propositions into which we enter their possible relation-ships. We then try to discover whether our inventions correspond to reality. If they do not, we have to construct other propositions. Data cannot think. They cannot speak. And we can only speak for them if we can interpret them. Hence my fear of the so-called shotgun studies in which large numbers of scores on gratuitously assembled process and product variables are fed into correlating machinery in the hope that what emerges may be interpretable. (That is not of course a procedure one would expect one of Piaget's formal operational thinkers to follow except under desperate circumstances.) More theory-driven data collection is likely to be to the benefit of both.

But what are the theoretical propositions to explain? Are they to describe and explain what is happening here and now in this situation or what *could* happen? Are they to describe and explain the current condition in samples of particular subcultures at particular points in time? Or should they be concerned with the psychological and sociological limits of what can be conceived within the parameters of contemporary imagination and experience? Psychological theories are normally expressed in what are presented as culture-free propo-sitions unconfined to space–time. To the extent that they do transcend those constraints they are representations of what could be rather than of what is. This is a dangerous area in which to risk quick pronouncements, but it would render our tasks easier if we were clearer in our objectives. Some explanations are clearly more idealistic and general than others. For example, Piaget's representation of intellectual development could not be asserted as a valid detailed description and explanation of the growth of intelligence in all human beings who have ever lived or will live. It does lean towards the *etic* of possibility while remaining anchored in the *emic* of contemporary reality. But even if his story represents an empirical possibility for contemporary man, it is subject to the limitation that the properties of future human beings may be different from ours – and let us hope they become so. Similar remarks might be made about theories relating to aspects of learning, motivational–emotional development, and social development relating to aspects of human action neglected in the Piagetian analysis of intelligence, but what are we to say about small emic studies?

What would we say about a study which showed that a small sample of 22-year-old primary schoolteachers believed that intelligence is a heavily inherited characteristic normally distributed in the population? Perhaps they could be persuaded very easily that their conceptualization of intelligence is wrong? Perhaps they could be persuaded very easily that its distribution in the population is irrelevant to their teaching practices? Perhaps they could be persuaded very quickly that the cues they use to assess a child's intelligence are unreliable and/or invalid? If we can devise procedures and situations that lead to rapid changes in belief and behaviour, then of what scientific interest are these temporary states? Clearly there is great educational relevance, especially for the children whose education is in the charge of such teachers, and presumably one persistent practical objective of social psychologists engaged in education is to promote greater correspondence between teachers' beliefs and reality. But such studies may not be of scientific significance. We 'know' that on an international and even on a national scale teachers differ enormously in their personal theories about child development, their beliefs about the proper purposes of education, and about much more. We may have good social psychological reasons for wishing to find out why and how particular teachers come to be what they are, but we have no reason to be surprised by the existence of the diversity that obtains. However, the fact of diversity makes it difficult to define many of our tasks. If we already know that the diversity is so great that true and useful statements beginning with 'All teachers . . .' are likely to be as rare as the sound of one hand clapping, what kinds of generalizations about them can be made? One answer is to say that all generalizations should be viewed as being subject to an implicit qualification, such as: 'In the studies conducted with samples A and B drawn from population C in place D at time E, it would appear that . . .'. This qualification has indeed to be entered for all the propositions that will be offered about teachers in this review. Many of the propositions are artefacts of the time–space culture from which they arise. Empirically this means that they represent conclusions drawn from Standard Average Americo-European culture post-1960. In so far as similar historical–sociological forces have been operative in other societies with formal educational institutions, the generalizations should be equally apposite. In so far as our own culture is subject to Newton's First Law that bodies progress as they are unless acted upon by other forces, the generalizations will continue to hold in our cultures. Some people are, however, trying to change educational practices and policies in those societies. With these worries and caveats in mind we can begin to ask some questions about efficient teaching, and attempt to make some generalizations (G).

EFFICIENT TEACHING

G1 Efficient Teaching Depends upon Teachers Engaging Teachable Pupils in Relevant Activities for Sufficient Time

This claim would be banal if its truth were not forgotten so often. The word 'efficient' is preferred to the more commonly used 'effective', because according to at least one dictionary the former term includes considerations of energy expended which the latter does not. 'Effective' involves simply a criterion of success; 'efficient' additionally means that this success is achieved with a minimum of energy expressed as time, effort, and error. If we consider briefly the role of time, we can quickly see its relevance to educational systems that use age as a major basis for assessment of achievement. Earliness of mastery dominates the norm-referenced systems extant. Rates at which children can render their achievements available for assessment are in fact as relevant to 'continuous assessment' as they are to time-restricted examinations. We have then to be concerned with efficiency and not just effectiveness.

'Teachable' has to be used to qualify pupils. On an international scale, UNESCO experts have argued that the most important variables affecting children's under-achievement are hunger and malnutrition. Within our own society the relevance of these and comparable factors which diminish the ease with which children can summon the energy to attend and to learn should not be discounted. Neither should the motivational–emotional considerations to be mentioned under G10. However, the main thrust of G1 is intended to be in the time devoted to appropriate teacher–learner–task interactions, a generally neglected source of variance.

Following Harnischfeger and Wiley (1975), Bennett (1978) initially emphasizes cross-cultural and within-cultural variations in nominal and actual quantities of schooling as demonstrably important factors affecting how much is learned. Within these constraints, he points to the variations in the amount of time allotted to particular curriculum activities as determinants of how much of what is learned. Nested within these, the amount of possible active learning time (as opposed to time devoted to administration and management for example) can also be shown to affect what is achieved. Approaching closer to the individual learning, Bennett quotes and develops Carroll's (1963) list of variables relevant to quality and amount of learning: pupil aptitude, clarity of instruction, and level, pace and sequence of content. He adds frequency and quality of feedback as additional features to be incorporated into a general model of teaching and learning.

Just as ideas of under-nourishment can broaden our perspectives, so Bennett offers a salutary reminder that social psychologists can ignore larger issues while focusing upon small ones. Although empirical studies claiming associations between 'teaching style' and pupil achievement may succeed in pinning down statistically significant variance (Bennett, 1976; Galton et al., 1980), the amount of variance attributable to these may be educationally trivial when compared with that attributable to variations in active learning time available – as some of the results reported by Bennett indicate. Neither can we forget learning is an interactive activity, necessarily involving three-way matchings of student characteristics, learning tasks, and teaching, in which variations in any one necessitate adjustments in one or both of the others in order to maximize progress.

This kind of differentiation emerges very forcibly in the project of Brophy and Evertson (1976), which will be considered in some detail as an exemplification of the kind of study that has linked process variables to products and simultaneously shown how generalizations offered can be subculturally specific. Brophy and Evertson isolated teachers of 2nd and 3rd Grade children whose classes had shown very consistent general profiles of achievement over the preceding three years. In terms of the annual average mean adjusted gains on academic achievement scores on Metropolitan Achievement Tests shown by their pupils, some teachers had consistently 'overachieved' for their pupils and others had 'underachieved'. For the cognitive domain at least, these teachers could be considered as differing in efficiency. Using data from interviews, questionnaires, and classroom observations, Brophy and Evertson found that the number of relationships between efficiency and these measurements could be greatly increased if teachers were subdivided according to whether or not they were teaching in Title 1 schools. 'Title 1' schools are those with a sufficiently high percentage of children from poor families to qualify for special assistance under the US Education Assistance Act. Non-Title I schools contained children from higher socio-economic status backgrounds.

Regardless of type of school, in comparison with less efficient teachers, more efficient teachers liked children more, were more concerned for them to learn and believed that they, the teachers, could affect and were responsible for this. They were more patient, more goodwilled and had more faith in the learning capacities of their children. They believed in not wasting time. Observations showed they were also in fact not spending as much time on administration and management. They were better prepared with well-planned lessons and were more likely to follow their plans.

However, for the teaching itself, differences between types of school became apparent. Relative to the efficient teachers in non-Title 1 schools, those in Title 1 schools paid more attention to basic skills and factual knowledge, structured the teaching/learning into smaller and more redundant steps, gave more predictable opportunities to practise and gave more immediate and corrective feedback. They tried to make sure all the children were keeping up before moving on.

In non-Title 1 schools the more 'efficient' teachers engaged in more indirect and more verbal teaching, allowing pupils greater freedom to choose assignments and work independently, alone or in groups. Instructional sequences were run through speedily. Both punishment and criticism for poor academic work were positively associated with higher learning gains.

These differences are predicated upon teachers' differential presumptions about and reactions to differences in their pupils' current capacities and dispositions. Efficient teachers are adaptive to such differences.

Brophy and Evertson do move down to a consideration of the details of non-verbal and verbal behaviour related to effective teaching. We have already mentioned some features of these efficient teachers' definition of their role and attitudes, particularly their beliefs that their children can and will learn if they are taught well. They were more likely to see teaching as an interesting and worthwhile challenge; not just a job where pupil failure can be assigned to shortages of resources. Their beliefs about management and their practice of it conformed closely to the prescriptions of Hargreaves (1975) and the findings of Kounin (1970). These need to be referred to because, as well as incorporating details of what happens in classrooms every day, they also draw attention to two aspects of longer and shorter term historical relevance. First, the more efficient teachers explicitly gave their children a small number of general rules about classroom conduct at the beginning of the school year; these were described and explained. This means that observations of subsequent activities in these classrooms could only be properly understood if these prior statements and negotiations were taken into account. Second, the more efficient teachers had thoroughly planned and prepared their lessons in advance; hence they were not having to make hasty and impulsive decisions *in situ*. What has happened earlier in the year, and what the teacher has done the week or evening before and outside the classroom are both relevant to effectiveness within the classroom – and to the correct interpretation of classroom events by observers.

In the daily management of their classrooms the more efficient teachers were rated higher on Kounin's categories of 'withitness', 'overlappingness', smoothness, and variety of activities. High ratings of these were found to be associated not only with lower frequences of inattention and discipline problems, as Kounin has reported earlier (1970), but also with higher achievement. Kounin had earlier argued that too low or too fine a level of observational analysis, for example counting and classifying particular acts, missed the meanings of acts and ignored their strategic significance. 'Withitness' involves being constantly aware of what is going on in all parts of the classroom and spotting potentially disruptive incidents before they have grown; its qualities are such that it can only be rated and not counted.

Just as 'withitness' potentially facilitates pupil concentration upon learning activities, so smoothness ensures an approach towards optimization of efficiency of conditions of learning, provided that is associated with matching of teaching tactics to student needs and abilities. Brophy and Evertson were able to translate these concepts into measurable observations such as rates of successfully answered teacher questions, waiting for and seeking improved answers, practice and feedback opportunities, and rewarding and punishing.

Bennett's review and the empirical work of Brophy and Evertson are important contributions for a number of reasons. Bennett reminds us that the social psychologists in education can miss the wood for the trees. We may be tempted to focus on individual differences in teaching styles, when, if we are really interested in pupil achievement, we might do better to argue for schools, classroom, and pupils being organized more efficiently. Brophy and Evertson offer a strong demonstration that thorough and intelligently planned investigations can yield substantial results linking pupil achievement to particular teaching practices, at least for 2nd and 3rd grade children in Austin, Texas, in the early 1970s.

Having been appropriately laudatory about Brophy and Evertson, we can study, note omissions, and some criticism may be allowed. The analysis is almost entirely pragmatic and atheoretical. That it accords with my common-sense may be sufficient reason for basing my teaching upon their conditional prescriptions, but as a social psychologist I need to know how and why their results are as they are. For example, it may be noted that there was no investigation of the children's perceptions of themselves and their situation or how these were relevant to their reactions and actions vis à vis teachers, the curriculum and its mode of presentation. The presumed linkages between teacher behaviour and pupil achievement could be made more explicit. It is not just these linkages that are left unspecified, however. There is no mention of theories of learning and development. With those approaches to learning are the teaching practices in the Title 1 group consistent – Piaget, Bruner, Skinner, Gagné, Ausubel or whose? If these children are afraid of failure, is the successful teaching consistent with Weiner's application of Attribution Theory to the classroom or Atkinson's (1964) theory of achievement motivation? Is it consistent with other theories that attempt to explain relationships between anxiety and performance (e.g. Sarason, 1960)? To ask that authors consider the theoretical foundations of their findings may be to demand much, but explanations are an (the?) essential objective of scientific activity.

This criticism in no way diminishes the value of the contribution of Brophy and Evertson to the field. Brophy and Evertson provide a strong example of a successful attempt to demonstrate process–product relationships in classroom interaction. It does point to its incompleteness and exemplifies the comment made earlier that explanations for phenomena have seldom been included as part of studies of classroom interaction. Other comparable contributions could have been cited (e.g. Stallings 1975), but the work of Brophy and Evertson additionally serves to illustrate the second point that different processes may be efficacious for children of different subcultures. While we can return to the issue of process–product relationships, it is desirable to take four steps backwards and ask about the perceptions of pupils by teachers that inform their behaviour towards pupils, if we are to see how sfp can have application in the classroom. To do that, the setting out of some conceptual model of information processing and decision-taking may be helpful.

DECISION-MAKING OF TEACHERS IN THE CLASSROOM

In order to gain some purchase on the staging of the internal acts of decision-making and decision-taking that intervene between a teacher entering an interactive situation and beginning to interact, Hargreaves (1975) sets down the boxes and arrows depicted in Figure 1. We can note that this flow diagram simplifies events in ways which might lead to unfounded adverse criticism.

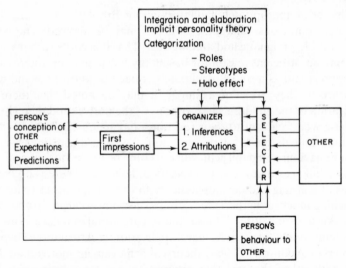

Figure 1

Only one person's thinking is displayed. 'Other' is of course engaging in similar processes, but Hargreaves is not pretending to represent the development of the interpersonal interactive sequence itself. Neither is he unaware that his diagram appears to be confined to a two-person rather than a multi-person situation. To represent the behaviour occurring in the first ten minutes of the first lesson of any new year could fill a book. Similarly to open up any one of the boxes is to become a victim of Pandora. The chart is similar in many important respects to those that can be found in standard accounts of person perception, and while we could quibble with its details, it will be more useful to comment on its major strengths and weaknesses, both for person-perception generally and

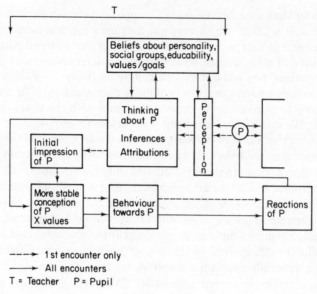

Figure 2

for teacher-pupil interaction in particular. Figure 2 offers some additions and alterations.

If we begin with the box labelled 'Implicit Personality Theory' we can note this emphasizes the possible processes relevant to assessments within a situation to the neglect of both the reasons why this assessment is being made and the manifold of 'data' stored away in the filing cabinet of the teacher's mind.

Why is any assessment being made at all? At the most general level we can agree that if any interaction is to occur the participants must select some actions for performance rather than others. At the specific level of deciding what is to be done in this situation people will be guided in that selection by the aims, goals, or purposes of that interaction. What do T and P intend to achieve through their interaction? T will have at least implicit values that will enable him/her to determine what he/she wants or needs to know about P. He/she will also have beliefs about data which will inform him/her what he/she needs to know. If this is so, we can immediately note an omission both from Hargreaves' diagram and from early work on person perception. Asch (1952) concerned himself with answering questions about perceived presumptive relationships between traits within persons and, perhaps unwittingly, set the scene for a divorce of the study of person perception from that of interaction. Why should T select some features of P for observation rather than others? Presumably because T believes that a knowledge of these is important for defining behaviour in that particular situation; they are relevant to the goals he wishes to pursue. As we shall see later (G2/G3) T's appear to emphasize features central to the T/P role relation, which may not be surprising, but nevertheless does serve to remind us that more generally we are likely to attend particularly to those features of other people which affect our interactions with them.

The 'Organizer' box will not only be calling up the goals of the interaction, but will also raise up relevant beliefs of more than one kind. The assumptions about P's we have to make in order to interact with them are not directly observable. We make inferences from observables to unobservables. What do T's believe are the relations between presumed symptoms and the characteristics of which they are believed to be symptoms? And once certain inferences have been drawn what other characteristics will also be attributed? As well as inferences from x to X there are inferences from X to Y; mediated as well as direct inferences are drawing on the store of beliefs in the filing cabinet. Proposed answers to questions of both kinds of what is connected with what have tended to assume simple all-or-nothing conjunctive relationships (Tagiuri and Petrullo, 1958), derived as these have been from experimental designs which have generally precluded respondents from registering tentativeness about probabilistically-related judgments. Whatever individual differences exist in beliefs about covariance of characteristics in others, research so far has certainly not done justice to the complexity which these 'implicit personality theories' can achieve. Neither have they paid attention to the situational constraints that can affect such judgments. While a teacher may muse for years about the characters of past pupils, in any classroom at a given point in time, he may not be able to afford such luxuries. Action of some kind is imperative and fast judgments have to be made on such evidence as is available.

Hargreaves' decision to highlight first impressions as especially significant is in full accordance with a longstanding literature. As Asch and others (Asch, 1952) demonstrated, data about persons are liable to be combined quickly into schemas that act as templates for the selection, integration, and interpretation of subsequent information. This established frame can be relatively resistant to change and will play a disproportionate role in the eventual stable conception of the other person.

While such experiments may underestimate the complexities of interpersonal perceptions of frequently interacting pairs of people who get to know each other well, intimacy is not the typical state of affairs existing in secondary schools in countries where teachers are subject specialists. In a British secondary school a teacher (junior high/high school) may teach over 100 pupils a day and perhaps 300 in the course of a week. These are large numbers, and beliefs about many of the pupils may hardly achieve the status of organized first impressions: judgments may have been made on very limited data. In primary schools (usually up to 11-year-olds) teachers can create and have much greater opportunities to get to know individual pupils.

The Conception box is subject to similar problems. We could add that some teachers may deliberately delay firming up impressions. They may be prepared to switch and consider alternatives.

Like the Implicit Personality Theory box, the Action box omits any reference to values. Decisions for action necessarily involve implicit or explicit values. One might also expect to find reference to situational factors as a set of considerations relevant to what is done.

Hence while the model includes much of relevance and salience, it does omit certain crucial features of general import such as values and goals. Its abstract quality may also tempt investigators to ignore the complexities of variations in situation and the teacher's experience of pupils being judged. The last time I had a class of primary teachers write character sketches of a pupil they wrote at great length. There was much qualification of the assessments offered. Very few stable traits or characteristics of social identity were assigned. Most comments related to behaviour in school contexts. It would have been very difficult to convert the sketches to ticks on an adjective check list!

A further worry is that all studies of teacher-pupil perception necessarily treat teachers as observers rather than as participants. That is, teachers are required to stand back and consider what they would say or write about pupils. Whether what they say *about* pupils is consistent with what they say *to* pupils about them is unknown. Whether what they say about pupils is dissociated from the way they actually treat them is unknown. A teacher might rate a pupil as unintelligent on a questionnaire, but this might be irrelevant to his treatment of that pupil. The importance of distinguishing between the role of observer and participant still needs to be examined and taken into account in person perception generally.

If we were to apply to studies so far conducted, even some of the basic questions arising from an improved version of Hargreaves' representation of the activities involved in moving from first sight to first action, we would find them unanswered, and even unconsidered. The most common technique has been to ask teachers to assign values of variables of personal or social identity to real pupils or mock-ups of pupils. Usually the variables have been predetermined by the investigator. Analyses either pursue the structure of the perceptions or demonstrate linkages between teachers' answers and the displayed characteristics of the 'pupils' presented. The ecological validity of the procedures has seldom been questioned. The dynamics of the linkages in teachers' minds that carry perception to action are not followed through. Hence, the generalizations to be suggested here are predicated on the results of studies whose status is far from satisfactory.

G2 Generally, but not Universally, Teachers Perceive Pupils in Terms of Individual and/or Socially-based Differences

This claim is an attempt to integrate the results obtained through empirical studies into as simple a single generalization as possible. It is not being claimed that *all* teachers always perceive *all* pupils only in terms of differences, and we shall even have to ask to what extent the empirical studies have misrepresented the perceptions of the teachers studied through the manner in which data have been collected. Typically teachers have been asked to rate pupils along certain dimensions already pre-defined by the investigator. Dissatisfaction with such pre-definitions led Nash (1973) to exploit Kelly's Repertory Grid, but although this technique initially frees respondents to choose their own labels for characteristics of children, the ultimate ratings or rankings are still in terms of differences (and similarities).

Although it is logically necessary that the assignment of any characteristic to a particular individual locates him/her in relation to all other people, psychologically this need not be so. When I judge X to be friendly, my reason for needing to make a judgment may be part of a decision-making procedure as to whether I should invite X to join me for a meal; the focus is upon actions which may or may not be performed. Similarly teachers' judgments may be related directly to decisions for particular actions. How shall I present this learning task? How shall I stop that fight now? One can envisage a teacher who had no beliefs about relatively stable characteristics of personality, but whose action-related decisions relied on assessments of the here and now dispositions and knowledge of pupils in relation to learning; they would be trying to match tasks to persons at this moment in this situation. To that extent their judgments would not be locating the child in relation to others.

However, studies show (see Hargreaves, 1977) that teachers are prepared to characterize pupils more generally either in terms of personality or social group membership or both. This contrast is not absolute, neither are the two independent. By 'personality' or 'individual differences' I intend to refer to characteristics that have a dimensional quality where the dimension can be at least crudely quantified on at least an ordinal scale – a person can be seen as more or less trustworthy, hardworking, or intelligent. 'Social identity' will be used to refer to qualitative differences definable in terms of social group membership. While some of these categorical distinctions are well-matched in terms of membership for the vast majority of the population, the membership can be more or less typical. Legally all children are either boys or girls, and the vast majority are biologically and socially defined as one or the other, but some girls are marginal, some typical, and others girls *par excellence* (Rosch, 1973). Inevitably a form of quantitative variation applies to the borders of categories, and the term 'fuzzy' has been used to refer to these. 'Socio-economic status' for example has achieved a measure of notoriety partly because features that co-vary generally can be clearly dissociated for many individuals, rendering firm allocations of these indefensible in the absence of operational definitions that may be too tight to be sociologically useful. The implications of Rosch's (1976) analysis of the categorical classifications have yet to be carried into the field of person perception to the extent that is necessary. In teacher–pupil perception studies social identity has most commonly been presented in terms of ethnicity or socio-economic status rather than sex, age, religious denomination, left-handedness, or colour of hair.

The distinction between personal and social identity itself has fuzzy borders. Some social identity characteristics have some dimensional properties (SES). Some personality variables may be phenomenologically and behaviourally reduced to binary categories, for example honest–dishonest, but this reduction still can be represented conceptually as a two-value ordinal dimension.

More directly relevant are the presumed relationships between the two. While it may be rare for people to make inferences from features from personality to social identity, these can and do occur. More commonly people have beliefs about personality characteristics associated with social identity, for example girls are expected to manifest certain characteristics just because they are girls. Two-way inferences are also possible. Presumptions of strong linkages between social identity and personality characteristics become educationally significant especially when identification of social group membership appears to provide a teacher with sufficient information to diagnose values of educationally relevant characteristics and act accordingly.

It is not clear under what conditions inferences from social identity to educationally relevant qualities are mediated through stereotypes and under what conditions they are direct. A mediated inference would be run: lower working class → unintelligent → low achievement; a direct inference would be: lower working class → low achievement. That the latter may be thought to be improper in the sense that there *must* be a mediating property would be a dangerous imposition on the thinking processes of others. If their thinking allows just an inference, then such is their reality, and that is what will guide their behaviour. It is after all not unknown for professional social scientists to assign causal significance to variables such as social class which are several levels away from pupil performance.

Some of the hazards of inference can be illustrated through a critique of a particular investigation. Seligman *et al.* (1972) collected coloured photographs, recordings of pupils' reading, and compositions and drawings from 9-year-old boys in two Canadian schools, one in a low SES area and one from a high SES catchment area. Controlling for non-verbal IQs they asked various panels of student teachers to assess each stimulus item on a variety of rating scales. The investigators utilized only the information for rated intelligence to select the 4 highest and 4 lowest voices and photographs. For compositions and drawings the values on the rating scale from poor to excellent were used for a similar selection. Drawings and compositions were combined as putative products of the same child and then composites were created of the three bipolarized variables: voice, photograph, and composition/drawing. The eight combinations from HHH to LLL were constructed, and 19 female student teachers saw the photo, heard the voice, and examined the composition and drawings prior to rating each child on 7-point scales for good–poor student, intelligent–unintelligent, privileged–not privileged, enthusiastic–not enthusiastic, self-confident–not self-confident, and gentle–tough. Analyses of variance were used to claim main effects for voice on all rating scales, and photographs and composition/drawings on three rating scales each, as well as for various inter-actions.

The authors state in their discussion (p.141)

> One would have hoped that teachers when evaluating a child's intelligence or academic potential, would have relied only on relevant information. Surely drawings and compositions reveal more about a student's creativity and capacity for self-expression than a photograph or speech sample. Yet, the results showed that Ss considered voice when judging intelligence, and both voice and physical appearance when rating student capability.

(Capability appears to refer to ratings on 'good–poor student'?)

That I select this study for criticism should not be taken to imply either disrespect for its authors or that it is peculiarly weak. Results of this kind have proved to be reproducible (e.g. Edwards, 1979; Eltis, 1978; Piche *et al.*, 1977; Williams, 1976). It does serve to highlight problems and difficulties. Questions can be asked about method, interpretation, and metholodogy.

The first issue would concern possibilities of generalizing about the samples of respondents, viz. teachers. Several investigations have used fewer than 20 respondents, which provides a flimsy foundation to write about teachers as a collectivity. In the UK for example the reliability and validity of estimates derived from 20 teachers would hardly constitute a warrant for writing about the 400,000 teachers in the community. Student teachers loom large in investi-gations. Seligman *et al.* used only female student-teachers, but in the discussion the word 'teachers' is not qualified or modified. Those investigators who have examined individual or socially-based differences among teachers as potential sources of variance have reported diverse results. For example, Edwards (1979) reports some sex differences; Eltis does not. Williams (1976) finds black and white, Afro-American, and Mexican teachers alike for some judg-ments and different for others. With a sample of 289 teachers, Eltis (1978) found either no or only weak associations between judgments and such teacher variables as sex, SES origins, own school career, and Rokeach's open-mindedness scores. Clearly such empirically driven investigations could be proliferated *ad infinitum*, and we must hope that some theoretical underpinning will be introduced to found differential predictions.

Conceptual analysis would also be welcome in respect of the judgmental processes. Of the studies referred to, only Edwards (1979) has asked the respondents to give accounts of their judgments, for example. We simply do not know how or why they made the ratings they did, just what beliefs mediate between stimuli provided and answers given. We have no idea of the ecological validity of the answers; whether these correspond to the kinds of judgments made about real children in real classrooms. (Reverting to the use of student teachers as respondents, one can see that people who have no or little experience of teaching pupils of the kinds portrayed could well have only cultural stereotypes on which to base their judgments.)

The demands of the task (Orne, 1962) have certainly structured the situation tightly for respondents in terms of the categories and range of both independent and dependent variables. When Seligman *et al.* comment on the relative weights assigned to the three independent variables, they miss the point that the *range* of each actually provided by the investigator will affect the outcome; they make an assumption that the Highs and Lows represent comparable extremes on the selected variables. Within the 36 examples of each product this may be a reasonable assumption, but do those 36 represent similar ranges for the three variables? We are not told how many voices came from the middle and lower SES schools, but perhaps accents and fluency in fact covered a very wide range of the possible spectrum whereas the photographs, compositions, and drawings did not. The relative power claimed for speech could be unwarranted, although it should be remembered that one of the intentions of the authors was to show that these other variables were relevant.

More worrying is the rush to structured studies. Ethologically-minded social psychologists would demand to know what kinds of variables are typically mentioned as dependent and independent. If a *T* heard a particular voice would he/she be prepared to draw inferences? If so, of what kind? Conversely if we had ascertained what kind of personality or other descriptions and evaluations of a particular *P* had been made by a *T*, we could ask how he/she had arrived at those judgments. Having started at what might resonably have been seen to be the beginning, 'experimental' studies would have emerged when the ecologically valid independent and dependent categories and/or dimensions had been specified. This criticism does not mean that investigators have in fact used invalid categories or dimensions. They may have guessed correctly at the characteristics of teachers' conceptualizations, but they cannot offer evidence to show that this is so. That the respondents have co-operated is not sufficient evidence for this. The co-operative and compliant respondent who will try to complete tasks as defined by investigators is a well-known friend and enemy of social psychological research.

Both Williams (1976) and Edwards (1979) introduced an important feature when they operationalized 'latitude of attitude acceptance' (Sherif *et al.*, 1965) subsequently labelled 'confidence'. This allows respondents to indicate a range of possible values on the dependent variables. With a very small sample of student teachers (7 male and 7 female), Edwards showed males to be simultaneously less confident and more positive in their ratings – and that degrees of confidence varied across scales.

With respect to speech as an independent variable, Seligman *et al.* simply used the tapes generated by the boys and were not able to say which features were relevant to the judgments of the respondents. In another study, Frender, *et al*. (1970) had a trained linguist rate the recorded readings of 93 lower class, 8-year-old boys. Higher academic achievers differed from lower academic achievers on amount and appropriateness of intonation, pitch and softness of voice quality using F tests, and confidence and speed using Mann–Whitney U tests. This would suggest that some indices are valid discriminators between higher and lower achievement, although we cannot say how useful these would be as markers without knowing more about the extent of covariance. It would be surprising if such were not the case for some speech variables. For lower class, 8-year-olds, reading will not be a fully mastered skill, and we might well expect that intonation would be sacrificed to accuracy of pronunciation and fluency if those characteristics had been accorded higher value by the teachers. Perhaps the same was true for the Seligman *et al*. study: perhaps the student teachers were utilizing speech cues that were valid markers of academic achievement. If so, then the conclusion quoted is doubly misleading. The authors may be denying the validity of a valid marker, while asserting the validity of other markers (drawings and compositions) whose relationships to achievement were not known. Empirical evidence on each would be necessary to justify the forlorn hope they expressed.

However, since SES may have been involved in the ratings, it might be suggested that 'accent' will have influenced judgments. In that case we might argue that there are no *direct* links discernible between accent and intelligence or academic achievement; one accent is unlikely to require greater cognitive capacity to produce than another. However, there is strong presumed covariance between use of accents and SES (Giles and Powesland, 1975). It is also true that there are significant correlations between SES and academic achievement (Reid, 1977) and between SES and verbal IQ (Butcher, 1968). There is also evidence to show that respondents can be accurate diagnosticians of SES from accent (see Robinson, 1979).

Hence, given *no other* information the following chain is a more valid pair of inferences than any alternative: certain accents → low SES → low IQ and/or low academic achievement. What is dangerous about the inference is that the relevant correlations fall well short of 1, and to pass diagnostic judgments on individuals on this basis would lead to many errors. While it may be true that in real life many teachers may assume higher correlations than the evidence would warrant (and that they may not realize an IQ score is a dependent as well as an independent variable) it would appear to be perverse to accuse them of 'prejudice' if their beliefs have a 'kernel of truth', and if the experimental design is partly responsible for exaggerating the resultant covariance.

Williams' (1976) factor analyses of teachers' ratings of speech variables led to him claiming there were two main dimensions of importance – confidence/ eagerness and ethnicity/non-standardness – where the latter factor confounds low SES and ethnicity (just as these are compounded in reality). Williams proceeded to try to identify from tapes what the teachers concerned were using as bases for their judgments. Non-standard grammatical variants were isolated in respect of non-standardness. Whether the teachers could have told him this is unknown. They might not have been able to do so. This doubt points to a weakness of reliance on respondents' accounts alone. Several possibilities exist. One is that teachers could specify the values of speech variables they use to make inferences either mediated or direct. Another is that they lack the technical jargon but could assign voices reliably. Another is that their judgments are unreliable, but that they continue to make them. Which of these is relevant we do not know.

We have examined speech in some detail not because it is necessarily so important in fact but because social psychologists have studied it. They have paid less attention to compositions or faces and virtually none to clothes, gestures, posture, movement, and so on. We have yet to conduct even a case-study in which the inference processes of a single teacher are fully displayed. What does the teacher think it is important to find out? How does he do so? How confident is he of his judgments? Are initial judgments subject to revision and if so what provokes change? How are these judgments associated with behaviour?

Do teachers' procedures of thinking about pupils change with time through experience? Hargreaves (1977) exposes the oddity of the assumption that pupil perception can be considered as though its characteristics do not develop with experience. He suggests six stages to a possible sequence:

(1) In the essentially hypothetical situation where T meets pupils as pupils for the first time in his career he is likely to have a stereotype (or stereotypes) and pupils will be seen in terms of correspondence to that stereotype (those stereotypes) (stereotype matching).
(2) With experience T will build up typifications of categories of Ps, and will match pupils to types (typical-matching).
(3) Within types comparisons will be made among pupils within the category (peer-matching).
(4) Conceptions of the ideal other develop and 'ideal matching' becomes an integral feature of typifying.
(5) 'A teaching typifying at this stage understands the characteristics he attributes to the pupil within a framework of the pupil's motives, the biography he imputes to the pupil, his knowledge of the pupil's home background, his relations with peers and so on.' (p.280)
(6) The still growing conception of (5): 'leads the typifier to typify in given ways as a function of the structure of that context (a particular context) and the intentions of the persons who interact in that context' (p.280)

This abbreviation distorts and over-simplifies Hargreaves' analysis, but it does highlight one possible course of development through time. Teachers are developing both their beliefs about pupils as a category and their beliefs about their ways of locating pupils within these categories. The system of typification is marked by an increasing number of cases experienced, with finer differentiation of differences combining with considerations of similarities with possible periodic reorganizations of the structural and substantive bases of classification. Regardless of the accuracy of the details, Hargreaves' analysis challenges us to study perception/conception through time in two respects: first, teachers from first pupils in first classrooms through later pupils in further classroom and second, teachers evolving conceptions of the same pupils through time.

One is left with a feeling that one is inspecting torn and faded photographs of the postures of people at particular points in time–space. It is very difficult to estimate the degree of correspondence between the snapshots and the realities they are intended to represent. That is, however, what we have to do.

G3 Generally, but not Universally, Teachers Make Inferences About Pupils in Respect of Characteristics Which are Believed to be Predictive of Eventual Academic Success and Failure

(They are also concerned to assess whether pupils will conform to their demands for order in the classroom.) Hallworth (1961) argued for the presence of two dimensions underlying the judgments of the teachers in his study, corresponding to the two components of G3, which in turn correspond to the most commonly asserted subroles of the teacher. Whatever else is also expected of them, teachers are expected to teach. Teaching requires instructional activities resulting in some academic progress by those being taught. Instructional activities cannot take place in chaotic classroom conditions. Hence, teachers need to assess pupils in relation to these two components. If we set aside teachers' judgments about the manageability of pupils, we may ask how teachers define eventual academic success and failure. First, do they define one pole explicitly and the other implicity or are both implicit or both explicit? What proportion of children clearly enter into one or other category?

Against which criteria are success and failure defined? Three contenders are commonly cited: criterion-reference, progress-reference, norm-reference. Pupils may be evaluated in terms of what they can and cannot do, their competencies in relation to actions regardless of all else. They may be evaluated by reference to the progress they are making; gains in proficiency through time would be the basis for comment and evaluation. While both occur, and there are no doubt wide individual differences in the extent to which each is used, it is the third normative frame of reference which is believed to be the most pervasive at the present time – as a matter of fact. The particular normative frame of reference most commonly used is age-related performance of others in mainstream school education. How well is this child performing relative to other children of the same biological age cohort?

The *de facto* existence of nationally-based examinations and curricula in a society ensure that one general frame of reference can be used to describe and evaluate performance in relation to these standards. In so far as school education is universal, and teachers subscribe to the beliefs that children have equal school-based opportunities to make academic achievements, that children grow uniformly in relation to others of the same age, they will tend to see eventuating differences as inevitable. If they do so, then there is no reason why they should not make inferences about eventual outcomes, provided they also have beliefs about the predictive validity of certain observable features. In the discussion of G2, we have encountered a number of studies which suggest that teachers do have beliefs which link aspects of personal and/or social identity to eventual outcomes.

In view of the amount of assessment of pupil work, the writing of reports, and the pressures to fit future opportunities to pupil aptitude, it would be surprising if the comparisons and categorizations teachers make did not exploit success/failure as a (the?) major dimension. What is surprising perhaps are the presumptions that long-term predictions can be made on so little data. Some investigators have been worried that teachers (and others) would assign a voice to an SES membership on the basis of less than half a minute's speech, but it is not clear why that particular judgment should be worrying. If speech (or any other variable) is to serve as a marker of social identity, it is important that the relevant characteristics be displayed very early in the interaction (Robinson, 1979); it is also important that the markers are distinctive. This is not to say that false identifications cannot be or are not made. What ought to be worrying are the possible beliefs associated with any such identification: for example, a strong prediction from social identity to presumed characteristics of the individual as a pupil or a strong belief in the irrelevance of teaching to eventual outcomes. It is crucial to distinguish between identifications themselves and the belief-systems associated with identities. It is also crucial to distinguish between predictions/expectations of a statistical kind and their application to individuals. It is finally crucial to realize that statistically valid expectations of the past are subject to change by changing the conditions which gave rise to them. (The more efficient teachers in the Title 1 schools studied by Brophy and Evertson (1976) appear to have been aware of the statistical probabilities, but it seems that they saw these were contingent only upon teachers acting as agents of the forces of social reproduction.)

G4 Generally, Teachers *Value* Success in Relation to Norm-referenced Standards of Academic Achievement

We have already mentioned that decisions to act require insertions of goals and aims as well as beliefs about what is true and false. We have already regretted the divorce of the study of person-perception from that of action in relation to others and suggested that this be remedied. In their accounts of the workings of the self-fulfilling prophecy, neither Brophy and Good (1974) nor Nash (1976) refer to the aims and objectives of teachers as essential components of the workings of the prophecy. What are teachers trying to achieve? Are they wanting all their pupils to make equal progress? Are they wanting to ensure that their very backward pupils make better than average progress? Are they wanting to maximize the percentage who will achieve some standard? As we have just suggested, teachers can confound their own initial expectations by adopting means to do so. To find out which pupils in a class are likely to receive better learning opportunities, one would expect to need to know the aims and objectives of the teacher.

It is clear from empirical studies (e.g. Ashton, *et al.*, 1971; Morton-Williams and Finch, 1968) that many teachers have aims which emphasize personal and social development as well as academic achievement, they are concerned with the education of citizens and human beings as well as successful examinees. Whether the curriculum they follow and the methods of teaching they actually use are consistent with their aims is beyond the present brief. It is also clear that success in relation to norm-referenced standards of academic achievement does have a strong place in the overtly expressed aims of teachers.

Since norm-referenced assessment necessarily withholds success from a proportion of candidates, then from G2 and G3 in combination with G4, it follows that some children are more likely to be seen as potential successes than others.

G5 Teachers have at Least Implicit Theories of Teaching and Learning

Although the statement might be considered to be obvious, the variety of theories extant among teachers, and the fact that many of these are likely to be valid only in specifiable and limited circumstances, have to be entered into the discussion as factors affecting the academic achievements of those being taught. Psychologists in education also disagree quite profoundly about these matters (see de Cecco, 1968 and Good and Brophy, 1980 for examples). Basing teaching on invalid theories of learning must be a major factor relevant to differences in subsequent achievements.

G6 Teachers Distribute Both the Quantity and Quality of Their Interactions Unevenly

Here the concern is not with the random variation that is inevitable, but with systematic discrimination, be this deliberate or accidental. Some measure of this is also inevitable. If a teacher is instructing a whole class, then the quantity of teaching potentially available to each child might be thought of as identical but the quality cannot be so. The lesson will make certain assumptions about current levels of knowledge, understanding, and interest, which will be more correct for some children than others, given that the children differ. Hence, apparent stimulus identity ensures differentials in the matching of pupils to lesson.

Where attention to groups or individuals is concerned it might be odd to expect teachers to hold a running account in their heads of how much help is given to each pupil and to ensure that the reality reflects intention. Even if it were to do so, then one has to know what principles are governing these intentions. Is it equality of time for all pupils? Is it rough equality of time with a little extra for the very fast and the very slow? Considerations of values (G4) might be expected to affect the distribution of attention.

G7 Differential Treatment of Pupils by Teachers Affects the Educational Development of the Pupils

We are now beginning to escape from the peculiar myth that teaching is irrelevant to learning with the aid of very clear demonstrations of the kinds of teaching behaviour that do make a difference (e.g. Brophy and Evertson, 1976; Evertson et al., 1978; Good et al., 1978; Good and Grouws, 1979; Stallings, 1975; Tikunoff et al., 1975). While these studies are focused on differences for pupils' achievements *between* teachers, others have examined within teacher differences among pupils. This has been the focus of attention in the pursuit of the self-fulfilling prophecy (Rosenthal and Jacobson, 1968; Elashoff and Snow, 1971). It has been relatively easy to demonstrate the conditions under which sfp is more likely to be operative. Some studies (e.g. Beez, 1970) have shown how even in experimental settings teachers' beliefs (and implicit values) can translate themselves into differentiating practices that give rise to differentiated outcomes. While the principle of sfp must be valid, the extent of its actual enactment across teachers, schools, and pupils is unknown and unknowable. Such estimates would require assessments of what could have happened if teachers' original expectations, etc. had been different. The prospective educational problems are to ensure that efforts be made minimize the influence of sfp in so far as it is viewed as an undesirable phenomenon. Those will not be easy to solve because the outcomes are consistent with original expectations, and the *attributions* of the causes of success and failure are likely to be consistent with the outcomes (Bar-Tal and Guttman, 1981; Weiner, 1980; Weiner *et al.*, 1971).

SELF-FULFILLING PROPHECY

The preceding generalizations enable us to specify two of the conditions under which sfp will operate. It will occur among teachers who make and maintain *either* relevant *false* inferences about particular children (G2) or relevant *true* inferences where these are linked in the teachers' minds to *false* beliefs (G2) about the inevitability of the eventual academic success and/or failure of these children (G3), provided that such teachers also:

(1) define success and failure in terms of norm-referenced standards (G4);
(2) value these standards (G4);
(3) act on implicit or explicit theories of teaching and/or learning which are sound (G5); and
(4) distribute the quantity and quality of their interactions in the classroom (G6) in such a manner as to render their predictions true.

In brief, in these circumstances, presumed potentially successful pupils will receive better learning opportunities than their peers, while presumed likely failures will receive worse learning opportunities than their peers.

These considerations will apply both to between-children differences within teachers (see Brophy and Good, 1974) and between-teacher differences across whole classes of children (see references cited under G1).

The starkest form of the self-fulfilling prophecy takes no cognizance of the perceptions, conceptions, and behaviour of its victims. In power-coercive situations the conduct of the victims makes no difference to the outcomes. However, children are not necessarily simply victims. If teachers have made false inferences about their characteristics, children (and significant others in their lives) may act to confound their teachers' definitions of them. Where children and their potential allies are relatively ignorant of their standing, however, they may well come to accept their teachers' views. If this results in children being defined as academic failures, then that may be incompatible with fundamental human aspirations. These points are taken up in G8–10.

G8 In the Absence of Contrary Influences Pupils' Perceptions of Themselves Will Come to Accord With Their Conception of How They Think Their Teachers see Them

Conflicting evidence can emanate from a number of sources: own perception of educational performance, own explanations of that performance, beliefs about other people's perception. Children may simply disagree with their teachers' assessments of their work. Or children may 'know' that the work they present does not reflect accurately what they could do. The judgments of parents, siblings, peers or any significant others may be in disagreement with those of their teachers. How the various influences are discounted, combined, weighted and entered into children's self-images is unknown, but we can be assured that in the absence of contrary views, pupils should accept their teachers' criteria and definitions. It therefore follows from G1, G2, and G3 that, generally, children will themselves be disposed to make *comparisons* and *categorizations* in relation to norm-referenced criteria of academic success and failure and will treat these as important.

While these comparison activities will lead to some children categorizing themselves as successful, others will see themselves as 'failures'. Is this latter acceptable to these children?

G9 Human Beings Strive to Gain High Self-esteem and/or Escape From or Avoid Low Self-esteem

This proposition is not so much an empirically-based generalization as a postulate or assumption in many amateur and professional theories about the fundamental nature of human beings. Some emphasize the aspiration to ideals, others emphasize the fear of condemnation. As with certain other motivational characteristics, it is almost certainly correct to include both approach and avoidance tendencies (Atkinson, 1964; Weiner, 1980) treating their relative strengths as a function of task, situational, and individual differences. While self-esteem has been a persistently popular concern of psychology and pre-psychology (see Gordon and Gergen, 1968), its conceptual status and that of cognate terms such as self, self-concept, self-image, ideal self, and ego-ideal remains muddy (Gordon, 1968). Certainly it is dangerous to treat self-esteem as a general unidimensional characteristic, although a number of theorists have done so (e.g. Coopersmith, 1967).

At least one important analytic separation is that emerging from Tajfel and Turner's (1979) theory of intergroup relations. They have drawn a distinction between acting as an individual person and acting as a member of a group. In respect of the latter, they have suggested that the content and processes of comparison, categorization, and evaluation in relation to social identity underpin crucial characteristics of intergroup behaviour. While Tajfel and Turner focus upon artificially created groups and naturally occurring groups based on ethnic discriminanda, their principles can be applied to educational categorizations.

Given the topic of the immediate argument, we can suggest that groups of academic failures will emerge in schools. When and where such groups emerge will depend upon the clarity with which the school authorities demarcate such a category and assign members to it. Pupil's beliefs about themselves will likewise be a determinant of membership. These influences will be sharpened if membership of certain other social groups is seen as a sufficient or contributory condition for being an educational failure. Hence, if the normative beliefs of the classroom or school presume that lower working-class males are prime candidates for failure, then having those characteristics will strengthen a child's conviction of his being a failure.

At present, we have no idea of the extent to which being an academic failure is construed as being an individual or group phenomenon in either its realization or its perceived origins, as far as pupils' perceptions are concerned, but whichever alternative or integration of the two occurs, it follows that pupils who categorize themselves as educational failures should strive to escape from this evaluation.

G10 Options for Enhancing Self-esteem are:

(1) **performing better academically;**
(2) **finding and accepting alternative dimensions of value which do not yield unfavourable comparisons;**
(3) **inverting the critical dimension of value, so that high self-esteem derives from being an academic failure**

In so far as the first is an individualistic solution, each child is theoretically capable of adopting it. However, its achievement requires both an improvement in academic performance and a redefinition of the child by the relevant teachers. In any system which utilizes norm-referenced criteria of comparison, it is inevitable that failures occur; escape by one individual means that another individual must take his place. The chances of a successful prosecution of this option are reduced to the extent that an individual pupil lacks the aptitude and foundations of past achievement necessary for the change of academic status – and a supportive context of necessary action.

The other two options are probably unlikely to be created successfully by an individual *de novo*. However, where precedents exist in earlier year groups and where other contemporaries are similarly placed, either or both become distinct possibilities. Hence where a social group of peers can establish itself as a counter-subculture to the establishment norms of the school, the two options can be successfully combined.

First, one would expect the academic failure to deny the values of educational success, emphasizing its disadvantages – hard work as a pupil, continuing to be a 'child', delayed earnings and freedom, and so on. Correspondingly, the advantages of emancipation would be stressed: behaviour associated with maturity, for example drinking alcohol, smoking, cross-sex relationships, independent transport, and probably delinquent acts as well.

Second, the classroom should become converted to a social situation in which group members challenge the establishment norms and lark about. Truancy should increase, and early leaving be seen as a final escape. Hence, self-esteem should become a matter of admiration by the other academic failures and of hostility, fear and/or rejection by other pupils and teachers.

SOCIO-ECONOMIC STATUS AND EDUCATIONAL FAILURE

For any particular teacher any feature of personal and/or social identity could be linked to a belief about likeiy academic success or failure. Teachers will differ considerably too in their definitions of success and failure. However, while some teachers may have beliefs about left-handed or red-headed children, children with dirty fingernails or cheeky smiles, or offspring of shoe repairers or second-hand car salesmen and these will be relevant to their personal treatment of children having these characteristics, we have to ask which beliefs about which social groups many teachers have in common. Any child will experience many teachers through a school career, and it is perhaps the general norms that will be generally relevant.

Certainly there are folk beliefs about sex differences, but perhaps the two most persistent and pervasive categories of concern and belief have been socio-economic status and ethnicity.

The facts about SES are not in dispute. Since surveys began and relevant records kept, lower SES children have been consistently less successful in schools than their middle SES peers on a wide variety of educational criteria: entry into higher education, examination successes at Advanced and Ordinary General Certificates of Education and Certificates of Secondary Education, scores on achievement and other tests of ability or motivation at all levels and stages. Low SES children leave earlier, truant more and are less likely to be in the higher streams in streamed schools. They have lower academic aspirations and are more likely to see school activities as irrelevant and useless to life outside school. Such evidence has been accumulated in a large number of national surveys as well as smaller scale studies (Bernstein, 1971; Central Advisory Council for Education (England), 1967; Douglas, 1964; Douglas, *et al.*, 1971; Husen, 1972; Kellmer-Pringle, *et al.*, 1966; Morton-Williams and Finch, 1963; Robinson, 1975).

There are many suggested explanations for these facts, ranging from almost wholly genetically determined inevitability to entirely socially determined inevitability. This is not the place to point to the extraordinary conceptual errors and muddles in that field. Suffice it to say that the quality and rate of learning and development of an individual will always be subject to limits from both directions. It is empirically clear that regardless of the favourability of environmental opportunities, genetically controlled factors will always constrain what is possible. But to suggest that any individual or social group has yet enjoyed an optimal environment for development would be impossible to demonstrate. Until such time as our understanding of growth and learning has been greatly improved and its consequences translated into practice, we had better ask what can be done to improve teaching of all children rather than engage in sterile debates based on ignorance. It has not been difficult to show that at least some of the variability in the achievement of low SES children is attributable to variations in teaching – across schools and within schools. The work of Brophy and Evertson (1976) is one thorough demonstration of this. As that study shows (see G1) efficient teachers in Title 1 schools (low SES) differ from less efficient teachers in just the characteristics mentioned in G2 through G7. Other investigations cited likewise show the potential relevance of teachers' judgments of and beliefs about SES to educational achievement. Certainly those cited under G2 suggest that teachers are prepared to identify SES on the basis of short extracts of the speech, photographs, or writing of pupils. While we do not know how accurate teachers generally are in such identifications, the empirical evidence is consistent with the potential validity of their judgments (see Robinson, 1979 for a review). It would be surprising if this were not so. If speech, for example, is to serve as a marker of significant components of social identity, then those markers need to be distinctive and to appear early in any interaction. Hence if SES is a significant social grouping influencing interaction, one would expect it to be marked, and that members of the community should be competent to make correct identifications.

The most likely invalid kinds of belief are at least two in number. The first is akin to the 'kernel of truth' theory of prejudice already mentioned earlier. While there are statistical associations between SES membership and eventual academic achievement, it may be the *degree* of this covariation that is exaggerated in the minds of many teachers; they may over-estimate the correlation. Beliefs which might merit weak generalizations about populations may be applied by teachers to individuals as expectations about their particular achievements. The second is that these identifications and expectations are sufficient grounds for not promoting the learning of low SES children. 'Poor home background' is a frequently voiced 'explanation' (and justification) for difficulties experienced in teaching low SES children (e.g. King, 1978). Beliefs about lower intelligence of low SES children may help to facilitate the society-wide intergenerational social reproduction referred to by Bourdieu and Passeron (1970). It may well prove to be difficult to persuade teachers that many of the SES differences observable among adolescents are consequences of differential teaching. In so far as low SES adolescents speak a 'restricted code' of language use (Bernstein, 1971) for example, it can be argued that this may well emerge as a consequence of the education received 'rather than its being a cause of failure' (Robinson, 1978, 1980).

To what extent the current 'facts' about SES and educational achievement could themselves be transformed we are not in a position to say, but to date the many biases in the system have been strongly tilted in favour of middle and high SES children and will probably continue to be so for the foreseeable future. Even if the life-chances were to be changed, the problem of failure would still remain; for every low SES child escaping, a middle or high SES child would have to join the failure category for as long as the system prescribes fail rates at current levels, and its executors practise in accordance with these principles.

For the present, low SES children are at particular risk for entering the failure category and the conduct of these pupils in secondary schools is consistent with G10. The investment of many low SES pupils in academic-related activities is low; relative to their middle SES peers they are more likely to perceive subjects studied as useless and irrelevant, to be bored by school, to be more withdrawn or aggressive, to have lower aspirations and to try less hard. They absent themselves from school more frequently and leave early (see Robinson, 1975 for a reanalysis of data collected by Morton-Williams and Finch, 1968). Very similar data are reported for Australia by Poole and Jones (1977).

That classrooms will be converted by such pupils to social rather than academic settings in which positively valued aspects of their personal and social identity can be displayed and reinforced is exemplified by the case study of Hargreaves (1967) – and attested by too many of their teachers. That such outcomes can be avoided by enhancing self-esteem in respect of academic achievement has been persuasively demonstrated by Brookover *et al.* (1965). However, enhancing self-esteem and enabling pupils to perform better is a constructive solution only for those particular pupils; where norm-referenced failure is part of the design of the system set percentages become failures. Dissociating the chances of failure from membership of particular social groups should reduce the unfairness of sfp; it should also reduce the incidence of sfp itself. In the longer term, however, it will be socially desirable to devise procedures in which those who fail to reach certain standards of academic performance are provided with socially desirable alternative dimensions on which to sustain their self-esteem. In the meantime those of us in education are obliged to rescue teachers from false beliefs and inferences that reduce the justice and efficiency of their educational activities, and SES is but one major variable of discrimination at the present time.

DISCUSSION

Depth of both conceptual analysis and data description and evaluation has been sacrificed in the interests of painting a larger picture of the classroom and its inhabitants. The broader canvas has been held at the social psychological level of analysis and thereby has ignored the perspectives of experimental psychology, linguistics, anthropology and, perhaps most dangerously, sociology.

The mechanisms through which social stratification is maintained and/or adjusted via the educational system are major factors permeating down into teacher-pupil-learning-task interactions in the classroom. Any social group finding itself discriminated against in the wider society is likely to find comparable forces in the educational system which act to lock it into a cycle that exerts its own intergenerational inertia. In so far as education is a horse race, the handicapping begins before school entry. And as Rist (1970) has illustrated, initial groupings in the infant school may already stratify children strongly on SES lines, and Newton's First Law holds – unless acted upon by other forces bodies continue along a predictable path. However, such wider considerations were not to be the immediate focus of attention here, but only their realization in the thoughts and actions of individual participants. The example of SES was selected as one social category among many in which it is possible to trace the operation of a self-fulfilling prophecy, both in a form which ignores the agentive properties of pupils and in one that includes those.

More generally, however, the concern has been with efficient and inefficient teaching and the social psychological factors relevant to the differences between the two. We have had occasion to refer to values and attitudes, person perception, decision-taking, teacher-pupil-task interaction, self-esteem, and intergroup relations in the course of the discussion. Strangely perhaps, the most educationally useful results obtained so far seem to have been constructed out of ideas that derive more from classroom folk wisdom than from theory in social psychology. Conversely, studies originating in social psychology are marked, by and large, by an aridity and distance from the complex mess of reality that renders them but points of departure for more thorough work which might aspire to a measure of ecological validity.

It could be interesting to compare social psychology in classrooms with social psychology in general to ask how each might profit from the other, given their current states of progress. It will not be possible to do justice to either, but such a comparison may encourage more social psychologists to become involved in education.

One advantage of the social psychology of teacher-pupil-task interactions in classrooms is that there is no escape from the intimate wholeness of behaviour in real situations. As we saw from Figure 1, it was unthinkable to exclude considerations of values and goals from perceptions and conceptions – and all these combine to yield actions. Individual actions have to be seen in terms of their past and future. They are part of smaller and larger sequences. In brief, one has to treat teachers and pupils as whole people engaged in interdependent activities that have foci and make up a continuing reality (or realities). The external system limits the possibilities. One cannot escape from the concrete and particular realities of classrooms and rise into abstractions that leave the parts unintegrated back into the whole; neither can the integrations escape from questions of ecological validity. These considerations are one of the reasons for the rather critical stance adopted in the section about teacher perceptions of pupils. Mainstream social psychology has been prone to abstract too much too soon, concentrating on quick judgments about strangers rather than extended commentaries about old acquaintances, gaining apparent control by supplying check lists of personality characteristics for respondents to tick, and then building up models to describe these phenomena, as though they were an adequate sampling of real-life person perception. What is emerging from teacher perception of pupils is that perceptions are likely to be related to the teacher's actions vis à vis pupils and that perceptual/conceptual processing can develop through experience. What do you need to know in order to have certain kinds of interaction with the other? How can you find out answers to these questions? How do the questions change with experience? In respect of the latter, I am tempted to wonder whether there are similarities between the development of teachers' perceptions of pupils and the ontogenesis of person perception in children. Hargreaves' stages may be wrong, but they are a point of departure for a neglected problem. Perhaps we in education find it easier to begin to pose such questions, because in real classrooms teachers have to continue to interact with their pupils (and vice versa) in a way that experimental subjects do not have to continue to interact with presented stimuli.

Although we have not examined goals/values, plans and attitudes to the same extent, the work of Brophy and Evertson (1976) highlights the necessity for adopting longer time perspectives than are traditionally adopted in social interaction studies. Some teachers make preparations on annual, termly, weekly, daily, and period bases, concerning themselves with management of behaviour as well as with instructional methods and procedures, believing that their efficiency is a function of their perceived credibility and trustworthiness as well as the procedures they adopt. It is only recently that students of social interaction (e.g. Clarke and Argyle, 1982) have begun to examine the sequential characteristics of conversations. They have begun to see we need to describe and explain films, not photographs.

Not that studies of classroom interaction have made great advances in this area. The many systems of observation catalogued by Simon and Boyer (1967) have not been that successful, partly perhaps because they have been used to count frequencies rather than sequences. Sequential analyses do exist. Sinclair and Coulthard (1975) have elaborated a system for describing units of classroom discourse, but unfortunately their elements are defined in terms of function in discourse rather than function in behaviour, and until these two are articulated, the linguistic descriptions will be of unknown status and value. It was also true that category systems such as Flanders Interaction Analytic Categories (1970) sacrificed meaning and significance (function in behaviour) to reliability of measurement and did so to such an extent that some researchers were prompted to switch to more anthropological analyses to recapture what had been lost (see Stubbs and Delamont, 1977). While this latter style of working takes account of the previous history of teacher–pupil relations, it unfortunately provides no means for handling descriptions and explanations of interactive sequences *per se*.

One can see advantages in studying classroom interaction rather than conversation. It is not clear how the latter is to be defined, but it is not uncommon for investigators to assume it is relatively goalless activity of general amiability, normative in certain situations in certain subcultures, and out of which possible goals may emerge. This very indeterminacy may mean that conversation has some peculiar rather than general interactive qualities. Classroom interaction is more likely to be guided by plans and purposes, of which accounts can be given. It may be easier to answer both 'why' and 'how' questions, when circumscribed 'whys' are likely to exist. It could be very interesting eventually to see comparative analyses of conversation, certain classroom lessons, and meal-ordering à la Schank and Abelson (1977) in terms both of descriptions and explanations, but those are heady prospects for the future. Meanwhile classroom interaction is still predominantly at the stage of relating frequencies of particular units or ratings of higher order variables such as 'withitness' to orderliness and achievement.

In view of its prominence in pure social psychology and the existence of applications to education, the omission of Attribution theory might be deemed eccentric. Studies have been made of both teachers' and pupils' attributions of academic success and failure (see Weiner, 1980) and these are clearly of potential relevance to the issues examined here. My initial impressions of early investigations unfortunately established a negative set. One might have hoped that by the early 1970s social psychologists would begin by collecting accounts of real-life academic successes and failures in deference to the pleas of Harré and Secord (1972). Instead one encountered students posing as teachers passing judgments on abbreviated forced-choice questionnaires in response to abbreviated scenarios, rapidly translated into dichotomized attributions of stable versus unstable and internal versus external causes. A snap judgment that this was a travesty of the complexities of reality was offset by the memory of 'poor home background' being a frequently voiced sole reason given by many teachers for the 'failure' of many pupils. The prejudice remains, however, that categories have been imposed when they should have been elicited. At least the work opens up the prospect of exploring a whole range of questions about teachers' and pupils' 'theories' of human activity.

What do teachers and pupils believe about the determinants of academic success and failure? How do they conceive of learning and development? Are their beliefs about individual and socially-based differences in achievement heavily hereditarian or wholly environmental or what? What do they see as amenable to change in themselves and others? What could bring about these changes? Just as developmental psychologists are beginning to ask about parents' theories of child development, so we ought to ask about teachers' theories – and about pupils' theories. In one sense we are all victims of our own theories about people, but some of us are more like victims than others. We are all constrained by our vision of what is possible and to that extent we are all victims of self-fulfilling prophecies. What is worrying educationally is that too many teachers have too limited theories of what is possible for themselves and their pupils, and it is only by extending their theories we can progress. In the Introduction we raised the distinction between social psychology as an etic and as an emic discipline, and suggested that the emic necessarily represents a temporary state of affairs. The description and explanation of the emic and its communication to the participants can vitiate its continued validity, especially if the communication includes considerations of alternative realities. To the extent that this is true, the social psychology of the classroom will be subject to continuing development and revision, and its constancies will be difficult to construct.

REFERENCES

Asch, S.E. (1952). *Social Psychology*, Englewood Cliffs, NJ: Prentice-Hall.
Ashton, P., Keen, P., Davies, F., and Holley, B.J. (1975). *The Aims of Primary Education: A Study of Teachers' Opinions*, London: Macmillan.
Atkinson, J.W. (1964). *Introduction to Motivation*, New York: Van Nostrand.
Bar-Tal, D. and Guttman, J. (1981). A comparison of teachers', pupils' and parents' attributions regarding pupils' academic achievements, *British Journal of Educational Psychology*, **51**, 301–311.
Becker, H.S. (1952). Social class variations in pupil–teacher relationships, *Journal of Educational Sociology*, **25**, 451–465.
Beez, W.V. (1970). Influence of biased psychological reports on teacher behaviour and pupil performance, in *Learning in Social Settings*, M.W. Miles and W.W. Charters (eds), New York: Allyn and Bacon.
Bennett, S.N. (1976). *Teaching Styles and Pupil Progress*, London: Open Books.
Bennett, S.N. (1978). Recent research on teaching: a dream, a belief and a model, *British Journal of Educational Psychology*, **48**, 127–147.
Bernstein, B. (1971). *Social Class, Codes and Control*, Vol.1: *Theoretical Studies towards a Sociology of Language*, London: Routledge & Kegan Paul.
Bourdieu, P. and Passeron, J.C. (1970). *La Reproduction, Eléments pour une Théorie du Système d'Enseignement*, Paris: Les Editions de Minuit.
Brookover, W.B., Le Pere, J.M., Hamachek, D.E., Thomas, S., and Erickson, E.L. (1965). Self concept of ability and school achievement. Final Report, Co-operative Research Project 1636, Bureau of Educational Research Services, East Lansing, Michigan.
Brophy, J.E. and Evertson, C.M. (1976). *Learning from Teaching*, Boston: Allyn and Bacon.
Brophy, J.E. and Good, T.L. (1974). *Teacher–Student Relationships*, New York: Holt, Rinehart & Winston.
Butcher, H.J. (1968). *Human Intelligence*, London: Methuen.
Carroll, J.B. (1963). A model of school learning, *Teachers' College Record*, **64**, 723–733.
Central Advisory Council for Education (England) (1967). *Children and their Primary Schools*, London: HMSO.

Clarke, D.E. and Argyle, M. (1982). Conversation sequences, in *Advances in the Social Psychology of Language*, C. Fraser and K.R. Scherer (eds), Cambridge: Cambridge University Press.

Coopersmith, S. (1967). *The Antecedents of Self-Esteem*, San Francisco: Freeman.

de Cecco, J.P. (1968). *The Psychology of Learning and Instruction*, Englewood Cliffs, NJ: Prentice-Hall.

Douglas, J.W.B. (1964). *The Home and the School*, London: MacGibbon and Kee.

Douglas, J.W.B., Ross, J.M., and Simpson, H.R. (1971). *All Our Future*, London: Panther Books.

Dunkin, M.J. and Biddle, B.J. (1974). *The Study of Teaching*, New York: Holt, Rhinehart & Winston.

Edwards, J. (1979). *Language and Disadvantage*, London: Arnold.

Elashoff, J.D. and Snow, R.E. (1971). *Pygmalion Reconsidered*, Worthington, Ohio: Chas. A. Jones.

Eltis, K. (1978). The ascription of attributes to pupils by teachers and student-teachers. Doctoral dissertation, Macquarie University, Australia.

Evertson, C., Anderson, L., and Brophy, J. (1978). Texas Junior High School Study. Final Report of process-outcome relationships (vol.1). Report No. 4061, Research and Development Center for Teacher Education, Austin, Texas.

Flanders, N. (1970). *Analysing Teaching Behaviour*, Reading, Mass: Addison-Wesley.

Frender, R., Brown, B., and Lambert, W.E. (1970). The role of speech characteristics in scholatsic success, *Canadian Journal of Behavioural Science*, **2**, 299–306.

Galton, M., Simon, B. and Croll, P. (1980). *Inside the Primary Classroom*, London: Routledge & Kegan Paul.

Gergen, K.J. (1971), *The Concept of Self*, New York: Holt, Rinehart & Winston.

Giles, H. and Powesland, P. (1975). *Speech Style and Social Evaluation*, London: Academic Press.

Good, T. and Brophy, J. (1980). *Educational Psychology: A Realistic Approach*, 2nd edn, New York: Holt, Rinehart & Winston.

Good, T., Ebmeier, H., and Bickerman, T. (1978). Teaching mathematics in high and low SES classrooms: an empirical comparison, *Journal of Teacher Education*, **29**, 85–90.

Good, T. and Grouws, D. (1979). The Missouri Mathematics Effectiveness Project: an experimental study in fourth grade classrooms, *Journal of Educational Psychology*, **71**, 355–362.

Goodacre, E.J. (1968). *Teachers and Their Pupils' Home Background*, Slough: NFER.

Gordon, C. (1968). Self conceptions: configurations of content, in *The Self in Social Interaction*, C. Gordon and K.J. Gergen (eds), Vol.I, New York: Wiley.

Gordon, C. and Gergen, K.J. (eds) (1968). *The Self in Social Interaction*, Vol. 1, New York: Wiley.

Hallworth, H.J. (1961). Teachers' personality ratings of high school pupils, *Journal of Educational Psychology*, **52**, 297–302.

Hargreaves, D. (1967). *Social Relations in a Secondary School*, London: Routledge & Kegan Paul.

Hargreaves, D.H. (1975). *Interpersonal Relations and Education*, London: Routledge & Kegan Paul.

Hargreaves, D.H. (1977). The process of typification in classroom interactions: models and methods, *British Journal of Educational Psychology*, **47**, 274–284.

Harnischfeger, A. and Wiley, D.E. (1975). Teaching/learning processes in elementary school: a synoptic view, *Studies of Education Processes*, No. 9, Chicago: University of Chicago Press.

Harré, R. and Secord, P. (1972). *The Explanation of Social Behaviour*, Oxford: Blackwell.
Husen, T. (1972). *Social Background and Educational Career*, Paris: OECD (CERI).
Kellmer Pringle, M.L., Butler, N.R., and Davie, R. (1966). *11,000 Seven-Year- Olds*, London: Longman.
King, R. (1978). *All Things Bright and Beautiful*, Chichester: Wiley.
Kounin, J.S. (1970). *Discipline and Group Management in Classrooms*, New York: Holt, Rinehart & Winston.
Merton, R.K. (1957). *Social Theory and Social Structure* (revised edition), Glencoe, Ill.: Free Press.
Morton-Williams, R. and Finch, S. (1968). *Young School Leavers*, London: HMSO.
Nash, R. (1973). *Classrooms Observed*, London: Routledge & Kegan Paul.
Nash, R. (1976). *Teacher Expectations and Pupil Learning*, London: Routledge & Kegan Paul.
Orne, M.T. (1962). On the social psychology of the psychological experiment: with particular reference to demand characteristics and their implications, *American Psychologist*, **17**, 776–783.
Piche, G., Michlin, M., Rubin, D., and Sullivan, A. (1977). Effects of dialect-ethnicity, social class and written compositions on teachers' subjective evaluations, *Communication Monographs*, **44**, 60–72.
Poole, M.E. and Jones, D. (1977). *Early School Leavers*. La Trobe 15 to 18 year old Project, Melbourne: La Trobe.
Popper, K.R. (1968). *Conjectures and Refutations*, London: Routledge & Kegan Paul.
Reid, I. (1977). *Social Class Differences in Britain*. London: Open Books.
Rist, R. (1970). Student social class and teacher expectations: the self-fulfilling prophecy in ghetto education, *Harvard Educational Review*, **40**, 411–451.
Robinson, W.P. (1975), Boredom at school, *British Journal of Educational Psychology*, **45**, 141–152.
Robinson, W.P. (1978). *Language Management in Education: the Australian Context*, Sydney: Allen & Unwin.
Robinson, W.P. (1979). Speech markers and social class, in *Social Markers and Speech*, K. Scherer and H. Giles (eds), Cambridge: Cambridge University Press, pp. 211–249.
Robinson, W.P. (1980). Language management, socio-economic status and educational progress, in *Language and Language Disorders in Childhood*, L.A. Hersov and M. Berger (eds). Supplement to *Journal of Child Psychology and Child Psychiatry*, No. 2.
Rosch, E. (1973). On the internal structure of perceptual and semantic categories, in *Cognitive Development and the Acquisition of Language*, T.E. Moore (ed.), New York: Academic Press.
Rosch, E. (1976). Human categorisation, in *Advances in Cross-Cultural Psychology*, N. Warren (ed.), 1. London: Academic Press.
Rosenshine, B. and Furst, N.F. (1971). Research on teacher performance criteria, in *Research in Teacher Education*, B.O. Smith (ed.), Englewood Cliffs, NJ: Prentice-Hall.
Rosenthal, R. and Jacobson, L. (1968). *Pygmalion in the Classroom*, New York: Holt, Rinehart & Winston.
Sarason, S.B. (1960). *Anxiety in Elementary School-Children*, New York: Wiley.
Schank, R. and Abelson, R.P. (1977). *Scripts, Plans, Goals and Understanding*, Hillsdale: Erlbaum.
Seligman, C.R., Tucker, G.R., and Lambert, W.E. (1972). The effect of speech style and other attributes on teachers' attitudes to pupils, *Language in Society*, **1**, 131–142.
Sherif, C.W., Sherif, M., and Nebergall, R.E. (1965). *Attitude and Attitude Change*, Philadelphia: Saunders.

Simon, A. and Boyer, E. (eds) (1967). *Mirrors for Behavior*. Philadelphia: Research for Better Schools.

Sinclair, J. McH. and Coulthard, R.M. (1975). *Towards an Analysis of Discourse*, London: Oxford University Press.

Stallings, J. (1975). Implementation and child effects of teaching practices in follow through classrooms, *Monographs of the Society for Research in Child Development*, **40**, no.163.

Stubbs, M. and Delamont, S. (1977). *Explorations in Classroom Interaction*, Chichester: Wiley.

Tagiuri, R. and Petrullo, L. (1958). *Person Perception and Interpersonal Behaviour*, Stanford, Cal: Stanford University Press.

Tajfel, H. and Turner, J.C. (1979). An integrative theory of intergroup conflict, in *The Social Psychology of Intergroup Relations*, W.G. Austin and S. Worchel (eds), Monterey, Cal: Brooks/Cole.

Thomas, W.I. (1928). *The Child in America*, New York: Knopf.

Tikunoff, W., Berliner, D., and Rist, R. (1975). An ethnographic study of the forty classrooms of the Beginning Teacher Evaluation Study Technical Report, 75-10-5. San Francisco: Far West Laboratory.

Weiner, B. (1980), *Human Motivation*, New York: Holt, Rinehart & Winston.

Weiner, B., Frieze, I., Kukla, A., Reed, L., Rest, S., and Rosenbaum, R.M. (1971). *Perceiving the Causes of Success and Failure*, New York: General Learning Press.

Williams, F. (1976). *Explorations of the Linguistic Attitudes of Teachers*, Rowley, Mass.: Newbury House.

Progress in Applied Social Psychology, Volume 2
Edited by G.M. Stephenson and J.H. Davis
© 1984 John Wiley & Sons Ltd

5

Pluralistic Ignorance, Revisited

H. TOCH and J. KLOFAS
State University of New York at Albany

Over 50 years ago, in 1931, the Craftsmen Press of Syracuse published *Students' Attitudes: A Report of the Syracuse University Reaction Study*, by Daniel Katz – who was then Instructor in Psychology at Princeton – and F(loyd) H(enry) Allport. The book-length report summarizes some surprisingly candid reponses of 3408 college students to a questionnaire circulated in 1926 by the School of Citizenship and Public Affairs of Syracuse. The analysis of these responses includes several almost throwaway lines that introduce a radical new concept, that of 'pluralistic ignorance'. We shall try to show that one is far from exhausting the research possibilities which this phenomenon suggests, and its implications for social reform.

Katz and Allport found that Syracuse students presented with a roster of roommates admitted that they would discriminate against twenty-six out of thirty 'types'. When asked for their reasons, 55 per cent of the students endorsed 'I have no personal objection to social contact . . . with most of these people; but, as things are at present in society it would lower the reputation of my fraternity to admit those I have not checked' (Katz and Allport, 1931, p. 149). Katz and Allport observe that

> The fact that 55 per cent of all fraternity members say they have no personal objection to certain groups, but exclude them because they are concerned about public opinion, is very significant. . . . They are, as individuals, unaware, in any statistically accurate sense, of one another's *private or personal feelings*; for in nearly every instance in which they express their feelings to one another, this illusion of 'what the group feels' enters to distort their expression. An inaccurate estimate of 'group opinion' is therefore universally accepted. This situation, which we may speak of as 'pluralistic ignorance,' has made possible an exaggerated impression of the universality of the attitudes in question. (Katz and Allport, 1931).

The paragraph is rich in hypotheses. It argues that erroneous assumptions about how others feel are self-perpetuating, because they discourage the expression of opinions that one (falsely) regards as non-conforming. There is an additional implication, *provided* the respondents are to be believed. It is that pluralistic ignorance inhibits conduct, and that it squelches the private preferences and sound inclinations of a majority-in-ignorance.

As we see in this paragraph, pluralistic ignorance is equated with estimates that tend towards an 'impression of universality'. Allport saw the widely shared impression of group consensus as evidence of induced conformity – of a successful gambit by institutionally supported opinion leaders to propagate their opinions (Allport, 1933). Only where *some* people in a group assume that there is consensus and others do not, the hypothesis that the consensus-estimators might be a special group motivated to 'project' their views seemed parsimonious.[1] In the case of student cheating, for example,

> Students who confess that they crib, in the majority of cases, give a higher estimate of the number of cribbers in Syracuse University than do those who deny participation in the practice. The size of the estimate increases, moreover, in direct ratio to the degree of cribbing acknowledged. (Katz and Allport, 1931, p. 227)

'Pluralistic ignorance' is sometimes referenced to an Allportian textbook by Katz and Schanck (1938); elsewhere, we are led to Schanck's *Psychological Monograph* (1932), which details a classic piece of field research on fundamentalist protestantism in a town called Elms Hollow. Schanck (1932) credits the term 'pluralistic ignorance' to F.H. Allport. Allport must have used the term in seminars; it does not appear in the index of his *Social Psychology* (1924) nor in that of his book about conformity (1933), where we expect a detailed exegesis. Relying on Schanck (as of 1932) we learn that

> Dr. Allport has called situations where individuals are unaware of the attitudes of others, situations of pluralistic ignorance. In such a condition, the feeling may be based often upon projection and not upon reality.... An individual may project an attitude into other group members from observations of their reactions to speeches, conversation, etc. As a result of the feeling that this projected attitude is universal among the group members, the individual may then desire to conform to the group standard and adopt the projected attitude himself. In this way an entire group may maintain a public position in contradistinction to the private attitudes of the majority or over. (Schanck, 1932, p. 101)

Like Katz and Allport (1931), Katz and Schanck (1938) place emphasis on the conformity-inducing power of pluralistic ignorance. They argue that 'people will stay in line because their fellows do, yet, if they only knew that their comrades wanted to kick over the traces too, the institutional conformity of the group would quickly vanish' (Katz and Schanck, 1938, p. 174). The assumption again is that people act in opposition to their convictions, under the impression that other people (who are similarly duped) disagree with them. This portrait is different from one in which pluralistic ignorance occasions public pretence, but leaves behaviour unaffected. This sort of view is illustrated by the following vignette from Elms Hollow, which is reported by Krech *et al.* (1962):

> Schanck (1932) found that the Methodist Church was dominant. The norms of this church prohibited card playing, smoking and drinking. When Schanck first investigated the attitudes of the people in Elms Hollows through interviews and questionnaires, the answers of nearly everyone reflected the norms of the church. Before he had left the community, however, he had played cards and had drunk hard cider with many individuals – behind locked doors and drawn blinds. Each individual believed that he was virtually alone in rejecting the norms of his church. (pp. 248–249)

Krech, *et al.* (1962) conclude that:

> Pluralistic ignorance results in public lip service to the norms of the group, and private recalcitrance. In such a state, the norms of the group have been called 'ideal' or 'fictitious' norms; the norms which govern the deviant private behavior have been termed the 'real' or 'actual' norms of the group. (p. 249)

Schanck's own conclusion was that pluralistic ignorance often (but not always) modifies conduct. His first example (unrelated to card playing) makes this point clearer:

> The Baptist preacher, for instance, was a warm friend and frequent visitor at the home of the investigator, possessed a multitude of liberal attitudes on religion which were inhibited in every situation in Elms Hollows except in his relationships with the investigator. A knowledge of these liberal and intimate attitudes, however, revealed very little of his actual behaviour in Sunday church services. Any stranger stopping at his door with a questionnaire would have obtained a more accurate account of his attitudes that actually function in community situations than the intimate accounts known to the investigator. (Schanck, 1932, p. 7)

As Schanck sees it, where almost everyone behaves similarly (where public behaviour follows a J-curve), we can infer that institutional norms, *or assumptions about institutional norms*, determine *public* conduct. *Private* conduct may vary, and may follow a normal curve.

Where persons-in-action deviate from a 'projected' (Schanck's term) majority sentiment, they may see themselves as risk-taking. This point is illustrated by the single pluralistic ignorance study cited in *The Handbook of Social Psychology* (Kelley and Thibaut, 1969), which derives from Roger Brown's (1965) text and refers to a dissertation by Hinds (1962). In Hinds' study, 'subjects very consistently guessed that others would choose more cautiously than did they themselves', and in Brown's replication 'not one subject guessed that these others would answer more riskily than themselves; they guessed the others to be the same as themselves or more conservative. It looks as if each person answering as an individual conceives of himself to be at least as risky as the average of a reference group' (Brown, 1965, p. 700).

In an accidental switch of Hinds' paradigm, a deviant group discussed their individual choices before committing themselves, and – having discovered the actual bravery of others – escalated their risks. This finding is related to the second Schanck corollary, which is that *behaviour based on pluralistic ignorance can be extinguished by discovering the preferences of others*, or – as Schanck put it – 'a dissolution of pluralistic ignorance is likely to result in the group members abandoning their public position and adopting their private attitude in public situations also' (Schanck, 1932, p. 101).

This 'solution' to the pluralistic ignorance problem (as the problem is portrayed by Allport, Katz and Schanck) runs into a difficulty that was alluded to by Katz and Allport (1931) themselves. The difficulty is elaborated upon by Krech, *et al.* (1962), who cite Cantril (1958) to the effect that

> the dissident individual's assumption (even though mistaken) that everyone else holds a certain belief on an issue often weakens his will to find out and to do something about it. Moreover, in 'real life' the crucial issues are often so complex that the individual cannot ask for evidence; the 'truth' cannot be objectively ascertained. He must then rely solely on his judgment and that of the group. . . . And yet in these circumstances he may still be *forced* to take a stand, denied the luxury of withholding judgment. (Krech, *et al.*, 1962, p. 512)

In other words, (i) individuals restrained by pluralistic ignorance could be freed from restraint if they discovered their peers' views, but (especially in the face of apparent consensus), (ii) they seem unable to afford this luxury. The implications of the dilemma are distinctly pessimistic.

POST-SYRACUSE RESEARCH

Our aim in this section is not to catalogue the pluralistic ignorance literature, but to characterize the state of the pluralistic ignorance art. The two enterprises, unfortunately, are hard to separate, because the material that is available is very sparse.[2] For arbitrary convenience, the extant body of research – excluding research about the misperception of groups (such as spouses) to which the perceiver does not belong – can be grouped in terms of its relationship to the Syracuse University survey.

We shall briefly review:

(1) Surveys of public attitudes toward discrimination (the Syracuse subject matter);
(2) Surveys of student opinion (the Syracuse sample);
(3) Portraits of delinquency, including in schools;
(4) Other studies of schools;
(5) Studies of more 'total institutions', including mental hospitals;
(6) Research in prisons.

Pluralistic Ignorance and Ethnic Discrimination

Breed and Ktsanes (1961) report two (small-scale) surveys in which groups of

Southern respondents estimated the prevalence of pro-segregation views. The main finding was that 'many persons guess that others share their views'. What pluralistic ignorance there was was relatively modest, but it was *almost* always in the direction of assessing public opinion as more conservative (i.e. pro-segregation)' (Breed and Ktsanes, 1961, p. 385). The hypothesis generated has to do with the *direction* of presumed opinion, tending to

> favour the older existing beliefs in the system rather than the direction of change. Thus when an individual is influenced by his assessment of others' views, a 'conservative bias may exist'. (Breed and Ktsanes, 1961, p. 383)

The conservative lag hypothesis is supported by O'Gorman (1975), who writes that

> It could well be the case that although fewer whites endorse segregation now, than ten, fifteen, or twenty years ago, their number still may be exaggerated by more liberal whites, whose mistaken beliefs inadvertently and paradoxically strengthen racial values they themselves do not hold: (O'Gorman, 1975, p. 314)

O'Gorman's studies (1975, 1979) dealt with *anti*-segregation samples, and the magnitude of pluralistic ignorance he found is appreciable. However, O'Gorman suggests that pluralistic ignorance probably has little impact on pro-segregationists or even anti-segregationists, but that it can mould the stance of undecideds, 'those whites who preferred neither desegregation nor segregation' (O'Gorman, 1975, p. 328). According to O'Gorman (1979) the data suggest (i) an overall, *reactionary*, direction to pluralistic ignorance; associated with (ii) a tendency for persons of any persuasion to presume that their own views enjoy public support. This tendency works *least* best for liberals, who *more often* feel outgrouped, while conservatives see themselves (frequently wrongly) *supported* (O'Gorman, 1979).

The same conclusions are drawn by Fields and Schuman (1976) based on data from the Detroit Area Study, who emphasize the role of assimilation or projection, which they call 'looking-glass perception'. Like O'Gorman (1979), Fields and Schuman saw assimilation as disproportionately reinforcing the conservative bias of conservatives. They infer that most people, but particularly conservatives – are not conforming – they are unlikely to shape behaviour based on perceived public opinion. This follows because if 'individuals themselves construct this aspect of reality, they are free to pursue their own beliefs, happily persuaded that these beliefs have the support of most others around them' (Fields and Schuman, 1976, p. 445).

This inference rejects conformity as a danger. The waters get muddied even further when pluralistic ignorance returns (after 40 years) to the college scene. Contrary to expectations, students are now found to *exaggerate radical student views and to short-change conservative (traditional) attitudes*. The direction of pluralistic ignorance seemingly shifts.

From Syracuse to Vassar

Korte (1972) finds undergraduates at Vassar College educationally traditionalist, sexually less-than-permissive, uninclined to favour drug use, and unattracted by agnosticism. Over time, this picture remains constant but there is an *increased* tendency for the students to feel themselves surrounded by drug-taking, secular, sexually liberated, anti-establishment peers.

Korte's respondents in two studies were administered the same 34-item questionnaire; they recorded their own position, and estimated the views 'they believed represented the most common or typical feeling' of the students in their group (Korte, 1972, p. 578). In the first (1970) study, 13 items showed statistically significant differences between real group opinions and estimates; of these, 11 items registered over-estimates of radicalism. In the second (1971) study, 20 (out of 34) items yielded significant differences, and 19 of these differences recorded a 'radical bias'. Like O'Gormon (1979) Korte (1972) encountered assimilation, in that two-thirds of his mis-estimates 'were displaced from the norm in the direction of the subject's own position' (p. 581).

In terms of pluralistic ignorance *direction*, Korte (1972) concludes that because 'espousing radical or nontraditional positions on contemporary issues exemplifies a shared value within a liberal college community . . . students over-estimated . . . the extent to which other students in their community would endorse the valued (i.e. radical) position' (p. 582). Korte (1972) traces the increase between 1970 and 1971 to 'the increased prominence of and attention given to the radical position and its advocacy, resulting in an increased impression of the unanimity of support for that position' (p. 586).

The question remains *why* radicalism 'exemplifies a shared value' that earns 'prominence and attention' in public, though not in the hearts of respondents. Why – to take the most dramatic differences Korte (1972) records – would students advertise an assumption they did not make that 'religious beliefs and doctrines are essentially self-deluding and false', or declare themselves hypocritically in 'favour of the use of soft drugs, such as marijuana'? (p. 580). A possibility that links such content is that it highlights *cynical*, rather than conservative or radical, views.

The projection-of-cynicism hypothesis is consistent with Newcomb's (1961) finding that college students tend to exaggerate the standoffishness of fellow-students. Another example of projection-of-cynicism is a 25-year follow-up study of graduates in clinical psychology, in which a majority (59 per cent) rated 'research experience in graduate school' extremely valuable, but only 28 per cent attributed the same view to fellow clinical psychologists (Kelly 1978, p. 753).[3]

Delinquency in the School and Elsewhere

In a study conducted by the Social Action Research Center (1978) 18,385 students who had been randomly selected in 92 schools completed a questionnaire about crime in their school. The questionnaire contained two questions that included estimates of how 'most students' would respond.

One question related to reactions to vandalism. Students were asked how they would feel if 'someone seriously damaged your school'. Many indicated they would feel 'angry' (28.6 per cent) or 'upset' (35.1 per cent). However, the modal response for how 'most students' would feel was that they 'wouldn't care' (36.2 per cent). Adjectives such as 'grateful' and 'amused' were applied 11.7 per cent for self, and 22.4 per cent for 'most students' (Social Action Research Center, 1978, p. 34).

Equally dramatic were responses to the questions 'If someone attacks you or threatens you with a knife at school, what would *you* do about it?' and 'What do you think *most students* in your school would do about it?' The choice of communicating with an adult (teacher, principal, police, parent) was selected 60 per cent for self and 40 per cent for 'most students'; violent options (get a weapon or a 'strong friend') were chosen almost twice as frequently (39 per cent) for 'most students' than for self (20 per cent). Such differences were *by far* most pronounced in crime-ridden inner city schools. In urban high schools, two-thirds of the students said they would contact an adult, but only 30 per cent thought 'most students' would; 25.1 per cent favoured retaliation, but 56.8 per cent thought 'most students' would fight (Social Action Research Center, 1978, pp. 37–38). The presumption arises that 'subculture of violence' peer norms (Wolfgang and Ferracuti, 1967), which we usually assume are prevalent among minority slum youths of the kind who comprise 76 to 100 per cent of this sample,[4] may be illusory.

This presumption is argued by David Matza (1964)[5], who contends that

> Each member of the company infers the subculture from the cues of others . . . the mutual inference is a delinquent subculture . . . Possibly, however, each member believes himself to be an exception in the company of committed delinquents. . . .
> Since the subculture must be constructed from the situation of company, it may be misconstructed. (p. 52).

In other words,

> commitment to delinquency is a misconception – first of delinquents and later of the sociologists who study them. Instead, there is a system of shared misunderstandings, based on miscues, which lead delinquents to believe that all others situated in their company are committed to their misdeeds, (Matza, 1964, p. 59)

Like Schanck (1932), Matza asks why pluralistic ignorance is not reduced through communication, and concludes that pluralistic ignorance subjects are emotionally charged, hence taboo. Issues related to sexuality are particularly amenable to obfuscation. As Brewster Smith notes, 'where there are taboos or strong barriers against free communication, as is likely to occur in sexual matters, states of pluralistic ignorance are especially likely to develop' (Smith, 1969, p. 302). Such is the case with machismo, or anxiety about 'manly' behaviour. Matza writes that 'the question of evaluation of delinquency is not put because it is almost immediately translated into a question of masculinity or membership' (Matza, 1964, p. 54). The problem is only solved (for some) when the advent of adulthood dispels self-doubts about gender-related identity.

The point is that pluralistic ignorance acquires survival-related overtones. One knows oneself to be – or suspects oneself of being – tender-minded, naive, vulnerable, and pro-social. One evolves a 'tough' facade to avoid being ridiculed. The source of ridicule one fears is the 'toughness' (invulnerability, tough-mindedness, cynical and asocial disposition) of peers. Some of one's peers – a clear minority – are *truly* tough; others – like the person himself – are 'facade-tough'. The combined impression (that of a 'tough majority') is the subculture that impresses the individual and the observer.

School Staff and Pluralistic Ignorance

Some observers of schools think that the 'tough' subculture in educational institutions is not confined to pupils. Licata (1981) points out that:

> A major conclusion of those who have studied the structural features of the school organization is that preoccupation with student control permeates the life of the school. The teacher subculture places great pressure on its members to maintain adequate student control. Younger teachers sometimes attempt to win the approval of their more conservative colleagues by talking or acting 'tough' with regard to students. . . . Examples of custodial school structure include norms in the teacher subculture that sustain the maintenance of social distance between teachers and students, organizational routines that promote universal treatment and processing of clients, or the system of rewards and punishments associated with the rules and regulations of the school organization. (p. 29)

Packard and Willower (1972) write that:

> Norms enjoining strictness toward students and the maintenance of social distance typically appear to mark the teacher subculture, and pressures for faculty members to exhibit a united front to guard against organizational problems resulting from pupil control breakdowns seem substantial. (p. 78).

Though the 'teacher subculture' is *not* traced, like that of disruptive students, to 'sexuality and identity problems', the subcultural *impact* that is described sounds reminiscent of Matza's picture of delinquents. Packard and Willower (1972) thus contend that teachers 'may feel obligated to represent their views on pupil control so that they appear to support prevailing norms'. They feel that school staff frequently 'are seen in on stage settings where support for the common defense against pupil recalcitrance and defiance is affirmed' (Packard and Willower, 1972, p. 80).

Are these 'on stage settings' scenarios of shadow boxing? Is there pluralistic ignorance among staff in schools as well as among students? Packard and Willower (1972) hypothesize that there is, that 'teachers will perceive the pupil control ideology of teachers to be more custodial than teachers, themselves, will report'. Teachers would hear fellow-teachers talk tough, and would assume that they were, in fact, tough. This assumption would encourage teachers to keep quiet about their real (non-tough) beliefs, and would reduce the visibility of their non-tough behaviour.

The findings of Packard and Willower's (1972) school survey, using an especially designed instrument (the PCI) confirmed the pluralistic ignorance hypothesis not only for teachers, but also for principals. (Counsellors were non-tough, and perceived themselves as non-tough.)

Institutions in which staff and clients suffer from the sort of pluralistic ignorance that centers on 'toughness' would be custodial settings. The paradigm is that of the 'total institution', a term coined by Erving Goffman (1961).

Pluralistic Ignorance and Total Institutions

Goffman (1961) recognized the existence of pluralistic ignorance in total institutions. He notes that 'typically, the inmate when with fellow inmates will support the counter-mores and conceal from them how tractable he acts when alone with staff'. He adds that:

> In the state mental hospital studied by the writer, even the few elite patients selected for individual therapy, and hence in the best position to espouse the psychiatric approach to self, tended to present their favourable view of psychotherapy only to members of their intimate cliques. (Goffman, 1961, p. 65).

Goffman refers to observations by Richard Cloward, which Cloward described at an HEW-supported conference on delinquency theory (Witmer and Kotinsky, 1955). Cloward was associated with an Army retraining centre, where soldiers were 'expected to express hostility toward the army' (Witmer and Kotinsky, 1955, p. 88). He notes that 'many respondents privately expressed skepticism about the standardized bravado which characterized informal relationships', but that the pattern 'was engaged in by a goodly number of them irrespective of their personal feelings' (p. 88).

The camp in which Cloward worked was rehabilitation-oriented, but rehabilitation-seeking soldiers were caught between staff goals and peer pressures. Cloward, who interviewed inmates, 'found that with rare exception, aspirants respond to this situation of conflict by more or less concealing their interest in restoration' (Witmer and Kotinsky, 1955, p. 90). There was no communication among soldiers about pro-army views, and 'the consequence of this is the fact that each conformist ultimately comes to believe that he is the only one who holds sentiments which support socially acceptable values' (p. 91). This dilemma is that of self-classed deviants where extreme pluralistic ignorance exists.

Research in Prisons

The pluralistic ignorance phenomena that were observed by Goffman and Cloward have been systematically confirmed in prisons. The seminal research centers primarily on prisoners (Wheeler, 1961), but it has been replaced both with inmates (Akers, et al., 1977), and with prison guards (Kauffman, 1981).

Wheeler (1961) relied on critical incidents. He reports that 'in each situation . . . inmate attitudes are perceived to lie at a point farther removed from staff norms than is indicated by the private responses of inmates' (p. 240). Among incidents, the largest difference was found between the real and estimated support for rehabilitation. For an inmate seeking therapy, peer support was virtually unanimous (99 per cent), though 'many inmates were quick to mention that *they* didn't need therapy, but weren't opposed to it for those who did' (p. 236).

Results for staff respondents were parallel to those for prisoners; Wheeler reports that 'the average custodial officer has opinions that are closer to those of inmates than they are perceived to be' (p. 246). In general, 'the most consistent finding revealed in the comparison of private with perceived opinions is the strong tendency toward overperception of conflict on the role expectations of staff and inmates . . . the *degree* of conflict is systematically perceived to be greater than it actually is. The tendency is most pronounced in the perception of inmate standards' (p. 248).

Pluralistic ignorance is a *divisive* force because the stance projects defensiveness (as in the desire for ethnic purity in Syracuse and among assorted poll samples), defiance (as among recalcitrant students and anti-therapeutic inmates), suspiciousness (as among custodial teachers and guards). Conflict is mutually reinforcing in that public behaviour that is conditioned by pluralistic ignorance not only encourages one's own pluralistic ignorance, but also that of one's 'opponents'. For example, students who appease an imaginary student subculture by play-acting delinquency play into the hands of control ideologists among teachers, whose 'crackdowns' spawn resentment.

Conflict-advocates have disproportionate visibility. This point is illustrated by Wheeler, who claims that inmates who live up to peer estimates thrive among council members and disciplinary cases, and in 'major' cell blocs. Wheeler concludes, 'much of the strength of the inmate culture may reside in the ability of anti-staff oriented inmates to attain positions of high visibility within the inmate system, thereby generating and reinforcing the image of a culture in marked conflict with the values of the administration' (Wheeler, 1961, p. 255).

Wheeler thought that pluralistic ignorance might be reduced in prisons that feature 'a closer liaison between inmates and the treatment staff' (p. 258), but Akers *et al*. (1977) report that 'the perception of a hostile inmate culture is found to very much the same extent in all types of prisons, from the most custodial-oriented to the most treatment-oriented institutions (p. 538). The level of staff-inmate conflict (which is highest in custodial prisons) is not predictive of the level of pluralistic ignorance.

Wheeler's observations about *staff* pluralistic ignorance have been confirmed in Connecticut (Kauffman, 1981), with an expanded roster of critical incidents. As in Wheeler's study, staff saw each other as 'more antagonistic to inmates and treatment than the reality of individual officers' attitude warrants' (Kauffman, 1981, p. 287). Though Connecticut guards proved liberal, they estimated themselves to be less liberal than they were. Nine out of ten respondents (91 per cent) approved a peer's 'decision' to affiliate with a treatment unit.[6] The median estimate was 65 per cent, and only 27 per cent of the officers guessed that 'almost all' would approve.

Like Katz and Allport (1931), Kauffman (1981) records a tendency for respondents to assume high degrees of peer consensus. Kauffman's study also surfaces assimilation, though she notes that custodially oriented officers 'were far more likely . . . to think that most of their fellow officers agreed with them than were officers giving inmate sympathetic responses' (Kauffman, 1981, p. 290). Hard-nosed staff could see themselves as 'main line', but 'those with sympathy for inmates and treatment' could not (p. 291).

THE CUMULATIVE PICTURE

How has our view of pluralistic ignorance evolved? Initially (Katz and Allport, 1931; Schanck, 1932; Breed and Ktsanes, 1961; Fields and Schuman, 1976; O'Gorman, 1975, 1979) pluralistic ignorance was a reactionary force, which appeared in reform situations in which a progressive majority assumed that a regressive majority exists. The illusion is fuelled by omission and commission. The omission is that of a silent majority – it is a *progressive* silent majority, which feels enjoined to be silent; the commission (Schanck, 1932) is that of self-appointed conservative spokespersons who pretend to be representative.

The Vassar studies (Korte, 1972) suggested that pluralistic ignorance can also advance the clock prematurely, through influence of visible (and intimidating) custodians of fads. The link between Vassar and Syracuse lies in an imagined student subculture whose norms affect behaviour (Syracuse) or cloak it in privacy (Vassar). Another common feature – which extends to the studies of discrimination in the community – is a theme of assimilation-based chauvinism and ingroup solidarity. A third theme – which stretches the import of Korte's data, but anticipates their link with other data – is one of contempt for beliefs and/or practices that are highlighted in socialization within the mainline culture (contra-cultural cynicism).

The school-crime and delinquency literature (Social Action Research Center, 1978; Matza, 1964) sharpens the hypothesis that pluralistic ignorance can sustain the impression of a cynical, hard-nosed, tough-minded group, immune to softening socialization influences. It suggests that cynicism and toughness can be a façade designed to reduce personal feelings of self-doubt and vulnerability. To live up to the presumed substance behind this facade, individuals are induced to engage in anti-social – or, at least, in antagonistic – behaviour.

The picture of illusory subcultures is interesting enough, but becomes fascinating where two 'subcultures' (staff and clients) intersect (Goffman, 1961). Such settings feature a dialectic of pluralistic ignorance in which one group play-acts 'resistant' clients, and the other 'custodially oriented' staff. The syndrome is highlighted for clients by Goffman (1961), Cloward, (in Witmer and Kotinsky) (1955), Wheeler (1961), Akers *et al.*, (1977), and the Social Action Research Center (1978); for staff, it is described by Packard and Willower (1972), Wheeler (1961), and Kauffman (1981). The combined picture (Wheeler, 1961) is one of pressure towards conflict. Community-oriented (caste-bridging) attitudes may be prevalent but are unrecognized, while defensive (separatist) views are advertised and believed to be prevalent. Each group faces unrepresentative spokesmen of both factions; it remains ignorant of majority sentiment in each. Collaboratively oriented individuals (who may constitute a group majority) are driven into the closet, leaving the minority as custodians of presumed 'subcultures'.

THE NEW YORK CORRECTION OFFICER SURVEY

The picture so far is plausible and coherent. The phenomenon is well-established and it conforms to impressionistic evidence from diverse settings, such as the proverbial locker room (in which mythology revolves around sexual and athletic prowess); pre-adolescent and adolescent hangouts (in which cliques pretend regimental status) and their adult versions, such as terrorist enclaves.

To undertake further research and to contemplate implications for reform we must go beyond confirming pluralisic ignorance and begin to break the phenomenon down into separate (differential) components. In other words, we can begin to take for granted that pluralistic ignorance *exists*, and consider its *sources* and *consequences*. Who are the carriers of pluralistic ignorance? Who in a group is likely to be affected and unaffected by the phenomenon? How do systemic variables (such as setting and group composition) impinge on pluralistic ignorance? Such questions can be pursued in real-life institutions in which pluralistic ignorance creates problems, and the neutralizing of pluralistic ignorance is socially relevant. The study we shall describe set itself this goal for pluralistic ignorance among correction officers.

Our research took place late in 1980, in four prisons in New York State. It was underwritten by the National Institute of Corrections and co-sponsored by the New York Department of Correctional Services and the officers' union (Council 82, AFSCME, AFL-C10). The purpose of the survey was to set the stage for a job enrichment/participatory management programme for correction officers. Data about *patterns* of correction officer pluralistic ignorance were compiled to give the officers insight, through data feedback, into the 'real' and 'assumed' climate of officer opinion.

Survey Content[7]

The survey instrument consisted of 50 items with Likert-type scales, plus 25 opinion estimates. Of the 50 self-ratings, half gauged the level of the officers' job-related alienation and half dealt with the officers' professional orientation – their interest in more-than-custodial involvement. Of the 25 opinion estimate items, most (17 out of 25) dealt with desire for job enrichment.

Alienation questions tapped feelings of powerlessness, meaninglessness, and self-estrangement (Seeman, 1959) and resentments inspired by perceived bureaucratic indifference. Professional orientation covered (i) interest in (or sympathy for) non-custodial work, and (ii) preference for low social distance from inmates; there were also some items that sampled a soft-nosed stance in penological matters.

The instrument evolved through two pre-tests. Items for which there was little variability in responses, or insufficient discrimination between high and low scorers in the summated scales, were rejected. The pre-test data and new proposed items were reviewed by an Officer Advisory Group, which included two union representatives.

Item to scale correlations on 46 of 50 retained variables (23 per scale) ranged from 0.31 to 0.72. Reliability indices proved respectable (Cronbach alpha, 0.92 and 0.85), and the product moment correlation between the scales approached zero in three samples out of four.

The items included in the pluralistic ignorance scale were those in which officers' estimates on the pre-test varied substantially from their responses. In the instructions, officers were asked to 'guess how other officers in your institution will answer each question'. The response choices were

Almost all agree ('over 80 per cent of officers would agree with the statement');
Most agree ('more than half but less than 80 per cent would agree');
Most disagree ('fewer than 80 per cent');
Almost all disagree ('80 per cent or more').

Survey Administration

The survey was administered to officers in four large New York State maximum security institutions, which were selected by a management–union group. The four prisons represent the range (from urban to rural) of the custodial officer spectrum. One institution (Clinton) is the largest complex in the state, and is located in a predominantly rural area near the Canadian border, with few available sources of employment. A contrasting prison is Ossining (Sing Sing), located 'up the river' (thirty miles north) from New York City. Most Ossining officers commute from the metropolitan area, and 85 per cent of them are black or hispanic.

Our other institutions (Auburn and Great Meadow prisons) range between these extremes. Auburn stands in a mid-sized (population 35,000) city of the same name; Great Meadow (Comstock) has a semi-rural location north of Albany, near Glens Falls. Almost all officers at Clinton, Auburn and Comstock are white.

At each institution, the survey was sponsored by local management and union representatives. Plans were announced during lineup; survey forms were then distributed to all available officers, to be returned to training staff or union officials. A total of 1739 survey forms were distributed, and 832 completed questionnaires (47.8 per cent) were returned. (Officers returning the questionnaire were demographicaly representative of their populations.) Most respondents (77 per cent) signed their questionnaires.[8]

Survey Results

The officers appeared to be quite disaffected, though their alienation levels ranged from very high to moderate. Response differences between urban and rural officers were appreciable, with a 40 per cent discrepancy far from unusual. In all samples, an appreciable minority recorded intense opinions in the alienated direction.

Alienation by officer experience level followed a consistent U-shaped distribution, with men of less than 5 years seniority and those with considerable experience (20 years or more) proving less alienated than those with 15 to 19 years of experience.

The professional orientation means for the four institutions reflect a mildly pro-job-enrichment orientation. What differences there are favour the rural prison (Clinton) over the urban prison (Ossining). Age differences suggest mellowing over time. High job enrichment shows a monotonic increase with age, and low job enrichment scores are concentrated in the youngest age group.

PATTERNS OF PLURALISTIC IGNORANCE[9]

We first faced the strictly applied task of sharing survey data with our respondents, who had never heard of 'pluralistic ignorance', but felt curious about their ability (or inability) to guess the opinions of peers. We responded by constructing tables for each item showing the proportion of agreement and the percentage who estimated each category of agreement.

This descriptive material showed that: (i) the number of 'surprise' tables was large, but varied from sample to sample;[10] (ii) the direction of discrepancy *invariably* over-estimated alienation and under-estimated the level of professional (human service) concern; (iii) pluralistic ignorance (majority estimating itself as minority and vice versa) was overshadowed by an *extreme subset* consisting of respondents who estimated *consensus* (almost all would agree) in the direction opposed to the actual majority sentiment. In one sample (Great Meadow) for example, tables included items in which 83 per cent of officers disagreed that 'The CO's only concern is with prison security', but 15 per cent estimated that 'almost all will agree'; 63 per cent disagreed that 'the best way to deal with inmates is to be firm and distant', and 20 per cent thought almost all would agree; 73 per cent disagreed with 'counseling .is a job for counselors, not correctional officers' but 22 per cent assumed total agreement; two-thirds (66 per cent) disagreed that 'any infraction of the rules by an inmate should result in disciplinary action', but one in five (19 per cent) expected affirmative consensus.

During feedback, respondents raised questions such as 'who are the 20 per cent?' and ventured hypotheses such as 'I guess those fellows must be a pretty die-hard bunch'. Psychological questions of this kind, which appeared largely unaddressed in the pluralistic ignorance literature, began to occupy our attention at this point.

Do Respondents Variably Project Their Views in Their Estimates?

To explore what the literature calls 'assimilation', we cross-tabulated estimates of peer opinion against Likert scale responses. We select five 'professionalism' items which most respondents answered in an enlightened direction, with a minority filing a strongly-felt pro-custodial dissent.

The results (Table 1) show that assimilation governs not only the direction of estimates, but that *intensity of personal opinion translates into magnitude of estimated plurality*. The most populated cells are 'I strongly agree and estimate that almost all will agree'; 'I agree and estimate that most will agree'; 'I disagree and estimate that most will disagree'; and 'I strongly disagree and estimate that almost all will disagree'. We additionally find that *by far the most strongly held views are those of the respondents who strongly dissent from the majority view and who assume that their own views are endorsed by a landslide*.

Are Respondents Consistent in Estimating Peer Opinion?

A psychological dissection of pluralistic ignorance becomes possible if one can

Table 1. Estimates by Respondents of Varying Opinion: Five items ($N - 806$)

Proportion who estimate that peers will:		Respondents' own opinion[11] Proportion who:			
		Strongly agree %	Agree %	Disagree %	Strongly disagree %
Almost All Agree					
	Item 1	64.1	29.4	5.0	6.2
	2	20.8	6.0	0.0	0.0
	3	75.0	33.3	7.3	13.3
	4	72.3	25.1	5.6	12.9
	5	69.0	35.2	7.8	6.9
Most Agree					
	Item 1	29.7	62.6	33.5	18.6
	2	43.4	60.8	5.1	4.3
	3	21.0	63.3	41.1	33.3
	4	23.4	69.6	37.2	12.9
	5	24.1	56.6	35.6	20.6
Most Disagree					
	Item 1	4.7	7.0	53.4	36.3
	2	24.5	30.1	72.6	30.4
	3	1.2	3.4	44.8	30.0
	4	0.0	4.7	51.7	40.0
	5	5.2	7.6	49.8	45.0
Almost All Disagree					
	Item 1	1.6	1.1	8.0	38.9
	2	11.3	3.1	22.3	65.2
	3	2.4	0.0	6.8	23.3
	4	4.3	0.5	5.4	37.1
	5	1.7	0.7	6.8	27.5
Total, per item		100	100	100	100
		Chi square for each item, significant beyond 0.001			

Item 1: Rehabilitative programmes should be left to mental health professionals.
Item 2: It's important for a CO to have compassion.
Item 3: Any infraction of the rules by an inmate should result in disciplinary action.
Item 4: If a CO wants to do counselling, he should change jobs.
Item 5: Counselling is a job for counsellors, not correctional officers.
(Actual responses: Agree, Item 1, 31.5%; Item 2, 75.2%; Item 3, 39.8%; Item 4, 29.8%; Item 5, 25%).

isolate groups or individuals who reliably demonstrate (or fail to demonstrate) a propensity for pluralistic ignorance. One question is whether there are consistencies in estimates of opinion to correlated items. This question is addressed in Table 2, which cross-tabulates estimates of responses to three professional orientation items which inter-correlate in the order of $r = 0.22$.

We find consistencies in the categories that are used to estimate peer

Table 2.   Consistencies in Estimations across Three Items, All Combinations $(N-815)$

Proportion who estimated that peers would:		Proportion who estimated that peers would:			
		Almost all agree %	Most agree %	Most disagree %	Almost all disagree %
		Item 1			
Item 2	Almost all agree	51.6	14.8	8.4	26.8
	Most agree	34.7	69.1	51.3	34.1
	Most disagree	12.1	15.1	38.6	28.1
	Almost all disagree	1.6	1.0	1.7	11.0
		100	100	100	100
		Item 1			
Item 3	Almost all agree	46.3	21.6	14.7	12.3
	Most agree	33.3	55.2	43.1	35.8
	Most disagree	14.6	21.0	38.1	33.3
	Almost all disagree	5.7	2.3	4.0	18.5
		100	100	100	100
		Item 2			
Item 3	Almost all agree	42.3	19.0	13.5	26.3
	Most agree	32.7	51.9	23.8	21.1
	Most disagree	17.9	25.9	34.5	26.3
	Almost all disagree	7.1	3.2	26.8	26.3
		100	100	100	100
		p, each table <0.001			

Item 1: The CO's only concern is with prison security (19.5% of respondents agreed).
Item 2: The best way to deal with inmates is to be firm and distant (41.8% agreed).
Item 3: Any infraction of the rules should result in disciplinary action (39.8% agreed).

responses for different items. *This tendency, however, is by far most dramatic in relation to estimates of concurrence with reactionary views held by a minority of respondents.* In fact, extremely erroneous estimates (such as assumptions of unanimity of opinion in relation to views held by a minority) are amazingly consistent, and four or five out of ten respondents who make such an error in relation to one item tend to make a commensurate error in estimating a related response. By contrast, the consistent tendency to estimate *accurately* is modest (28 per cent for Items 1/2; 33.3 per cent for 1/3 and 34.5 per cent for 2/3), though it is far from insignificant.

Evolving an Index of Pluralistic Ignorance

Pluralistic ignorance is systematic inaccuracy of estimates of group opinion by members of a group. One arrives at a measure of pluralistic ignorance by comparing the distribution of responses to a set of items, to a distribution of estimated responses to the same items by the same respondents.

The task is facilitated if one evolves a distribution of difference scores. A difference score can be computed by converting the response to each item (in our case, percentage of agreement) into categories comparable to those used by respondents to estimate responses to the item (magnitude of estimated agreement). For each individual, then, his estimate of the level of response can be subtracted from the actual level of response of his group to obtain a difference score. In our case, the difference score indicates whether the individual over-estimated his peers' alienation or professional orientation, under-estimated it, or estimated it accurately.

Distributions of difference scores for individual items confirm a modal tendency to under-estimate professional orientation and over-estimate alienation. This holds for 15 (out of 17) professionalism items, and 4 (out of 7) alienation items. Among top-ranking errors, 84 per cent over-estimated agreement with 'The CO's only concern is with prison security', and in the alienation roster, 58 per cent over-estimated concurrence with 'Supervisors care more about the inmates than about the COs'.[12]

Difference scores varied with the settings.[13] The 'concern with prison security' item, for example, yielded differences ranging from 50 per cent in one prison to 93 per cent in another; over-estimates of responses to the alienation item ('Supervisors care more about inmates . . .') ranged from 28 per cent in the most alienated setting to 80 per cent in the least alienated one.

Item differences can be summed for each respondent to arrive at a personal index of pluralistic ignorance. (If a respondent accurately predicted responses to every question, his score would be 'zero'.) We plotted the composite difference scores of our combined sample for each variable, and obtained bell-shaped curves. The mean of the professional orientation difference curve was 10.2 in the expected direction with a sigma of 7; the mean of the alienation difference distribution was 2.8, with a standard deviation of 3.4.

Differences in Distributions of Pluralistic Ignorance

Tables 3 and 4 display differences in distributions of pluralistic ignorance. Table 3 shows pluralistic ignorance levels of respondents who hold different views, and confirms that high pluralistic ignorance is clustered among cynical respondents. The table also shows a monotonic increase in accuracy as the desire for professionalism increases.

What holds for individuals does not hold for settings (Table 4). The alienated institution (Ossining) differs from the unalienated prison (Clinton) in that the former has the fewest 'high pluralistic ignorance' respondents, and the latter has the most. The alienated setting has more accurate estimators among its respondents. If we recall that the estimates relate to *one's own peer group* (respondents in the same prison), Table 3 summates the estimates of alienated respondents who are sometimes (in Clinton) in the minority, and sometimes (in

Table 3. Pluralistic Ignorance (about Professional Orientation) by Respondents
          Varying in Professional Orientation

| Difference scale score | Respondent's professional orientation | | | |
	Low %	Mid-low %	Mid-high %	High %
Reverse (over-estimate of professionalism	0.0	0.0	2.0	4.3
Accurate	2.2	13.4	23.2	28.6
Moderate pluralistic ignorance	36.7	59.2	58.6	42.2
High pluralistic ignorance	61.2	27.4	16.3	24.8
	100	100	100	100
	(139)	(201)	(203)	(161)

$P < 0.001$

Ossining) in the majority. Table 4 suggests that where cynical respondents are
in the minority they have scope for pluralistic ignorance, but that a cynic can be
a prophet among alienated peers.

Table 4. Pluralistic Ignorance (about Professional Orientation) or Respondents in
          Four Different Institutions

Difference scale score	Ossining Prison %	Auburn Prison %	Great Meadow Prison %	Clinton Prison %	Total %
Reverse (over-estimate of professionalism)	7.9	0.5	1.3	0.6	1.9
Accurate	30.7	15.3	22.8	11.7	17.9
Moderate pluralistic ignorance	44.1	56.6	47.5	50.0	50.2
High pluralistic ignorance	17.3	27.6	28.5	37.7	30.0
	100	100	100	100	100
	(127)	(196)	(158)	(308)	(789)

$P < 0.001$

Subcategorizing the Pluralistic Ignorance Universe

One of our aims was to construct a typology of respondents who make up the
pluralistic ignorance spectrum, by locating persons who consistently respond
and estimate in a patterned fashion.

We started with responses and estimates to seven professional orientation items for which the modal response category was in the professional (liberal) direction, and was the same across the four samples. A respondent acquired membership in a type by producing the same combination of responses and estimates on four or more of the seven items. In considering the typology, it must be born in mind that in each of the seven items the majority of each sample took a professional (liberal) position. Estimates of professionalism are therefore accurate, and those of non-professionalism inaccurate.

Table 5 shows that 78 per cent of the combined sample was 'typable', in the sense that the respondents responded consistently. One cell contains not a single respondent. This type (which we have labelled 'discouraged subculturists') would have contained any non-professional respondent who (correctly) estimated the majority view as professional. Against a backdrop of pluralistic ignorance, we find that the largest type is the 'supported majority', the professionally oriented persons who accurately estimate the professional orientation of their peers. The next largest cell is that of 'lonely braves' – professionals who (wrongly) see themselves surrounded by non-professionals. Lastly are the non-professionals who (wrongly) feel themselves supported. We call this group 'subculture custodians' because fictitious norms seem largely generated by this group.

Table 5.   Typology of Respondents in Terms of Own Orientation and Presence/
Absence of Pluralistic Ignorance

Number and percentage of respondents who

	See others as:	
	Professional	Not professional
See self as:		
Not professional	None (0%) *(Discouraged subculturalists)*	$N - 130$ 17% of total 21.8% of 'pure' types *(Subculture custodians)*
Professional	$N - 265$ 34.7% of total 44.5% of 'pure' types *(Supported Majority)*	$N - 200$ 26.2% of total 33.6% of 'pure' types *(Lonely braves)*

Missing cases: $N - 69$
Total not typed: 168 (22.1%)

The types are differently distributed among our samples. What we see (Table 6) differs markedly from the 'raw' pluralistic ignorance index (Table 4). The setting with low raw accuracy (Clinton) has a large supported majority but few subculture custodians; and Ossining's apparent accuracy translates into inconsistency (unclassifiability), rather than a large supported majority. Ossining's (low) pluralistic ignorance ditributes unevenly, yielding subculture custodians, but few lonely braves.

Table 6. Distribution of Types in the Four Settings

		Ossining %	Auburn %	Great Meadow %	Clinton %
Proportion of the type in the sample:	Subculture custodians	22.3	16.6	13.7	13.1
	Supported majority members	23.7	27.3	31.5	38.4
	Lonely braves	12.2	30.2	23.8	25.3
	All other	41.7	25.9	31.0	23.1
		100	100	100	100
		(139)	(205)	(168)	(320)

$P < 0.001$

Pluralistic Ignorance Extremists

We began our analysis by pointing out that in many items a large (15 – 20 per cent) group of respondents wrongly estimate a consensus, holding cynical (alienated, non-professional) views. To pinpoint these respondents, we selected seven professionalism items in which over 15 per cent estimated a non-professional consensus. Considering only the estimates, we located respondents who estimated a non-professional consensus in four or more of the seven items. The group totalled 78 respondents, or 9.8 per cent of our combined sample. The distribution of this group across the four samples is depicted in Table 7, which shows a disproportionate prevalence of such individuals in the alienated group (Ossining) and an under-representation in the non-alienated setting (Clinton).

We are not surprised to find (Table 8) that 'subcultural consensus estimaters' (as we call them) are disproportionately alienated. We also find, however (Table 9), that over half the group is low in professional orientation, compared to 16 per cent of remaining respondents. Only one-fourth of consensus estimators (compared to over half of the remaining respondents) show interest in job enrichment.

Our final table (Table 10) relates our typologies. It shows overlap of subculture custodians with consensus estimators. Clearly pluralistic ignorance of subculture custodians is extreme, compared to the pluralistic ignorance of lonely braves. Subculture custodians see themselves as (incorrectly) supported.

Table 7.   Distribution of Extreme Pluralistic Ignorance Syndrome, by Setting, in the
Composite Sample

| | Distribution of: | |
	Subculture consensus Estimators %	All others %
By setting		
Ossining	29.5	14.4
Auburn	14.1	26.0
Great Meadow	26.9	19.2
Clinton	29.5	40.4
	100	100
	(78)	(720)

P <0.0004

Table 8.   Distribution of Extreme Pluralistic Ignorance Syndrome among Respondents
Varying in Alienation

| | Prevalence of: | |
	Subculture consensus estimators %	All others %
At alienation level		
Low	9.9	24.6
Mid-low	21.1	27.4
Mid-high	28.2	27.1
High	40.8	21.0
	100	100
	(71)	(639)

P <0.0005

One out of two such persons sees himself (incorrectly) as *unanimously* cheered
on by an imaginary consensus.

IMPLICATIONS OF THE PATTERNS

Merton has pointed out that 'there are two patterns of pluralistic ignorance –
the unfounded assumption that one's own attitudes and expectations are
unshared and the unfounded assumption that they are uniformly shared'
(Merton, 1957, p. 377). These two 'patterns' describe two of the three stable
frames of reference that are manifest within the pluralistic ignorance universe.

Table 9.   Distribution of Extreme Pluralistic Ignorance Syndrome among Respondents Differing in Professional Orientation

	Prevalence of:	
	Subculture consensus estimators %	All others %
With professional Orientation		
Low	52.1	15.9
Mid-low	23.3	29.0
Mid-high	11.0	31.0
High	13.7	24.1
	100	100
	(73)	(630)

P <0.001

Table 10.   Distribution of Extreme Pluralistic Ignorance Syndrome Among Pluralistic Ignorance Types

	Prevalence of:	
	Subculture consensus estimators %	All others %
Among Types		
Subculture custodians	50.0	9.7
Supported majority	0.0	34.9
Lonely braves	24.4	25.0
All others	25.6	30.4
	100	100
	(78)	(720)

p <0.0001

(The third denotes the *absence* of pluralistic ignorance in a subset of the spectrum. A residual group includes approximations of patterns.)

Merton uses the word 'uniformly' when he describes the second pattern, but not when he discusses the first: in doing this, he implies a hypothesis that our data confirm. We have shown that the assumption of consensus – Allport's impression of universality – is centered among subculture custodians, the group making 'the unfounded assumption that (their beliefs) are uniformly shared'. Partly because of this fact the *magnitude* of pluralistic ignorance is more appreciable for this group than it is for the lonely braves, those who assume that their 'attitudes and expectations are unshared'. Unlike all the other estimators,

the subculture custodians not only avoid regressing towards moderate estimates, but they never (or rarely ever) assume a direction of opinion that is
opposed to their own estimates. These facts imply that (i) the conformity-
inducing potency of pluralistic ignorance is mitigated by the distribution of
extreme conformity-inducing assumptions, which are more prevalent among
conformity inducers than among their targets; (ii) given the totalistic (all-or-
none) form that assimilation takes among subculture custodians, their projection of likemindedness increases the recorded level of pluralistic ignorance,
because other groups who project their views do so more temperately; and (iii)
subculture custodians would be poor prospects for conversion because they
seem to be unresponsive to interpersonal cues and indicators of public opinion.
Our cell for 'discouraged subculturists' is thus empty.

Patterns of pluralistic ignorance vary from one sample to another. The
highest-alienation institution (Ossining) shows the lowest pluralistic ignorance,
but contains the largest proportion of subculture custodians (and of subculture
consensus estimators) in its ranks.

Subculture custodians are alienated persons with over-determined, strong
feelings. The public statements of such individuals are distorted and distorting.
Alienation-carriers perceive cynicism in themselves, and are blind to its
absence elsewhere. The magnitude of pluralistic ignorance among subculture
custodians – their propensity to see consensus-of-cynicism – is 'projection': it
mirrors a need for assumed unanimity around a jaundiced world view. Pluralistic ignorance is not a *source* of their cyncism – subculture custodians do not
feel supported by public opinion, or reassured by it, or content. The alienation
of such persons feeds on itself, and social perceptions subserve the self-
destructive cycle.

Where individuals such as these exist in *large* numbers they are spared the
need to filter and distort. They simultaneoulsy gain credibility because they
accentuate prevalent views – at least, around alienation. The lot of the subculture carrier is not strained where alienation is prevalent; there is a chance of
feeling part of the group. At the same time, the destructive potential – the
self-assured, intimidating presence among self-doubting susceptibles – is
largely missing. For that matter, it is probably also largely missing elsewhere.
This fact can be better understood by contrasting the high-alienation setting
with our lowest-alienation setting.

Pluralistic ignorance is highest among respondents at Clinton, but there is a
large supported majority, many lonely braves, and few subculture consensus
estimators. This means that if there is a subculture, Clinton would be the last
place to find it. This fact surprises, because the setting is noted for its solidarity
and 'hard-nosed', end-of-the-road reputation. It is the sort of prison where the
guard business runs in families and car pools contain siblings and cousins, or
fathers and sons. On the other hand, the prison has an 'Annex' (formerly, a
mental health facility) with a 'therapeutic' (inmate-centered) tradition.

We mention these facts because contexts give shape to pluralistic ignorance. The shape varies, and the symptom (high pluralistic ignorance) tells us little. On the one hand, pluralistic ignorance denotes destructive conformity. It describes high-crime schools and delinquent gangs in which deviants (lonely braves) are terrorized into subservience by toughs (subculture custodians) and opposing factions are reciprocally intimidated.

Pluralistic ignorance can also be conflict-reducing and socially stabilizing – as at Vassar and in Elms Hollow – by creating an assumptive framework that allows extremists to cohabit with a moderate majority. The difference between contrasting paradigms relates to (i) the coercive or non-coercive impact of subculture custodians on lonely braves; (ii) the role of a 'liberated' group not blinded by pluralistic ignorance; (iii) the dialectic (or its absence) of intersecting pluralistic ignorance.

The pre-Allportian view presumed group-based pressures. Consensus creates 'norms' which influence conduct. Pluralistic ignorance modifies the equation because it divorces the originators of norms (influential minority) from those who are influenced by them (intimidated majority). The paradigm is one of manifest cynicism, covert idealism, and limited communication. The group whose majority are lonely braves has its tone set by its lowest denominator (subculture custodians).

To the extent to which the scenario obtains (as in some low cynicism–high pluralistic ignorance settings), we understand the reason why it does. Subculture custodians can disproportionately influence because they are most consistent in their views, care more deeply about their beliefs, feel more certain of support, and are themselves immune to influence.

But we have suggested that scenarios that are much less threatening (and even self-correcting) emerge when we disaggregate actors and refine their plots. For one, a submerged progressive faction that does not feel subjected to influence (the supported majority) emerges where we least expect it. More important, subculture custodians do not arise (like fruit flies) where they can damage most, but appear to be by-products of high-alienation climates where pluralistic ignorance is low and lonely braves are few.

Organizations sometimes generate alienating climates, but can also be their beneficiaries. Ossining is thus not an enclave of burnout, but an employer of unhappy urban workers. Among such workers are some who are more embittered than others (the prototypical young rebellious recruit), but the largest group at Ossining is that of unhappy persons whose perspective is poorly defined. The same complexity arises at Clinton, where the most prevalent 'type' is a non-cynical, non-alienated group which sees itself as non-cynical, *despite* undifferentiated data (pluralistic ignorance marginals) and folklore (a reputation for backwoodsy clannishness).

The point is simply that differential (typological) diagnosis defines change problems that are not only obscured by poll data but are insufficiently illuminated by unrefined indices of pluralistic ignorance. It matters a great deal who believes and estimates what, how such believers and estimators are distributed, whence they arise and how they interact. Our data are primitively illustrative, but they have propaedeutic research implications that go beyond variations on Allport. The change implications are less obvious. They probably have to do with (i) increasing the potential of change; (ii) defining the targeting of change; and (iii) suggesting a responsive technology short of therapy for subculture custodians.

IMPLICATIONS FOR PLANNED CHANGE

Pluralistic ignorance was born with two strikes against its acceptability as a social phenomenon to be lived with: (i) pluralistic ignorance was tantamount to conforming to destructive norms; which were (ii) based on mistaken and erroneous assumptions. The remediating strategy – disseminating knowledge about 'real' majority opinion – faced a third problem: (iii) the victims of pluralistic ignorance were uncooperative (reluctant) consumers of data.

The early perspective was not only compatible with Allport's concern about the insidious potency of conformity-inducing institutions (Allport, 1933), but it made unambiguous sense of the research-supported portraits of discrimination in Syracuse and of fundamentalist religiosity in Elms Hollow. In such views of pluralistic ignorance, conformity was largely passive. Motivation entered as assimilation, which modulates pluralistic ignorance. The exception was the suggestion (Schanck, 1932) that unrepresentative self-appointed (specially motivated) spokespersons can play a disproportionate role in influencing others.

Motivation comes to the forefront in Matza's theory (Matza, 1964), which illuminates a diverse body of pluralistic ignorance research by highlighting the function that is served by cynical facades in reducing self-doubt and buttressing self-images of 'toughness'. The reform implications of this view are (if anything) more pessimistic than those of earlier perspectives. Motivated conformity is self-cycling and it is incestuous; the norm is induced by its targets, and has obvious survival value. To be enlightened is uninviting because it means that one must face one's vulnerability.

A more recent development – which is particularly salient in the studies we reviewed of client–staff settings – is the pluralistic ignorance contra-culture view, which stresses the reinforcing role of ignorance-based conflict. This body of impressive research (beginning with Wheeler, 1961) explodes the myth of ordained staff–client warfare in institutional settings. The view it substitutes – which highlights make-belief subcultures in lieu of real ones – is, however, no less promising of change, in that reform targets (whether clients or staff) suffer from double ignorance. They suffer from (i) pluralistic ignorance relating to contra-cultural norms of their own group, and (ii) the impression of hostile norms generated by pluralistic ignorance of the opposing faction.

Our own research is not destructive of these perspectives. What it does is to soften them so as to suggest possibilities for planned change. Specifically, (i) we describe several pluralistic ignorance syndromes with different change implications, and (ii) we isolate contrasting target-of-change subgroups within the pluralistic ignorance spectrum.

We agree with Matza that pluralistic ignorance *in individuals* is strongly motivated (sometimes extremely so), but may be self-correcting. Where a young 'tough' or a cynical recruit manages to survive – where an offender remains out of jail, a truant remains in school, and an alienated worker refrains from resigning – personal mellowing often occurs. Alienation and self-doubts may dissipate, facades may be abandoned, and the person may leave the ranks of subculturists. This, however, solves only the *individual's* problem, not that of the group; new subculturists take the place of those who mature out; ex-subculturists (for consistency's sake) may continue to play their game.

Cycle-breaking interventions are called for, not to 'correct' ignorance (which has limited or short-term impact), but to generate pressures opposing those that reinforce pluralistic ignorance. In undertaking this task, contemporary planned change literature (Bennis, *et al.*, 1969) may prove helpful, and the work of Lewin (1947) offers especially pointed guidelines. The Lewinian perspective calls attention to the primacy of group norms, and offers techniques for changing group norms that affect personal attitudes. The strategy invites us to mobilize social forces *of the same kind that shape pluralistic ignorance* to neutralize its impact. The premise is that group process must counteract group process. Among the obvious action implications are the following:

(1) The prime change targets must be lonely braves, whose self-interest lies in escaping group norms, so that they can engage in principled (pro-social) behaviour that is congruent with their goals.

(2) Survey feedback is useful, but has limited impact, because it is 'rational' and non-experiential. Feedback must be embedded in, and must be buttressed with, group experiences.

(3) The groups of lonely braves that are to be changed must contain other lonely braves, as well as 'liberated' peers who can serve as group primers; (in other words, the supported majority become primary change agents).

(4) The content of the group sessions must center on *dynamics* of pluralistic ignorance. Group members must (a) review the sources of their erroneous impressions of public opinion, and they must (b) isolate the effects of pluralistic ignorance on their own behaviour.

(5) 'Positive' success stories can neutralize pessimism and combat an

inviting sense of impotence; they can illustrate the permeability of subcultural pressures.

(6) Group members must commit themselves to take 'liberated' actions
(either as individuals or as groups).

(7) Anticipated reactions of subculture custodians must be accommodated
as 'resistances' in force field analyses of proposed courses of action. Such
resistances must be placed in perspective as strongly motivated, unrepresentative pressures.

Subculturalists (subculture custodians) become *secondary* targets of change:
the strategy for changing them must rely on mixed groups of sub-culturalists
and ex-lonely braves, or of would-be-subculturalists and accurate estimators.
Young candidates for subcultural custodianship (such as recruits) can be
tackled before their cynicism solidifies. In such efforts, 'liberated' senior
citizens of the peer group may be change-agents-of-choice. Peer veterans have
credibility and charisma. They are also the *assumed* subculture custodians, and
their disavowal of views that are ascribed to them can expedite unfreezing.

Further preventive work requires organizational support of individuals,
such as recruits, who are vulnerable and are susceptible to self-doubt. The
young and the new must be furnished with opportunities to cement their
self-esteem through pro-social, personally effective, enriching behaviour.
Failure to offer such opportunities invites facade-building and constricts the
range of accepted behaviour to anti-social, chauvinistic, cynical, 'toughness-
advertising' conduct. This contingency is self-defeating and it is unsatisfying; it
is also dysfunctional and socially disruptive.

ACKNOWLEDGEMENTS

We are indebted to the National Institute of Corrections of the United States
Bureau of Prisons for supporting much of the work on which this chapter is
based. The opinions we express, however, are ours, and should not be taken to
reflect the views of the federal prison service.

NOTES

1. The word 'projection' reflects a contemporary usage. Allport employed the word
   'project' as a synonym of 'ascribe'. He did not anticipate more psychoanalytic
   implications, including the assumption that people attribute unto others what they
   ignore in themselves.
2. We say 'sparse' after having unsuccessfully reviewed social psychology textbooks,
   psychological abstracts, and computerized information printouts for references to
   pluralistic ignorance or pluralistic ignorance research.
3. A parallel picture is presented by Weiss (1980), who studied the extent to which
   government officials make use of research findings. Most of the policy-makers who

were surveyed by Weiss reported extensively relying on research themselves, but they all felt that other policy-makers did not use research, or read it.

4. The concept 'subculture of violence' refers to shared assumptions or values which imply that violence may be used (or should be used) in a variety of situations.
5. Though Matza's discussion is the most sophisticated available, Matza uses the phrase 'pluralistic ignorance' only in passing, and does not refer to pluralistic ignorance literature.
6. The response to this item does not imply endorsement of therapy: instead, it approves the officer's right to select his assignment. In a second Kauffman (1981) item, eight out of ten officers endorsed a peer's decision to seek placement in a guard tower.
7. The methodology and survey results are described in detail in another publication (Toch and Klofas, 1982).
8. Officers were not required to identify themselves, but they were requested to sign their questionnaires if they felt free to do so.
9. Some of the material in this section has been dealt with in a criminal-justice-related context (Klofas and Toch, 1982), where we examine the implications of the data for the existence of a corrections officer subculture. Tabular material is here reproduced from our earlier publication courtesy of the National Council on Crime and Delinquency.
10. Differences between agreement and estimates of agreement on the 25 estimate items were significant beyond the 0.05 level on 17 items in the Ossining sample and on all items for the Auburn, Great Meadow, and Clinton samples. Only the most dramatic of these differences were shared with the respondents as 'surprise' tables.
11. Data for each sample were analysed separately and later pooled. Each sample was within ten percentage points of the aggregated totals for each item.
12. The magnitude of these differences could be due to randomly distributed error being subtracted from an extreme score. However, item analysis in the construction of the instrument diminished the possibility of extreme scores, and in fact only three of the items achieved over 70 per cent agreement or disagreement in any of the sample.
13. Variation in difference scores is attributable to differences in estimates and in the actual level of agreement at each institution. The scores are used here only to examine the accuracy of perceptions of peers.

REFERENCES

Akers, R.H., Hayner, N.S., and Gruninger, W. (1977). Prisonization in five countries: type of prison and inmate characteristics, *Criminology*, **14**, 527–554.
Allport, F.H. (1924). *Social Psychology*, Boston: Houghton Mifflin.
Allport, F.H. (1933). *Institutional Behaviour*, Chapel Hill: University of North Carolina Press.
Bennis, W.G., Benne, K.D., and Chin, R. (eds) (1969). *The Planning of Change* (2nd ed.), New York: Holt, Rinehart and Winston.
Breed, W. and Ktsanes, T. (1961). Pluralistic ignorance in the process of opinion formation, *Publ. Opin. Quart.*, **25**, 382–392.
Brown, R. (1965). *Social Psychology*, New York: Free Press.
Cantril, H. (1958). *The Politics of Despair*, New York: Basic Books.
Fields, J.M. and Schuman, H. (1976). Public beliefs about the beliefs of the public, *Publ. Opin. Quart.*, **40**, 428–447.

Goffman, E. (1961). *Asylums: Essays on the Social Situation of Mental Patients and other Inmates*, Garden City, LI: Doubleday (Anchor).

Hinds, W.C. (1962). Individual and group decisions in gambling situations. Unpublished Master's Thesis, School of Industrial Management, MIT.

Katz, D. and Allport, F.H. (1931). *Student Attitudes: a Report of the Syracuse University Research Study*, Syracuse: Craftsman Press.

Katz, D. and Schanck, R.L. (1938). *Social Psychology*, New York: Wiley.

Kauffman, Kelsey (1981). Prison officer attitudes and perceptions of attitudes, *J. Res. Crime Delinquency*, **18**, 272–294.

Kelley, H.H. and Thibaut, J.W. (1969). Group problem solving, in Lindzey, G. and Aronson, E. (eds), *The Handbook of Social Psychology*, Vol. 4, (2nd ed.), Reading, Mass.: Addison-Wesley, 1–101.

Kelly, E.L. (1978). Twenty-five years later: a follow-up study of graduate students in clinical psychology assessed in the VA selection research project, *Amer. Psychologist*, **33**, 753–755.

Klofas, J. and Toch, H. (1982). The guard subculture myth, *J. Res. Crime & Delinquency*, **19**, 238–254.

Korte, C. (1972). Pluralistic ignorance about student radicalism, *Sociometry*, **35**, 576–587.

Krech, D., Crutchfield, R.S., and Ballachey, E.L. (1962). *Individual in Society: a Textbook in Social Psychology*, New York: McGraw-Hill.

Lewin, K. (1947). Group decision and social change, in Newcomb, T.M., Hartley, E.L. and editorial committee for SPSSI (eds), *Readings in Social Psychology*, New York: Henry Holt, pp. 330–344.

Licata, J.W. (1981). Student brinkmanship and school structure, *Amer. Educator*, **5**, 26–29.

Matza, D. (1964), *Delinquency and Drift*, New York: Wiley.

Merton, R.K. (1957). *Social Theory and Social Structure* (rev. ed.), Glencoe, Ill.: Free Press.

Newcomb, T.M. (1961), *The Acquaintance Process*, New York: Holt, Rinehart & Winston.

O'Gorman, H.J. (1975). Pluralistic ignorance and white estimates of white support for racial segregation, *Publ. Opin. Quart.*, **39**, 313–330.

O'Gorman, H.J. (1979). White and black perceptions of racial values, *Publ. Opin. Quart.*, **43**, 48–59.

Packard, J.S. and Willower, D.J. (1972). Pluralistic ignorance and pupil control ideology, *J. Educ. Admin.*, **10**, 78–87.

Schanck, R.L. (1932). A study of a community and its groups and institutions conceived of as behaviour of individuals, *Psychol. Monographs*, **43**, Whole No. 195.

Seeman, M. (1959). On the meaning of alienation, *Amer. Sociol. Rev.*, **24**, 783–791.

Smith, M.B. (1969). *Social Psychology and Human Values: Selected Essays*, Chicago: Aldine.

Social Action Research Center (1978). *Students Say it as They See it: a Report on the School Climate Survey*, San Rafael, Calif.: Social Action Research Center.

Toch, H. and Klofas, J. (1982). Alienation and desire for job enrichment among correction officers, *Federal Probation*, **46**, 35–44.

Weiss, D.H. (with Bucuvalas, M.J.) (1980). *Social Sciences Research and Decision-Making*, New York: Columbia University Press.

Wheeler, S. (1961). Role conflict in correctional communities, in Cressey, D.R. (ed.), *The Prison: Studies in Institutional Organization and Change*, New York: Holt, Rinehart & Winston.

Witmer, Helen L. and Kotinsky, Ruth (eds) (1955). *New Perspectives for Research on Juvenile Delinquency*, Washington: US Department of Health, Education and Welfare, Children's Bureau.

Wolfgang, M.E. and Ferracuti, F. (1967). *The Subculture of Violence: towards an Integrated Theory in Crimonolgy*, London: Tavistock.

SECTION B

Group Decision-making

Progress in Applied Social Psychology, Volume 2
Edited by G.M. Stephenson and J.H. Davis
© 1984 John Wiley & Sons Ltd

6

The Role of Judgment in Small-group Conflict and Decision-making

B. BREHMER

University of Uppsala, Sweden

Those who want to understand and explain a decision made by an individual or a group face what seems to be an unsolvable problem: that the important determinants of the decision cannot be observed. We recognize two such determinants: the decision-maker's motive or goal, and his understanding of the decision problem. Neither of these can be observed. What can be observed is the relation between some description of the decision problem and the actual decision or the consequences of the decision. Thus, we face an impossible problem: we have *two* unknowns, but only *one* equation. The problem can be solved only if we eliminate one of the unknowns. The only way of doing this is by making some assumption about the decision-maker's goal or about his understanding of the decision problem.

The customary assumption, made by scientists and non-scientists alike, is that of rationality. That is, one assumes that the decision-maker has perfect understanding of the decision problem. Consequently, he is able to select that course of action which leads to his goal. His decision, therefore, mirrors his motives perfectly, and the actual consequences of the decision are the consequences that the decision-maker intended. This solves the problem of explanation, because we are now able to ignore one of the unknowns, and we can concentrate on the other unknown, that is the decision-maker's motives. Explanation now becomes a matter of inferring these motives. Once the motives have been inferred, the decision-maker's behaviour is fully explained.

We recognize this paradigm as the general paradigm of lay psychology, as well as the paradigm of most sciences. In political science, for example, the paradigm is called the 'rational actor paradigm' and guides important research on international and national politics (e.g. Allison, 1971). In psychology, the paradigm is a well-known explanatory device in clinical psychology. Psycho-analysis despite its reputation of being a science of the irrational is also founded on the rational actor paradigm. Thus, psychoanalysts assume that although a person's behaviour may look irrational, it is nevertheless an expression of rational cognitive processes; the problem is that these rational processes are employed to pursue irrational motives. However, using the assumption of rationality, the psychoanalyst is nevertheless able to infer what these motives are, despite the fact that the person being so explained may strenuously object to explanation.

As pointed out by Allison (1971), the rational actor paradigm provides us with efficient means to handle problems in the area of international politics. It always leads us to expect the worst, and as a consequence, we are not likely to be taken by surprise. It may be conjectured that the paradigm serves similar objectives in the everyday lives of people. It does so, however, only at the cost of fostering distrust, and it makes lack of trust a primary motive when dealing with our fellowmen. It does, of course, not take too much effort to find self-serving motives that explain the behaviour of others, so the rationality assumption is not easily refuted.

Even though the rational actor paradigm is so common that it may seem almost self-evident, it cannot, however, account for any but the simplest decisions. First, it seems unlikely that people have the perfect understanding of what will lead to what in a decision problem assumed in the rational actor paradigm. For example, decisions are often based on projections of what the future may be and many unforeseen things may intervene between the decision and that future state. This introduces an element of uncertainty in the relation between the decision and the consequences. For example, the increase in the price of oil since 1973 obviously came as a surprise to many decision-makers and made it impossible to achieve many of the things expected when the decisions were made. Therefore, the decision-maker's motives cannot be infer-red from the consequences of his decisions.

Second, decisions often require the decision-maker to rely on new and perhaps unique configurations of information. Consequently, the decision-maker cannot rely on any particular past experience, and if he turns to science, he will often find that theories there are not powerful enough to deal with the complexity of the problems facing him; recall, for example, the problems now facing Keynesian (and other) economists trying to deal with stagflation.

Third, decision problems often require the decision-maker to integrate a considerable amount of information. Given that he has but a limited capacity for processing information, he may not always be able to find the decision that would lead to exactly those consequences which he sought to achieve. Conse-quently, his decisions would not reflect his motives with any great fidelity.

Thus there are good reasons for doubting that a decision-maker's motives can be inferred from his decisions. Therefore the usefulness of the rational actor paradigm for explaining the behaviour of real people in real decision problems is in doubt also and we would do well to look for an alternative.

To develop such an alternative we take as our point of departure the consequences of the purely epistemological problems mentioned above, which are to force the decision-maker to rely on something other than facts and a full understanding of the decision problem for his decisions. Instead of facts, he will have to rely on what Hammond (1974) has so aptly called 'the cognitive process of last resort': human judgment. Consequently, the basic premise of the rational actor paradigm, that the decision-maker has perfect understanding of the decision problem, cannot be upheld for any but the simplest and most trivial of decision problems. Therefore this paradigm is not likely to serve us well in solving the problems in the real world either. This conclusion is certainly not contradicted by any great number of success stories from social scientists helping to solve important decision problems.

The purpose of the present chapter, therefore, is to argue for an alternative to the rational actor paradigm for anlaysing decision-making. Provisionally, we will call this alternative paradigm the judgment paradigm to underline its most important feature: that it sees decisions as based on judgment rather than on fact, and that it considers the analysis of these judgments to be the key to understanding decisions. This entails giving up the basic tenet of the rational actor paradigm: that decisions are based on a complete understanding of the decision problem (which amounts to the same thing as assuming that judgments are based on fact).

Analysis of decisions using the judgment paradigm requires that the decision-maker's motives are presumed to be known. Such an assumption is no more problematic than the basic assumption in the rational actor paradigm. It is only by the fruitfulness of the analyses that follow from it, that the value of an assumption can be assessed.

The move away from the rational paradigm is currently gaining popularity in psychology, mainly as a result of the work of Tversky and Kahneman (e.g. 1974) on probabilistic reasoning, which has shown that judgments based on probabilistic information often do not follow the rules of probability theory. Another important source has been Simon's (e.g. 1953) work on 'bounded rationality', that is the hypothesis that people often do not strive to do what is best because this requires too much effort. Instead, they just try to get what is good enough, that is, in the words of Simon (1953) people are 'satisficers' rather than 'optimizers'. Dawes (1976) summed up these developments when he called for a 'shallow psychology' of cognitive processes instead of a depth psychology of motives to explain behaviour.

The present chapter, however, does not have these traditions as its point of departure. Instead, it is grounded in an earlier tradition, that of Social Judgment Theory, SJT (Hammond, et al., 1975). SJT stems from Brunswik's probabilistic functionalism (e.g. Brunswik, 1952), which has been adapted to the task of analysing human judgment and decision-making by Hammond and his collaborators.

SJT AND THE ANALYSIS OF JUDGMENT

SJT defines human judgment as the process of using information from probabilistic cues to arrive at an inference which can serve as a basis for a decision. An example is the cognitive activity of a physician making a diagnosis on the basis of a set of symptoms to guide his selection of a treatment, or a stockbroker inferring what the future value of some stocks may be to provide a basis for deciding whether or not to buy.

In problems requiring judgment, there is no fail-safe algorithm for computing the answer (not much of a restriction when it comes to real decision problems). Judgment, therefore, becomes a matter of relying on two sources of information: whatever rules may be available from textbooks and the like, and one's experience with cases of a similar kind. This amalgam of analytical knowledge of rules and specific case-by-case experience defines the process of judgment in SJT. The details of this process are not known, but there seems to be general agreement about at least one aspect of the process: that it is covert, that is to say, although a person may be able to make judgments, he may nevertheless not be able to report on how he actually arrived at these judgments (see e.g. Slovic and Lichtenstein, 1971 for a review of the evidence).

The covert nature of the process is the source of three kinds of problems:

(1) It is impossible to ascertain whether or not a person has taken a certain factor into account or not. Consequently, it is impossible to assess whether or not a person's judgment is biased.

(2) It is difficult to teach judgment. Even though an expert diagnostician may be able to make successful diagnoses, he often cannot teach his students to make these diagnoses, leaving the students to learn from their own experience, which in no way guarantees that the students will become experts (see Brehmer, 1980).

(3) Conflicts are hard to resolve. Suppose that two persons, A and B, have arrived at different decisions and start questioning each other. A then finds that B's explanations of his decisions cannot account for these decisions. What could A then possibly conclude? Following the rational actor paradigm, he must assume that if B does not give a satisfactory explanation, this is because there is something B does not want him to know. And what B does not want him to know is probably something that is going to hurt him. Consequently, A can only conclude that B is up to no good, and that he cannot be trusted. Thus, something that started as a simple disagreement develops into a full-scale conflict which becomes impossible to solve because it is perceived incorrectly.

These three problems could presumably be solved if the judgment process could somehow be made overt.

At first, this may seem like an unsolvable problem. However, the problem is no worse than that facing most other sciences: many of the phenomena of interest to, for example, physics, are covert and cannot be observed directly. There is a solution to the problem. It takes as its point of departure that if one knows a person's judgments and the information upon which they are based, it is possible to develop a mathematical model which relates the judgments to the information. If one is successful in this enterprise, the model, when given the same information as a person, will produce the same judgments as the person. The model may then be said to simulate the person's judgment process. But because it is a simulation, it has a great advantage; it is overt, rather than covert. Consequently, it is possible to inspect the model and find out how it works. By doing so, one can learn about the covert system being modelled.

The problem, then, is to select a mathematical model. For reasons that we shall not go into here (but see Brehmer, 1976b, 1979), Social Judgment Theorists have chosen linear statistical models for the purpose of modelling human judgment.

A linear model describes a judgment, J, as a weighted sum of the cues, x_i, upon which it is founded.

$$J = b_0 + b_1x_1 + b_2x_2 + \ldots b_nx_n \tag{1}$$

when $b_1 \ldots b_n$ are weights determined by fitting the model to the judgments and b_0 is the intercept.

Such a model gives information about four aspects of the judgment process:

(1) What cues are used. This is shown by what cues receive significant weights in the analysis.
(2) The relative weights given to different cues.
(3) The functional relation between each cue and the judgments. This relation may be linear, that is, the higher the value of the cue, the higher the judgment, or it may be non-linear, for example, quadratic, so that there is an optimum value, leading to a high judgment with values above and below this optimum leading to lower values.
(4) The organizing principle, that is, the rule used for combining the information from the different cues. This rule may be additive and compensatory, or configural, such that the weight given to one cue depends on the value of another cue. Given the form of Equation (1), it may not seem possible to assess configural rules. However, Equation (1) can easily be expanded to include higher order terms, for example cross-product terms. If these terms receive a significant weight in the analysis, deviations from additivity are indicated.

These four aspects of the process as described by a linear model are easy to understand, and it is clear that an analysis by this kind of model answers exactly the kind of questions anyone would want to ask:

(1) What factors did the judge use?
(2) What was the relative importance of these factors?
(3) How were the factors used?
(4) How did the person put the different factors together?

There may be some doubt about exactly which of the measures available should be used (see Brehmer and Qvarnstöm, 1976, for a study of what people understand by the concept of weight), but it is clear that the linear model will provide answers to the kinds of questions anyone would want to ask about the judgment process. However, these kinds of analysis also give information about an aspect which people may not think of asking about: the *consistency* of the process.

Basically, the term consistency refers to the degree to which a person makes his judgments in the same manner from case to case. If the person is inconsistent, this means that she/he will not make the same judgment when the same case is presented over again. Thus the rules used for making judgments will differ from case to case. The degree of consistency is usually measured by inserting replicates among the cases presented for judgment. The degree of consistency is then given in the manner of a test–retest reliability coefficient by the correlation between the judgments for the replicates. Alternatively, if there is evidence that a linear model adequately describes the process, the degree of non-consistency is simply given by the proportion of variance that cannot be accounted for by the model (see Brehmer, 1978). The actual estimation of the parameters of the judgment process by means of multiple regression offers a number of problems not mentioned here, and anyone who wants to use these techniques should start by consulting a good textbook on the subject.

OVERVIEW OF RESULTS FROM STUDIES OF JUDGMENT

Linear models have been used to analyse judgment processes in a variety of experts, including stockbrokers (Slovic, 1969) clinical psychologists (Goldberg, 1970; Hammond, 1955; Hoffman, 1960), radiologists (Hoffman, *et al.*, 1968), and physicists (Hammond and Marvin, 1981); see Goldberg (1968), or Slovic and Lichtenstein (1971), for reviews.

The results are easily described because the results of all of the analyses so far are quite similar. They can be summarized under four headings.

The Judgment Process is Simple

First, it is simple in the sense that judges seem to rely on very little information. Thus, a judge may ask for a lot of information, say ten or more cues, but s/he is usually found to use no more than three or four cues. Second, the process is simple in that it usually follows a simple linear model. If deviations from an additivity are found, they are usually small and have little systematic importance (e.g. Hoffman *et al.*, 1968; Wiggins and Hoffman, 1968). However, the fact that a linear model fits the judgments must not be interpreted to mean that the judge simply adds up the information from the various cues. An additive model is only a paramorphic representation of the process (Hoffman, 1960). Thus it may be consistent with different kinds of psychological process. One likely candidate is a general compensatory process where different cues are traded-off against one another (see Einhorn, *et al.*, 1979, for a discussion of this problem). This trade-off may, of course, not be perceived by the judge as a particularly simple process, despite the fact that the mathematical description of the result is simple.

The Process is Inconsistent

A typical finding in these analyses is that the judges are inconsistent. Thus, judgment processes are not perfectly regular, and there is a measure of unpredictability, or randomness, in these processes. The nature of this inconsistency is not known. Inconsistency is, however, not a constant, but varies with the characteristics of the judgment task. At least two characteristics are known to affect consistency: task complexity and task uncertainty. As for task complexity, the results show that consistency is lower when the task has many cues, rather than few cues, and lower when the task requires the subjects to use non-linear rules, rather than linear rules (Brehmer *et al.*, 1980). This has been interpreted to mean that judgment, at least in part, may be seen as a matter of *skill*. This means that even though a person intends to use a certain rule, his judgments may not necessarily follow that rule, just as wanting to make a certain stroke in tennis does not automatically produce that particular stroke. However, in the case of tennis, it is immediately apparent that the results are not what one intended. In the case of judgment, this is not always true because there may be no immediate feedback informing the judge about his success. Furthermore, it is not possible, for a judgment task of even very moderate complexity, to ascertain what rules were actually followed. Therefore it is usually not possible for a person to detect that his judgment does not follow the rule s/he intended it to follow. This is illustrated in the study by Brehmer, *et al.*, (1980).

In this study, subjects were asked to use specified configural rules for making judgments. Despite the fact that they tried to use these rules and believed that they had used them, their judgments nevertheless tended to follow a simple additive model without any configural components. That is, the subjects' judgments did not follow the rule that the subjects intended to use, but they were not aware of this.

Task predictability is a measure of the extent to which the criterion can be predicted from the cues, for example, the degree of certainty with which a disease can be diagnosed from the symptoms. A common measure is the multiple correlation between the cues and the criterion.

According to statistical decision theory, which is the appropriate normative theory for these kinds of tasks, task predictability should not affect the utilization of the cues; regardless of the predictability of the task, the cues should be used maximally, that is to say, such that the multiple correlation between the cues and the criterion is unity. Human judges do not follow this recommendation, however. First, they are inconsistent: that is, the multiple correlation between cues and judgments is not unity. Moreover the consistency varies with the predictability of the task, such that as predictability decreases, so does consistency (Brehmer, 1976a). This result has been obtained in a wide variety of circumstances, both in laboratory studies of learning (e.g. Brehmer, 1978) and conflict (Brehmer, 1973) and in studies of clinical judgment (Brehmer, 1976a). The explanation for these results is not clear. Two hypotheses about possible explanations have been investigated.

The first of these hypotheses is that people simply do not know that they have to use statistical rules, rather than deterministic rules, when faced with probabilistic cues, or that they do not recognize a probabilistic task when they see one. This hypothesis has been tested in a series of studies (Brehmer and Kuylenstierna, 1978, 1980; Johansson and Brehmer, 1979; Kuylenstierna and Brehmer, 1981) in which subjects have been given various kinds of information about the nature of the task, thus relieving them of the requirement to ascertain that the task is, in fact, probabilistic, and of deciding whether they should use a statistical rule or not. This has not affected their behaviour. When information about the nature of the rule to be used has been given, this has led to some improvement in performance. However, even with this information, subjects remain inconsistent, and the relation between inconsistency and task predictability does not change. This suggests that lack of knowledge about the appropriate rule is at best part of the explanation for the effects of task predictability on the subjects' behaviour in judgment. This leads to the second hypothesis, which is that subjects lack the cognitive capacity required to perform optimally in these kinds of tasks. Specifically, to find the optimal statistical rules, it is necessary not only to have the correct kind of rule, it is also necessary to use rather large amounts of data; to focus on single hits and misses can only lead the person astray.

To test this hypothesis, the effects of various means of decreasing the cognitive strain imposed by these tasks have been investigated. Hagafors and Brehmer (1980a, b) studied the effects of how information was presented, and Kuylenstierna and Brehmer (1981) the effects of memory aids. Again, some effects were found, but the subjects still behaved in a fundamentally non-optimal way. Thus lack of optimality cannot be explained in terms of cognitive strain.

A possible explanation for these results, and one that would tie them to other results on how people handle uncertain information, is what Tversky and Kahneman (1971) have called 'Belief in the law of small numbers'; that is the belief that the characteristics of the task can be inferred from small samples. This may be interpreted to mean that people have adapted their rules of inference to their limited capacity for processing information; if one has limited processing capacity it does one no good to use rules which require large amounts of information such as the full-fledged statistical rules.

Because the judges rely on small samples, their rules change and they become inconsistent, and more so the greater the inconsistency of the task. This hypothesis thus explains the results on inconsistency, as well as those from a variety of other statistical tasks of the kind used by Tversky and Kahneman.

There is Considerable Disagreement

This is true also when the subjects are experts who are making the kinds of judgments they usually make, and have been making for years and years. That there will be disagreement follows from the fact that people are inconsistent. If two persons are inconsistent, their judgments cannot be perfectly correlated, even if they use the same rules for making their judgments. However, lack of consistency is not the only explanation for the disagreement among experts. There are also systematic differences, and experts such as physicians are found not only to rely on different symptoms, but also to give different weights to the same symptoms and, occasionally, to use different rules for combining the information from different symptoms (e.g. Hoffman et al., 1968).

This means, in fact, that people who work at the same task, for example diagnosing a set of diseases, may learn very different things from what they have to learn from experience in probabilistic tasks. This is not surprising. In such a task (as in any inference task) the hypotheses that the persons bring to the task are as important as the information, but the hypotheses cannot, of course, be derived from the information. Therefore there is no guarantee that people will learn the correct rules from a given task, or even that they will learn the same rules (see Brehmer, 1980 for a discussion of this issue). For the physicians studied by Hoffman et al., it was indeed shown that no physician used the most useful of the available symptoms:

Subjects lack Insight into Their Own Rules

In many cases, investigators have collected not only judgments from their subjects but also subjective descriptions of how they have been making these judgments. From these descriptions, it has then been possible to construct models of the judgment process, and these models have then been compared to the models fitted to the actual judgments. The extent to which these models agree gives a measure of the degree of insight people have into their own judgment processes. An alternative is to compare subjective reports about specific aspects of the process, for example about the relative weights they give to different cues, by comparing what the model fitted to the judges' judgments yields. The results of both these kinds of studies (e.g. Hoffman, 1960; Summers *et al.*, 1969; Stewart and Carter 1973; Slovic, 1969) show that subjects do not have very good insight into their judgment processes, a finding in line with many other studies using retrospective reports about cognitive processes (Nisbett and Wilson, 1977).

Taking all of the available results in this field into account, an interesting pattern emerges: objective models fitted to the actual judgments tend to be simpler than subjective models. That is, people seem to believe that their judgment processes are more complex than they actually are. There are at least two possible explanations for this.

First, as pointed out by Einhorn *et al.* (1979), many different kinds of processing information will result in a linear model. A linear model is a compensatory model, implying that the person makes trade-offs. The process of making trade-offs may very well be experienced as being quite complex.

Second, as shown by Brehmer *et al.* (1980), lack of cognitive skill may prevent a person from actually following the rule s/he intends to use. Specifically, the results show that even when subjects are trying to follow a configural model, and believe that they are following such a model, their judgments nevertheless fail to exhibit configural properties. That is, the subjects are simply unable to follow the model they intend to follow. It is possible that verbal descriptions of judgment processes give information about what model a person intends to follow but not necessarily about the actual process.

In summary, the results from studies on judgment indicate that judgment processes are simple and inconsistent and that people have limited insight into these processes.

Hammond and Brehmer (1973) have termed such processes *quasi-rational processes*, and hypothesized that their characteristics stem from their being midway between analytical and intuitive thinking. Basically, a quasi-rational process is seen as a process that is partially rule-bound (analytical thinking) and partly relying on specific experience (intuitive thinking). Thus a person may have rules for making judgments, but the judgments derived by these rules are checked against specific experience from cases similar to that at hand. If the rule-derived judgment does not agree with whatever specific case that the person happens to remember, the judgment is modified. As a consequence, the process is not completely determined by the rules, that is, it is inconsistent.

Although this is an attractive explanation for inconsistency, it is admittedly *ad hoc*. However, whatever the explanation, the fact of inconsistency remains, and it has unfortunate consequences for human social interaction, as we shall see as we now turn to the problem of conflict.

COGNITIVE CONFLICT IN SMALL DECISION-MAKING GROUPS

One reason for letting a group, rather than an individual, make decisions is that many kinds of expertise may be needed, or because experts differ in their opinions. Another reason is, of course, that there are conflicting interests that may be involved and need to be reconciled, but such a case will not be considered here.

Within SJT, differences in expertise are interpreted in terms of differences in how the cues in a judgment task are used. Thus one expert may know how to use some cues, while another may know how to use some others. These experts may then need to co-operate to produce an optimal decision for a decision problem which requires the use of both sets of cues. This will entail the reconciling, or integration, of judgmental differences which stem from differences in how the cues are used. Such a reconciling will, of course, often imply a change in judgmental strategies.

However, judgmental differences may also occur in the absence of any real differences in expertise. As described above, experts may also differ within their area of expertise, especially when the expertise is derived from their own experience, either because they have learned different rules from this experience, or because they are inconsistent. Of course, people do not have to be experts to make different judgments; this can also happen when ordinary people make decisions about everyday problems, such as when a husband and wife try to agree on where their vacation should be spent.

As should be clear from what has been said above, both of the cases described, that involving persons with different expertise, and that involving persons with the same kind of expertise, may lead to conflict caused by judgmental differences.

Conflicts of this kind have not received very much attention from social and behavioural scientists, presumably because the prevalence of the rational actor paradigm leads them to focus on conflicts caused by motivational factors, and to interpret cases of conflict in terms of motivational differences. An additional reason for the relative neglect of these kinds of conflicts may be that there has not been any well-developed experimental paradigm comparable to those developed for the study of conflict of interest, such as the prisoner's dilemma game.

Hammond (1965) has, however, developed a paradigm for the study of judgmental conflicts and this paradigm has now generated a considerable number of empirical results both in the laboratory and in applied settings. In the next section we will describe this paradigm and give a brief overview of the results obtained.

THE SJT PARADIGM FOR THE STUDY OF INTERPERSONAL CONFLICT

The SJT interpersonal conflict (IPC) paradigm was first suggested by Hammond (1965) as a simulation of the essential characteristics of judgment conflicts. Experiments in this paradigm are conducted in two stages. The first stage serves to create, or assess, the relations between the cognitive systems of the persons involved. In most laboratory studies, this first step is a training stage in which two or more persons are trained to have the judgmental policies required for the experiment. The training usually follows a multiple-cue probability learning (MPL) paradigm.

Experiments in an MPL paradigm require subjects to learn to infer the state of a criterion variable from that of a set of cue variables which are imperfectly correlated with the criterion, thus introducing uncertainty into the task.

The MPL paradigm incorporates many of the important features of the situations requiring judgment, as these situations are conceptualized within SJT. Most important are (i) that the subjects have to learn to use uncertain information, and (ii) that a number of cues have to be used.

The policies acquired in MPL share the important features of the cognitive systems involved in judgment as these features have been revealed in, for example, studies of clinical judgment. Thus, the policies acquired in the MPL are inconsistent (e.g. Brehmer, 1976a), and the subjects have limited insight into their policies; they cannot fully describe how they arrive at their judgments (Brehmer, et al 1974). Thus the MPL paradigm produces cognitive systems which have the important features of quasi-rational cognition.

However, training is not the only method of obtaining subjects with different cognitive systems. It is also possible to select subjects whose policies towards some issues differ as a consequence of their pre-experimental experience. It does not seem to make any difference in the results of these experiments if subjects are trained to have different policies or if they are selected because of different policies (Hammond and Brehmer, 1973).

Conflict Stage

In the conflict stage pairs of subjects are brought together to work on a new task for which their policies are only partly relevant. This may be arranged in different ways. One possibility, used in many experiments, is to train subjects to use different cues and then put them together in a situation requiring the use of all the cues. This may be seen, either as a situation where two persons with different expertise are brought together to co-operate and benefit from each other's specialist knowledge, or as a situation where two persons with different ideologies have to resolve differences in how they view the world. The general context will determine which of these possibilities is relevant, but so far, experiments have generally been set up to study the latter possibility, which is how people who see the world differently are able to resolve their differences.

In the conflict stage, subjects are given a series of problems of the same kind. For example, they may receive a series of 20 different countries, each described in terms of the same economic indices, and asked to predict the future economic growth for each of these countries. In those cases about which the subjects disagree, they are asked to discuss their differences until they can reach a joint answer agreeable to both of them.

The trial then usually ends with a feedback, when the subjects are informed of the correct answer for the trial, but this feedback may be omitted (see e.g. Brehmer, 1971).

In the conflict stage, as in the training stage, probabilistic tasks, that is tasks in which the correlation between the cues and the feedback values is less than unity, are used in accordance with the general analysis of the nature of judgment tasks in SJT.

Experiments in this paradigm yield a variety of measures, (Hammond, 1965) but in actual practice only the relation between the initial judgments is analysed as this provides a measure of the amount of conflict. In addition, analyses of the subjects' policies – how they use the cues, and their consistency – are performed.

In the early experiments, various distance measures were used, such as the absolute differences between the initial judgments, $S_1 - S_2$, often weighted by the expected difference, $T_1 - T_2$, where T_1 and T_2 are the judgments predicted from regression equations fitted to the subjects' responses in the final part of the first stage, for example the last 15 trials in training or selection (see e.g., Miller *et al.*, 1970). These kinds of measures were later called 'surface measures'. They were found to have unfortunate characteristics and were later abandoned (see Brehmer, 1969a, 1974b), in favour of a correlational analysis, using the so-called 'lens model equation', LME (Hursch, *et al.*, 1964; Tucker, 1964). This equation was first developed to analyse the relation between the cognitive system of a person and a cognitive task, but was adapted to the analysis of cognitive conflict by Brehmer (1969b).

For analyses of conflict, the LME takes the following form

$$r_A = G R_{S_1} R_{S_2} \tag{2}$$

where r_A is the correlation between the judgments made by subject S_1 and those made by subject S_2, G is the correlation between the linearly predictable variance in the cognitive systems of the two subjects, that is, $G = r_{\hat{J}S_1 \hat{J}S_1}$ is the judgment predicted for subject S_1 from a regression equation fitted to the relation between the judgments of S_1 and the cues, and $\hat{J}_{S_2}$ the judgment predicted for S_2 from a regression equation fitted to the judgments of S_2 and the cues, R_{S_1} the multiple correlation between the judgments of S_1 and the cues, and R_{S_2} the corresponding multiple correlation for the judgments of S_2.

In Equation (2), r_A is a measure of the level of agreement between S_1 and S_2 and G shows the extent to which the systematic aspects of the policies of S_1 and S_2 are similar, that is, the extent to which they use the cues in the same way. R_{S1} and R_{S2}, finally, show the consistency of the policies of S_1 and S_2.

Equation (2) shows that two things are required for perfect agreement, that is, for r_A to reach unity: that the subjects use the cues in the same way, that is, so that $G = 1.00$, and that they are perfectly consistent, that is, so that $R_{S1} = R_{S2} = 1.00$. Therefore it is not sufficient that the subjects have the same policies, they must also apply these policies with perfect consistency. Disagreement does not therefore imply that there are fundamental policy differences; because of inconsistency, we may have cases of agreement in principle but disagreement in fact. Indeed, inconsistency may also produce the opposite problem, agreement in a concrete instance, despite fundamental policy differences. This means that it is not possible to draw any firm conclusions about the nature of a conflict from observations of the relations between the decisions of two persons: a structural analysis of the kind provided by the LME is needed. Yet most analyses of conflict outside SJT unually rely only on the actual decisions and no structural analysis is performed. This is, of course, especially true in analyses performed in the rational actor paradigm. In this paradigm, inconsistency is, of course, totally unthinkable, so a structural analysis may not seem all that necessary.

OVERVIEW OF RESULTS OBTAINED WITH THE SJT PARADIGM

There have been a number of quite detailed reviews of the results from various perspectives (Brehmer, 1976b; Brehmer and Hammond, 1977; Hammond et al., 1975; Hammond et al., 1977), so we will only give a brief overview of two of the most important results: those pertaining to the structure of conflict and those concerning the importance of the task, before we turn to a review of some of the applied work.

The Structure of Conflict

The early results obtained with the SJT paradigm were surprising in that they yielded no evidence of conflict reduction over a 20-trial conflict sequence (e.g. Hammond et al., 1968; Miller et al., 1970). Thus it seemed that people were unable to change their policies.

However, these studies were limited in that they used only surface measures of conflict. The first studies using LME analyses gave an entirely different picture (Brehmer, 1968), and showed that although there was little reduction in surface conflict, there was a radical change in the structure of the conflict. Specifically, the results showed that the systematic differences between the subjects' policies decreased rapidly. At the same time, however, the consistency of the policies also decreased. Thus in the beginning of the conflict stage, most of the conflict was caused by systematic differences in policy, that is by a low G value, but at the end, most of the conflict was caused by lack of consistency, that is, by low values of R_{s1} and R_{s2}.

Further analysis showed that the decrease in consistency was due to the manner in which the subjects changed their policies as a consequence of their interaction with each other and with the task. Thus, contrary to expectation, the subjects did not stick to their initial policies, but gave up these policies and acquired new ones. However, they gave up their old policies faster than they learned new ones, and as a consequence, their consistency decreased.

These results have subsequently been replicated over a wide variety of circumstances, including subject characteristics such as their sex (Hammond and Brehmer, 1973) and nationality (Brehmer et al., 1970), and task characteristics, both with respect to substantive characteristics, such as task content, (Hammond and Brehmer, 1973) and formal characteristics such as task predictability (Brehmer, 1973) the distribution of the validities of the cues (Brehmer, 1974; Brehmer and Kostron, 1973), the forms of cue-criterion relations (Brehmer and Hammond, 1973) and the intercorrelation between the cues (Brehmer, 1974b).

The adverse effects of inconsistency are also obtained when the subjects start with similar policies, but are required to change because their policies are not optimal for the task at hand. Under these circumstances, inconsistency causes persons who start out with near perfect agreement to disagree more and more as they change their policies, even though they do not develop any systematic differences in policy (Brehmer, 1972). These results suggest a new kind of explanation for why groups break up when their environment changes.

Inconsistency is not an artifact, caused by the particular way in which the data from the experiments are analysed; it also has behavioural consequences. Thus Brehmer (1974c) showed that when inconsistency is high the subjects ask their partners more questions about what they are doing and what their policy is. This indicates that inconsistency leads to lack of interpersonal understanding. In a reanalysis of some data collected by Brown and Hammond (1968), Hammond and Brehmer (1973) found that inconsistency hindered the subjects in four-person groups in identifying who had the same policy and who had a different policy with respect to the evaluation of presidential candidates. This is a remarkable result given that the four-person groups were composed of two students from the radical Students for a Democratic Society and two students from the conservative Young Americans for Freedom.

Hammond and Brehmer (1973) have discussed these results in detail, and hypothesized that inconsistency will prevent the persons from realizing the true nature of their conflict, and because they are likely to employ the rational actor paradigm, they are likely to explain their differences in motivational terms, rather than in cognitive terms. As a consequence, they will not only fail to resolve their conflict, but attempts to resolve the conflict may actually lead to exacerbation when the subjects start searching for the motives that will explain their differences. This attribution process has, however, not yet been investigated empirically.

The Importance of the Task

In standard analyses of conflict following the rational actor paradigm, conflicts are seen as involving only the two persons in conflict. According to the present analysis, this is not sufficient. Instead, the analysis must involve three systems: the two parties to the conflict and the task for which the conflicting policies have been developed. This is because the characteristics of this task will have important effects on the policies of the people in conflict. In the earlier part of this paper, we mentioned two important task characteristics that affect the consistency of policies: complexity and uncertainty. Since the policies in the conflict stage are changed to cope with the task in that stage, we would expect that the characteristics of the task would affect the consistency of the policies developed and that the level of conflict would vary with the characteristics of the task. This prediction is supported in studies by Brehmer (1973) and Brehmer and Hammond (1973). The former study shows that conflict varies with task predictability, and that disagreement is greater when predictability is lower because the subjects' policies are then less consistent. The study by Brehmer and Hammond (1973) suggests that complex non-linear tasks tend to lead to higher conflict because of lower consistency.

These results are important because they show that the level of conflict cannot be understood only in terms of the persons in conflict and their characteristics. The nature of the task facing the persons has to be considered as well. In short, the analysis of conflict must involve three, rather than just two, systems. Clearly, it may be just as reasonable to look for an explanation of conflict in the task as to look for it in the people in conflict.

Summary

The results obtained with the SJT paradigm in the laboratory show that interpersonal conflict can be caused by purely cognitive factors, that is, by differences in policies, and that the level of conflict can be understood in terms of the cognitive systems involved. An important determinant of the level of conflict is the nature of the task which affects the conflict by its effects on the policies of the persons involved.

These results were, however, all obtained in laboratory simulations of conflict. We now turn to some applications of these results in real settings.

STUDIES IN APPLIED SETTINGS

There have been a number of studies in applied settings. These studies have been reviewed in Brehmer and Hammond (1977) and Hammond *et al.*, 1977). Later studies add little to what is in these reviews, except to add to the variety of settings in which SJT methods have been applied.

Except for the first study by Balke *et al.* (1973), which was a re-enactment of a labour-management conflict, the applied work has been concerned with real conflict which had existed for some time before the Social Judgment Theorists became involved. The conflicts studied include, among other things, disagreement over the choice of handgun ammunition for a metropolitan police force (Hammond and Adelman, 1976), conflict over policy in a governmental organization (Adelman *et al.*, 1975), and disagreement among experts over judgments of cancer risk (Hammond and Marvin, 1981).

In all of these studies, it proved possible to identify the cognitive differences that caused the conflicts by means of the kinds of techniques for judgment analysis described in this paper. These results thus give evidence that these techniques are useful, but, more important, they demonstrate the utility of analysing conflict in terms of cognitive differences, and not only in terms of differences in interest. In short, they underline the importance of developing an alternative to the rational actor paradigm for understanding decision-making and conflict.

As would be expected from the laboratory results, the judgment policies in these studies were found to be inconsistent, and the parties to the conflicts had little insight into the real causes of their disagreement and what differences actually existed between their policies (see Balke *et al.*, 1973, for a particularly clear demonstration of this).

These results suggest that it is important to develop new methods for communication to help resolve conflict. A first step in this direction was taken by Hammond and Brehmer (1973). They developed a computer graphics system which presents cases for judgment, accepts judgments via a keyboard, performs a judgment analysis according to the principles described in this paper and displays the results graphically so that the parties to the conflict can see what their differences actually are with respect to what cues are used, which weights are given to these cues, the functional relations between each cue and the judgments, and their consistency, thus relieving the persons of having to rely on their limited insight and on the imprecise medium of words for communicating about their policies. The current version of this system (Stewart and Carter, 1973) is available through the General Electric international time-sharing system.

The system has been used in many of the applied studies referred to above, but there has been no evaluating of its usefulness compared to other techniques for communication, nor has there been any study comparing conflict reduction with the system and without the system. Despite the fact that there are good theoretical reasons for expecting positive effects from the system on conflict reduction through improved communication there are, as yet, no empirical results to demonstrate that the system actually serves the function it is supposed to serve. To perform such an evaluation is a task of utmost importance for future studies in SJT.

CONCLUSIONS

The main argument in this paper is that the complexity of the problems facing decision-makers prevents them from having the complete understanding presumed in the rational actor paradigm. As a consequence, decisions have to be based on judgment, rather than on fact, that is to say, cognitive processes intervene and have to be taken into account. Clearly, the characteristics of the judgmental processes involved contribute to conflict, and judgmental differences seem sufficient to create disagreement, even in the absence of motivational differences, as is demonstrated in both laboratory and applied studies. These results substantiate the claim that an alternative to the rational actor paradigm is needed to supplement the analysis performed in this paradigm. While it is clear that considerably more theoretical and empirical work is needed before we achieve any reasonably complete understanding of human judgment and its role in decision-making and conflict, I hope that this chapter has at least convinced the reader that work conducted towards this end will prove worthwhile.

REFERENCES

Adelman, L., Stewart, T.T., and Hammond, K. R. (1975). A case history of the application of social judgment theory to policy formation, *Policy Science*, 6, 137–159.

Allison, G.T. (1971). *Essence of Decision. Explaining the Cuban Missile Crisis*, Boston: Little, Brown.

Balke, W.M., Hammond, K.R., and Meyer, G.D. (1973). An alternative approach to labor–management relations, *Administrative Science Quarterly*, 18, 311–327.

Brehmer, B. (1969a). Sequence effects on conflict, Umea Psychological Reports, No. 17.

Brehmer, B. (1969b). The roles of policy differences and inconsistency in policy conflict, Ume'a Psychological Reports, No. 18.

Brehmer, B. (1971). Effects of communication and feedback on cognitive conflict, *Scandinavian Journal of Psychology*, 12, 205–216.

Brehmer, B. (1972). Policy conflict as a function of policy similarity and policy complexity, *Scandinavian Journal of Psychology*, 13, 208–221.

Brehmer, B. (1973). Policy conflict and policy change as a function of task characteristics. II. The effect of task predictability, *Scandinavian Journal of Psychology*, 14, 220–227.

Brehmer, B. (1974a). Policy conflict and policy change as a function of task characteristics. III. The effect of the distribution of the validities of the cues in the conflict task, *Scandinavian Journal of Psychology*, 15, 273–276.

Brehmer, B. (1974b). A note on the cross-national differences in conflict found by Hammond et al., *International Journal of Psychology*, **9**, 51–56.

Brehmer, B. (1974c). Policy conflict, policy consistency, and interpersonal understanding, *Scandinavian Journal of Psychology*, **15**, 273–276.

Brehmer, B. (1975). Policy conflict and policy change as a function of task characteristics. IV. The effect of cue intercorrelations, *Scandinavian Journal of Psychology*, **16**, 85–96.

Brehmer, B. (1976a). Note on clinical judgment and the formal characteristics of clinical tasks, *Psychological Bulletin*, **83**, 778–782.

Brehmer, B. (1976b). Social judgment theory and the analysis of interpersonal conflict, *Psychological Bulletin*, **83**, 985–1003.

Brehmer, B. (1978). Response consistency in probabilistic inference tasks, *Organizational Behavior and Human Performance*, **22**, 103–115.

Brehmer, B. (1979). Preliminaries to a psychology of inference, *Scandinavian Journal of Psychology*, **21**, 193–211.

Brehmer, B. (1980). In one word: Not from experience, *Acta Psychologica*, **45**, 223–241.

Brehmer, B. and Hammond, K.R. (1973). Cognitive sources of interpersonal conflict. Analysis of ineractions between linear and nonlinear cognitive systems, *Organizational Behavior and Human Performance*, **10**, 290–313.

Brehmer, B. and Hammond, K.R. (1977). Cognitive factors in interpersonal conflict, in D. Druckman (ed.), *Negotiations: A Social Psychological Perspective*, New York: Sage.

Brehmer, B. and Kostron, L. (1973). Policy conflict and policy change as a function of task characteristics. I. The effects of cue validity and function form, *Scandinavian Journal of Psychology*, **14**, 44–55.

Brehmer, B. and Kuylenstierna, J. (1978). Task information and performance in probabilistic inference tasks, *Organizational Behavior and Human Performance*, **22**, 445–464.

Brehmer, B. and Kuylenstierna, J. (1980). Content and consistency in probabilistic inference tasks, *Organizational Behavior and Human Performance*, **26**, 54–64.

Brehmer, B. and Qvarnström, G. (1976). Information integration and subjective weights in multiple-cue judgments, *Organizational Behavior and Human Performance*, **17**, 118–126.

Brehmer, B., Azuma, H., Hammond, K.R., Kostron, L., and Varonos, D.D. (1970). A cross-national comparison of cognitive conflict, *Journal of Cross-Cultural Psychology*, **1**, 5–20.

Brehmer, B., Kuylenstierna, J., and Liljergren, J. (1974). Effects of cue validity and function form of the subjects' hypotheses in probabilistic inference tasks, *Organizational Behavior and Human Performance*, **11**, 338–354.

Brehmer, B., Hagafors, R., and Johansson, R. (1980). Cognitive skills in judgment: Subjects' ability to use information about cue weights, function forms and organizing principles, *Organizational Behavior and Human Performance*, **26**, 373–385.

Brown, L. and Hammond, K.R. (1968). A supra-linguistic method for reducing intra-group conflict. Institute of Behavioral Science, University of Colorado: Program on Cognitive Processes Report, 108.

Brunswik, E. (1952). *Conceptual Framework of Psychology*, Chicago: University of Chicago Press.

Dawes, R.M. (1976). Shallow psychology, in J.S. Carroll and J.W. Payne (eds), *Cognition and Social Behavior*, Hillsdale, NJ: Earlbaum.

Einhorn, H.J., Kleinmuntz, B., and Kleinmuntz, D.N. (1979). Linear regression and process tracing model of judgment, *Psychological Review*, **86**, 395–416.

Goldberg, L.R. (1968). Simple models or simple processes? Some research on clinical judgment, *American Psychologist*, **23**, 483–496.
Goldberg, L.R. (1970). Model vs model of man. A rationale, plus some evidence for a method of improving on clinical judgment, *Psychological Bulletin*, **73**, 422–432.
Hagafors, R. and Brehmer, B. (1980a). Effects of information-presentation mode and task complexity on the learning of probabilistic inference tasks, *Scandinavian Journal of Psychology*, **21**, 109–113.
Hagafors, R. and Brehmer, B. (1980b). Effects of information-presentation mode and learning paradigm on the learning of probabilistic inference tasks under different levels of memory strain, *Scandinavian Journal of Psychology*, **21**, 249–255.
Hammond, K.R. (1955). Probabilistic functioning and the clinical method, *Psychological Review*, **62**, 255–262.
Hammond, K.R. (1965). New directions in research on conflict, *Journal of Social Issues*, **21**, 44–66.
Hammond, K.R. (1974). Human judgment and social policy. Institute of Behavioral Science, University of Colorado: Program on Human Judgment and Social Interaction, Report No. 170.
Hammond, K.R. and Adelman, L. (1976). Science, values, and human judgment, *Science*, **194**, 389–396.
Hammond, K.R. and Brehmer, B. (1973), Quasi-rationality and distrust. Implications for international conflict, in L. Rappoport and D. Summers (eds), *Human Judgment and Social Interaction*, New York: Holt, Rinehart & Winston.
Hammond, K.R. and Marvin, B.A. (1981). Report to the Rocky Flats Monitoring Committee concerning scientists' judgments of cancer risk. Institute of Behavioral Science, University of Colorado: Report No. 232.
Hammond, K.R., Bonauito, G.B., Faucheux, C., Moscovici, S., Frohlich, W.D., Joyce, C.R.B. and DiMajo, G. (1968). A comparison of cognitive conflict between persons in Western Europe and the United States. *International Journal of Psychology*, **3**, 1–12.
Hammond, K.R., Stewart, T.R., Brehmer, B., and Steinmann, D.O. (1975). Social judgment theory, in M. Kaplan and S. Schwartz (eds), *Human Judgment and Decision Processes*, New York: Academic Press.
Hammond, K.R., Rohrbaugh, J., Mumpower, J.L., and Adelman, L. (1977). Social judgment theory: Applications in policy formation, in M. Kaplan and S. Schwartz (eds), *Human Judgment and Decision Processes in Applied Settings*, New York: Academic Press.
Hoffman, P.J. (1960). Paramorphic representation of clinical judgment, *Psychological Bulletin*, **57**, 116–131.
Hoffman, P.J., Slovic, P., and Rorer, L.G. (1968). An analysis-of-variance model for the assessment of configural cue utilization in clinical judgment, *Psychological Bulletin*, **69**, 338–349.
Hursch, C.J., Hammond, K.R., and Hursch, J.L. (1964). Some methodological considerations in multiple-cue studies, *Psychological Review*, **71**, 42–60.
Johansson, R. and Brehmer, B. (1979). Inferences from incomplete information: A note, *Organizational Behavior and Human Performance*, **24**, 141–145.
Kuylenstierna, J. and Brehmer, B. (1981). Memory aids in the learning of probabilistic inference tasks *Organizational Behavior and Human Performance*, **28**, 415–424.
Miller, M.J., Brehmer, B., and Hammond, K.R. (1970). Communication and conflict reduction: A cross-national study, *International Journal of Psychology*, **5**, 44–56.
Nisbett, R.E. and Wilson, T.D. (1977). Telling more than we can know: Verbal reports on mental processes, *Psychological Review*, **84**, 231–259.
Simon, H.A. (1953). *Models of Man*, New York: Wiley.

Slovic, P. (1969). Analysing the expert judge: A descriptive study of a stockbroker's decision processes, *Journal of Applied Psychology*, **53**, 255–263.
Slovic, P. and Lichtenstein, S. (1971). Comparison of Bayesian and regression approaches to the study of information processing in judgment, *Organizational Behavior and Human Performance*, **6**, 649–744.
Stewart, T.R. and Carter, J. (1973). POLICY: An interactive computer program for externalizing, executing, and refining judgmental policy. Institute of Behavioral Science, University of Colorado: Program on Human Judgment and Social Interaction, report No. 159.
Summers, D.A., Taliaferro, D.J., and Fletcher, D.J. (1969). Subjective vs. objective description of judgment policy, *Psychonomic Science*, **18**, 249–250.
Tucker, L.R. (1969). A suggested alternative formulation in the developments by Hursch, Hammond, and Hursch and by Hammond, Hursch, and Todd, *Psychological Review*, **71**, 528–530.
Tversky, A. and Kahneman, D. (1971). Belief in the law of small numbers, *Psychological Bulletin*, **76**, 105–110.
Tversky, A. and Kahneman, D. (1974). Judgment under uncertainty. Heuristics and biases, *Science*, **185**, 1124–1131.
Wiggins, N. and Hoffman, P.J. (1968). Three models of clinical judgment, *Journal of Abnormal Psychology*, **73**, 70–77.

Progress in Applied Social Psychology, Volume 2
Edited by G.M. Stephenson and J.H. Davis
© 1984 John Wiley & Sons Ltd

7

The Role of Justice and Power in Reward Allocation

S. S. KOMORITA
University of Illinois, Urbana-Champaign

THE ROLE OF JUSTICE AND POWER IN REWARD ALLOCATION[1]

In their book *The Social Psychology of Bargaining*, Morley and Stephenson (1977) claim that laboratory studies of bargaining are extremely artificial and are poor simulations of actual bargaining situations. However, it can be argued that all experiments attempt to simulate some aspect of the real world. Although many laboratory experiments are indeed very poor simulations of the real world, the results of laboratory studies can have significant implications for social policy. Laboratory experiments can provide valuable insights into the nature of relations between the relevant variables, and they provide an efficient method of detecting promising relations that can subsequently be tested in field settings. Moreover, the sometimes perplexing findings of field studies may be refined in laboratory studies before attempting additional field work.

Figure 1 illustrates my ideas about the implications of laboratory experiments for social policy. The upper-left box represents the real world, including the consequences of implementing various social policies. There are several paths or routes that lead to social policy decisions. Social policies are frequently based on social-political philosophy, which I have labelled 'arm-chair speculation'. In other cases, the results of field studies (surveys, field experiments, case-studies, and so on) have been used to implement social policies. Solutions based on data certainly increase our confidence that a given policy is likely to lead to certain consequences, but it would also be desirable to show that such solutions are consistent with our theoretical understanding of the phenomenon.

Now, turning to the upper-right box, we have laboratory experiments which

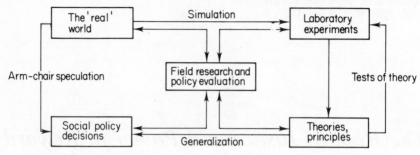

Figure 1. The role of laboratory and field research for social policy

are fórmulated on the basis of simulating some aspects of the real world. According to Figure 1, it is implied that the further the distance to the right, the more artificial the situation (poorer the simulation). The main advantage of laboratory experiments – because of cost, convenience, and the relative ease of controlling extraneous variables – is that they provide rigorous tests of theories about the phenomenon, shown in the lower-right box. Thus another path to reach policy decisions is through laboratory experiments, cycled through tests of theories, and then to deduced effects of policies. However, if a theory that has not been tested in field settings is used to derive hypotheses about a given policy, the obvious problem is external validity, denoted 'Generalization'. This is, of course, the main problem with theories based exclusively on laboratory research.

The main advantage of field research, shown in the centre of Figure 1, is that it closely simulates the real world and provides a direct connection between social policy and its possible consequences in the real world. However, I submit that field research has contributed much less towards the development and test of theories (shown by the arrow linking field studies and theory) than have laboratory experiments. Thus the two types of research approaches comple- ment each other, and more attempts should be made to conduct laboratory experiments derived from the results of field research, and vice versa. This is shown by the arrow connecting field research and laboratory experiments. Similarly, more attempts should be made to test theories in field situations, so that different paths, or cycles of paths, are used to make social policy decisions. If both laboratory and field studies support a given theory, it would certainly increase our confidence that a given policy decision will have certain conse- quences in the real world.

It should be obvious by now that activities involving the left side of Figure 1 are frequently called 'applied research', while activities involving the right side are called 'basic research'. But note that field research bridges the gap between the two types of activities; consequently, communication between investigators committed to field research and those committed to laboratory research should be much more frequent than in the past. In accordance with this view about the role of laboratory and field research for social policy, the purpose of this chapter is twofold: to describe some laboratory studies that suggest hypotheses that might be tested in field settings, and to suggest some new directions for theory and research on reward allocation in groups.

For the purpose of this chapter, several important assumptions will be made. First, it will be assumed that there is a positive relation between the total rewards allocated to the members of a group (or organization) and the effectiveness of the group. The classical approach to this problem is based on varying reward magnitude and observing its effect on learning and performance. However, even if we found a direct relation between reward magnitude and group performance, in most situations there are constraints on the amount of reward that is available for distribution. Hence the problem of reward allocation involves not only maximizing group performance, but also minimizing internal conflict among the members. Moreover, there is considerable evidence to suggest that it is not necessarily the absolute magnitude of reward that enhances group performance but the relative magnitude of reward, compared to one's reference or comparison group. Hence in most situations it is neither feasible nor necessary to allocate large rewards to all members of the group. Given these assumptions, a pervasive problem for the leader or head of an organizational unit is how limited resources should be divided among the group members.

CRITIQUE OF EQUITY RESEARCH

In contrast to the classic approach, I want to focus first on the processes of allocation and describe some of the limitations of theory and research on justice norms, particularly studies based on the reward allocation paradigm. This paradigm was first used by Levanthal and Michaels (1969) and consists of asking two or more persons to perform a task. Based on their performance, a reward is given to the group and one of them is selected to divide the reward. Empirical studies using this paradigm have generally supported the predictions of Adams' equity theory (1963) and Homans' concept of distributive justice (1961), which assume that an individual's output (share of reward) should be directly proportional to the input (contribution). Although there is considerable evidence to support this assumption (cf. Walster *et al.*, 1973; Levanthal, 1976), some studies have shown that an equality norm also influences reward allocation (e.g. Morgan and Sawyer, 1967).

One of the main limitations of theory and research on equity, in my opinion, is that most investigators have emphasized judgments of equity and have not adequately examined behavioural reactions to inequitable allocations, especially on the part of those who perceive they have been under-rewarded. Although Adams' (1963) theory predicts that those who are under-rewarded should decrease their inputs (performance), while those who are over-rewarded should increase their inputs, so as to restore equity, these reactions are by no means the only method – nor the most common method – of restoring equity. Probably the initial reaction to perceived inequity (in addition to distress and tension) is to seek restitution (Leventhal and Bergman, 1969; Walster *et al.*, 1973). If appeals to justice and inequity are unsuccessful, however, there are several behavioural options available to the parties besides decreasing input. Indeed, in some situations a victim of inequitable allocation may actually increase performance (input) so as to achieve a greater share of the reward in a subsequent allocation period. Thus it is essential to investigate how individuals are likely to behave in response to inequitable outcomes, and in particular, how such behaviour may vary as a function of the situation.

A related but equally important process that has not received sufficient attention is the role of power (bargaining strength) in reward allocation. There is no reason to believe that the basic functions of justice norms differ from the functions of other norms, and if norms develop through a process of informal exchange (bargaining), as hypothesized by Thibaut and Kelley (1959), then the bargaining strength and the power structure of the group must be incorporated into any theory of equity and justice. In an employer–employee relationship, for example, salaries are not typically negotiated on the basis of justice but on the basis of the power (bargaining strength) of the respective parties. Some pitchers on a professional baseball team, or some quarterbacks on a football team, receive ten times the salary of some of their team mates. Is this fair and do they deserve such a large salary? According to Homans' concept of distributive justice, the pitcher (or quarterback) has special skills (abilities) and these skills are inputs that determine his output (reward).

The main point is that the marketplace dictates that some members of a baseball team receive higher rewards, not simply because of justice norms, but because it would cost much more to replace that person than to replace other members of the team. Thus certain persons deserve a much larger share of the reward because they cannot be replaced or are very difficult and costly to replace. Hence to maintain a given level of group effectiveness, reward allocation cannot be based solely on justice norms, but must also incorporate the effects of the marketplace.

This interpretation is consistent with the assumption that members of a group negotiate their share of the reward and those who are in a stronger bargaining position are likely to receive a higher share of the profits. My definition of bargaining strength (Komorita, 1977) is based on Thibaut and Kelley's (1959) concept of 'comparison level for alternatives' (CLalt), defined as the maximal reward an individual can expect in alternative relationships. An individual has greater bargaining strength to the extent that he(she) has better alternatives than the others. This interpretation of reward allocation is, of course, perfectly consistent with the marketplace. The basic problem is to incorporate the effects of bargaining strength and the effects of justice norms into a single theoretical scheme, and as we shall see, there are several possibilities for accomplishing such an integration.

It might be argued, at this point, that these are obvious hypotheses about the allocation problem. Pruitt (1972), for example, has pointed out that conflicts are resolved either through bargaining *or* through the application of norms, and Mikula and Schwinger (1978) feel that this distinction between the two modes of resolving conflict of interests is a useful one. I do not disagree with either Pruitt or Mikula and Schwinger, but I do insist that bargaining precedes the acceptance and application of normative rules. Moreover, norms are not static and frequently dissatisfied members attempt to renegotiate which norms apply (both social and legal contracts). The provocative question is what happens if appeals to justice are unsuccessful in renegotiating one's contract? My main thesis is that it depends on the alternatives (CLalt) available to the parties, and we should examine how justice norms develop and how they might change as a function of changing circumstances. In this context, the studies by Thibaut and Faucheux (1965) and by Thibaut (1968), on the development of contractual norms, are extremely important, and extensions of these studies are certainly warranted. Their results indicate that threats and counterthreats, based on the power of the parties, are important variables that determine the nature of contractual agreements (norms); hence it would be desirable to examine how norms might change when the power of the parties changes over time.

Some Evidence for the Importance of Power

Let me turn to some evidence to support my hypothesis that power, based on alternatives, may be equally important, or indeed, more important than justice norms. First, let me briefly describe a conversation I once had with a black activist during the late 1960s in the United States. He indicated that he had previously accepted Martin Luther King's policy of peaceful demonstration to correct past injustices to blacks, but had rejected this policy during the mid-1960s. He claimed that peaceful demonstrations would be effective only to the extent that the white majority felt guilty about such injustices, but the guilt aroused by peaceful demonstrations had not been sufficient to correct past injustices. Hence power – black power – was the only effective means of achieving civil rights for blacks and other minority groups. The riots in several cities in the United States were the first instance of this use of black power, and the mass registration of black voters to influence political candidates is another example of this change in strategy. Judging from the number of black leaders subsequently appointed to high government positions in the Carter administration, this change in strategic use of power seems to have been quite effective.

Now let me describe some results of coalition experiments to support my hypothesis. A commonly used procedure to test coalition theories is to assign weights to the parties such that the weight of any single person is not sufficient to win a specified prize. Hence, a coalition based on the combined weights of two or more persons is necessary to win. In Gamson's (1961a) political convention paradigm, the weights are represented by votes controlled by each person, and a majority of the votes is necessary to form a winning coalition. Gamson's (1961b) Minimum Resource theory assumes that reward distribution will be based on the parity norm, which prescribes that each person's share should be directly proportional to the number of votes controlled by each person. For example, in a three-person game with weights (votes) of 40, 30, and 20, Gamson's theory predicts that the shares for the 40–30 coalition should be 4/7 and 3/7, respectively; shares for the 40–20 should be 4/6 and 2/6, respectively; and shares for the 30–20 coalition should be 3/5 and 2/5, respectively. Since the prescribed shares for the 30–20 coalition mutually maximize reward for the two players, Gamson's theory predicts that the 30–20 coalition should be most frequent.

Note that Gamson's theory is based exclusively on an equity norm and ignores the role of power, based on alternatives. There are several studies showing that the 30–20 coalition occurs most frequently, thus supporting Gamson's theory, but the mean reward division is midway between an equal split and the 60–40 split predicted by the parity norm. However, Kelley and Arrowood (1960), found that the 30–20 coalition occurred most frequently in the early trials, but with repeated plays of the game, no significant differences were found in the frequencies of the three possible coalitions. Since all two-person coalitions are winning coalitions, Kelley and Arrowood argued that their subjects learned through repeated plays of the game that power – based on the weights of the players – was really illusory; hence, power, based on alternatives (CLalt) became the dominant factor in later trials of the game.

We have found similar results in our own laboratory using four-person games. In our most recent study (Komorita and Tumonis, 1980), we compared the effects of assigning resource weights vs. not assigning such weights to determine the relative effects of justice norms and power on coalition behaviour. In one of the resource weight conditions, the following weights were assigned: 60, 40, 20, and 10, and a majority (70) was required to form a winning coalition. If the players are denoted, A, B, C, and D, in descending order of assigned weights, the following are minimal-winning coalitions: AB, AC, AD, and BCD. A minimal-winning coalition is one in which the deletion of any single member converts it into a losing coalition, and all descriptive theories of coalition formation predict that only minimal-winning coalitions are likely to form. When resource weights were not assigned, subjects were simply informed that only the AB, AC, AD, and BCD coalitions were winning coalitions. Since weights were not mentioned and the players differed only in their alternatives to form winning coalitions, a comparison of the two conditions provided a means of assessing the effects of equity norms.

Table 1 shows the results of the two experimental conditions. It can be seen that the differences between the two conditions are negligible, and indicate that equity norms, based on resource weights, had surprisingly little effect. Similar results were also obtained in a recent study by Miller (1979), who found that resource weights had negligible effects on coalition behaviour.

Table 1. Frequency of Coalitions and Mean Reward Division (shown in parentheses) [a]

| | Coalitions | | | |
Weights	AB	AC	AD	BCD
Assigned	0.35 (58–42)	0.21 (62–38)	0.33 (61–39)	0.11 (37–33–30)
Not assigned	0.33 (56–44)	0.21 (56–44)	0.38 (60–40)	0.08 (34–34–33)

[a] When resource weights were assigned, weights of 60, 40, 20 and 10 were assigned to Players A, B, C and D respectively. There were eleven tetrads in each condition and each tetrad played the game for six trials.

For this distribution of resource weights (60, 40, 20, 10), Gamson's Minimum Resource theory predicts that the AD or BCD coalitions are most likely to occur, with predicted pay-off splits of 86–14 for A and D (in AD), respectively, and 57–29–14 for B, C, and D (in BCD), respectively. Table 1 shows that the AD coalition occurred frequently, but the BCD coalition rarely occurred. The predicted pay-off splits are clearly inaccurate, but this should not be surprising because Gamson's theory is based on equity (parity), and equity norms (based on resource weights) had neglible effects.

In contrast, our Bargaining Theory of coalition formation (Komorita and Chertkoff, 1973) predicts that the AD coalition should be most frequent, and it correctly predicts that the BCD coalition should be least frequent. The predicted pay-off splits in these coalitions are 69–31 for A and D, respectively, and 33–33–33 for B, C, and D, respectively. It can be seen that these predictions are much more accurate than the predictions of Minimum Resource theory. The main reason for the greater accuracy of the Bargaining theory is that it assumes that both justice norms (parity and equality) and power, based on the alternatives of the players, affect coalition behaviour.

CONFLICT BETWEEN JUSTICE NORMS AND POWER

Although my comments thus far suggest that justice norms are dominated by the marketplace (power), i do not wish to imply that we should ignore such norms. On the contrary, I believe that justice and power are complexly intertwined in reward distribution, and we must untangle these two sets of forces. For example, in our research in dyadic bargaining (Komorita and Esser, 1975), we have found that the most effective means of inducing concessions is a bargaining strategy that is moderately tough. An extremely tough bargaining stance was likely to be perceived as unfair and was typically met with resistance. Thus, a 'firm but fair' strategy was most effective in reaching a mutually agreeable settlement.

Moreover, Mikula (1980) suggests that the equality norm may be more salient in groups with positive socio-emotional relations while the equity norm may be salient in negatively affected groups. Mikula's hypothesis suggests that justice norms may serve to maintain the cohesiveness of the group while power (based on the marketplace) functions to maximize group performance. Mikula's hypothesis is consistent with Deutsch's (1975) hypothesis that the equity norm is likely to be salient in groups that are motivated to maximize productivity, while the equality norm is more likely to be salient in groups that are motivated to maintain positive social relations.

If Mikula's and Deutsch's hypotheses are valid, it is plausible that justice and power may serve complementary functions and the critical problem for a group or organization is to determine the optimal weights that should be assigned to the two factors. It is plausible that members of cohesive groups, if they operate mainly on the basis of the equality norm, may become overly concerned with meeting socio-emotional needs, and may decline in group performance. Conversely, groups operating mainly on the basis of the equity norm – or on the basis of the marketplace – may inhibit co-operation in performing the task and may lose cohesion to such an extent that performance may suffer. Thus, there may be two opposing forces that affect performance, and a delicate balance between these forces may be necessary to maximize satisfaction and group performance (cf. Bales, 1950, 1953).

There is no simple solution to the problem of balancing forces, of course. Investigators in other areas of social interaction are equally concerned with this problem. It is plausible, for example, that various theories of leadership differ in the assumptions they make regarding the weights assigned by effective leaders, and how they change the weights depending on the situation (cf. Fiedler's model of leadership effectiveness, 1967).

Egocentric Motives and Conflict

The basic problem in formulating an optimal policy of assigning weights to justice and power is that members of the group are not likely to agree on the weights. Consensus regarding weights may be exceedingly difficult to achieve because of egocentric motives to maximize one's share of the reward (McClintock, in press). Such egocentric motives are relevant not only for the weights assigned to justice and power, but also for the weights assigned to various types of inputs. Those who are older will want to weight experience and seniority higher than those who are young; those who have special skills will want to weight such skills higher than those without such skills.

Indeed, our Bargaining theory of coalition formation (Komorita and Chertkoff, 1973) is based on such egocentric motives and postulates that those who have few resources (inputs) will appeal to and demand a share of the reward based on equality (equal shares), while those who have larger resources will demand and expect a share based on parity (proportional to inputs). However, our Bargaining theory also predicts that such inputs are weighted heavily only in the early trials, and at the asymptotic level (after many trials), the relative bargaining strengths of the players – based on their alternatives (CLalt) – determine the final outcomes. These predictions are, of course, consistent with the hypothesis proposed by Kelley and Arrowood (1960), discussed earlier.

Another example of such egocentric motives is a study I conducted many years ago to simulate a buyer–seller relationship. As a classroom demonstration I administered a short questionnaire to a large undergraduate class, and asked students to role-play a situation in which they were selling a used typewriter. They were to assume that they could sell it to a dealer for $30, and to assume that if someone wanted to buy a comparable typewriter from a dealer, the buyer would have to pay $70 to the dealer. The students were then asked to indicate what selling price they believed would be 'fair' (or reasonable). The fair-price estimates of the subjects, as sellers, were normally distributed around $50, the split-the-difference point between what the seller could receive from the dealer, and what the buyer would have to pay the dealer. I was pleased with this result because some of my earlier research also showed that the split-the-difference point was a good estimate of a bargainer's 'fair' agreement value. However, one half of the students had been asked to play the role of the seller, and the other half had been asked to play the role of the buyer. For subjects as buyers, estimates of a fair-agreement value was much lower than the split-the-difference point: about a third of these subjects thought that the split-the-difference value of $50 would be fair, but another third of the subjects thought that $35 would be fair, resulting in a bimodal distribution. These results suggest that there are implicit norms of justice operating in a buyer–seller relationship, and what is judged to be fair depends on one's role in the situation.

In a larger social-cultural context, such egocentric motives are the underlying basis of labour-management disputes and the conflict between capitalist and socialist countries. Each individual (group, collective) is likely to demand a share based on weights that maximize the individual's share of the reward. When such conflicts over the weighting of inputs and norms arise, each individual (or organizational unit) will want to influence the decision, and conflict over procedural rules and norms of procedural justice comes into play. A provocative question for social policy is how such conflict might be resolved to maximize satisfaction and group performance. Deutsch (1975), for example, hypothesizes that methods by which decisions are made (procedural justice) may be more important than the actual allocation decision, and suggests that member participation in the decision-making may minimize feelings of injustice.

Coalition Formation To Reduce Power Imbalance

If allocation decisions are based on egocentric motives and those who have the authority to make such decisions use their power to gain a disproportionately large share of the rewards, those who disagree with the decision will be dissatisfied and believe they are being exploited. If appeals to justice (through persuasion) are ineffective, there are two basic options for the 'victim': leave the situation for better alternatives or remain and attempt to restore equity by other means. Assuming there is no better alternative for the 'victims', what methods are available to restore equity within the group? In such a situation, Emerson's (1962) theory of power-dependence relations in groups suggests that the weaker members will attempt to reduce the imbalance of power. One obvious method of restoring balance is to use violence and aggression so as to change the power structure of the group; however, aggression is typically used as a last resort, when all other methods fail.

The history of the labour movement suggests that an effective non-violent method of reducing power imbalance is to form a coalition of the weak, sometimes called the 'weak-union' (Rapoport, 1970). Now how does coalition formation reduce an imbalance of power? According to my definition of bargaining strength (Komorita, 1977), if the weaker members act as individuals, their alternatives (CLalt), relative to the alternatives of the stronger members, are severely restricted. If the weak members form a coalition and act as a single unit, however, they can markedly decrease the alternatives of the stronger members.

Let me illustrate this idea with a principle derived from my Weighted Probability model of coalition formation (Komorita, 1974). The basic assumption of this model is that large coalitions, because of the logistic problem of communicating offers and counter-offers, are more difficult to form than small ones. As the size of a potential coalition increases, the problem of achieving reciprocity and achieving unanimous agreement on the terms of the offer also increases. Thus, the Weighted Probability model generally predicts that the coalition of minimum size will form.

Table 2 shows the predictions of the model for a class of coalition situations called an apex game. In an apex game there is a single strong player and $N-1$ weaker players, and there are two possible minimal-winning coalitions: the coalition of the strong player and one of the weak players, called the strong-weak alliance, and a coalition of all of the weak players, called the weak-union. For such games, Minimum Resource theory predicts that either the strong-weak alliance or the weak-union will form. In contrast, the Bargaining theory and the Weighted Probability model both predict that the strong-weak alliance is most likely, and the Weighted Probability model makes an exact prediction about the probability of each coalition. It can be seen that the probability of the strong-weak alliance increases with the number of weak players, and that the proportional share of the reward for the strong player also increases as the number of weak players increases.

Table 2.   Predictions of the Weighted Probability Model for Apex Games Varying in Group Size

Group size	Quota[a]	Resource distribution	Apex coalition	
			Probability	Division
4	3	2–1–1–1	0.86	67–33
7	6	5–1–1–1–1–1–1	0.97	83–17
11	10	9–1–1 ... 1–1	0.99	90–10

[a]   Quota denotes number of joint resource weights required to form a winning coalition.

The psychological basis for these predictions is that as group size increases, the number of alternative coalitions for the strong player increases, but the number of alternative coalitions for the weaker players remains constant (choice of strong-weak alliance and the weak-union). The Weighted Probability model postulates that an individual's bargaining strength is proportional to the number of alternative coalitions an individual can form, and the greater the bargaining strength, the greater the share of the reward. Empirical support for the predictions of this model, especially its predictions of coalition formation (e.g. Komorita and Moore, 1976; Komorita and Meek, 1978), lends some support for the effects of alternatives in bargaining. Moreover, it can be shown that in this type of coalition game, the formation of interim (non-winning) coalitions of some of the weaker members reduces the number of alternatives available to the strong player, and thereby reduces that player's share of the reward. Also, restrictions on communication among the players enhances the power of the strong player by making it more difficult to co-ordinate and organize the weak-union.

Power, Contributions, and Deservingness

Although I have thus far emphasized the effects of bargaining power of the 'victims' of injustice, an equally important factor in reward allocation is the consequence to the group if a given member decides to defect and seek better alternatives. Assuming that the members of a group or organization are interpreted as a coalition, suppose the defection of a given member has little effect on the outcomes for the remaining members of the group. In such cases, even if the individual has many attractive alternatives – since the defector is not making a significant contribution to group performance – the group will be indifferent towards the defection, and the individual in question will have little bargaining strength. However, if the defection of a given member will result in a serious decrement in outcomes to the group, the individual will have considerable bargaining strength in demanding a larger share of the reward.

This interpretation of bargaining strength is consistent with Emerson's (1962) hypothesis that power is the inverse of dependence. The power of a given member of a group is a function of the dependence of the group on the individual for achieving the goals of the group. This interpretation is also consistent with Shapley and Shubik's (1954) index of pivotal power. The concept of pivotal power is based on the Shapley value (1953) and assumes that an individual has power to the extent the person's addition to a coalition transforms a losing coalition into a winning coalition. The Shapley value is more general in that it does not assume that coalitions are either winning or losing, and allows for the possibility that the addition or deletion of members has differential effects on the outcomes for the group, depending on which particular member is added or subtracted. For example, if the defection of one member of a potential coalition will result in a small decrement in the pay-offs to the remaining members, while the defection of a second member will result in a large decrement, the Shapley value assumes that the second member can demand and negotiate a larger share of the reward than the first member.

Normative (prescriptive) theories, such as the Shapley value, assume that what one 'deserves' depends on: (i) what one contributes to the coalition if one joins it (or the loss to the coalition if one leaves it), and (ii) what one can obtain in alternative coalitions. Thus, a coalition situation is ideally suited to examine the effects of alternatives in bargaining, and it also provides a convenient method of studying the concept of 'deservingness' based on the contribution of each member towards group goal achievement.

THEORETICAL INTEGRATION OF POWER AND JUSICE NORMS

Since the effects of both justice norms and of power (bargaining strength) are important factors in reward allocations, it would be desirable to organize and integrate the two sets of forces into a single theoretical framework. For this purpose, one simple approach is to base justice norms exclusively on power, rather than on the concept of inputs (age, seniority, abilities, skills, and so on). According to this approach, the marketplace dictates what is fair, and whatever an individual can negotiate is fair. This approach is represented by game theoretic solutions to the general bargaining problem (e.g. those offered by such theorists as Nash, Raiffa, Shapley, and Harsanyi). In Nash's solution (1950, 1953), for example, a person's share of the reward is based on the 'disagreement' (or *status quo*) point, the outcomes of the parties if an agreement cannot be reached. Nash has shown that given a set of 'rationality' axioms (e.g. symmetry, Pareto optimality), his solution is unique and prescribes an agreement that maximizes the product of the utility increments of the bargainers. Solutions to the bargaining problem, such as those proposed by Nash, are sometimes called 'arbitration schemes' because the axioms that they are intended to satisfy can be interpreted as criteria that an arbiter would use to justify his recommended solution (Luce and Raiffa, 1957; Rapoport, 1970).

The main weakness of such arbitration schemes is that they ignore the relation between various inputs and the bargaining strength of the respective parties. This approach would be viable if there were a one-to-one correspondence between inputs and the alternatives of the parties, but in real life situations the relations between inputs and alternatives vary widely. Moreover, if the argument is made that bargaining strength, based on alternatives, is directly related to inputs, the results of a bargaining study we recently conducted (Komorita and Kravitz, 1979) suggest that Adams' equity formula is invalid. The results of our study indicate that an allocation norm based on the *differences* rather than the *ratios* of inputs and outputs is more accurate. However, since we did not manipulate inputs in our study, the assumption of a one-to-one correspondence between inputs and alternatives is questionable.

Another approach is to treat bargaining strength as one of many types of inputs and then specify a transformation rule that combines these inputs into a single measure. This approach would be consistent with Homans' and Adams' theoretical approach, but in order to derive predictions it would be necessary to specify the importance or salience of various possible inputs, as well as the function used to combine them (cf. Farkas and Anderson, 1979). One possible solution is to treat special skills and abilities as inputs, as proposed by Homans, and assign weights to these attributes as a function of three factors: (i) the importance of these attributes for group success; (ii) the scarcity of these attributes among the group members; and (iii) the cost to the group of replacing a person with such attributes who might threaten to leave. Suppose, for example, that a given attribute is critical for group goal achievement. If many members of the group possessed the attribute, the loss of one person with the attribute would not be critical. Such threats would not be very effective because the person could be easily replaced. However, if no other member possessed such attributes the bargaining power of the critical member would be considerably enhanced, especially if it would be costly to replace such a person. In this case, the group would be highly dependent on the person because there would be no alternative persons to perform this critical function; thus the more the group depends on a given person to satisfy needs, the greater the power of that person. This example illustrates why a coalition is effective in enhancing bargaining power. If there are several members who posses an important skill, the threat of any single person with the skill is not likely to be effective;

however, if all members with the skill collectively threatened to leave, it would reduce the alternatives for the group, and enhance the bargaining power of the coalition.

The above formulation also suggests that some inputs have direct consequences for group performance, and the bargaining power of a given member depends not only on personal alternatives but on the alternatives of the group. This hypothesis follows directly from my conceptualization of bargaining strength (Komorita, 1977). Other inputs, on the other hand, have very little effect (if any) on group performance. What I am suggesting here is a classification of inputs: those that are relevant in achieving the goals of the group, hereafter called task-relevant, and those that are less task-relevant. Some attributes, such as age and sex, are less task-relevant than others, and if the primary goal of the group is to maximize performance, task-relevant inputs would be assigned the greatest weight in allocating rewards. On the other hand, if tension and internal conflict is a problem, and satisfaction and group maintenance functions are perceived to be equally important, then task-irrelevant inputs might be weighted appropriately.

To illustrate this conceptualization, consider Equation (1):

$$R_i = aX_i + bY_i + c(1/N), \tag{1}$$

where R_i denotes the reward (output) of individual i, $i = 1, 2, 3, \ldots N$; X_i, and Y_i denote task-relevant and task-irrelevant inputs, respectively; a and b denote the weights assigned to these inputs; and c denotes a parameter representing the salience of the equality norm.

Equation (1) is similar to one proposed by Levanthal (1976), who restricts his weights to various types of justice rules, such as equity, equality, and the needs rule (allocation based on the needs of individual i). The basic difference between Levanthal's formulation and Equation (1) is that task-relevant and task-irrelevant inputs are distinguished. More importantly, power, based on the marketplace, is assumed to affect task-relevant weights a. Task-relevant inputs would include skills, abilities, experience, and training, and the a-parameter is based on the importance of such skills in achieving the goals of the group, the number of other members in the group who possess such skills, and the cost of replacing such persons. Task-irrelevant inputs would include sex, religion, nationality, the 'need principle', and so on. It can be seen that if $a = b = 0$, and $c = 1$, rewards would be based on the equality principle. If $b = c = 0$, rewards would be based purely on the marketplace (e.g. the Nash solution).

The Nature of the Task and Assignment of Weights

It is reasonable to assume that the optimal input weights will vary with the nature of the situation. In particular, there seem to be two related factors that have been ignored in equity research: the nature of the task and the nature of interdependence between the group members. Borrowing from Steiner's (1972) classification of tasks, it is plausible that the optimal weights may depend, at least in part, on whether the task is disjunctive, conjunctive, or additive. In a disjunctive task, group performance (success) depends primarily on the performance of the most competent member(s), while in a conjunctive task group performance is based on the performance of the least competent member(s). On an additive task, group performance is based on the sum of the performance of the individual members.

It is also reasonable to assume that judgments regarding the share of the reward each member deserves will depend on judgments regarding the contribution of each member towards success on the task. On a disjunctive task, since success is based on the most competent persons, it is plausible that the most competent persons will feel that they deserve a much larger share of the reward. However, on a conjunctive task group performance depends on all members of the group, including the least competent members; consequently, the equality norm should be more salient. Finally, an additive task should evoke judgments of deservingness that are intermediate between disjunctive and conjunctive tasks.

To complicate matters, in many real world situations there are several organizational units and successful performance within each unit may be conjunctive or disjunctive, but the ultimate success of the organization may be based on an additive function of the separate units. For example, Steiner (1976) reports a study by Gurnee (1937) in which the group task was divided into subparts such that the total task was additive but each subtask was disjunctive. Steiner interprets such a situation as an organizational problem requiring an optimal assignment of members to subtasks in which each person is most qualified to perform.

This problem of dividing a group task into subtasks and assigning members to subtasks directly leads to the problem of assigning weights to various inputs. What weight should be assigned to attributes that are critical for some subtasks when there are few members who possess such attributes? One obvious solution is to divide the task so that at least several members have the attributes to perform each subtask. In this way, no single person (or subset of persons) will have enormous power to demand a disproportionately large share of the reward, thus minimizing feelings of injustice. In most situations, unlike a football game, the rules of the 'game' can be changed so that group performance does not depend critically on any single person (the quarterback). In cases where the rules cannot be changed, or there are constraints on possible changes, it is plausible that the marketplace may lead to the optimal input weights.

A related factor that has received insufficient attention is the effect of interdependence between the members in performing the task. If we define interdependence as the degree to which group performance depends on the actions of the individual members, there is a direct relation between Steiner's classification of tasks and the degree of interdependence: the group's dependence on the least competent members is maximal on a conjunctive task and is minimal on a disjunctive task. This correspondence between interdependence and the nature of the task suggests that Adams' equity norm is most likely to be salient when there is low interdependence, while the equality norm is likely to be salient under high interdependence. This hypothesis is consistent with Mikula and Schwinger's (1978) contention that the contribution principle is more important and appropriate '. . . when the reward held in common has been achieved by the independent work of the group members without any interdependence.' (p. 236).

There are several related factors that support this hypothesis. First, under high interdependence, the group depends on everyone for success on the task, including the least competent person, resulting in pressure towards equal shares; under low interdependence, however, the group is less dependent on the less competent members, with less pressure to reward the less competent. Secondly, under high interdependence, if the least competent members are given smaller shares, they may decrease their effort on subsequent trials, resulting in a corresponding decrement in group performance; under low interdependence, however, decreased effort on the part of the less competent member would have less effect on group performance on subsequent trials. Thus, under high interdependence, the co-operative requirements of the task is maximal (cf. Shaw, 1976), and the group cannot afford to have any dissatisfied members because such members, despite their competence, can markedly affect success on the task.

It is interesting to note that equity research, based on the reward allocation paradigm, has ignored this important factor. In such studies subjects have been asked to perform a task in a coaction-type situation where each person performs the same task independently. They are given feedback on their individual performance, and based on their joint performance, they are informed that they earned a group reward that must be divided among them. Almost all studies, with a few notable exceptions (e.g. Burnstein and Katz, 1972), have used an independent rather than an interactive (interdependent) situation; this may seem paradoxical but there is a reasonable explanation for this restriction. In an interactive situation, it is very difficult to assess unambiguously the relative contribution of each person towards success on the task. Hence, in order to manipulate the inputs of each member, the performance of each person must be clearly distinguishable. But in many real-life situations, the group task cannot be divided into clearly defined independent subtasks, and it is plausible that the results of equity studies may not generalize to highly interdependent situations.

In a highly interdependent situation, the input of each member is more susceptible to perceptual distortion because the relative contribution of each member towards group success is more difficult to assess. Consequently, if some members are allocated much larger shares than others, dissatisfaction and disagreements over the reward allocation may be greater and more likely in an interdependent situation than in a coaction-type situation. In order to minimize such potential conflicts, it is plausible that the variability of rewards in a group is an inverse function of the degree of interdependence among the members. This hypothesis is consistent with my earlier hypothesis that the equality norm should be more salient in a conjunctive task than in a disjunctive task.

A related problem with the reward allocation paradigm is that the relation between inputs and success on the task is rarely specified. After subjects are given feedback about their individual performance, they are simply informed that they have succeeded and earned a given amount of reward. In the few cases where the relation was clearly specified, subjects have been informed that success on the task depends on the sum of performance of the individual member, an additive task. However, the results might be quite different if different functional relations were to be specified, and it is plausible that judgments of what each member deserves may be based on how the pattern of inputs determines success on the task, rather than on individual inputs.

As a test of this hypothesis, let me describe a study conducted by Leung (1980). Leung used a variant of the reward allocation paradigm with three-person groups, and asked each subject to perform an ambiguous dot-estimation task. Before performing the task they were informed that if their scores exceeded a certain criterion of accuracy, the group would be awarded $5.00 that would be divided among the three persons. All groups were given false feedback about their accuracy scores and informed that their scores were as follows: 71, 54, and 38, hereafter denoted as subjects A, B, and C, in descending order of their scores.

The main independent variable was the criterion of success on the task. There were five conditions (i) *Conjunctive*: all three members of the group had to exceed a score of 35 to earn the $5 prize; (ii) *Additive*: the sum of scores of the three members must exceed 140; (iii) *Disjunctive*: at least one member must exceed a score of 65; (iv) *Majority*: at least two members must exceed a score of 50; and (v) *Control*: subjects did not perform the task and were randomly assigned numbers (71, 54, 38).

All groups were informed that they had succeeded in earning the $5 prize (scores of 71, 54, and 38 met the criterion of success in all conditions). They were then asked to vote to form a two-person decision committee to allocate the $5 prize among the three members. Table 3 shows the mean allocations of the decision committees, where A/C denotes the ratio of Person A's share divided by Person C's share (an index of deviation from the equality norm). Assuming that the performance scores of 71, 54, and 38 are measures of the

PROGRESS IN APPLIED SOCIAL PSYCHOLOGY

inputs of the three members, Adams' equity theory predicts that the $5 prize should be allocated $2.18, 1.66, and 1.17 for A, B, and C, respectively. Hence, the mean values of A/C should be 2.18/1.17 = 1.86, according to the equity norm. For the equality norm, mean A/C should be 1.0.

Table 3.   Mean Reward Allocations for Players A, B and C, and Mean Values of A/C[a]

| | | Experimental conditions | | | |
	Control	Conjunct.	Additive	Disjunct.	Majority
A	1.72_p	1.79_p	1.89_p	1.98	2.01_e
B	1.56	1.70	1.66	1.60	1.68
C	1.72_p	1.51_p	1.45_p	1.42	1.31_e
A/C	1.002_p	1.253_p	1.356_{ep}	1.871	1.691_e

[a] Subscripts e and p denote that the mean deviates significantly from the equality norm and from the equity norm (proportionality), respectively. The means for the disjunctive condition did not differ significantly because of the extremely large variability and skewness of the distribution.

As hypothesized, Table 3 shows that the control and conjunctive conditions yielded values of A/C that are closest to equality (1.0); the disjunctive and majority conditions yielded values closest to equity (1.86); and the additive condition was intermediate. The subscripts e and p denote that a given mean deviates significantly from the equality norm and from the equity norm (proportional to inputs), respectively. Thus these results provide partial support for our hypothesis that allocations, based on inputs, depend in part on the nature of the relation between inputs and success on the task.

These results also suggest some intriguing questions for future research. First, we do not know what indiviudal members would have allocated if each person had been given the power to do so. Secondly, the allocations were based on a two-person (majority) committee who negotiated the allocation, and it would be desirable to compare such allocations with a situation in which all three members negotiated the allocation. Third, success on the task was all-or-none and all groups were led to believe that they had succeeded in earning a constant prize. In many real life situations, however, reward magnitude may vary, depending on the pattern of individual performances on the task, and we have very little information about the effects of changes in reward magnitude on changes in reward allocation (cf. studies by Burnstein and Katz, 1972).

Finally, with regard to possible implications for social policy, this conceptualization suggests that the salience of the equity norm (task-relevant inputs), in contrast to norms based on equality and needs (task-irrelevant inputs), may be a function of the clarity and reliability of such inputs, and the degree of correspondence between individual inputs and success on the task. To the extent that this hypothesis is valid, if those in authority to make the allocation wish to emphasize group performance, the relation between individual inputs and group performance should be specified clearly. If some members are to be allocated larger shares than others, their inputs and contributions to group goal achievement should be communicated to all members of the group, so as to justify their larger share. It is plausible that such a procedure may not only motivate members to increase their inputs but may minimize feelings of injustice.

SOME CONCLUDING COMMENTS

My description of the role of power and justice in reward allocation suggests that the optimal distribution of rewards in a group depends on many factors. Theory and research on justice norms, on the one hand, have not paid sufficient attention to the effects of power, while theory and research on bargaining, on the other hand, have not adequately incorporated the effects of justice norms. Thus the search for an optimal policy of reward distribution must include both types of factors in the allocation scheme.

Some theorists (Deutsch, 1975; Mikula, 1978) have implied that co-operatively oriented groups are more likely to weight equity (contributions) more heavily than competitively oriented groups. Deutsch (1975), in particular, suggests that if productivity is the primary goal of the group, equity rather than equality or needs will be the primary rule of distributive justice. As an extension of this hypothesis, it is plausible that if maximizing group performance is the primary goal of the group, power should be weighted more heavily than justice norms. But there is a danger of weighting power too heavily: the competitive tendencies of the group may be heightened, and depending on the co-operative requirements of the task, group performance may suffer. Moreover, as I described earlier, if power is weighted too heavily, those who are weak are likely to form a coalition (the weak-union) so as to strengthen their bargaining power. Indeed, attempts may be made to change the decision-making structure of the group so as to change the weights. As in many industrialized societies, when the weak-union becomes formalized, reward allocation is likely to be based on collective bargaining, and the problem is to resolve conflict constructively rather than through strikes and lockouts.

These observations suggest that valuable insights may be gained by examining the processes of collective bargaining. In particular, an extremely important problem is the effects of third-party intervention and the conditions under which the parties (union, management) are likely to accept solutions offered by third parties. When individual citizens are involved in disputes, laws require conflict resolution through the courts, for example, in a divorce case involving the distribution of the couple's assets, a judge serves as an arbitrator and prescribes a property settlement. When a business firm is involved in a dispute with another firm, the dispute is settled through arbitration by a judge or jury.

By similar reasoning, it is not unreasonable to require arbitration of union-management disputes before a costly strike, lockout, or other destructive acts are implemented. But arbitration involves a process of weighting justice and power of the disputants and recommending a solution based on such weights. Thus, theory and research on reward allocation, based on both laboratory and field studies, may provide valuable information regarding social policy decisions. In a larger context, however, it is obvious that criteria other than maximizing group performance and maximizing satisfaction of group members must be considered, and the social welfare of the society as a whole must also be weighted.

NOTE

1. The preparation of this report was supported in part by a research grant from the National Science Foundation (BNS 79-11103). Portions of this report were presented at a conference on 'Social Psychology and Social Policy', University of Kent, Canterbury, England.

REFERENCES

Adams, J.S. (1963). Toward an understanding of inequity, *Journal of Abnormal and Social Psychology*, **67**, 422–436.
Adams, J.S. (1965). Inequity in social exchange, in L. Berkowitz (ed.), *Advances in Experimental Social Psychology*, Vol. 2, New York: Academic Press.
Bales, R.F. (1950). *Interaction Process Analysis: A Method for the Study of Small Groups*, Cambridge, Mass.: Addison-Wesley.
Bales, R.F. (1953). The equilibrium problem in small groups, in T. Parsons, R.F. Bales, and E.A. Shils (eds), *Working Papers in the Theory of Action*, New York: Free Press.
Burnstein, E. and Katz, S. (1972). Group decisions involving equitable and optimal distribution of status, in C.G. McClintock (ed.), *Experimental Social Psychology*, New York: Holt, Rinehart & Winston.
Deutsch, M. (1975). Equity, equality, and need: What determines which value will be used as the basis of distributive justice? *Journal of Social Issues*, **31**, 137–150.
Emerson, R.M. (1962). Power-dependence relations, *American Sociological Review*, **27**, 31–41.
Farkas, A.J. and Anderson, N.H. (1979). Multidimensional input in equity theory, *Journal of Personality and Social Psychology*, **37**, 879–896.
Fiedler, F.E. (1967). A theory of leadership effectiveness, New York: McGraw-Hill.
Gamson, W.A. (1961a). An experimental test of a theory of coalition formation, *American Sociological Review*, **26**, 565–573.
Gamson, W.A. (1961b). A theory of coalition formation, *American Sociological Review*, **26**, 373–382.
Gurnee, H. (1937). Maze learning in the collective situation, *Journal of Psychology*, **3**, 437–443.
Homans, G.C. (1961). *Social Behavior: Its Elementary Forms*, New York: Harcourt, Brace, & World.
Kelley, H.H. and Arrowood, A.J. (1960). Coalitions in the triad: Critique and experiment, *Sociometry*, **23**, 231–244.
Komorita, S.S. (1974). A weighted probability model of coalition formation, *Psychological Review*, **81**, 242–256.

Komorita, S.S. (1977). Negotiating from strength and the concept of bargaining strength, *Journal for the Theory of Social Behavior*, **7**, 65–79.
Komorita, S.S. and Esser, J.K. (1975). Frequency of reciprocated concessions in bargaining, *Journal of Personality and Social Psychology*, **32**, 699–705.
Komorita, S.S. and Chertkoff, J.M. (1973). A bargaining theory of coalition formation, *Psychological Review*, **80**, 149–162.
Komorita, S.S. and Kravitz, D. (1979). The effects of alternatives in bargaining, *Journal of Experimental Social Psychology*, **15**, 147–157.
Komorita, S.S. and Meek, D. (1978). The generality and validity of some theories of coalition formation, *Journal of Personality and Social Psychology*, **36**, 392–404.
Komorita, S.S. and Moore, D. (1976). Theories and processes of coalition formation, *Journal of Personality and Social Psychology*, **33**, 371–381.
Komorita, S.S. and Tumonis, T. (1980). Extensions and tests of some theories of coalition formation, *Journal of Personality and Social Psychology*, **39**, 256–268.
Leung, A.S. (1980). Effects of task requirements on equity and coalition formation. Honours thesis, University of Illinois (unpublished).
Leventhal, G.S. (1976). Fairness in social relations, in J. Thibaut, J. Spence, and R. Carsons (eds), *Contemporary Topics in Social Psychology*, Morristown, New Jersey: General Learning Press.
Levanthal, G.S. and Bergman, J.T. (1969). Self-depriving behavior as a response to unprofitable inequity, *Journal of Experimental Social Psychology*, **5**, 153–171.
Leventhal, G.S. and Michaels, J.W. (1969). Extending the equity model: Perception of inputs and allocation of reward as a function of duration and quantity of performance, *Journal of Personality and Social Psychology*, **12**, 303–309.
Luce, R.D. and Raiffa, H. (1957). *Games and Decisions*, New York: Wiley.
McClintock, C.G. (in press). Equity and social exchange, in J. Greenberg and L. Cohen (eds), *Equity and Justice in Social Behavior*, New York: Academic Press.
Mikula, G. (1980). The role of justice in allocation decisions, in G. Mikula (ed.), *Justice and Social Interaction*, Berne: Huber.
Mikula, G. and Schwinger, T. (1978). Intermember relations and reward allocation: Theoretical considerations of affects, in H. Brandstatter, J.H. Davis, and H. Schuler (eds), *Dynamics of Group Decisions*, Beverly Hills, Cal: Sage.
Miller, C.E. (1979). Coalition formation in triads with single-peaked payoff curves, *Behavioral Science*, **24**, 75–84.
Morgan, W.R., and Sawyer, J. (1967). Bargaining, expectations, and the preference for equality over equity, *Journal of Personality and Social Psychology*, **6**, 139–149.
Morley, I.E. (1978). Bargaining and negotiation: The character of experimental studies, in H. Brandstatter, J.H. Davis, and H. Schuler (eds), *Dynamics of Group Decisions*, Beverly Hills, Cal: Sage.
Morley, I.E. & Stephenson, G.M. (1977), *The Social Psychology of Bargaining* London: Allen and Unwin.
Murnighan, J.K. and Roth, A.E. (1977). The effects of communication and information availability in an experimental study of a three-person game, *Management Science*, **23**, 1336–48.
Nash, J.F. (1950). The bargaining problem, *Econometrica*, **18**, 155–162.
Nash, J.F. (1953). Two-person cooperative games, *Econometrica*, **21**, 128–140.
Pruitt, D.G. (1972). Methods for resolving differences of interest: A theoretical analysis, *Journal of Social Issues*, **28**, 133–154.
Rapoport, An. (1970). *N-Person Game Theory*, Ann Arbor: University of Michigan Press.
Shapley, L.S. (1953). A value for n-person games in H.W. Kuhn and A.W. Tucker (eds), *Contributions to the Theory of Games*, Princeton: Princeton University Press.

Shapley, L.S. and Shubik, M. (1954). A method for evaluating the distribution of power in a committe system, *American Political Science Review*, **48** 787–92.

Shaw, M.E. (1976). *Group Dynamics: The Psychology of Small Group Behavior*, New York: McGraw-Hill.

Steiner, I.D. (1972). *Group Process and Productivity*, New York: Academic Press.

Steiner, I.D. (1976). Task-performing groups, in J. Thibaut, J. Spence, and R. Carsons (eds), *Contemporary Topics in Social Psychology*, Morristown, New Jersey: General Learning Press.

Thibaut, J. (1968). The development of contractual norms in bargaining: Replication and variation, *Journal of Conflict Resolution*, **12**, 102–112.

Thibaut, J. and Faucheux, C. (1965). The development of contractual norms in a bargaining situation under two types of stress, *Journal of Experimental Social Psychology*, **1**, 89–102.

Thibaut, J. and Kelley, H.H. (1954). *The Social Psychology of Groups*, New York: Wiley.

Walster, E., Berscheid, E., and Walster, G.W. (1973). New directions in equity research, *Journal of Personality and Social Psychology*, **25**, 151–176.

Progress in Applied Social Psychology, Volume 2
Edited by G.M. Stephenson and J.H. Davis
© 1984 John Wiley & Sons Ltd

8

Environmental Uncertainty, Power, and Effectiveness in Laboratory Organizations

J.M. Rabbie and J. van Oostrum
Institute of Social Psychology
University of Utrecht, The Netherlands

INTRODUCTION

One of the major themes of modern organization theory has been that organizational structures and processes are affected by the various contingencies the organization has to cope with, including the uncertainty of the environment, the type of technology it uses, the scale and size of its operations, and the kind of people it employs (Child, 1976). The idea that organizational structures and processes depend or are contingent upon the requirements the organization faces, lies at the heart of various contingency-theory approaches (Lawrence and Lorsch, 1967).

The basic assumption of the contingency-theory approaches is that there is 'no one best way of organizing', but that some structural arrangements are more appropriate than others in enabling the organization to survive or at least to be more effective than others in a uncertain, competitive environment. Despite their popularity, the contingency approaches have been severely criticized on various conceptual and methodological grounds. In an effort to deal with some of these criticisms, two laboratory experiments were conducted, designed to study the impact of variations in environmental uncertainty on the power structure and effectiveness of our laboratory organization.

In the first section of the chapter there will be a general discussion about the contingency approach in the organizational literature. Two major models will be contrasted with each other, and the basic assumptions, concepts, empirical evidence, and current research methodology will be critically evaluated.

Next, specific hypotheses are developed about the effects of variations in environmental uncertainty on the total amount of control, hierarchization of perceived power, and organizational effectiveness. The question is raised to what extent these structural power variables contribute significantly to the subjective and objective indices of organizational effectiveness. These hypotheses are partly derived from the control graph theory of Tannenbaum (1968) and Tannenbaum and Cooke (1979). For this reason the control graph theory will be discussed in some detail.

These hypotheses are tested in two laboratory experiments, the results of which will be reported in the last section of this chapter. In conclusion there will be a short discussion of some of the implications of these findings for future work in this area.

CONTINGENCY APPROACHES IN ORGANIZATIONAL THEORY

Most of the structural-contingency models (Pennings, 1975) consist of two related propositions: (i) the environment-structure hypothesis, relating the environmental and/or technological demands to the structure of the organization, and (ii) the congruence hypothesis that relates the degree of congruence or fit between the organizational structure and its environment to organizational effectiveness. The environment-structure hypothesis assumes that the uncertainty due to a turbulent, unstable, and dynamic environment (Duncan, 1972) or to a non-routinous and unpredictable technology (Perrow, 1970) is associated with a more 'organic' rather than with a more 'mechanistic' or bureaucratic management system. The congruence hypothesis assumes that the greater the congruence or fit between the environment and/or technology on the one hand and the organic or mechanistic management system on the other hand, the more effective the organization will be.

Theorists differ in their conception how the congruence between the organization and its environment is achieved: whether they give greater weight to the environment or to the organization in selecting the most appropriate structures. This difference in conception depends in part how they view the environment. Aldrich and Mindlin (1978) suggest that there have been two major perspectives on how organizations relate to the environment. *The information-approach* treats the environment primarily as a source of information and focuses on the degree of uncertainty in the environment (Dill, 1958; Lawrence and Lorsch, 1969; Duncan, 1972). The second approach views the environment mainly as a *source of (scarce) resources* for which populations of organizations have to compete (Aldrich and Pfeffer, 1976; Pfeffer and Salancik, 1978).

The main concern of the *information-processing* approach is how individual decision-makers in groups, departments, or organizations perceive, filter, and interpret the flow of information that emanates from the environment. The question is how structure and processes are designed to enable them to cope effectively with the perceived uncertainty. In this context uncertainty is sometimes defined as: 'a lack of information about future events, so that alternatives and outcomes are unpredictable' (Hickson *et al.*, 1971, p. 219).

The main concern of the *resource-dependence* approach is how decision-makers try to minimize their dependence on other organizations, for example by making others depend on them (Aldrich, 1979). The basic objective is to gain sufficient control over the strategic resources on which their survival, growth, and effectiveness depend. It has been noted that the resource approach more or less ignores the process by which information about the environment is apprehended by decision-makers (Aldrich and Pfeffer, 1976, p. 92). The resource approach tends to emphasize the 'objective' characteristics of the environment. Environmental dimensions such as resourcefulness, hetero-geneity, complexity, stability, and turbulence are characterized in terms of the resources they make available to the organization (Aldrich, 1979, pp. 63–70).

Advocates of the information and resource approaches also tend to use different selection models to explain how the congruence or fit between the environment and the organization is achieved. Aldrich (1979, p. 107) has described two ideal typical selection models: the rational selection or learning model and a natural selection or population ecology model. When the environ-ment is viewed as a source of scarce resources, those organizations are selected, according to the natural selection model, that are superior in acquiring the necessary resources over others who fail to match the environmental require-ments. In this view it is the environment, not the organization, that selects the most appropriate structures. Particular units, that is individuals, groups, or organizations, play only a minor role in achieving the fit. According to Aldrich (1979, p. 107). ' . . . the environment selects the most fit organizations and individual units are relatively powerless to affect the process'.

The information approach tends to lean towards the rational selection model. In this model, learning, planned variation, and rational choices are emphasized, although it is recognized that there are severe limits to cognitive rationality and that decision-makers strive for 'satisficing' rather than for 'optimal' solutions for their problems (March and Simon, 1958). In view of these differences in perspective, it is striking that the research stimulated by the information and resource approaches has come to very similar conclusions concerning how the environment affects the structures and processes in the organization. Whether they stress dependence or uncertainty, both agree that a high degree of dependence or uncertainty tends to be associated with more organic management systems as characterized by Burns and Stalker (1961), and Aldrich (1979, pp. 122–124).

This agreement between the two approaches becomes understandable when it is recognized that the reduction of environmental uncertainty is often aimed at acquiring the critical resources for the organization. The experiments to be reported in this chapter try to construct organizations in the laboratory that have to reduce the uncertainty in the environment in such a way that it enables them to attain the resources necessary for gaining an acceptable level of effectiveness.

Empirical Evidence

The empirical evidence for the contingency-theory approach is weak and conflicting (Hazewinkel, 1980, p. 13). Some investigators find positive evidence (e.g. Perrow, 1967; Lawrence and Lorsch, 1967, 1969; Hinings et al., 1974; Khandwhalla, 1973; Blau et al., 1976; Neganda and Reimann, 1973). Others obtain mainly negative evidence (e.g. Mohr, 1971; Pennings, 1975), while a third group of researchers qualify the hypothesis by noting that the predicted relationships between the contextual and structural variables are obtained or enhanced only under rather specific conditions, such as whether organizations find themselves in a very competitive environment (DuBick, 1978); whether the perceived uncertainty of the relevant subenvironments of the functional departments rather than the total environment of the organization is taken into account (Sullivan, 1977); whether only those respondents are questioned who are highly involved in the 'boundary-spanning activities of the organization', that is members who are responsible for the information-processing task at the boundary of the organization (Leifer and Huber, 1977).

It has also been argued that often no relationship is found between uncertainty and structure because the relationship between these two variables may be curvilinear rather than linear as is often assumed (Reimann, 1974). Rabbie et al., (1976) have suggested that there might be a positive relationship between the perceived environmental uncertainty and more organic structures when the environment is seen as moderately uncertain but still manageable. As soon as the environment is perceived as highly uncertain and difficult to control crisis-like conditions may develop, especially when vital issues are at stake (Mulder et al., 1970, p. 433). Under these conditions centralized structures may be more appropriate than less hierarchical methods of co-ordination and information-sharing (Mulder and Stemerding, 1963; Rabbie and Wilkens, 1971; Bourgeois et al., 1978). This argument could imply that a positive relationship between contextual and structural variables will only be obtained within 'normal' ranges of environmental uncertainty, although it is difficult to specify beforehand what these 'normal' ranges may be. Contingency theories in other areas are fraught with the same kind of problems (Fiedler, 1978; Korman, 1973).

Conceptual and Methodological Problems

The structural-contingency model has been criticized on conceptual and methodological grounds. Central concepts such as environment, technology uncertainty, structure, and effectiveness are multi-dimensional concepts that are often represented by categories or clusters of variables. Very often these concepts are operationalized in many different ways that make it very difficult to compare them from one study to another (Veen, 1980a). Sometimes a relationship between such variables as structure and technology is inferred because researchers tend to overlook the area of overlap between the clusters of dimensions and indices that are used to represent these variables. In that case it is more appropriate to draw conclusions only in terms of specific variables instead of inferring a relationship between general categories or clusters of variables (Stanfield, 1976, p. 491). Therefore in the experiments to be reported we have tried to delineate the relevant variables as clearly as possible from one another.

According to Pennings (1975) there is a great deal of conceptual confusion between environment and technology. He defines environment as '. . . the organization's source of inputs and sink of outputs' and technology as '. . . internal operations of the organization; that, is the means that the organization uses to convert inputs into outputs' (Pennings, 1975, pp. 393–394). In his view the confusion between environment and technology can be explained by the concept of uncertainty: the inability to predict future events. Penning asserts that the environment can be described in many different ways: for example in terms of stability, complexity, resourcefulness, and competitiveness, but in his opinion all these variables are characterized by uncertainty. In his view technology, too, is commonly defined in terms of uncertainty since technology may also lead to certain or uncertain outcomes (Perrow, 1967, 1972; Hunt, 1970; Mohr, 1971; Hage and Aiken, 1969).

In view of this conceptual confusion between environment and technology and to disentangle the effects of these variables on structure and effectiveness, it is necessary to manipulate the degree of environmental uncertainty independent from the kind of technology the organization is using. In the laboratory studies to be reported in this chapter we have attempted to achieve this objective.

Whether investigators focus on the external uncertainty generated by the environment or the internal uncertainty due to technology, all agree that uncertainty, complexity, and heterogenity of inputs are related to a lower degree of centralization and a de-emphasis of rules and procedures (Pennings, 1975, p. 375).

The results of the research about the structural-contingency model are also unsatisfactory because of methodological shortcomings. Pennings has pointed out that studies relying on subjective data (questionnaires or interviews) to assess the uncertainty of the environment have obtained stronger evidence for the notion that environmental variables have structural correlates (Lawrence and Lorsch, 1967; Duncan, 1972; Pfeffer and Leblebici, 1973) than studies that employ more objective data, such as company records. Moreover, the measures of perceived environmental uncertainty developed by Lawrence and Lorsch (1967) and Duncan (1971) have been sharply criticized (Tosi *et al.*, 1973; Downey, *et al.*, 1975; Rabbie *et al.*, 1976). The reliability and internal consistency of the subscales, especially of the Lawrence and Lorsch scales, appear to be very low. More important, there is a lack of significant association between these subjective and the more 'objective' indices of the environment that are supposed to relate to environmental uncertainties. If one wants to assess the effect of the 'objective' or 'subjective' uncertainty on organizational structure and effectiveness it is necessary to manipulate the 'objective' environmental uncertainty independent from the members' perceptions about it. That is what we have tried to do in our experiments.

Perhaps one of the most critical problems with the research stimulated by the structural-contingency approach is that it is very difficult to make causal inferences about the organization-environment relationships. Most research in the contingency tradition has used cross-sectional and correlational data that do not allow a specification of the causal direction of these relationships Although it has often been hypothesized that environmental uncertainty leads to more organic management structures, it has also been argued that 'complex and contingent structures simply perceive more of the uncertainty in the environment' (Aldrich and Pfeffer, 1976, p. 92). In fact it has been found that changes in structure led to changes in perceived environmental uncertainty (Huber et al., 1975). Child (1977) has pointed out that the discovery of a simple correlation between organizational design and level of performance does not convincingly demonstrate that organizational structure is a causal factor: '. . . in addition to the possible effect the organization has on performance, the performance achieved constitutes a vital feedback of information to managers which may stimulate them to make adjustments to structure' (Child, 1977, p. 165). Indeed Bourgeois et al. (1978) have obtained some empirical evidence in management exercises for the notion that managers confronted with a very poor performance react by 'pulling in the reins', leading to a tighter and more centralized management structure.

In an effort to gain more insight into the causal relationships between the uncertainty of the environment, organizational structure, and the level of effectiveness, two laboratory studies were conducted in which an attempt was made to investigate the effects of the manipulated or 'objective' and 'perceived' environmental uncertainty on the emergence of a differentiated structure, particularly on the hierarchization and total amount of perceived power in the organization. These structural variables are derived from the control graph theory of Tannenbaum (1968; Tannenbaum and Cooke, 1979). Moreover, we were interested in the question to what extent these structural variables contributed significantly to the subjective and objective indices of organizational effectiveness.

Laboratory Groups and Complex Organizations

Individuals, groups, and organizations can be considered as open goal-directed systems that have to cope with the uncertainties in the environment in order to acquire the resources necessary for their survival and/or relative effectiveness. Groups differ from organizations in their orientation towards specific goals, size, complexity, and often in the duration of their existence and interchangeability of membership. Organizations can be viewed as intergroup systems (Horwitz and Rabbie, 1982), or as a 'group of groups' (Simon, 1957). Because of the size and complexity of the organization, differentiation and integration are achieved through formalized role prescriptions and hierarchical control and decision structures (Veen and Van Haren, 1980, p. 98). To Katz and Kahn (1978, p. 242): 'The essential difference between social organizations and less structured social systems is the greater reliance on formal prescriptions of acceptable versus unacceptable behavior in the organization.' It is assumed that in spite of these differences in size, complexity, and degree of formalization small groups and large organizations are both open social systems and can therefore be described by means of the same general principles (Berrien, 1968). Whether this assumption is correct or not is an empirical issue.

In the first experiment we were interested in what kind of power or influence structures would emerge as a function of the variation in environmental uncertainty the organization has to cope with and how these influence structures would affect the level of effectiveness of our laboratory organization. In this experiment there were three conditions of environmental uncertainty: highly uncertain (HU), increasingly certain (IC) and highly certain (HC). It was left to the members of our three-man laboratory organization how they would organize themselves for work when they were confronted with these three types of environmental uncertainty.

The second experiment can be considered as a partial replication of the first. Instead of three, two conditions of environmental uncertainty were manipulated: a highly uncertain (HU), and an increasingly certain (IC) condition. The environmental uncertainty variable was crossed with a second variable: the degree of formalization which consisted of specific 'organizational features' such as formalized role prescriptions, and hierarchical control and decision structures. We are interested in the combined effects of these variables on the degree of participation in the decision-making process, on the attribution of influence of the members to themselves and others, and on the effectiveness of the organization.

This chapter is based on data collected in earlier studies by Hemmer (1972), Vreugdenhil (1972) and Van Oostrum (1973). These studies were stimulated by the contingency theory of Lawrence and Lorsch (1969) and included their measures of differentiation such as the interpersonal orientation of the members as measured by the LPC-scale of Fiedler (1978), the goal-orientation of the members, and the degree of task-specialization. In this report we limit ourselves to a discussion of the data that seem most relevant to the control graph theory of Tannenbaum (1968) and Tannenbaum and Cooke (1979). A more detailed report of the method and results of the two experiments is presented in the original studies and in more recent articles by Rabbie, Van

Oostrum and Hemmer (1983) and Rabbie, Van Oostrum, and Vreugdenhil (1983).

UNCERTAINTY AND INTRAORGANIZATIONAL POWER

Environmental Uncertainty and the Total Amount of Perceived Power

In his control graph theory Tannenbaum is concerned about the distribution and total amount of perceived power in the organization. In his research, the degree of perceived control, power, or influence – he uses these terms interchangeably (1968, p. 5) – is measured by asking the respondents in the various hierarchical echelons: 'how much say or influence' each group, including one's own, has on 'what is going on in the organization'. The perceived influence of each level is computed through an averaging procedure with a horizontal axis representing the hierarchical scale of the organization and the vertical axis representing the amount of power or social influence perceived by the respondents belonging to each of the hierarchical levels. The resulting control graph usually has a negative slope, indicating that more influence is attributed to the higher levels than to the lower ones. The more negative the slope the higher the degree of hierarchization of perceived power. Since a slope may vary over a graph (Jennergen, 1981, p. 40) an average slope is used (Tannenbaum, 1968, pp. 174–201). Alternatively, the difference in attributed influence between the highest and lowest level has been used as an indicator of the degree of hierarchization in complex organizations as well as in small groups (Pennings, 1976, p. 692; Rabbie *et al.*, 292; Rabbie and Wilkens, 1971, p. 226). The height of the curve, or more precisely the area under it, represents the total amount of perceived power, influence, or control.

Despite the many criticisms that have been raised against the control graph method (Levine, 1973; Gundelach and Tetzschner, 1976; Rabbie and Van Oostrum, 1981) the major advantage of this technique is that it permits a description of groups and organizations at a system level and not at the level of the individual. Whether one studies small groups in the laboratory or highly complex organizations, the two social systems can be described by means of the same two power dimensions: the hierarchization and the total amount of perceived power. Tannenbaum (1968, p. 5) believes that these two dimensions of power may vary independently from each other. He questions the assumption of the traditional management theories that there is a 'fixed influence pie' in groups and organizations in which more influence for one group or individual will always imply less influence for another. For him control or power is not a zero-sum concept in which one individual or group wins at the cost of another, but the 'influence pie' is expandable so that all members in an organization or group can 'win'. Tannenbaum's notion of an influence pie of expandable proportions depends on the assumption whether the people in an organization emphasize a communality of interests or a conflict of interests. In the first case we deal with persuasive processes, in the latter with an outright power struggle (Katz and Kahn, 1978, p. 322; Rabbie and Van Oostrum, 1981). Tannenbaum's view of conflict-free organizations contrasts sharply with the ideas of Pfeffer (1978) who stresses the importance of power politics in the organization.

Uncertainty and Total Amount of Power

Most of the research of Tannenbaum and his associates has focused on the importance of *internal* structural and motivational factors. Much less attention has been paid to the impact of the *external* environment on the 'expansion of power' and control in the organization, the issue we are most interested in. According to Tannenbaum (1968, pp. 14–18) the expansion of the total amount of control or power in the organization can be viewed as a result of exchange processes as discussed by Blau (1964) and Homans (1961) for example. The exercise of control is seen as an exchange of some valued resource dispensed by one person in return for compliance on the part of the other: 'the total amount of control or power in a system may therefore be seen as a function of the amount of exchange involving compliance' (Tannenbaum, 1968, p. 15).

Allport (1933) has suggested that only segments of people's needs and behaviour are included in the organization. Members are only 'partially included'. According to Tannenbaum mutual influence processes and participation in a decision-making process include the person more fully in the organization. Tannenbaum (1968, p. 16) views this greater inclusion as an example of the expansion of the organization into its environment: 'because the newly included segments were heretofore outside the organization'. It should be noted that even in this case internal rather than external factors are emphasized as possible determinants of the total amount of control in the organization.

Finally the total amount of control makes organizational behaviour more orderly and predictable. Tannenbaum assumes, in line with general systems theory, that every living system tends towards disorder and entropy. The total amount of control is one of the means to negate this entropic tendency. In Tannenbaum's view the greater the total amount of control, the smaller the degree of random and unpredictable behaviour and the higher the negative entropy (cf. Pennings, 1976, p. 689).

Although Tannenbaum generally emphasizes the importance of the internal structure and motivational factors leading to an increase in the total amount of influence in the organization, there are a few places in his work in which he also discusses the possible impact of 'external' factors such as environmental uncertainty on the distribution and the total amount of control in the organization (Tannenbaum and Georgeopoulos, 1957 – reprinted in Tannenbaum, 1968, p. 54 and Tannenbaum and Cooke, 1979, p. 195). In his most recent statement he writes:

decision units may need to react participatively with substantial input from lower level-members, when responding to non-routine decision situations, but may have to apply hierarchical and non-participative procedures for dealing efficiently with routine matters. *A high amount of control would be expected in effective organizational sub-units not only as a result of the participative procedures used for non-routine decision-making but also as a result of the control maintained at upper levels for routine decision-making.* (emphasis added)

If it is assumed that the uncertainty associated with non-routinous decision-making can be equated with the uncertainty generated by complex and unpredictable environments (Pennings, 1975), one implication of Tannenbaum's version of the structural-contingency model could be that the greater the environmental uncertainty the greater the amount of total perceived influence or power in the organization. The idea is that the complexity and unreliability of the environment requires a greater amount of participation in the decision-making process to deal with the environmental uncertainty and as a consequence of these mutual influence processes within and between levels a greater amount of total control is generated and perceived. In Tannenbaum's view a greater environmental uncertainty is positively associated with a greater participativeness and hence with a high level of total amount of perceived power. It should be noted, however, that Tannenbaum's hypothesis holds only for 'effective organizational subunits'. If these 'subunits' are incapable of coping with the environmental uncertainty effectively – for example, because the environment is too uncertain or the members are lacking sufficient expertise to reduce the uncertainty effectively – a very high environmental uncertainty will probably lead to a lower level of total perceived power in the group or organization rather than a high level of perceived power as Tannenbaum seems to assume. If this reasoning is correct two hypotheses can be formulated:

(H1) The greater the uncertainty of the *external* environment – and the lower the effectiveness of the members of the organization to cope with it – the lower the amount of perceived power in the organization.

(H2) The greater the increase in effectiveness in coping with the uncertainty in the *external* environment over time the greater the increase in the perceived power in the organization.

There is some question in the literature whether it is the 'objective' or 'perceived' environmental uncertainty that affects the social structure of the organization (Aldrich and Pfeffer, 1976, p. 92). As we have noted before, part of the problem has been that the correlations between the 'objective' and 'subjective' indices of environmental uncertainty are rather low and often insignificant (Tosi *et al.*, 1973; Downey *et al.*, 1975; Pennings, 1975). These low correlations between the objective and perceived indices of uncertainty can be partly attributed to the fact that complex organizations are segmentized in many different ways. Each segment has to cope with various uncertainties that differ in degree and relevance from those that are faced by other segments (Friedlander and Pickle, 1968; Lawrence and Lorsch, 1969; Duncan, 1972). In our experiments the manipulated environmental uncertainty is much more simple and can be measured in more reliable ways. We are therefore able to assess more easily than in field studies the effects of the 'objective' and 'perceived' uncertainty on the structure and effectiveness of the organization.

External and Internal Uncertainty

Until now we have focused on the effects of the *external* environment on intraorganizational power. However, in the organizational literature a distinction is made between the external and internal environment of a system. Rice (1963) defines the internal environment in terms of the interpersonal relations of the members with each other while the external environment refers to other individuals, groups, and institutions. Duncan (1972, p. 314) offers a more comprehensive definition. In his view not only social factors, but also physical factors within and outside the boundary of the organization are relevant for the decision-making behaviour of individual units within the system. The unpredictability of other people within and outside the system is perhaps one of the most important sources of uncertainty the organization has to deal with (Thompson, 1968, p. 99). Indeed, according to Kahn and Katz (1978, p. 41) the core problem of any social system can be defined as 'reducing the variability and instability of human action'. This reduction and control is brought about by environmental pressures, shared values, expectations, and rule reinforcements. It is rather obvious that there will be a high degree of internal uncertainty in complex organizations, but even in laboratory groups a great deal of internal uncertainty has to be reduced in order to allow the members to work effectively on the experimental tasks. In such 'laboratory organizations' subjects are randomly assigned to conditions and they have no prior experience with one another. Prior to the entrance in the group, shared expectations and values among the members regarding the specific task they are faced with could not develop. Subjects may have a variety of motives and goals to participate in experiments that might be quite different from the major goals imposed on them by the experimenter. Apart from the goals directly related to their participation in an experiment, such as getting money for their efforts, learning about social-psychological experiments, adhering to the implicit contract between the subjects and the experimenter to participate in the study, how to approach the experimental tasks and so on, subjects might also have more personal concerns: how they will be evaluated by the experimenter and their fellow subjects, how they should present themselves to others, how much say or influence they would like to have in this situation, whether people like them or not, etc.

The internal uncertainties generated by these initial differences in motives, goals, expectations, and behaviour should be reduced to a level that allows members to act in an orderly co-ordinated fashion and to behave in accordance with the demands of the experimenter. Through processes of social comparison (e.g. Festinger, 1954; Rabbie, 1963) and attribution (e.g. Kelley and Michela, 1980; Veen and Van Haren, 1980) a social reality is constructed (Berger and Luckman, 1967) and interpersonally negotiated (Day and Day, 1977) that is sufficiently shared and orderly to enable the members to work together on the organizational tasks. As people have more experience with one another, the uncertainty of the internal environment will be reduced and hence will become more orderly and predictable than before. Since an increase in certainty leads to a greater sense of control over the (internal) environment, it is to be expected that the total amount of perceived power will be greater at the end than at the beginning of the experiment. Earlier experimental studies support this proposition (Visser and Groot, 1970; Visser, 1973; Rabbie and Visser, 1976).

(H3) It is predicted that the greater the effectiveness in reducing the uncertainty of the *internal* environment the greater the perceived power in the organization.

Obviously – from an open system perspective – the *internal* uncertainty generated by the internal environment will be affected by the instability and variability of the *external* environment. When the external environment remains highly unpredictable over time stable patterns of behaviour cannot be developed and as a consequence the internal uncertainty will remain at a very high level.

(H4) It is expected that there will be an increase in the total amount of perceived power when the external environment becomes more predictable over time, but a decrease of the total amount of perceived power when the uncertainty of the external environment remains at a very high level despite the efforts of the members to reduce it.

Uncertainty and Hierarchization

According to Tannenbaum there is a universal tendency towards hierarchical control even in organizations in which the members are strongly committed to a participative and democratic ideology as exemplified by industrial organizations in Israeli *kibbutzim* and in 'socialist' countries such as Yugoslavia and Hungary (Tannenbaum and Cooke, 1979, p. 185). From this point of view it is expected that there will be a significant degree of hierarchization or negative slope in our laboratory organization regardless of the uncertainty of the environment the members are faced with. A hierarchical structure will emerge even in 'leaderless' groups on which no structure is imposed and which consist of members who are known to have very strong egalitarian values (Rabbie *et al.*, 1974). In earlier experiments this hypothesis received strong support (Rabbie and Van Oostrum, 1981).

The structural-contingency model, including the contingency hypothesis formulated by Tannenbaum and Cooke (1979), assumes that hierarchical methods of communication and control are more efficient the more the organizational task can be routinized and programmed (Perrow, 1970, pp. 78–84). A certain environment permits a greater routinization of the decision-making tasks than a more uncertain environment. If reasons for efficiency prevail – such as maximizing outcomes or effectiveness at minimal costs – there will be a greater need for a co-ordinator or leader.

Thus it is expected (H5) that the greater the certainty of the environment, the greater the need for a leader who assigns tasks and co-ordinates the activities in the organization.

If people act on these needs for a greater task co-ordination, it is hypothesized (H6) that the greater the certainty of the external environment, the greater the degree of hierarchization of perceived power in the organization.

This hierarchization of influence depends mainly on the 'expert power' (French and Raven, 1959) of the most influential person, since some members are better able to deal with the environment than others.

Davis (1982, p. 43), in a recent review of his research on social decision schemes, concludes '. . . that substantial task uncertainty, whether a problem to be solved or a sequential decision-making task, forces an egalitarian–equiprobability social process'. Socio-metric and observational data confirm this impression. An egalitarian social process is a process in which members participate equally in the decision-making process whether or not they are 'good' or 'bad' problem-solvers. Under less uncertain task conditions there is a tendency towards a more hierarchical social process in which the 'best' problem-solvers participate proportionally more often in the decision-making task than the more 'incompetent' ones. In highly uncertain conditions, the environmental uncertainty might be so high that one member cannot become a better problem-solver or develop a greater expertise in reducing the external uncertainty than another. If the environment is very certain all members are equally competent to deal with it and again no differential expertises can be developed. Only in a condition in which it is possible to discover predictable patterns and trends in the environment over time may some members become more proficient than others in reducing the external uncertainty.

Thus it is expected (H7) that more power will be attributed to those subunits in the organization which are most effective in reducing the critical uncertainties in the environment.

Hypothesis H7 is very similar to the one proposed by Hickson and his associates (1971) in their strategic-contingencies theory of intraorganizational power. Their argument is that power is conferred to those subunits that are most effective in coping with the most critical uncertainties in the environment. In their own words: '. . . uncertainty itself does not give power . . . but those subunits that cope most effectively with the most uncertainties should have the most power in the organization' (Hickson et al., 1971, p. 219). In addition they stress the importance of the substitutability and the centrality of the subunits in gaining power.

In an empirical test of their theory, Hinings, Hickson et al, (1974) found some support for their hypothesis. They obtained moderate positive correlations – levels of confidence were not reported – between perceived and more objective measures of environmental uncertainty (unpatterned variability) on one hand and their indices of perceived, participative, and position-power on the other hand (Hinings, Hickson et al., 1974, p. 34). For our present purposes it is interesting to note their measures of perceived power, are derived from the scales used by Tannenbaum. The scores of these scales correlated highly with the more objective indices of power, including participation and position power. These findings suggest that their measure of perceived power, which is also used in this study, may provide a valid indicator of the actual exercise of power (Hickson et al., 1971, p. 32).

Uncertainty and Effectiveness

Effectiveness is often defined in terms of goal attainment (Steers, 1975). Since often a variety of goals exist, effectiveness is a multi-dimensional concept which might be measured in many different ways (Veen, 1980a). For example Tannenbaum and Cooke (1979, p. 193) use subjective criteria of effectiveness such as satisfaction, morale, or loyalty of the members, or employ more objective indices such as productivity, efficiency, profitability, and adaptability to a changing environment. Other writers make a sharp distinction between efficiency and effectiveness: 'effectiveness is an external evaluation of what an organization is doing, while efficiency is an internal evaluation of the amount of resources consumed in the process of doing this activity' (Pfeffer and Salancik, 1978, p. 37). In this context we will use effectiveness as an external criterion of organizational performance. Profitability will be employed as the main 'objective' criterion of effectiveness, while the reported task satisfaction will be used as the main 'subjective' criterion.

In many organizations the reduction of environmental uncertainty is aimed at acquiring the resources necessary to attain an acceptable level of effectiveness. The environmental uncertainty of our laboratory organization was manipulated by varying the predictability of the 'input' and 'output' markets the members had to deal with and the degree to which they received clear and definite feedback about the results of their actions. The 'input' or 'raw materials' markets provided the raw materials to make the organizational products, while the 'output' or 'product markets' determined the price they could get for their finished products.

The greater the ability of the organization to reduce the uncertainty associated with the unpredictability of the market patterns, the more resources become available to the organization. When we talk about resources we are not only referring to the 'material' resources such as the raw materials or prices that are related to these markets, but also to the 'personal' and 'social' resources that are utilized as soon as the environment becomes more predictable and controllable. When the market patterns are fully known from the start, as in the highly certain condition, or become completely predictable after some time, as in the increasingly certain condition, the members are able through logical analysis and calculation (March, 1976) to minimize the amount of scrap (for which fines have to be paid) by planning the correct sequences of raw material purchases in an efficient way. Complete knowledge about the product market permits the members to choose a product to be manufactured of the kind of complexity that offers the highest pay-off at the lowest cost and effort. In a highly uncertain condition both market-patterns remain unpredictable until the very end of the experiment.

It is predicted (H8) that the greater the certainty of the environment, the more material and social resources become available and the greater the effectiveness as measured in terms of task satisfaction and profitability.

Total Amount of Power and Effectiveness

In their version of the structural-contingency model Tannenbaum and Cooke (1979) have suggested that hierarchical and non-participative procedures may be more efficient for dealing with routine matters, while more participative and less hierarchical procedures may be more effective in non-routinous decision-making. A higher total amount of control is expected in 'organic' effective organizational subunits, not only as a result of the participative procedures used, but also as a consequence of the greater hierarchical and 'mechanistic' control required in routine decision-making. To some extent this hypothesis conflicts with an earlier non-contingent statement of Tannenbaum that it is the total amount of control and not the hierarchization of perceived power that is always positively related to organizational effectiveness. In reviewing a great number of studies Tannenbaum (1968, p. 10) concludes: '. . . within 'normal' ranges variations in power between persons of different rank are *not* likely to be associated with criteria of performance' (emphasis by Tannenbaum). His general, somewhat idealized argument, in support of the notion that it is the total amount of perceived power that is conducive to organizational effectiveness, can be summarized as follows. Participation in the decision-making process involves mutual interaction and influence within and between hierarchical levels. These mutual influence processes lead to an increase in the perceived total amount of control in the organization for officers as well as for the rank and file. The exercise of power is a major basis for the psychological integration of the member in the social system. It tends to foster a high degree of identification, involvement, and loyalty to the organization. The greater the inclusion of the member within the system – the organization or work group – the more of his resources and information become available that are necessary to perform the organizational task efficiently and with greater effectiveness. The involvement, identification, and shared responsibility enhances the motivation of the members and will give rise to a greater attraction to the group or cohesiveness that in turn will lead to a greater uniformity and conformity to the work-group standards (Cartwright and Zander, 1968, pp. 139–150). This uniformity in behaviour and attitudes facilitates the co-ordination and acceptance of the decisions that are made collectively. People are also more likely to implement the decisions they have taken part in. All these processes lead to greater efficiency and effectiveness in solving the problem the organization is faced with (Tannenbaum, 1968, pp. 307–312). Thus in Tannenbaum's view it is the mutual influence within and between levels that results in an increase in the total amount of control leading to an increase in involvement, cohesiveness, and resourcefulness that enhances effectiveness. In his review of studies summarized in Tannenbaum and Cooke (1979, pp. 197–206) he finds generally positive evidence for this hypothesis.

It should be pointed out, however, that this positive relationship between total amount of control and effectiveness might also be ascribed to a self-serving bias: when groups or organizations are effective it is more likely that they attribute their success to their own efforts rather than to the environment and hence will attribute more control and power to themselves and others in the group (Streufert and Streufert, 1969). Moreover, research on the relationship between participation in the decision-making process, on the one hand, and satisfaction and productivity on the other hand, indicates that this relationship is much weaker and is only obtained under much more limiting conditions than Tannenbaum seems to assume (e.g. Locke and Schweiger, 1979).

Whatever the causal direction of the relationship, it is expected (H9) that the total amount of perceived power in the organization is positively associated with organizational effectiveness.

Hierarchization of Power and Effectiveness

The evidence regarding the relationship between hierarchization and effectiveness is less often reported than the relationship between total control and effectiveness (Tannenbaum and Cooke, 1979). This is not too surprising since Tannenbaum has emphasized that hierarchization is not generally related to effectiveness. When evidence is available the relationship tends to be negative: the greater the hierarchization the lower the effectiveness. This negative relationship has been found in research in complex organizations (Tannenbaum and Cooke, 1979) as well in small laboratory groups (Rabbie and Van Oostrum, 1981). A possible explanation of this relationship is suggested by Tannenbaum when he writes: 'Hierarchy is designed to solve a universal problem of organization, the need for co-ordination. But hierachy in turn creates problems of its own, division between persons of different rank and the seeds of disaffection and conflict implicit in that division' (Tannenbaum et al., 1974, p. 208). If hierarchization leads to alienation and dissatisfaction, especially among our egaliterian subjects who do not see the need for it, it is expected

(H1.0) that there will be a negative relationship between degree of heirarchization and task satisfaction.

The two experiments to be reported in this paper were designed to test these ten hypotheses

EXPERIMENT I. UNCERTAINTY, POWER AND EFFECTIVENESS

Method

Subjects

A total of 90 male students at the University of Utrecht took part in the experiment. They received Dfl 7.50 (approximately US $3.00) for their participation in the study. An extra bonus of Dfl 10.00 was promised to each of the members of the three-man organization when they attained a better performance than any other group that participated in the experiment.

The Experimental Task

A modification of an organizational task, developed by Weick, Allegro et al. (1970) in our laboratory was employed in this experiment. In designing this task an effort was made to manipulate the environmental uncertainty associated with the input and disposal of outputs without affecting the process of the 'throughput' to any significant degree (Hickson et al., 1971, p. 214). In other words, only the 'knowledge technology' was varied, particularly the extent to which effective performance of the task required logical analysis or guess work (Perrow, 1970). This was accomplished by keeping the operations to be performed or the kind of materials to be used as constant as possible. Thus the 'operation technology': the equipping and sequencing of activities in the work-flow and the 'material technology': the action that the indiviudal performs on an object in order to make some changes in it (Perrow, 1967) remained very similar from one experimental condition to another. In this way the perform-ances of groups operating under different conditions of environmental uncer-tainty could be directly compared with each other.

In our version of the 'Market Co-ordination' or 'Marco' task, three-man groups were asked to construct geometric figures made from pieces of paper varying in form and colour. The raw materials could be 'bought' on a 'raw materials' or 'input' market and the products made of these materials were 'sold' on a 'product' or 'output' market. Fifteen standard products could be made. These products varied as to the kind and amount of materials needed to make them, their complexity, and the price they would make on the product market.

The raw materials market consisted of a matrix of 8 rows and 18 columns. The eight types of raw materials (squares and triangles of different size and colour) were listed on the left-hand side of the matrix. At the top of the matrix, letters from A to R identified the 18 columns of the market. Each of the 144 cells contained a number varying from 0 to 8, indicating the amount, size, and colour of the squares and triangles that the group could buy with each purchase. When the group decided to work with particular kinds of materials they selected a particular row in the matrix. The experimenter, acting as supplier, chose the supply column on the basis of a pre-arranged pattern.

The product market was constructed in a similar way. The 15 rows of the output matrix corresponded with the 15 standard products that could be made. The 12 columns were identified with the letters A to L. Each of the 180 cells contained an amount of money ranging from Dfl 0.80 to 1.80. The amount of money the groups could gain or lose depended on the particular product they had made and the column that was chosen by the observer/consumer, again according to a pre-arranged pattern. Although there were exceptions, a com-plex product yielded on the average a higher price on the product market than a more simple one.

Manipulation of Environmental Uncertainty

In the *Highly Certain* (HC) condition the pre-arranged patterns of the in- and output market were fully known from the start and were listed under the matrices of the two markets and were displayed on the walls in front of the subjects.

In the *Increasingly Certain* (IC) condition the pre-arranged patterns were so complex that it took the subjects on the average 30 to 45 minutes to detect a predictable pattern. After the first 45 minutes, just before the pause, in general complete certainty about the market patterns were attained.

In the *Highly Uncertain* (HU) condition, the market patterns were so complicated that none of the groups were able to detect a predictable pattern within the 90 minutes available for each of the experimental sessions. With respect to the raw materials market, some members in the group were sometimes able to predict one or two column choices correctly, but after these correct trials the market patterns were so complicated that they found themselves on the wrong track again.

Complete knowledge about the raw materials market made it possible for the subjects to assemble an acceptable product within the eight 'purchases' or requests allowed by the experimenter. When a product was not completed at the end of these eight purchases, it was destroyed and the group had to pay a fine to the experimenter because of the 'pollution' involved. Since for each product only eight purchases could be made, the subjects were inclined to make simple products, that is products that required fewer materials to produce them. On the other hand, the product had to be 'sold' on the output or product market. On the average a complex product yielded more profits on the product market than a simple one. Thus a dilemma was created which necessitated a group decision in choosing a product which was both feasible and profitable. In order to prevent groups from making two identical products in a row, subjects were told after a product was completed, that the market for that product was 'satiated' and a different product had to be made. They had to wait four trials before the same product could be made again. Each organization received Dfl 5.00 as 'working capital'. From this amount of money fines had to be paid and the capital could increase or decrease as a function of the gains and losses obtained on the product market.

Experimental Setting

The three subjects worked at a round table rather than at a square one, in an effort to eliminate effects due to the seating positions of the subjects at the table (cf. Shaw, 1981, pp. 148–150). At the experimenter's table next to it, there were trays containing the raw materials, money, and working sheets on which the products had to be pasted. In front of the experimenter/supplier there was a stack of delivery cards. Each supply card had the letter of the column choice of the raw materials market. After each request for materials, the experimenter turned a card and announced the supply column choice for that request. The members took the task very seriously. An assistant of the experimenter, the observer/consumer, was seated at a separate table and had a stack of product cards in front of him. The finished products were brought to him and after inspection the consumer turned a card and announced the 'market-decision' for that trial and the gains or losses incurred by that decision. On the wall in front of the subjects the matrices of the two markets were displayed. Next to the markets the subjects could see a full display of the 15 standard products that could be made.

Procedure

The subjects received their instructions by means of tape-recorded and written instructions. They were urged to make as much money as they could: 'The objective is to earn as much money as possible. This goal can be accomplished by a thorough study of the two markets and a fast production . . .'. After the first 'practice' trial there were two periods of 45 minutes in each experimental session. At the end of the first period their work was interrupted and question- naires were administered to them which included seven-point scales on which they could indicate how certain they were about the raw material and product markets, how satisfied they had been, how much they were attracted to the group, and so on. The control graph question of Tannenbaum was phrased in the following way: 'Could you indicate on the scale below how much influence each one of you has exercised, including yourself, on the way the group has approached this task?'.

These and other questions were repeated at the end of the second period to register possible changes over time with regard to the self-reports of the subjects. In addition to these questions attempts were made by the observer/ consumer to observe some aspects of the behaviour of the subjects. In the result section we will refer more specifically to the kind of observations that were made.

Results

Effectiveness of the Experimental Manipulation

In view of the low and insignificant correlations between 'objective' and 'subjective' indices of environmental uncertainty which are often found in the literature (Aldrich, 1979, p. 129) it is important to show that the manipulated 'objective' uncertainty in this experiment is strongly related to the subjective or perceived uncertainty of the market patterns. The subjects were asked on a seven-point scale how certain they were about the raw materials and product markets. An analysis of variance on these data presented in Table 1(a) indi- cates that the subjects in the HU condition are much more uncertain about their column choices of the raw materials market than subjects in the two other conditions ($F=21.16$, df 2/27, $p<0.001$). The time of measurement did not make any difference. (For the subjects in the HC condition, the questions with regard to the uncertainty about the column choices of the two markets were clearly irrelevant, since these choices were completely known from the start. We included them to make the experimental conditions as comparable as

Table 1.   Mean Perceived Uncertainty Scores about the Market Patterns [a]

		HU	IC	HC
(a)	*Raw materials market*			
	Time 1	34.0	62.1	53.2
	Time 2	34.6	67.5	56.1
		34.3	64.8	54.6
(b)	*Product market*			
	Time 1	29.2	48.5	54.7
	Time 2	36.1	64.9	57.4
		32.6	56.7	56.1

[a]   Higher scores indicate higher certainty.

possible. Our impression was that the subjects in the HC condition answered these questions in terms of the difficulty experienced in making decisions about the feasibility and profitability of the products they chose to make.)

As can be seen in Table 1(b) there is, on the average, an increase in certainty about the product market in all experimental conditions ($F=21.16$; $df\,1/27$; $p<0.001$), and as expected this increase is greater in the IC than in the two other conditions. The interaction between conditions and time of measurement is statistically significant ($F=4.57$; $df\,2/27$; $p<0.05$). Also consistent with our expectations; at the end of the experiment, at time 2, the certainty about the product market is significantly greater in the IC than in the HU condition ($F=19.23$; $df\,2/27$; $p<0.001$). These results indicate that we have been successful in inducing the expected differential degrees of environmental uncertainty in the three experimental conditions.

There is a close correspondence between the objective, manipulated uncertainty and the subjective, perceived uncertainty of the markets. In Table 2 the results of a 'Manova'-regression analysis are summarized (SPSS, Update 7–9, 1981) in which the experimental conditions are included as D or 'dummy' variables. $D1$ represents the difference between the HU versus IC and HC, while $D2$ reflects the difference between the IC versus the two other experimental conditions. Rows 1 and 2 of Table 2 indicate that the manipulated uncertainty accounts for 62 and 48 per cent of perceived uncertainty of the raw materials and product markets at time 1. At time 2 these figures are respectively 76 and 60 per cent. All these relationships are significant beyond the 0.001 level. Behavioural measures: whether subjects made guesses or calculated judgments is another indication of the close correspondence between the manipulated and the perceived uncertainty about the markets (Hemmer, 1972, p. 39).

Table 2. Regression Analysis

	RM1	RM2	PM1	PM2	INFL1	INFL2	HIER1	HIER2	ATG1	SAT1
RM¹	0.62[a]									
RM²	0.76[a]	0.84[a]								
PM¹	0.48[a]	0.73[a]								
PM²	0.60[a]	0.66[a]								
HIER. 1	0.12	0.74	0.15		0.40[a]					
HIER. 2	0.10	0.26	0.13		0.31[b]					
INFL. 1	0.00	0.18	0.20[a]	0.30[a]		0.35[b]	0.46[b]			
INFL. 2	0.16[b]	0.30[a]	0.26[b]	0.30[a]	0.27[b]					
ATG. 1	0.12	0.12	0.24	0.27	0.26	0.30	0.27			
ATG. 2	0.22[a]	0.24[b]	0.26[b]	0.38[b]	0.48[a]		0.53[a]			
SAT. 1	0.21[a]	0.36[a]	0.37[a]	0.43[a]	0.43[a]			0.53[a]	0.62[a]	
SAT. 2	0.25[a]	0.45[a]	0.46	0.46[a]	0.49[a]	0.58[a]	0.58[a]	0.60[a]	0.60[a]	
PROFITS	0.73[a]	0.75[a]	0.82[a]	0.82[a]	0.82[a]	0.82[a]	0.67	0.82[a]	0.82[a]	0.82[a]
d1, d2 (certainty)	0.75[a]	0.75[a]	0.82[a]	0.82[a]	0.82[a]	0.82[a]	0.82[a]	0.85[a]	0.82[a]	0.83[a]

[a] $p < 0.05$
[b] $p < 0.10$

The numbers in the table refer to the amount of explained variance (R^2).

RM   = Raw materials market ('1' refers to phase 1, '2' to phase 2 of the experiment)
PM   = Products market
INFL = Total amount of influence
HIER = Hierarchization
ATG = Attraction to group
SAT = Task satisfaction.

Table 3. Mean Total Amount of Perceived Power Scores in the Experimental Conditions[a]

	HU	IC	HC
Time 1	139.7	140.0	137.0
Time 2	135.6	148.3	148.0
	137.6	144.1	143.6

[a] Higher scores indicate more perceived power.

Uncertainty and the Total Amount of Control

The data presented in Table 3 offer some partial support for hypotheses H1 and H2. Although there was no significant main effect difference between the experimental conditions, a significant interaction between conditions and time ($F=10.71$; $df\ 2/27$; $p<0.001$), shows that there is a significant increase over time in perceived power and control in the HC and IC conditions ($t=3.89$; $p<0.01$), but a slight decrease in the HU condition. Apparently an increasing sense of control over the environment leads to a higher perception of total amount of power in the organization, while a loss of control has the opposite effect.

Table 3 also shows a significant increase in the total amount of perceived power over time ($F=11.33$; $df\ 1/27$; $p<0.001$). The same finding has been obtained in other experimental studies (Rabbie and van Oostrum, 1981).

It should be stressed once again that in the HC condition the market patterns were fully known from the start. With a few exceptions this was also the case in the IC condition at the beginning of time 2. Thus the increase in the total amount of power over time can be mainly ascribed to the reduction of uncertainty generated by the *internal* environment. The significant main effect over time is consistent with our hypothesis (H3) that the uncertainty about the internal environment decreases over time, especially when the external environment remains relatively stable. As the internal environment becomes more certain, predictable, and orderly there is an increase in the total amount of perceived control in the group. In the absence of any independent measure of internal uncertainty this interpretation of the time effect remains speculative.

The regression analysis presented in Table 2 suggests that a combination of manipulated and perceived uncertainty is a better predictor of the total amount of influence than the manipulated uncertainty alone. Especially at time 2 the inclusion of the perceived uncertainty of the market patterns, particularly of the input market ($t = 2.37$; $p <0.03$) almost doubled the explained variance in the total influence scores. Apparently it is the experience as well as the actual control over the environment that leads people to attribute more power and influence to each other and themselves.

Environmental Certainty and Hierarchization

Tannenbaum and Cooke (1979, p. 195) have claimed that '. . . hierarchy in one form or another is a universal although controversial aspect of organization'. This conclusion is based on their research with the control graph method in large-scale complex organizations. This conclusion applies also to our small laboratory groups: regardless of the environment they faced, a significant degree of hierarchization of perceived power occurred, that is significantly more influence was attributed to the high than to the low-influence person ($F=13.99$; $df\ 2/27$; $p<0.001$).

Table 4.   Mean Hierarchization Scores of Perceived Power in the Experimental Conditions[a]

	HU	IC	HC
Time 1	25.1	43.1	34.1
Time 2	20.4	27.0	17.9
	22.8	35.1	26.0

[a]   Higher scores indicate higher hierarchization.

Hypothesis H5 receives some support: on the question asked at the end of the experiment: 'How appropriate do you think it is to appoint a leader who assigns tasks and co-ordinates activities of the group?' the average expressed need for a leader was 41.8 in the HC, 42.1 in the IC and 32.8 in the HU condition ($F = 3.75$; $df\ 2/27$; $p < 0.05$). This finding seems at odds with a common notion that in extremely uncertain and threatening conditions there is a call for strong leadership (Coser, 1956; Mulder and Stemerding, 1963; Rabbie and Wilkens, 1971; Bourgeois et al., 1978). This centralization of power occurs mainly in groups which are engaged in intergroup conflict and when vital issues are at stake. In our experiment the environmental uncertainty is probably less threatening. Moreover, the subjects in the HU condition learned that none of them was better able to master the environment than any of the others. None had found a better 'path' to this goal than other members in the group (House, 1971). Under certain environmental conditions there is a greater need for co-ordination that seems instrumental in reaching the goal than in highly uncertain conditions in which a greater co-ordination does not appear to solve the problems the members are faced with. Contrary to our expectations (H6) there is no greater degree of hierarchization of perceived power in the IC than in the two other conditions. Although the data presented in Table 4 are in the predicted direction, the difference is not significant ($F = 2.43$; df 2/27; p <0.17).

Consistent with previous research (e.g. Rabbie and Visser, 1976) the degree of hierarchization decreases strongly over time ($F = 21.11$; df 2/27; p <0.001). This greater 'power equalization' (Leavitt, 1965) over time can mainly be attributed to the increase in influence attributed to the lower power person. (For a discussion of this finding having been obtained more often, see Rabbie, Van Oostrum, and Visser, 1983).

The regression analysis presented in Table 2 indicates that it makes little or no difference in the degree of hierarchization whether the perceived uncertainty of the market patterns is included in the regression analysis. Only at the end of the experiment, at time 2, the degree of hierarchization seems to be somewhat affected by the perceived uncertainty of the input or raw materials market ($t=2.04$; $p<0.05$).

On the basis of the contingency theory of intraorganizational power of Hickson *et al*. (1971) it was expected that more influence would be attributed to those subunits at the boundary of the organization that appeared to be the most effective in coping with the critical uncertainties in the environment, that is in reducing the uncertainty contained in the input and output markets. There is some indirect support for this hypothesis. The observer made a record for each trial of which members were most responsible for making the decisions about the kind of products and the materials to be selected. These decisions were based on the study of the market patterns. In our internal analyses each member obtained a decision score based on the number of decisions he announced, divided by the total number of decisions in the group. The average correlation between the decision score of a member and the amount of influence attributed to him by the two other members in the group was highly significant over all the conditions combined ($r=0.59$; df 98, $p<0.01$). Within the three experimental conditions the correlations between decision score and attributed influence in the HU, IC and HC were, respectively, 0.46 ($p<0.02$), 0.75 ($p<0.01$) and 0.55 ($p<0.01$). Assuming that these decisions are based on the study of the market patterns, these correlations suggest, in line with hypothesis H7, that more power will be attributed to the members who cope more effectively than others with the critical uncertainties in the environment. In addition, these members seem to be more able to make acceptable decisions for the group, based on their greater insight into the uncertainties of the environment relative to other members in the organization. It is interesting to note that the correlation between the decision scores of the members and the attributed influence is highest in the IC condition, in which the uncertainties about the external and internal environment could be reduced more effectively than in the other two conditions. Generally, these significant correlations between a behavioural measure of the decision power of a member and the perceived power attributed to him by the two other members strengthens our confidence in the validity of these measures.

Uncertainty and Effectiveness

The data of the profitability of the organization presented in Table 5 show strong support for Hypothesis H8. As expected, the most money was earned in the HC and the least in the HU condition. The profitability in the IC condition was at an intermediate level of effectiveness ($F=36.75; df 2/27; p<0.001$). The figures in Table 5 include the initial working capital of Dfl 5.00. In comparison with the other two conditions, the subjects in the HU condition lost part of the money that was given to them as working capital ($t=8.56; p<0.001$).

Table 5. Mean Profitability Scores in the Experimental Conditions in Guilders (Dfl)[a]

	HU	IC	HC
Time 1	4.08	5.70	10.83
Time 2	4.43	11.46	15.95
	4.26	8.58	13.39

[a] Higher scores indicate higher profitability.

Since market patterns in the HU condition remained highly uncertain over time more scrap was produced in the HU than in the IC condition ($t=2.35$; $p<0.05$) and in the HC condition much less than in the IC condition ($t=3.62$; $p<0.001$). In the second period, at time 2, the market patterns were completely predictable in the IC as well as in the HC condition. As a consequence no significant difference was obtained between the amount of scrap produced in the IC and in the HC conditions at time 2, but both were significantly different from the HU condition ($t=2.81$; p<0.01).

Our measure of *subjective* effectiveness, the degree of task satisfaction, showed a similar pattern of results. As can be seen in Table 6, as predicted, more satisfaction is experienced the greater the certainty of the environment ($F=4.45; df 2/27; p<0.05$). This difference in satisfaction is significant at time 1 ($F=3.59; p<0.05$) as well as at time 2 ($F=4.67; p=<0.02$).

There is also a significant interaction between time and conditions ($F = 6.59$; $df 2/27; p<0.05$). In the IC condition the increasing mastery over the environment produces a greater task satisfaction over time while in the two other conditions there is a slight and non-significant tendency in the opposite direction. This increase in task satisfaction for the IC as compared with the two other conditions is highly significant ($t=3.24; p<0.003$).

These patterns of results provide strong support for the hypothesis (H8) that

Table 6.   Mean Task Satisfaction Scores in the Experimental Conditions [a]

	HU	IC	HC
Time 1	53.1	52.2	59.1
Time 2	52.1	57.3	57.7
	52.6	54.7	58.4

[a]   Higher scores indicate higher task satisfaction.

a greater predictability of the environment produces a greater profitability and more task satisfaction. This hypothesis is less obvious than one would think. In an earlier pilot-study (Hemmer, 1971) it was found that the members in the highly certain condition were so concerned with the more interesting task of reducing scrap, that they neglected to make sufficient products to earn them the maximum amount of money on the product market. This result implies that the goals imposed by the experimenter may have had a different weight and importance to the subject than was intended.

The regression analysis in Table 2 shows that a major portion (75 per cent) of the profit score can be accounted for by the *manipulated* uncertainty of the market patterns. The *perceived* uncertainty, especially of the product market, contributes significantly to the amount of explained variance of the profitability score (up to 82 per cent; $t=2.95$; $p<0.01$).

The satisfaction scores are less affected by the manipulated uncertainty: about 21 per cent in time 1 and 25 per cent in time 2. When the perceived certainty scores are added as predictors in the regression analysis, the variance acounted for in the satisfaction score is raised to 36 per cent, especially by the scores of the raw materials market ($t=2.51$; $p<0.02$) at time 1, and 45 per cent at time 2 ($t=3.00$; $p<0.006$). These results indicate that the perceived uncertainty scores account for a considerable amount of the 'subjective' task satisfaction in the organization.

Power and Effectiveness

Our position has been – at least in the present experiment – that the effectiveness of the organization is mainly determined by the amount of material (and social) resources that are made available through reduction of the environmental uncertainty rather than by the influence structures that emerge as a reaction to the variations in environmental uncertainty. The results of the regression analysis presented in Table 2 provide some support for this point of view. As far as the objective index of effectiveness is concerned the manipulated and perceived uncertainty explain most of the variance (82 per cent of the profit scores), and the inclusion of the total amount of power and hierarchization does not add significantly to the prediction of the profitability of the organization. A similar statement can be made about the additional effects of the degree of cohesiveness and satisfaction that are supposed to accrue from the total amount of perceived power according to Tannenbaum (1968, p. 310).

The subjective index of effectiveness, the reported task satisfaction, appears to be more sensitive to variations in the power structure of the organization. The effects of the total amount of influence and hierarchization show up more clearly at the end of the experiment at time 2, when the power structure was relatively stabilized, than in the first period before the pause. At time 2 about half or 48 per cent of the satisfaction scores can be explained by the manipulated and perceived environmental uncertainty. When the total amount of perceived power is included in the regression analysis it appears that 10 per cent more of the satisfaction scores can be accounted for ($t = 2.78$; p<0.01), by the total influence scores.

Hierarchization and Effectiveness

In accordance with our expectation (H9), the total amount of influence contributes *positively* to the task satisfaction, while hierarchization, as measured in time 1 – which explains an additional 9 per cent of the variance – is *negatively* related to task satisfaction ($t = -1.95$; $p < 0.06$). Although these two dimensions of perceived power may vary independently from one another (Tannenbaum, 1968, p. 5) the perceived total amounts of power and hierarchization appear to have opposite effects on the task satisfaction in the organization. Participation in the decision-making process enhances the total amount of perceived power and increases task satisfaction. The hierarchization of power among equals, on the other hand, seems to lead to greater dissatisfaction amongst our subjects.

As can be seen in Table 2, the addition of the cohesiveness scores in the regression analysis produces a considerable increase of the variance in the task satisfaction scores accounted for during the first period (from 33 to 62 per cent) but contributes very little to the task satisfaction scores at the end of the experiment. Apparently when the members do not have much experience of one another, during the first period of the experiment, their satisfaction with the task is mainly determined by the in-group cohesiveness they experience. At a later phase in the development of the group other factors such as the experienced control over the environment and the consequent influence processes appear to become more important in determining the degree of task satisfaction.

Discussion

At the individual level of analysis it has been argued that coping effectively with an uncertain environment tends to induce a sense of competence (White, 1955), self-efficacy and behavioural efficacy (Bandura, 1977), control

(Langer, 1975), and personal power, while a loss of control seems to have the opposite effects (Seligman, 1975).

The present experiment suggests that very similar phenomena can be observed at the level of groups and organizations. A sense of power and control over an increasingly certain and predictable environment leads to a greater increase in the total amount of perceived power in the group, while a loss of control has the opposite effect. Both the actual and the perceived control over the external environment enhanced the perception of (social) power in the organization. According to Tannenbaum, the increase in the total amount of perceived power is due to participation in the decision-making process. In Experiment I we had no measure of the participation rates of the members in the discussion. In the following experiment we will correct this omission. By obtaining a measure of the frequency of participation of the individual members we are able to test the control graph theory of Tannenbaum at the individual as well as the system level of analysis.

It was predicted that there would be a greater hierarchization of perceived power in the increasingly certain than in the two other experimental conditions. The argument was that the greater the increase in control over the environmental uncertainty, the greater the participation of the more competent relative to the less competent members in the discussion (Davis, 1982). In the highly certain (HC) condition all members were equally competent, while in the highly uncertain condition all members were equally incompetent to deal with the organizational task. Since the rate of verbal participation is often positively associated with the attribution of social power (Lord, 1977), the degree of hierarchization would be greater in the increasingly certain than in the two other conditions. Although the data were in the predicted direction no significant differences between the conditions were obtained. In Experiment II, we will test this hypothesis once again, but at this time we will use only two uncertainty manipulations: an Increasingly Certain (IC) and a Highly Uncertain (HU) condition.

As expected, there was a greater need for a leader who would co-ordinate the activities of the members in the certain than in the uncertain conditions, but this greater need did not lead to a significant difference in the hierarchization of power between the conditions. Some indirect support was found for the hypothesis of Hickson et al., (1971), that most power will be attributed to those decision units that are most effective in coping with the most critical uncertainties in the organization. In the following experiment a more direct test of this hypothesis will be provided by manipulating the degree of formalization of structure and leadership in the group. In the High Formalization (HF) condition the members will be assigned to specific tasks; in the Low Formalization condition (LF) the members are free to organize themselves as they wish, just as in Experiment I.

As predicted, the total amount of perceived power had a positive effect on the task satisfaction, while a greater degree of hierarchization diminished the task satisfaction of our equalitarian subjects. It is not clear, however, whether a greater hierarchization led to a lower task satisfaction or whether a low task satisfaction induced a greater centralization of leadership or hierarchization in the group. In an effort to obtain more information about this issue we will attempt to manipulate the degree of hierarchization by appointing a leader in the high formalization condition, but not in the low formalization condition.

Since there is some overlap in design between the two experiments it is possible to ascertain which of the findings of Experiment I can be replicated. Moreover, by measuring the degree of participation in our laboratory organization, we may gain more insight in the processes which may have accounted for the findings of Experiment I.

EXPERIMENT II. UNCERTAINTY, FORMALIZATION, AND PATTERNS OF PERCEIVED POWER

Uncertainty, Formalization, and Participation

In Experiment I it was predicted that there would be a greater differentiation in participation between the most and the least competent members and consequently a greater hierarchization of perceived power among them in the increasingly certain than in the two other experimental conditions (Davis, 1982). In a partial replication of the previous experiment we will compare in Experiment II an Increasingly Certain (IC) with a Highly Uncertain condition (HU). Participation in the decision-making process is measured by noting at 5-second intervals which members were speaking. Measuring the frequency of the verbal participation of the members also permits a test of the hypothesis

(H11) that an organization faced with an increasingly certain and controllable environment will develop a more stable, differentiated and orderly rate of participation among the members as compared to an organization in which the members are faced with a highly uncertain uncontrollable environment that remains uncertain despite the efforts of the members to reduce it.

It is also expected (H12) that the greater the increase in environmental certainty the greater will be the participation in the decision-making process.

This hypothesis was suggested by a field study among University Institutes in a University department in The Netherlands (Rabbie et al., 1976). In that study we found, to our surprise, that a high degree of formalization was associated with a high rather than a low degree of reported participation in the decision-making process. We had expected that a low degree of formalization of structure – due to a highly uncertain environment – (Lawrence and Lorsch, 1967) would have led to a higher degree of participation. In a post hoc explanation of this finding it was argued that in the highly uncertain environments of these Institutes there should be some minimal internal and external certainty about the predictability of the effects of one's actions in inducing the faculty members to participate in the decision-making process at all. Apparently a high degree of formalization in these institutes provided the minimal certainty required to participate in the decision-making process. Likewise, in the highly uncertain environment of our laboratory organizations, in which the members were continuously confronted with their failure to make the internal and external environment more predictable and controllable, there will be less participation in the group discussion, since people do not know where it leads to as compared to organizations in which the members are increasingly successful in coping with the uncertainty in the environment.

This argument could imply that the high degree of formalization of structure, defined as 'pre-existing programmes and controls' (Lawrence and Lorsch, 1967, p. 5) would lead to more rather than less participativeness since formalization makes the internal environment more certain. It should be noted, however, that this hypothesis would only hold under a very high level of external environmental uncertainty. It also depends on the kind of formalization imposed on the organization. When the imposed structure does not match the prevailing contingencies another source of uncertainty may arise. In the present experiment, within each of the two uncertainty conditions, a High degree of Formalization (HF) was manipulated by appointing one member, B, to a leadership position. He had the task of co-ordinating the activities of the group. Another member, A, had to study the raw materials market, while C had two tasks: to study the product market and to paste the product on the work-sheet. In fact the production task took most of his time. A and C had only visual access to their 'own markets', while B could see both markets at the same time. There were also communication restrictions between the members: A and C could not talk directly to each other, but had to channel their communications through B. The appointed leader B could talk directly to anyone. He occupied a central position in the communication network (Leavitt, 1951). In the Low Formalization condition (LF) it was left to the members to organize themselves, as was the case with the groups in the first experiment.

Because of the restrictions in communications the degree of participation could be less in the High Formalization (HF) than in the Low Formalization (LF) condition. In view of these contradictory hypotheses it is difficult to make a prediction about the total amount of participation in the HF and LF conditions.

At the level of the individual member, however, it is expected (H13) that members who have a central position in the communication network and are assigned to the task of reducing the external uncertainty and of co-ordinating the activities of the group will participate more often in the decision-making process than members who are assigned, or happened to perform, the more menial production tasks.

These task assignments in the HF condition were not made at random. In the previous experiment it was found that the seating arrangement of the members, despite the round table, affected the 'spontaneous' division of labour in the organization. B (the person who occupied the middle seating position at the table) was more likely to work on the production activities than A and C, who were more involved in studying the market patterns ($X^2 = 21.97$, df 2, p<0.001)

In general it has been observed that seating arrangments influence the rate of participation and emergence of leadership in the group (e.g. Strodtbeck and Hook, 1961; Howells and Becker, 1962). Consistent with these findings, we expected that B in the LF condition would work mainly as a production worker and hence participate less often in the discussion than the other members in his group. To counteract the possible effects of the seating arrangements on the participation and attribution of influence of the members we decided in the HF condition to appoint B as the leader of the group and to give him the most central position in the communication structure. Despite the identical seating position it was expected that B will be the highest participator in the group in the HF condition but the lowest participator in the LF condition.

Uncertainty, Formalization, and Hierarchization of Influence

We hypothesized (H12) that an increasingly certain environment would lead to a greater differentiation in the participation rates of the members than the highly uncertain environment. Since participation and the attribution of influence are assumed to be positively related to each other (Lord, 1977) it is predicted:

(H14) that the patterns of influence attribution among the members in the experimental conditions will closely correspond with the participation of those members in the decision-making process.

This hypothesis implies that the hierarchization of perceived power will be greater in the increasingly certain (IC) than in the highly uncertain (HU) condition, particularly in the LF condition in which the members are free to organize themselves. In the HF condition, the hierarchization of perceived power would be less dependent on the degree of the certainty of the environment, but would be more determined by the manipulated structure imposed on the organization.

At the individual level of analysis it is expected that the attribution of influence to each of the members would closely correspond to the difference in participation rates between them. For the HF condition this hypothesis implies that most of the influence would be attributed to B, the appointed leader, less to A and the least to C, the production worker. For the LF condition the least influence would be attributed to B, who is likely to be involved in the production activities of the organization, than to the two other members of his group, who are involved in the boundary-spanning task to reduce the uncertainty of the environment. These predictions are consistent with the hypothesis of Hickson et al. (1971), who propose that the most social power will be attributed to those organizational units which are most effective in reducing the greatest number of critical uncertainties in the organization.

In the first experiment it was found that the degree of hierarchization decreased over time. A similar time effect is expected in this experiment, particularly in the LF condition, in which the members could choose any task they wanted.

In addition, it is hypothesized:

(H15) that the greater the decrease in environmental uncertainty, the greater the hierarchization of perceived power, particularly in the condition under which no control structure is imposed on the organization; (H16) that the greater the participation of the individual member in the decision-making process the more influence will be attributed to him; and (H17) that there will be a decrease in hierarchization of perceived power over time.

Uncertainty, Formalization, and Total Amount of Influence

In Experiment I support was found for the hypothesis (H1) that the greater the certainty and controllability of the environment the higher the amount of perceived (social) power in the organization. The same hypothesis will be tested in this experiment.

Since the uncertainty of the *internal* environment will decrease over time, there will be an increase of the total amount of perceived power from time 1 to time 2 in this experiment, since people will experience a greater sense of control over the internal environment over time (H3).

It is difficult to make predictions about the effects of formalization of structure on the total amount of perceived power in the organization. A greater degree of formalization will lead to a greater internal certainty and controllability of the internal environment and therefore should enhance the participation rate and total amount of perceived power in the group. On the other hand, the restrictions in the communications between the members in the HF condition may lower the degree of participation and total amount of influence. Moreover, there is some question whether the structure that is imposed on the laboratory organization is congruent with the one that will emerge 'spontaneously' in the LF condition. When a discrepancy is perceived in the HF condition between an emergent structure – one induced by the seating arrangements for example – and the structure imposed on the members by the experimenter, another source of internal uncertainty is created which may tend to lower the degree of participation and total amount of influence. In view of these difficulties we will refrain from making a prediction on this point.

Formalization, Involvement, and Task Satisfaction

In the communication network studies (cf. Shaw, 1981, pp. 153–155) it has been shown that the member who occupies a central position in the communication network has a high probability of emerging as a leader in the group. Moreover, persons in a central position are also more involved and satisfied than members occupying a peripheral position in the communication network. These findings are consistent with Tannenbaum's control graphy theory. Although his theory has been formulated at a system level rather than at the level of the individual members, it would imply that a high level of influence – due to a greater participation in the decision-making process – would lead to a high degree of involvement and task satisfaction of the more central, as compared with the more peripheral, members. If this derivation of his theory is correct, it is predicted:

(H1.8) that a central highly participative member such as B in the HF condition will feel more involved and satisfied with the organization as compared to more peripheral members such as A but particularly C.

At a system level of analysis Tannenbaum would predict that the total amount of control in an organization contributes positively to the involvement and the task satisfaction of the members (H1.9).

Although Tannenbaum has asserted that hierarchization is not necessarily related to the subjective indices of effectiveness such as involvement and task satisfaction, we found in the previous experiment

that a high degree of hierarchization of perceived power is negatively associated with task satisfaction (H2.0).

Apparently, among our equalitarian subjects a greater hierarchization of power diminishes task satisfaction. In the present experiment we will try to replicate this finding.

Uncertainty, Formalization, and Effectiveness

Just as in the first experiment we predicted that the greater the certainty and controllability of the environment, the more resources will become available and the greater the effectiveness of the organization (H8). A combination of the 'objective' and 'perceived' environmental uncertainty will be a better predictor of the effectiveness than the manipulated certainty alone.

Earlier we have argued that the effectiveness of the organization will be mainly determined by the amount of resources made available to the organization rather than by the variations in power structures that emerge as a consequence of the manipulation of the environmental uncertainty. With regard to the *objective* indicator of effectiveness, the profitability of the organization, this argument received some support. With respect to the *subjective* indicator of effectiveness we observed that these power structures – total amount of power and hierarchization – did indeed contribute significantly to the reported task satisfaction of the members but, as we noted before, in opposite ways. A regression analysis will be performed to explore the relative contribution of these factors to the subjective and objective effectiveness.

According to the congruence hypothesis contained in most contingency theories (Lawrence and Lorsch, 1967; Tannenbaum and Cooke, 1979) an interaction should be expected between the formalization and the degree of environmental uncertainty if it is assumed that the manipulated structure fits the environmental demands of the organization. If that is the case, a highly formalized structure would be more congruent and would lead to a greater effectiveness in an increasingly certain than in a highly uncertain environment. On the other hand, a lower degree of formalization would be more congruent and effective in a highly uncertain than in an increasingly certain environment. This hypothesis stands or falls with the assumption that the imposed structure is indeed congruent with the environmental demands. We already expect that the formalization and influence structures in the HF conditions will be quite different from the ones that emerge spontaneously in the LF condition. If the assumption is made that emergent structures are more appropriate than the imposed ones no interaction between formalization and uncertainty is to be expected.

Method[1]

Subjects

Ninety-six male students at the University of Utrecht volunteered to take part in the experiment. They received Dfl 7.50 for their participation. In addition

[1] For a more detailed description of the method and results see Vreugdenhil, 1973; Van Oostrum, 1973; and Rabbie, Van Oostrum and Vreugdenhil, 1983.

they were promised a bonus of Dfl 10.00 per person for the 'best performing group'. Each experimental session took about 90 minutes. After the first 45 minutes, at time 1, there was a pause in which various questionnaires were administered. At the end of the experiment, at time 2, most of these questionnaires were administered again.

Experimental Conditions

The experimental 'Marco-Task' setting and procedure was identical to the one used in Experiment I. However, the experimental instructions differed. In a 2 × 2 factorial design half of the subjects were randomly assigned to the *Highly Uncertain* (HU) condition and the other half to an Increasingly Certain (IC) condition. Within each of these two experimental conditions the degree of formalization of structure was varied. In the *Low Formalization* (LF) condition half the subjects were free to organize themselves just as in the first experiment. In the High Formalization (HF) condition the other half of the subjects were told: 'As you can see each of you has a letter, *A*, *B* or *C*. Person *B* has the task to act as a leader of the group. Person *A* has the task to study the patterns of the raw materials market and to make a record of the column choices that are made. It is the task of *C* to study the patterns of the product market, to take notes of the column choices of the product market and to make the product (i.e. paste the materials on the working sheets).' It is the task of the leader (*B*) to make decisions, in consultation with *C*, about what kind of products have to be made. He also makes the decisions about the sequence of the purchases of the raw materials market, in consultation with *A*. The leader can help *A* and *C* with their tasks and he has to co-ordinate their activities. He is also the person who contacts the experimenter and the consumer (observer) by writing the request notes and by bringing the finished products to the consumer and keeping the cash. To reinforce these task assignments, the communication structure between the members was arranged by means of wooden partitions in such a way that *A* and *C* could only pay attention to their respective input and output markets, while *B* had visual access to both markets. Moreover, *A* and *C* were not allowed to talk directly to each other about the market patterns they had detected but had to channel their communications through *B*. No one else than *B* could write the purchase and delivery notes and only *C* had the pasting-stick, ruler, and mould that were necessary to make the products. In the LF condition there were no specific task assignments, each member had the same legitimate authority as any other one. There were no communication restrictions and no difference in visual access to the markets. Each member in the LF condition could perform any task he wanted. For example, each member had a pasting-stick before him that could be used to paste the product on to the working-sheet if he wished to do so.

Measures

The same measures as in the first experiment were used. In addition the observer registered the rate of participation of each subject. He had a tape-recorder before him which emitted a soft click at 5-second intervals. At the moment of a click the observer noted who was speaking at that time. An early study has shown (Van Oostrum, 1973) that this method of sampling the rate of participation in the group is a highly reliable method of assessing the talkativeness of the members. Several other questionnaires were administered at the pause (time 1) and at the end (time 2) of the experiment, besides the ones which were used in the first experiment.

Results

Manipulated and Percieved Uncertainty

The manipulation of the Raw Materials (RM) and Product Market (PM) had the intended effects on the perceived uncertainty of the two markets. The average perceived uncertainty of the RM and PM markets were respectively 64.0 and 56.0 in the IC and 34.3 and 33.1 in the HU condition ($F=71.18$, $df=1/28$, $p<0.001$ and $F=49.6$, $df=1/28$, $p<0.001$). There was a significant increase in certainty about the PM from time 1 ($M=37,4$) to time 2 ($M=51,58$; $F=33.59$, $df=1/28$, $p<0.001$) but no increase in certainty in the RM (The means are 48.0 at time 1 and 50.3 at time 2.)

According to the regression analyses presented in Table 7 73 per cent of the perceived uncertainty score of the RM and 41 per cent of the PM patterns can be accounted for by the manipulated uncertainty of the market patterns. For time 2 these figures are respectively 63 and 60 per cent. Thus it can be concluded that we have been successful in inducing different degrees of perceived uncertainty as a function of variations in the predictability and complexity of the market patterns.

Observations indicate that the division of labour was in accord with the task assignments made by the experimenter in the high formalization condition. In general there was more task specialization in the HF than in the LF conditions, but on some tasks like 'pasting' and 'writing notes', the spontaneous division of labour in the LF was as great as in the HF condition (Vreugdenhil, 1973, p. 50). As expected it turned out that *B* in the LF condition, just as in the first experiment, was more engaged in the production task than were the two other members in his group. In general the variation in the formalization of structure had the desired effects.

Table 7. Regression Analysis

	D1 (IC/HU)	D2 (HF/LF)	RM1	RM2	PM1	PM2	PART1	PART2	INFL1	INFL2	HIER1	HIER2	INV1	INV2	SAT1	SAT2
RM_1	0.73ᵃ	0.74ᵃ														
RM_2	0.61ᵃ	0.63ᵃ														
PM_1	0.41ᵃ	0.42ᵃ														
PM_2	0.59ᵃ	0.60ᵃ														
			(0.79)ᵃ													
PART.1	0.08	0.10	0.10		0.13											
PART.2	0.12ᵃ	0.16ᵇ		0.16		0.22										
			(0.34)ᵃ		(0.38)ᵃ											
INFL.1	0.17ᵃ	0.19ᵃ	0.19		0.22		0.24									
INFL.2	0.07	0.14		0.18		0.18		0.20								
			(0.19)ᵃ		(0.26)		(0.28)									
HIER.1	0.14ᵃ	0.20ᵃ	0.25		0.36ᵃ		0.40ᵃ		0.40ᵃ							
HIER.2	0.07	0.05		0.05		0.07		0.07		0.10						
			(0.07)		(0.01)		(0.15)		(0.33)							
INV.1	0.11ᵇ	0.13	0.27ᵃ		0.35ᵃ		0.36ᵃ		0.44ᵃ		0.49ᵃ					
INV.2	0.01	0.02		0.03		0.08		0.08		0.16		0.29				
			(0.12)		(0.12)		(0.15)		(0.23)		(0.36)				
SAT.1	0.03	0.03	0.08		0.12		0.14		0.28		0.30		0.35			
SAT.2	0.05	0.05		0.07		0.14		0.14		0.19		0.29		0.33		
			(0.24)		(0.26)		(0.31)		(0.34)		(0.46)		(0.60)			
PROFITS	0.55ᵃ	0.57ᵃ	0.72ᵃ		0.72ᵃ		0.73ᵃ		0.75ᵃ		0.77ᵃ		0.77ᵃ		0.77ᵃ	
			(0.74)ᵃ		(0.78)ᵃ		(0.79)ᵃ		(0.80)ᵃ		(0.81)ᵃ					

ᵃ = p .05
ᵇ = p .10

The numbers in the table refer to the amount of explained variance (R^2).
The numbers between parentheses ( ) refer to the percentage of explained variance of the variables measured at the second end phase of the experiment, when they are included in the regression equation.
RM = Uncertainty about raw materials market
PM = Uncertainty about products market
PART = Total amount of participation (verbal output)
INFL = Total amount of influence
HIER = Hierarchization
INV = Involvement
SAT = ...

Certainty, Formalization and participation

If we may use the total verbal output as an indicator of the degree of participation in the decision-making process, Hypothesis H12 is supported. There is a greater degree of participation in the IC ($M = 132.5$) than in the HU condition ($M = 112.5, F = 3.48, df = 1/28, p < 0.05$). Thus a highly uncertain environment, which stays that way over time, stimulates less participation than an increasingly certain environment. It was also predicted (H1.1) that organizations confronted with an increasingly certain environment would develop a much more stable, differentiated, and orderly rate of participation among the members than an organization in which the members were faced with a highly uncertain environment, that remained uncertain despite their strenuous efforts to reduce it. This difference between the IC and HU would be stronger the greater the opportunity of the members to organize themselves rather than being faced with a formal structure imposed on them by an external authority. As can be seen in Figure 1, there is some support for this hypothesis. The triple interaction between the two experimental conditions and the seating-position (A, B, C) of the members is significant beyond the 5 per cent level ($F = 3.25$, $df = 2/56, p < 0.05$).

As predicted, within the LF condition, there is a more stable, differentiated and orderly rate of participation in the IC/LF (1a) than in the HU/LF (1b) condition. In the latter condition the participation rates seem to reflect the temporary successes and failures of the members in coping with a highly uncertain environment. As expected, the imposed structure almost obliterated the impact of the variation in environmental uncertainty on the participation rates of the members. Nevertheless, it is interesting to note that the participation rates of the high and low participators B and C in the HU/HF condition (1d) approached each other over time, while in the IC/HF condition (1c) the participation rates of B and C remained very stable. It seems as if B, the appointed leader, did his utmost to do the job required of him, but after about an hour or so he gave up on it and did not talk as much as before. In about the same time A, but particularly C, tried to fill the void and participated more often than before, each apparently trying to make *his* contribution to solving the problem. Unfortunately we made no tape-recordings of the discussion to check on these speculations.

It was expected that in the HF condition B, the appointed, legitimate leader, would participate more than A who had to study the RM markets. Both A and B would participate more in the discussion than C, the production worker. As can be seen in Figures 1c and 1d there is some partial support for this hypothesis. Contrary to our prediction A and B did not differ significantly from each other in the HF/HU and HF/IC conditions: the average participation rates were respectively 148.9 for A and 129.9 for B. As expected both A and B talked much more than C ($M = 89.6, F = 13.35, p < 0.001, df 2/56$). Consistent

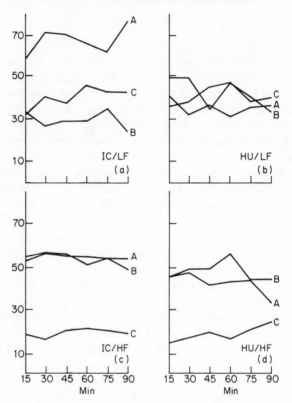

Figure 1.   Verbal participation of each member in the experimental conditions

with our hypothesis (H1.3) it appears that members engaged in the 'boundary-spanning activities' and task co-ordination participated more often in the discussion than C, who worked mainly as a production worker. It seems as if A and B talked a great deal with each other, leaving the production task to C. That is perhaps the reason that B, as the appointed leader, did not talk more than A, who was responsible for studying the raw materials market. A was often the first person who made suggestions, on the basis of his input market, as to what product should be chosen. In the IC condition he was often successful in his choice, which stimulated him to talk more than the others. In the uncertain condition he failed most of the time which may have led to a reduction of his talkativeness.

Generally, regardless of the experimental conditions there is a strong position effect ($F=15.35$, $df=2/56$, $p<0.001$), that is to say that members differ significantly from each other in their participation rates. This result is in line with previous findings (e.g. Bales *et al.*, 1951; Van Kreveld, 1968) that *inequality*, not equality, is the most frequent consequence of social interaction (Webster, 1975, p. 135).

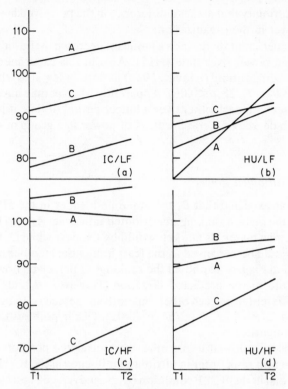

Figure 2.   Attribution of perceived power to each member in the experimental
conditions

Uncertainty, Formalization and Distribution of Power

Consistent with Hypothesis H16 the graphs in Figures 1 and 2 are remarkably
similar. In general the overall correlation between the verbal participation and
attributed influence is highly significant ($r=0.63$, $df=94$, $p<0.001$).

It was expected that the greater the environmental certainty the higher the
hierarchization of perceived power, particularly in the LF condition in which
no external structure was imposed. Generally at time 1, after the group had
worked for about 45 minutes, there was a significant greater degree of hierarchization in the IC than in the HU condition ($F=4.88$, $df=1/28$, $p<0.04$). In
the second part of the experiment, at time 2, there was no difference between
the IC and the HU condition.

The regression analysis presented in Table 7 indicates that the degree of
hierarchization in phase 1 can be primarily attributed to the perceived uncertainty of the RM market ($t=2.27$, $df=26$, $p<0.04$) and the PM market ($t=2.07$,
$df=26$, $p<0.05$) rather than to the manipulated uncertainty ($t=0.39$, $df=26$,
$p<0.70$). These results suggest that it is the perceived rather then the

'objective' uncertainty that makes a difference in the perceived hierarchization of (social) power in the organization.

In the first experiment there was a significant decrease in the hierarchization of the perceived power over time (H17). Also in this experiment there is a greater 'power equalization' (Leavitt, 1965) at time 2 ($M = 30.4$) than at time 1 ($M = 36.9, F = 3.91, df 1/28, p < 0.06$). Apparently when people have the opportunity to interact with each other over a longer period of time it is difficult to maintain a high degree of hierarchization of power in a group of equalitarian subjects.

Position and Attributed Power

Generally it was expected that B, the appointed leader in the HF condition, would receive the highest ranking in attributed influence; A, who had the task of studying the raw materials market, would be the next while C, the 'production worker', would be perceived as the least influential member in the group. As can be seen in Figures 2c and 2d the rankings of perceived power between the members are in the predicted direction. However, B and A were not significantly different from each other, but both are perceived to be much more influential than C ($F = 5.22, df = 2/56, p < 0.01$). Our hypothesis thus received some partial support.

When groups are allowed to organize themselves the position at the table produces a different rank order in attributed influence in the IC/HF condition ($A, C,$ and B) than in the IC/LF condition ($C, B,$ and A, see Figures 2a and 2b). Consistent with the hypothesis of Hickson *et al.* (1971) (H13), it was found that more influence was attributed to members who were involved in the boundary-spanning activities of the organization (studying the market patterns) than the members who were more involved in the production tasks (Rabbie, Van Oostrum and Vreugdenhil, 1983). This relationship between uncertainty-reducing activities and attributed influence was much stronger in the IC condition, in which the uncertainty could be reduced successfully, than in the UC condition, in which the members were ineffective in reducing the uncertainty contained in the market patterns. In the highly uncertain conditions almost no task specialization did occur (Van Oostrum, 1973). These findings underline once more that it is the *effective* reduction of uncertainty that confers power to the organizational unit (Hickson *et al.*, 1971).

The power structure which emerged 'spontaneously' among the members in the LF condition was quite different from the one that was imposed on them by an outside authority. As expected, the power structure in the LF condition was partly determined by the seating arrangement at the table. In both the HF and the LF condition B was randomly assigned to a seating position between A and C. In the LF condition he was mainly engaged in the menial production task, in the HF condition he was assigned to a leadership position by the experimenter.

As predicted (H13) much more influence was attributed to B in the HF condition than in the LF condition ($F=8.90$, $df=2/56$, $p<0.001$). This result indicates once more that less power is conferred on a member who is assigned or happens to perform a production task that does not allow him to reduce the critical certainties in the organization. These results also suggest that we have not been successful in providing a structure that is congruent with the physical and social requirements of the internal and external environment in the high formalization condition.

Certainty and the Total Amount of Perceived Power

As can be seen in Figure 2 in support of Hypothesis H1 more total power is attributed to the members in the IC than in the HU condition ($F=4.51$, $df=1/28$, $p<0.05$), but this difference is more pronounced at time 1 ($F=6.30$, $df=1/18$, $p<0.02$) than at time 2 ($F=2.32$, $df=1/28$, $p<0.11$).

The regression analyses presented in Table 7 suggest that the variance in influence scores of 19 per cent in phase 1 and 14 per cent in phase 2 can mainly be ascribed to the manipulated rather than to the perceived uncertainty of the market patterns. As expected (H2 and H3) the greater the increased uncertainty about the internal and external environment over time the higher the level of perceived total power in the group. The increase in total amount of (social) power from time 1 ($M=87.2$) to time 2 ($M=94.3$) is highly significant ($F=35.96$, $df=1/28$, $p<0.001$).

Contrary to our hypothesis, the average increase in total amount of influence in the IC condition is somewhat *lower* than in the HU condition. This suggested interaction between time and uncertainty ($F=3.76$, $df=1/28$, $p<0.10$) is difficult to understand unless it is assumed that 'ceiling' effects prevented the influence score from rising as freely in the IC as in the HU condition. The initial level at time 1 of the total amount of influence was already much higher in the IC ($M=90.8$) than in the HU condition ($M=83.6$) and was raised to 95.6 in the IC and 92.9 in the HU condition at time 2.

Generally, however, the results support the hypothesis that the greater the 'grip' or controllability of the external and internal environment the greater the total amount of perceived social power in the organization.

Formalization, Total Amount of Perceived Power, Task Satisfaction and Involvement

The average amount of perceived power in the L.F. condition ($M=87.7$) is almost identical to the one in the H.F. condition ($M=88.9$). Thus at least in these experimental conditions a greater formalization of organizational structure does not lead to a lower nor to a higher degree of experienced power in the group. The data presented in Table 8 present some partial support for Hypothesis H1.8 as far as involvement is concerned. C, the least influential member,

Table 8.   Mean Involvement Scores of the Members in the Experimental Conditions[a]

	A	B	C
IC/LF	58.2	46.9	53.8
IC/HF	49.5	57.0	42.6
HU/LF	49.7	44.2	51.1
HU/HF	50.2	51.1	44.7

[a]   The higher the score the higher the involvement.

appeared to be less involved ($F=4.99$, $df=2.56$, $p<0.05$) than his more participative and influential fellow members. Although the data were in the predicted direction, no significant differences in task satisfaction between the members were obtained. When we use the degree of 'interest in their own task' as an indication of task satisfaction a similar significant interaction is found ($F=5.14$, $df=2.56$, $p<0.01$) (see Table 9). Thus Tannenbaum's hypothesis also receives some support at the individual level of analysis.

Table 9.   Mean Interest Scores in Own Task of Members in Experimental Conditions [a]

	A	B	C
IC/LF	57.1	41.0	46.2
IC/HF	44.7	53.1	40.1
HU/LF	39.4	36.2	46.6
HU/HF	47.4	50.7	41.8

[a]   The higher the scores the higher the task interest.

Total Influence, Involvement, and Task Satisfaction

Contrary to Tannenbaum's theory, we have found support for our hypothesis that hierarchization of power is negatively related to task satisfaction. It was expected that the higher the total amount of perceived power the greater the involvement and task satisfaction would be, while the hierarchization of power would have the reverse effects on these two variables (H2.0). The regression analyses provide some support for these two hypotheses. In agreement with the control graph theory the total amount of power contributes positively to the degree of involvement ($t=1.95$, $df=25$, $p<0.06$) and task satisfaction ($t=2.24$, $df=25$, $p<0.04$) in the first phase (time 1) of the experiment but not in the second phase (time 2). The degree of hierarchization in the *first* phase contributes negatively to the involvement ($t=2.08$, $df=24$, $p<0.05$) and task satisfaction ($t=1.80$, $df=24$, $p<0.08$) in the *second* phase of the experiment. Apparently it takes some time before hierarchization affects the degree of involvement and task satisfaction. These results imply once more, contrary to Tannenbaum's opinion, that at least in small groups, both dimensions of social power may affect the subjective aspects of effectiveness but in an opposite direction.

Certainty and effectiveness

With respect to the 'objective' indicator of effectiveness, the profitability scores, there is strong support for Hypothesis H8. In the IC condition more money was earned ($M=$ Dfl 19.38) than in the HU condition ($M=$Dfl 10.72, $F=37.12$, $df=1/64$, $p<0.001$).

The regression analyses in Table 7 indicate that the manipulated uncertainty accounts for about 55 per cent of the variance of the profitability scores. When the perceived uncertainties of the RM and PM markets are included in the analyses the amount of explained variance in the profitability scores raises to about 72 per cent for the RM ($M=3.83$, $p<0.001$), but not for the PM market. Thus the combination of objective and subjective indicators of the environmental uncertainty appear to be better predictors of the profitability of the organization than the manipulated uncertainty alone.

The hypothesis that a greater certainty and controllability would lead to greater effectiveness did not receive support when a subjective indicator of effectiveness was used. The task satisfaction in the IC condition ($M=50.5$) is not significantly different from the mean task satisfaction in the HU condition ($M=47.5$).

When the perceived uncertainties of the market patterns are included in the regression equation there is no significant increase in the task-satisfaction scores. This result is different from that obtained in the first experiment. Since we used a very similar measure of task satisfaction in both experiments this difference between the two experiments is difficult to understand.

We expected that a highly formalized structure would lead to more positive

Table 10.   Mean Profitability Scores [a] in Guilders (Dfl) in the Experimental Conditions [b]

	LF	HF	
IC	18.76	20.00	19.38
HU	10.00	11.45	10.72
	14.38	15.73	15.05

[a]   The higher the scores the higher the profitability.
[b]   The working capital of Dfl 5.00 is induced in these figures.

outcomes in a certain than in a highly uncertain environment, while a low degree of formalization would be more effective in an uncertain than in a certain environment. As can be seen in Table 10 this hypothesis receives no support. Apparently, as noted before, we have not been able to design a structure that was congruent with the environmental contingencies the organization was faced with.

Summary and Future Research Implications

The greater the effectiveness in coping with the environmental uncertainty, the greater the amount of power and control over environment and the greater the total amount of social power that is attributed to the members in the organization. The significant increase of social power over time suggests that this hypothesis also holds for effective coping with the internal environment. Thus effective coping with the external and the internal environment leads to an expansion of the total amount of perceived social power in the organization.

The inability to cope with a highly uncertain environment produces a less differentiated power structure than the capability to deal with an increasingly certain environment. In the latter condition the efforts of some members appeared to be superior to others in reducing the environmental uncertainty. As a consequence a greater expertise and social influence was attributed to some members rather than to others. In a highly uncertain condition, however, none of the members appeared to be more successful in reducing the uncertainty than the others and as a result no stable and orderly participation and influence structure could develop.

In both experiments there was a decrease in hierarchization over time. This greater power equalization has been observed before (e.g. Rabbie and Visser, 1976). One possible explanation could be that a greater certainty of the internal environment over time – after an initial power struggle – provides an opportunity, particularly for the less dominant and more timid members, to participate more often in the decision-making process than before, leading to a more equal attribution of power to the members in the last phase of the development of the group (Rabbie, Van Oostrum, and Visser, 1983).

Generally, there was a close correspondence between the participation rates of the members in the various experimental conditions and the attributions of influence to each of them. Consistent with the contingency theory of intra-organizational power of Hickson et al., (1971) it was found that more power was attributed to members who appeared to be more effective in reducing the critical uncertainties in the environment than to members who were less successful in this respect and who were more involved in the production tasks of the group. In fact, whether they were assigned to these production tasks, as in the high formalization condition, or happened to be engaged in these tasks as a function of the seating arrangements between the members, as in the low formalization condition, in both instances the production worker received the lowest influence score in the organization. Apparently, to be involved in the production task interfered with the ability to pay attention to the environmental uncertainty contained in the market patterns.

Although hierarchization may solve 'the universal problem of co-ordination' (Tannenbaum, 1974), it may be that the inequality of power is 'controversial', because hierarchization also produces alienation and dissatisfaction. In accord with this hypothesis it was found in both experiments that the greater the hierarchization the lower the task satisfaction of the members. Tannenbaum (1968) has asserted that it is the total amount of control, not hierarchization, that contributes significantly to task satisfaction, a subjective indicator of effectiveness. These data suggest that these two dimensions of power – the total amount of control and the slope of the control curve – also have effects on effectiveness, but in the opposite direction. In the long run the lower task satisfaction in more hierarchical organized groups may also interfere with the profitability of the organization, since people may not be very motivated to earn as much as they can, when they are dissatisfied with their position. It is possible of course that the causal relationship between hierarchization and dissatisfaction may point the other way. Dissatisfaction, for whatever reason, may induce members to take control, leading to a greater hierarchization of perceived power the greater the dissatisfaction in the group or organization (Lowin and Craig, 1968).

The resource-dependence approach emphasizes the objective characteristics of the environment and tends to neglect the ways in which decision-makers perceive, filter, and interpret their organizational environment, which is the main emphasis of the information-processing perspective (Aldrich and Pfeffer, 1976). Sometimes the information-processing approach tends to disregard the importance of the objective environment. For example Weick (1969, p. 27) has stated: 'Rather than talking about adapting to an external environment, it may be more correct to argue that organizing consists of adapting to an enacted environment, an environment which is *constituted* by the actions of interdependent human actors'. In a more recent statement of his position Weick (1979, p. 169) has argued: 'If environments are enacted then there is no such thing as a representation that is true or false, there simply are versions that are more or less reasonable'. The present findings indicate that *both* the objective and the subjective aspects of the environment have to be taken into account to predict the effectiveness of the organization. In fact the manipulated uncertainty of the 'objective' environment explained most of the variance in the effectiveness scores. However, *both* the manipulated and the perceived environment provided better predictors of the profitability of the organization than the manipulated environment alone. Apparently it is not only the actual amount of resources that become available through the controllability of the 'objective' environment but it is also the perceived sense of control that contributes significantly to profitability.

The introduction of a formalized structure had a strong impact on the participativeness of the members and the distribution of power in the group, but the contribution of these imposed structural arrangements on performance was insignificant. One explanation could be that the imposed organizational design did not match the prevailing internal and external contingencies. Another, more likely interpretation, is that the variations in environmental uncertainty had an overwhelming influence on performance since our laboratory organizations were highly dependent on the resources that were made available through the control over the environmental contingencies. When organizations are less dependent upon their environments the arrangements of intraorganizational power may have a greater impact on performance, allowing decison-makers to make 'strategic choices' to select, shape, or even create the kinds of environments they want to deal with. To test this hypothesis, however, a completely different experimental design is required.

IMPLICATIONS FOR FUTURE RESEARCH

The importance of the ability to control and to cope effectively with the environment has also been a crucial feature in various expectancy-value theories formulated at an individual level of analysis. For example, the attribution of (social) power to oneself has been conceptualized by Bandura (1977) in terms of personal efficacy. According to Saltzer (1982) the belief in personal efficacy comprises several components: the belief of self-efficacy (Bandura, 1977), a person's belief or expectation that he or she can successfully perform a given behaviour; behavioural efficacy: the expectancy or estimate that a given behaviour will lead to valued outcomes (Rotter, 1966; Seligman, 1975) and causal attributions how the outcomes come about.

Several theories have focused on outcome attributions. For example, Weiner et al. (1971) have studied the conditions under which outcomes can be ascribed to 'ability', 'effort', 'task difficulty', and 'luck'. Rotter (1966) and Phares (1976) contend that individuals differ in their 'locus of control': whether they attribute their outcomes to their 'internal' factors such as ability and behaviour or to 'external' forces beyond their control. A state of 'learned helplessness' occurs when individuals develop a belief or expectancy that they cannot control the environment after they have been repeatedly exposed to situations in which outcomes appear to be non-contingent on their behaviour. These and other theories have been useful in understanding the aetiology of depression (Seligman, 1975; Abrahamson et al., 1978); psychological stress (Lazarus et al., 1974); problems of health and ways of dealing with them (Rodin, 1978); and even in conditions accelerating or retarding death of elderly hospitalized patients in old-age homes (Rodin and Langer, 1978). We believe that very similar 'pathologies' such as hopelessness, loss of morale, lack of cohesion, disintegration, and bankruptcy can be observed at the level of groups and organizations as well. To study these phenomena comparative research is needed which examines changes in cognitions and behaviour of individuals and groups when they are confronted with environments that differ in uncertainty. One of the attractive features of the Market-Co-ordination or 'Marco task' is that it can be performed by individuals as well as by groups. Moreover, the Marco task allows us to manipulate the degree of environmental uncertainty without affecting the structure of the task to any significant degree. The Marco task can also be extended in another direction. The decisional subunits in the present experiment were individuals rather than groups or departments as in some organizational studies (Hickson *et al.*, 1971; Duncan, 1972). In a recent study (Van der Linden and Rabbie, 1976) dyads instead of individuals were assigned to the task of studying the raw materials and product markets under the supervision of a co-ordinator.

We have used Tannenbaum's control graph question to measure the total amount and distribution of perceived social power in the organization. Significant correlations between the reported influence assessed by this scale with behavioural measures such as the verbal participation of a member in the discussion and the number of accepted decisions he made for the group increase our confidence in the validity of Tannenbaum's scale. However, the control graph method has been criticized on several grounds (Levine, 1973; Gundelach and Tetzschner, 1976). For example, it has been pointed out that respondents may use a variable frame of reference from one respondent to another, and from one hierarchical level to another. Influence and control are used as unidimensional concepts and no distinctions are made among several aspects of control such as decisions about pay, task structure, work activities, and so on. One of the main difficulties in using the Tannenbaum scale in our experiments has been that it does not differentiate between the control exerted over the internal and over the external environment. In future research this omission should be corrected. Experiments using the Marco task are under way, studying what kind of strategies and measures members are using to gain power in the group (Falbo, 1977) and how a balance of power between the members is to be achieved.

Contingency-theory approaches assume that the greater the fit or congruence between the uncertainty of the environment and the formalization of structure the greater the organizational effectiveness. However, in our second experiment the statistical interaction between these two variables was far from significant. One explanation could be that the formalized structure imposed on the organization was in fact incongruent with the environmental demands and because of this mismatch may have created various uncertainties of its own. Furthermore, it appeared that the organizational effectiveness was overwhelmingly determined by the availability of environmental resources and that variations in internal structure had only minor effects on effectiveness. These results suggest that a further specification is needed of what is meant by concepts such as 'congruence', 'fit', 'appropriateness' and other terms used by contingency theorists to indicate the match between structure and environment. It also appears that the theory may hold under only a limited range of environmental uncertainty. Research to test this proposition is in preparation.

NOTE

1. The authors are indebted to G.J.F. Hemmer and G.C. Vreugdenhil for their assistance in designing, execution, and analysis of the experiments reported here. They also wish to thank A. Hazewinkel, D. van Kreveld and W. Polet, all members of the Institute, for their constructive criticism of a first version of this manuscript. The research was supported by the Netherlands Organiztion for the Advancement of Pure Research (ZWO, grant 57.7).

REFERENCES

Abrahamson, L.Y., Seligman, M.E.P., and Tesdale, J.D. (1978). Learned helplessness in humans: Critique and reformulation,*Journal of Abnormal Psychology*, **87**, 49–74.
Aldrich, H.E. (1979). *Organizations and Environments*, Englewood Cliffs, NJ: Prentice-Hall.
Aldrich, H.E. and Mindlin, S. (1978). Uncertainty and dependence: Two conceptions of the environment, in *Organization and Environment*, L. Karpik (ed), New York: Sage.
Aldrich, H.E. and Pfeffer, J. (1976). Environments of organizations, in *Annual Review of Sociology*, Vol. II, A. Inkeles, (ed.), Palo Alto: Annual Review, pp. 79–105.
Allport, F.H. (1933). *Institutional Behavior*, Chappel Hill, NC: The University of North Carolina Press.
Bales, R.F., Strodtbeck, F.L., Mills, T.M., and Roseborough, M.E. (1951). Channels of communications, *American Sociological Review*, **16**, 461–468.
Bandura, A. (1977). Self-efficacy: Toward an unifying theory of behavioral change, *Psychology Bulletin*, **84**, 191–215.
Berger, P.L. and Luckman, T. (1967). *The Social Construction of Reality*, Garden City, NY: Doubleday Anchor Books.
Berrien, F.K. (1968). *General and Social Systems*, New Brunswick (NJ): Rugers University Press.
Blau, P.M. (1964). *Exchange and Power in Social Life*, New York: Wiley.
Blau, P.M., McHuge, Falbe, McKinley, W., and Tracy, P.K. (1976). Technology and organization in manufacturing, *Administrative Science Quarterly*, **21**, 20–40.
Bourgeois, L.J., McAllister, D.W., and Mitchell, T.R. (1978). The effects of different organizational environments upon decisions about organizational structure, *Academy of Management Journal*, **21**, no. 3, 508–514.
Burns, T. and Stalker, G.M. (1961). *The Management of Innovation*, London: Tavistock.
Cartwright, D. and Zander, A. (1968). *Groups Dynamics — Research and Theory*, London: Tavistock.
Child, J. (1972). Organization structure, environment, and performance – the role of strategic choice, *Sociology*, **6**, 1–22.
Child, J. (1976). Organizational design and performance: contingency theory and beyond, *Organization and Administrative Sciences*, 8/2 and 3: 169–183.

Child, J. (1977). *Organization, A Guide to Problems and Practice*, London: Harper & Row.

Davis, J.H. (1982). Social interaction as a combinatorial process in group decision, in Brandstätter, H., Davis, J.H. and Stocker-Kreichgauwer (eds), London: Academic Press, pp. 27–58.

Day, R. and Day, J.V. (1977). A review of the current state of negotiated order theory: An appreciation and critique, in S.K. Benson (ed.), *Organizational Analysis: Critique and Innovation*, Beverly Hills: Sage Publications, pp. 128–144.

Dill, W.R. (1958). Environment as an influence on managerial autonomy, *Administrative Quarterly*, **2**, 409–443.

Downey, H., Kirk, D., Hellriegel, D., and Slocum, J. (1975). Environmental uncertainty: the construct and its application, *Administrative Science Quarterly*, **20**, 613–629.

DuBick, M.A. (1978). The organizational structure of newspapers in relation to their metropolitan environment, *Administrative Science Quarterly*, **23**, 383–395.

Duncan, R. (1972). Characteristics of organizational environments and perceived environmental uncertainty, *Administrative Science Quarterly*, **17**, 313–327.

Falbo, T. (1977). Multidimensional scaling of power strategies, *Journal of Personality and Social Psychology*, **35**, 537–547.

Festinger, L. (1954). A theory of social comparison processes, *Human Relations*, 271–282.

Fiedler, F.E. (1978). Recent developments in research on the contingency model, in L. Berkowitz (ed.), *Group Processes*, New York: Academic Press, pp. 209–225.

French, J.R.P. Jr. and Raven, B.H. (1959). The bases of social power, in D. Cartwright (ed.), *Studies in Social Power*, Ann Arbor: University of Michigan, pp. 150–167.

Friedlander, F. and Pickle, H. (1968). Components of effectiveness in small organizations, *Administrative Science Quarterly*, **13**, 289–304.

Gundelach, J. and Tetzschner, H. (1976). Measurement of influence in organizations – critique of the control-graph method, *Acta Sociologica*, **19**, 49–63.

Hage, J. and Aiken, M. (1969) Routine Technology, Social Structure and Organizations Goals. *Administrative Science Quarterly*, **14**, 538–561.

Hazewinkel, A. (1980). Organisatiestructuur en contingentietheorie, in *Arbeids- en Organisatiepsychologie*, afl. **1** (February 1980), 4.3 1–23.

Hemmer, G.J.F. (1971). *Verslag van een exploratief onderzoek op basis van de theorie van Lawrence and Lorsch*, intern rapport ISP, Universiteit van Utrecht.

Hemmer, G.J.F. (1972). *Het effect van omgevingszekerheid op een aantal individuele en intragroepsvariabelen*, Afstudeerproject ISP, Universiteit van Utrecht.

Hickson, D.J., Hinings, C.R., Lee, C.A., Schneck, R.E., and Pennings, J.M. (1971). A strategic contingencies' theory of intraorganizational power, *Administrative Quarterly*, **16**, 216–229.

Hinings, C.R., Hickson, D.J., Pennings, J.H., and Schneck, R.E. (1974). Structural conditions in the organizational power, *Administrative Science Quarterly*, **19**, 22–24.

Homans, G.C. (1961). *Social Behavior: its Elementary Forms*, New York: Harcourt, Brace & World.

Horwitz, M. and Rabbie, J.M. (1982). Individuality and membership in the intergroup system, in *Social Identity and Intergroup Relations*, H. Tajfel (ed.), Cambridge: Cambridge University Press, Paris: Editions de la Maison des Sciences de l'Homme.

House, R.J. (1971). A path goal theory of leadership effectiveness, *Administrative Science Quarterly*, **16**, 321–338.

Howells, L.T. and Becker, S.W. (1962). Seating arrangement and leadership emergence, *Journal of Abnormal and Social Psychology*, **64**, 148–150.

Huber, G.P., O'Connell, M.J., and Cummings, A. (1975). Perceived environmental uncertainty: Effects on information and structure, *Academy of Management Journal*, **18**, 725–740.

Hunt, R.G. (1970). Technology and organization, *Academy of Management Journal*, **13**, 235–252.

Jennergren, L.P. (1981). Decentralization in organizations, in P.C. Nystrom and W.H. Starbuck (eds), *Handbook of Organizational Design*, Oxford: Oxford University Press, pp. 39–59.

Katz, D. and Kahn, R.L. (1978). *The Social Psychology of Organizations*, New York: Wiley.

Kelley, H.H. and Michela, S.C. (1980). Attribution theory and research, *Annual Review of Psychology*, **31**, 457–502.

Khandwalla, P.N. (1970). Viable and effective organizational designs of firms, *Academy of Management Journal*, **16**, 481–495.

Korman, A.K. (1973). On the development of contingency theories of leadership: Some methodological considerations and a possible alternative, *Journal of Applied Psychology*, **38**, 384–387.

Kreveld, D. van (1968). Vrijwillige samenwerkingsgroepen in de gezondheidszorg, *Tijdschrift Sociale Geneeskunde*, **46**, 828–832.

Langer, E.J. (1975). The illusion of control, *Journal of Personal and Social Psychology*, **321**, 311–328.

Lawrence, P.R. and Lorsch, J.W. (1969). *Organization and Environment*, Cambridge, Mass.: Harvard University Press.

Lawrence, P.R. and Lorsch, J.W. (1967). Differentiation and integration in complex organizations, *Administrative Science Quarterly*, 1–48.

Lazarus, R.S., Averill, J.R., and Opton, Jr., E.H. (1974). The psychology of coping. Issues of research and assessment, in Coelho, G.V., Hamburg, D.A., and Adams, J.E. (eds), *Coping and Adaptation*, New York: Bulbe Books.

Leavitt, N.J. (1951). Some effects of certain communication patterns on group performance, *Journal of Abnormal Social Psychology*, **46**, 38–50.

Leavitt, H.J. (1965). Applied organizational change in industry: structural technological and humanistic approaches, in March, J.G. (ed.), *Handbook of Organizations*, Chicago: Rand McNally.

Leifer, R. and Huber, G.P. (1977). Reactions among perceived environmental uncertainty, organizational structure and boundary spanning behavior, *Administrative Science Quarterly*, **22**, 235–247.

Levine, E.L. (1973). Problems of organizational control in microcosm: Group performance and group member satisfaction as a function of differences in control structure, *Journal of Applied Psychology*, **38**, 186–196.

Linden, W. van der and Rabbie, J.M. (1976). Doel differentiatie en-integratie in gesimuleerde organisaties, *Nederlands Tijdschrift voor de Psychologie*, **31**, 305–320.

Locke, E.A. and Schweiger, D.H. (1979). Participation in decision-making: one more look, in Shaw, B.H. (ed.), *Research in Organizational Behavior*, Vol. 1., Greenwich (Conn.): JAI Press, pp. 265–334.

Lord, R.G. (1977). Functional leadership behavior: Measurement and relation to social power and leadership perceptions, *Administrative Science Quarterly*, **22**, 114–133.

Lowin, A. and Craig, J.R. (1968). The influence of level of performance on managerial style: an experimental object-lesson in the ambiguity of correlational data, *Organizational Behavior and Performance*, **3**, 440–458.

March, J.G. (1976). The technology of foolishness, in March, J.G. and Olsen, J.P., *Ambiguity and Choice in Organizations*, Bergen.

March, J.G. and Simon, H.A. (1958). *Organizations*, New York: Wiley.

Mohr, L.B. (1971). Organizational technology and organizational structure, *Administrative Science Quarterly*, **16**: 444–459.
Mulder, M., Ritsema van Eck, J.R., and De Jong, R.D. (1970). Het systeem van functioneren on der verschillende omstandigheden in een grote organisatie, in P.J.D. Drenth, P.J. Willems, and Ch.J. de Wolff (eds), *Bedrijfspsychologie*, Kluwer: Van Loghum Slaterus, Deventer.
Mulder, M. and Stemerding, A. (1963). Threat, attraction to group, and need for strong leadership, *Human Relations*, **16**, 317–334.
Neganda, A.R. and Reimann, B.C. (1973). Task environment, decentralization and organizational effectiveness, *Human Relations*, **26**, 203–214.
Oostrum, J. van (1973). *Spreektijd en de toekenning van invloed*, Intern rapport ISP, Universiteit van Utrecht.
Oostrum, J. van (1979). *Spreektijd en leiderschap*, Afstudeerproject ISP, Universiteit van Utrecht.
Pennings, J. (1975). The relevance of the structural contingency model for organizational effectiveness, *Administrative Science Quarterly*, **20**, 393–410.
Pennings, J. (1976). Dimensions of organizational influence and their effectiveness correlates, *Administrative Science Quarterly*, **21**, 688–699.
Perrow, C. (1967). A framework for comparative organizational analyses, *American Sociological Review*, **26**, 194–108.
Perrow, C. (1970). *Organizational Analyses: A Sociological View*, Belmont, Cal.: Brooke-Cole.
Perrow, C. (1979). *Complex Organizations: A Critical Essay*, Glenview, Ill.: Scott, Foresman & Company.
Pfeffer, J. (1978). The micropolitics of organizations, in M.W. Meijer and associates (eds), *Environments and Organizations*, San Francisco: Jossey-Bass.
Pfeffer, J. and Leblebici, H. (1973). The effects of competition on some dimensions of organizational structure, *Social Forces*, **52**, 268–279.
Pfeffer, J. and Salancik, G.R. (1978). *The External Control of Organizations, A Resource Dependence Perspective*, New York: Harper & Row.
Phares, E.J. (1976). *Locus of Control in Personality*, Morristown, US: General Learning Press.
Rabbie, J.M. (1963). Differential preference for companionship under threat, *Journal of Abnormal and Social Psychology*, 586–592.
Rabbie, J.M. (1981). Desindividuacao e emergência de normas sociais numa audieca: experiência de campo sobre o comportamento colectivo, *Psicologia*, **11**, 4, 343–360.
Rabbie, J.M., Benoist, F., Oosterbaan, H., and Visser, L. (1974). Differential power and effects of expected competitive and cooperative intergroup interaction and intragroup and outgroup attitudes, *Journal of Personality and Social Psychology*, **30**, 45–56.
Rabbie, J.M. and Visser, L. (1976). Gevolgen van interne en externe conflicten op verhoudingen tussen groepen, *Nederlands Tijdschrift voor de Psychologie*, **31**, 233–251.
Rabbie, J.M., Visser, L., and Vernooy, L. (1976). Onzerkerheid van omgeving, differentiatie en invloedsverdeling in universitaire instituten, *Nederlands Tijdschrift voor de Psychologie*, **31**, 285–303.
Rabbie, J.M. and Wilkens, G. (1971). Intergroup competition and its effect on intra- and inter-group relations. *European Journal of Social Psychology*, **1**, 215–234.
Rabbie, J.M., Van Oostrum, J., and Hemmer G.J.F. (1983). *Onzekerheid, macht en effectiviteit, een experimentele toets van de contingentietheorie*. Ongepubliceerd intern rapport van het ISP Universiteit van Utrecht.
Rabbie, J.M. and Van Oostrum, J. (1981). *Patterns of Influence in Groups and*

Organizations. Paper presented to the General Meeting of the European Association of Experimental Social Psychology, Brighton, Sussex, 5–9 April, 1981.

Rabbie, J.M., Van Oostrum, J., and Visser (1983). *Machtsnivellering in kleine groepen*, intern rapport ISP, Universiteit van Utrecht.

Rabbie, J.M., Van Oostrum, J., and Vreugdenhil, G.C. (1983). *Omgevingsonzekerheid, formalisering en effectiviteit in laboratorium organisaties*, intern rapport ISP, Universiteit van Utrecht.

Reimann, B.C. (1974). Task environment and decentralization: A cross-national replication, *Human Relations*, **27**, 677–695.

Rice, A.K. (1963). *The Enterprise and Its Environment*, London: Tavistock.

Rodin, J. (1978). Somatopsychics and attribution, *Personality and Social Psychology Bulletin*, **4**, 531–540.

Rodin, J. and Langer, E.J. (1978). Long-term effects of a control relevant intervention with the institutionalized aged, *Journal of Personality of Social Psychology*, **36**, 988–999.

Rotter, J.B. (1966). Generalized expectancies for internal versus external control of reinforcement, *Psychological Monographs*, **80** (1), Whole no 609.

Saltzer, E.B. (1982). The relationship of personal efficacy beliefs to behavior, *British Journal of Social Psychology*, **21**, 213–221.

Schreyögg, G. (1980). Contingency and choice in organization theory, *Organization Studies*, 1/4, 305–326.

Seligman, M.E.P. (1975). *Helplessness: on Depression, Development and Death*, San Francisco: W.H. Freeman.

Shaw, M.E. (1981). *Group Dynamics, The Psychology of Small Group Behavior*, New York: McGraw-Hill.

Simon, H.A. (1957). *Administrative Behavior*, New York: Free Press.

Sorrentino, R.M. and Boutillier, R.G. (1975). The effect of quantity and quality of verbal interaction on ratings of leadership ability, *Journal of Experimental Social Psychology*, **11**, 403–411.

Stanfield, G.C. (1976). Technology and organizational structure as theoretical categories, *Administrative Science Quarterly*, **21**, 489–492.

Steers, R.M. (1975). Problems in the measurement of organizational effectiveness, *Administrative Science Quarterly*, **20**, 546–558.

Streufert, S. and Streufert, S.C. (1969). Effects of conceptual structure, failure and success on attribution of causality interpersonal attitudes, *Journal of Personality and Social Psychology*, **11**, 138–147.

Strodtbeck, F.L. and Hook, L.H. (1961). The social dimensions of a twelve man jury table, *Sociometry*, **24**, 397–415.

Sullivan, D.B. (1977) Task Environments and Organizations Structure, *Organization and Administrative Science*, **8**, nrs. 1–3, 185–202.

Tannenbaum, A.S. (1968). *Control in Organizations*, New York: McGraw-Hill.

Tannenbaum, A.S. and Cooke, R.A. (1979). Organizational control: A review of studies employing the control graph method, in Lammers, C.J. and Hickson, D.J. (eds), *Organization Alike and Unlike. International and interinstutional studies in the sociology of organisations*, London: Routledge & Kegan Paul.

Tannenbaum, A.S. and Georgeopoulos, B.S. (1957). *The Distribution of Control in Formal Organizations*, In: A.S. Tannenbaum (1968), pp. 45–71. *Control in Organizations*, New York, McGraw-Hill.

Tannenbaum, A.S., Kavcic, B., Rosner, M., Vianello, M., and Wieser, G. (1974). *Hierarchy in Organizations*, San Francisco, Jossey-Bass.

Thompson, J.D. (1968). *Organizations in Action*, New York: McGraw-Hill.

Tosi, H., Aldag, R., and Storey, R. (1973). On the measurement of the environmental:

an assessment of the Lawrence and Lorsch environmental subscale, *Administrative Science Quarterly*, **18**, 27–36.

Veen, P. (1980a). Kenmerken van organisaties, *Arbeids- en organisatiepsychologie*, afl. 2 (July, 1980), 4.1–38.

Veen, P. (1980b). Organisatietheorieën, in *Arbeids- en Organisatie-psychologie*, afl. 1 (February, 1980), 4.2 1–41.

Veen, P. and Van Haren, Th. (1980). Gedrag in organisaties, in J.M.F. Jaspars and Van der Vlist (eds), *Sociale Psychologie in Nederland*, Vol. III December: Van Loghum Slaterus, 81–150.

Visser, L. and Groot, R. (1970). *Appointed and Emergent Leadership in Competitive and Cooperative Intergroup Relations*, internal report ISP, University of Utrecht.

Visser, L. (1973), *Hierarchization of Influence as a function of Differential Information*. Unpublished Internal Report ISP, University of Utrecht.

Vreugdenhil, G.C. (1972). *De invloed van omgevingsonzekerheid en orga nisatiestructuur op taakuitvoering en doelbetrokkenheid*, Afstudeerproject ISP, Universiteit van Utrecht.

Webster Jr., M. (1975). *Actions and Actors, Principles of Social Psychology*, Cambridge Mass.: Winthrop Publishers.

Weick, K.E. (1969). *The Social Psychology of Organizing*, Reading, Mass.: Addison-Wesley.

Weick, K.E., Allegro, J.T., Bekkers, F., Binkhorst, D., Van der Horst, C. Mulder, M., Ritsema van Eck, F., Smeenk, G., and Veen, P. (1970). *A Laboratory Replica of Socio-technical systems: Rationale, Procedures and Pilot Results*, unpublished internal report ISP, University of Utrecht.

Weick, K.E. (1979). *The Social Psychology of Organizing*, 2nd edition, Reading, Mass., Addison-Wesley.

Weiner, B., Frieze, L., Kukla, A., Reed, L., Rest, S., and Rosenbaum, R.M. (1971). *Perceiving the causes of success and failure*, in E.E. Jones, D.E. Lanouse, H.H. Kelley, R.E. Nisbett, S. Valins, and B. Weiner (eds), *Attribution — Perceiving the Causes of Behavior*, Morristown, NJ: General Learning Press.

White, R.W. (1955). Motivation reconsidered: The concept of competence, *Psychological Review*, **66**, 297–323.

SECTION C

Psychology and Law

Progress in Applied Social Psychology, Volume 2
Edited by G.M. Stephenson and J.H. Davis
© 1984 John Wiley & Sons Ltd

9

Legal Literature, Dialogue with Lawyers, and Research on Practical Legal Questions: some Gains and Pitfalls for Psychology

S.M.A. LLOYD-BOSTOCK
Centre for Socio-Legal Studies
Wolfson College
Oxford

Although psychology and law is primarily thought of as a branch of applied psychology which may benefit law, it has frequently been commented that psychology as well as law has much to gain from research in the area (e.g. by Tapp, 1976; Farrington and Hawkins, 1979; Saks and Hastie, 1978). As Saks and Hastie put it, '. . . the law-psychology interface is not a one-way street . . . science profits handsomely from the connexion' (1978, p. 3). But such statements have tended to be acknowledgments that there are possible gains for psychology as a preface to the actual topic – the gains, or potential gains, for law. Thus, Saks and Hastie (1978), after stating in their opening pages that both sides could profit from more interaction, devote the rest of their book to the profit for law and lawyers. The form that the pay-offs for psychology might take are little more than hinted at – and indeed it is probably not feasible to develop both angles at once. However, it is worth taking the opposite emphasis and looking explicitly at the various ways that psychology can gain from the legal literature, and dialogue with lawyers; from research on practical legal questions; and from the development and/or application of psychological theory in legal settings. Research in this area not only presents psychology with the challenge of 'real-world' settings and problems; it also involves relating the concerns of psychology and psychologists to those of another discipline or group – law and lawyers – relationships which are further complicated by the fact that lawyers themselves, like psychologists, fall into a number of distinct groups with different concerns. I hope to show that a closer examination of the possible benefits of these interrelationships has implications for research strategy in the psychology and law area in particular, as well as more general implications for social psychological research and theory. The gains are diverse and not always obvious. I shall try to suggest possible gains as much as indicate actual ones. The first two sections look at the possible advantages, for research in psychology and law and in other areas, of closer dialogue with lawyers of different kinds and familiarity with legal literature. The second two sections look at some possible types of theoretical and methodological feeback into psychology from research in psychology and law.

DEFINING THE QUESTIONS AND DIALOGUE WITH LAWYERS

Alongside references to a more literally profitable feature of problem-oriented research – that it attracts funding – the most usual sense in which writers refer to the gains for psychology in psychology and law research is through challenges to theory. (This is discussed below.) If such research is to succeed in achieving its primary goals, rather than incidental ones, however, psychologists need to consider carefully what practical problems they are seeking to help to understand or solve, how they are defined, and by whom. There are a great many opportunities for psychologists to miss the point, or as King (1981) shows, to focus on part of the issue from one particular angle at the expense of the rest. If narrowness of focus and bias are to be avoided in psychological approaches to law, it is important to extend the basis of research to include lawyers', sociologists' and others' perspectives on legal phenomena, and definitions of practical 'problems'.

At the simplest level it is obviously important that psychologists should be familiar with the realities of the processes they are ostensibly researching. This is so for any applied research, but represents a problem in different ways and to different degrees. Where applied cognitive problems such as landing aeroplanes or monitoring air traffic are concerned the problem is, for the purposes of doing the research, probably fairly easily defined. It is clear enough what the pilot or air traffic controller's task is, and what constitutes more or less successful performance. Consultation with various personnel will probably be essential, but the outcome is unlikely to be too seriously ambiguous. Legal applied problems are a different matter. Psychology and law is particularly vulnerable to inadequate or mistaken definitions of research questions for a variety of reasons.

Bias Arising from Psychologists' Theoretical Interests

One reason for this vulnerability is that the practical problems researched are frequently defined as much by psychologists as by lawyers, and from an angle commensurate with certain theoretical interests within psychology. Thus, for instance, the way in which studies of the jury are conceived would seem as often to reflect theoretical interests in small group decision-making as any initiative from lawyers. Farrington and Hawkins (1979) point out that jury research provides a tempting opportunity to test psychological theories such as group polarization or equity theory. The amount and type of attention given to the identification parade would appear to result as much from its adaptability as a quasi-laboratory recognition task, its amenability to analysis in terms of signal-detection theory, and other virtues of convenience for psychological study, as any notion of its legal significance. This is partly, but not simply, psychology and law's version of what Baddeley calls the 'high-speed serial exhaustive scanning in female black homosexual drug addicts' problem (Baddeley, 1979) which involves taking a laboratory technique one happens to be interested in and applying it in a way which will attract large amounts of research funds. Certainly the need to raise funds has attracted some workers into the psychology and law field, especially in North America, but the concern of researchers in this field to promote justice and improve procedures is generally speaking genuine enough. The problem is also partly one of a failure to recognize some of the assumptions on which the research is proceeding.

Psychologists' Preconceptions About Law

This points to a second reason for the vulnerability of psychology and law research, which is that as members of the society whose legal system they are studying, psychologists inevitably have preconceptions about the nature and functions of law and may approach psychology and law research on this basis. It may *seem* clear enough what juries, identification parades, courts, and so on are there for, but this can be deceptive and may be one source of a certain lack of success in applying psychology in the area of law. Greer (1971) (a lawyer) suggests for example that one reason why attempts to apply eyewitness research have on the whole not been welcomed by lawyers is that psychologists have worked with a limited view of legal objectives – for instance, failing to grasp the fundamental point that establishing the truth is not the only, or perhaps even the main, goal of the criminal trial. As Twining (1983) shows, if psychologists approach research in psychology and law without paying sufficient attention to the *legal* models and theories they are implicitly adopting, they are likely to fall into the trap of adopting uncritically and unreflectively only one of a number of competing perspectives on law, to take legal rhetoric too much at face value, and to tend to place the courts or jury trials too much at the centre of the stage. These tendencies can be interrelated: research which reflects chiefly the rhetoric of justice can also tend to over-emphasize the jury trial rather than other trials; to give a corresponding under-emphasis to pre-trial processes; to view court processes in isolation as if self-contained; and to take what is going on at face value. The connection between a view of legal processes coloured by the ideology and rhetoric of justice and the temptation to give disproportionate attention to particular parts of the criminal justice system is shown in this passage from McBarnet's analysis of the process of conviction:

> Trial by jury may be one of the cornerstones of the ideology of justice but it is a rare event in criminal justice. So is the participation of the judiciary. So is the provision of legal representation for the defence . . . [T]he Crown Courts, where the ideology of justice is displayed in the form of judge, jury, and barrister for the defence deals with only 2 per cent of the business of the courts; 98 per cent of cases are dealt with in the lower courts by summary justice and that is a different brand of justice altogether. (McBarnet, 1981, p. 122)

Of course, the importance of the jury as a topic of research for psychologists is not to be measured solely in terms of the proportion of all cases heard in this way. There are plenty of considerations besides the relative (or absolute) frequency of its use which determine its practical legal significance. But the effort devoted to its study by psychologists does seem disproportionate to the topic. While there is clearly some justification in treating courts as quite central, over-emphasis on contested trials has thus had implications for a large proportion of psychology and law research, in the topics selected as the focus of research, and also in the assumptions underlying the ways in which research on legal processes outside the courts is approached. Less obvious than the focus on juries are strands running through research on non-court topics. For example Twining (1983) has suggested that much eyewitness research has tended to proceed as if the identification parade were solely an evidence-generating advice, leading to a contested trial. But the parade has multiple functions, and may, for example, at least as often serve the purpose of persuading a guilty suspect that the game is up and he or she might as well plead guilty – so that the need to introduce and assess identification evidence at the trial does not arise (see further below).

In another area of research – decisions on taking children into care – Dingwall (1984) shows how misleading it can be to detach court hearings from their institutional setting. He illustrates the point with a case from his own study (Dingwall et al., 1983) of a six- and an eight-year-old where care proceedings were taken – and succeeded – on truancy grounds. However, it would have been quite wrong to conclude that the children had been taken into care merely because of their poor school attendance. It was established in the course of interviews with social workers that this was a means of avoiding dragging the mother's history before the court, possibly at the risk of precipitating her suicide, while securing the children's well-being.

The Variety of Legal Standpoints and Legal Debates

A third closely related source of difficulty for psychologists in defining applied problems in this area is that there are alternative viewpoints amongst lawyers about how such problems ought to be defined. It is important to differentiate different groups of lawyers, and the different standpoints and perspectives of participants in legal processes. The standpoint of the law-maker differs from that of the judge; that of the advocate from that of the cautious solicitor; that of the police or other enforcer from all of these; and so on. Some of these differences between the perspectives of participants are reflected (not necessarily directly) in academic law. Thus, some legal scholarship is restricted to expounding rules, some to proposing improvements in the law, some to advising on methods of effective participation, and some to describing and explaining – often from the outside – the actual workings of legal processes and institutions. There are differing traditions within legal scholarship which imply different roles for the psychologist; and legal sources (such as the *Devlin Report* and various texts on evidence) that have been influential in directing the attention of psychologists to particular issues, are themselves the products of particular trends and bodies of legal thought. Moreover, even a defined group such as, for example, 'American academic lawyers of a given period', may be so individualistic as to make generalization dangerous (see Twining, 1972). There are therefore serious pitfalls for the unwary psychologist who comes into contact with only selected parts of the legal literature: psychologists often need to be aware of at least certain major legal traditions and debates.

One implication of this is that it is not safe simply to consult 'a lawyer' to make sure the legal side of one's research is not off-beam. The issue has been recently analysed by Twining in a discussion of the question of defining 'the problem' of identification and misidentification in legal processes, and hence the role of psychological research (Twining, 1983). Psychologist have tended to proceed on the assumption that the legal questions and problems surrounding eyewitness evidence to which they have directed their attention are reasonably clear, and that there would be broad agreement amongst lawyers on how these questions ought to be defined. Twining shows some of the dangers in such assumptions. He contrasts two general approaches to the study of law – the Expository Tradition and the Contextual Approach – and examines how far biases generally associated with the former, much narrower approach are to be found in the legal and psychological literature on identification. He shows that some, but not all, of these biases are indeed reflected in the ways in which psychologists have approached research in this area. In particular, he suggests that psychological research on witness reliability has been dominated by a view of the problem is primarily one of *admissible evidence* in the legal sense, which may ultimately be presented in court and used towards a decision on guilt, probably by a jury. This perspective is compatible with the much narrower legal tradition he outlines. Even when psychologists have moved their attention away from the courts, they frequently retain elements of this perspective, indicating the legal relevance of their work by reference to questions about evidence, courts, or juries. Twining suggests that psychologists and lawyers working in the area of identification need explicitly to free themselves from the 'evidence' model and replace it with a broader 'information model' which substitutes the notion of information for that of evidence and which takes a very broad view of 'legal processes' and 'the problem' of identification and misidentification.

Adopting an approach closer to the Contextual Approach would mean that at least some of the questions psychologists have been investigating could be cast in a quite different form, while other, quite new questions would be raised. For instance, as well as paying little attention to the multiple functions of identification parades, studies of the identification parade generally implicitly assume that the only evil of misidentification is wrongful conviction. A great deal of research has therefore been devoted to possible ways of modifying parade procedures such as to maximize true identifications while also minimizing false positives. A parade on which an innocent suspect is *not* identified would be regarded as satisfactory. However, such a parade may have had extremely undesirable consequences. The suspect may have suffered a great deal from 'misidentification' before being eliminated as a suspect following an identification parade. Moreover, most who suffer in this way probably never even take part in a parade at all. Yet researchers proceeded as if the identification (or lack of identification) of major concern is that which takes place at the parade. What is more, the scale of the problem of misidentifications of this sort, which do not result in a prosecution nor even in an identification parade, let alone wrongful conviction, may be far greater than the 'problem' in terms of wrongful convictions. The problem may for example cause as much harrassment to innocent persons as did the notorious 'sus' laws. As Twining points out, no-one really knows the scale of the problem because, despite the volume of literature, legal as well as psychological, on the topic, no-one has done the necessary demographic work.

Increasingly the tendency in academic law is away from the narrower legal traditions towards the broader (in Twining's terms, from the Expository Tradition towards the Contextual Approach), and certainly the latter is more in keeping with the development of a role for research in social sciences and the law. The contributions over the past 30 years or so of economics, anthropology, and sociology to the study of law have probably themselves contributed to these trends in present-day legal thought. Psychologists might do well to keep up with the times, especially if, in defining their research questions, they are implicitly buying into a view of legal processes which is widely and increasingly questioned within law.

Conclusions

The purpose of this section has been to suggest that more dialogue with lawyers and increased familiarity amongst psychologists with law and with the perspectives on law of other social sciences, might benefit law and psychology research. In particular some areas of law and psychology research seem to be in danger of stagnation and to have begun to contribute to a closed literature and peer group within psychology. This is not to undervalue the achievements of research which has been done: in the past ten years, achievements in the law and psychology field have been remarkable. It is rather to argue for the development of a wider and perhaps more sophisticated base to research in law and psychology as the next step. Psychology and law is such a diverse field that this kind of development needs to come mostly from within the work of specialists in particular areas. It has been possible only to throw out a few illustrations of the kinds of possibilities I believe a more open approach might indicate.

COMMON INTERESTS IN LAW AND PSYCHOLOGY

Although the various aims of legal discussion and of legal processes are quite different from the aims of psychology their concerns can be in some respects very close. The value of dialogue with lawyers and familiarity with the legal literature therefore need not lie only in defining the parameters of applied research in psychology and the law. There are also further, much wider ways in which legal material can be of relevance and value for work in psychology that is not necessarily applied – nor even necessarily concerned with understanding behaviour in legal contexts. Legal approaches to explaining and understanding human behaviour can sometimes be seen as a kind of commonsense psychology. In fact, this is what lies at the basis of much psychology and law research: psychological assumptions, implicit or explicit in legal rules or legal practice or legal discourse are regarded as prone to error because they are 'unscientific' and psychology's contribution is viewed as being to identify and test these unscientific assumptions, and replace them with something more reliable. But increasingly the legal literature surrounding such topics as responsibility, rules, *mens rea*, and probability, is being recognized as a resource by psychologists in a diversity of fields of psychology. On the topic of rules, for example, Hart's *Concept of Law* (1961) is closely concerned with rules and rule-governed behaviour; and Twining and Mier's *How To Do Things with Rules* (1982), while intended primarily as a student text, contains analyses of rule interpretation and so on, which could be of considerable interest to psychologists in some fields. Other examples are mentioned below. However, while I believe that psychologists have much to gain from familiarizing themselves further with legal material, and through more dialogue with lawyers, I do not wish to imply that lawyers' concepts, definitions, distinctions, and models can simply be lifted, whole or piecemeal, and used by psychologists; nor that legal cases proved ready-made stimulus material for psychology experiments. Gains will be most not from a one-way or a two-way street, but from integration. This requires a critical approach and a reasonably clear idea of how the legal material actually relates to psychologists' concerns.

Mens Rea

One of the most interesting explorations of this relationship between legal and psychological bodies of literature is that by Blackman (1981). Blackman discusses how the issue of *mens rea* is confronted in law; and how this relates to behaviourist approaches to understanding human behaviour. He suggests that both the criminal law and contemporary psychology have at their core similar questions about the relationship between mental life and overt behaviour, and the problem of interpreting the mental life of other people. If the questions for law and for psychology are indeed similar, and legal writers and practising lawyers have grappled with these problems for very many years, then it seems only sensible for psychologists to take every possible advantage of their thinking and the working solutions they have reached. Blackman shows how this might be done, integrating radical behaviourism with the apparently totally opposed legal model which accords a primary role to man's conscious monitoring and control of his own behaviour.

Blackman's analysis touches on questions at the heart of the relationship between psychology and law. The apparently fundamental divergence between legal and psychological models of man is often seen as an obstacle to interdisciplinary co-operation. Bentley (1979), discussing some reasons why lawyers may be unenthusiastic about psychology, quotes a judgment by Lord Simon of Glaisdale in a case in which duress was raised as defence to murder,[1] in which he sets out some basic principles:

> The law accepts generally two concepts as axiomatic, even though acknowledging that metaphysicians and psychologists have amongst themselves differing views on the subject. The first concept which the law accepts generally as a datum is that of the conscious mind. Of course the law recognises that exceptionally the mind may be absent, as with a person of severely subnormal mentality. And of course the law does not deny the existence of subconscious psychic activity. But it remains generally true that it is of conscious and provable mental processes that the law takes cognisance. . . . Largely concomitant with this first datum, the law also accepts generally as an axiom the concept of the free human will – that is, a potentiality in the conscious mind to direct conscious action – specifically, the power of choice in regard to action. Even the most devout predestinarian puts off his theology when he puts on his legal robe. The law may be an ass, but it is not Buridan's ass. (pp. 688–689)

Bentley goes on to say 'the lawyer then will not be impressed by the argument that men are machines: rightly or wrongly, between input and output the lawyers inserts free will' (p. 36). The idea that psychologists (and other social scientists) regard consciousness as not relevant to the explanation of behaviour, treat men as machines and try to do away with the concept of free will has sometimes become rather caricatured. Kenny, for instance, envisages the law taken over by social scientists in the following terms:

> To many people the apparatus of responsibility as administered in the criminal courts seems antiquated and inhumane: many social reformers look forward to a day when

the courts have gone the way of rotten boroughs and ordeal by combat. They look forward to a time when the law courts are replaced by something more scientific and clinical: when the determination of responsibility and the handing down of penalties by judicial bodies is replaced by the diagnosis of social illness and the prescription of appropriate medicinal procedures by teams of social scientists. (Kenny, 1978, p. 3)

Analyses such as that by Blackman might help dispel some misunderstandings about psychology, and about radical behaviourism in particular, as well as being of more direct value to psychology itself. It is to be hoped that the approach will be pursued further in this area.

Probabilities

Another general area with further potential is discussions of probability and reasoning which arise in many different ways in connection with the law – especially in connection with the meaning of proof, but also in other contexts such as defining what risk it is reasonable to take. These discussions, in common with psychological research in such areas as attribution and subjective probability (e.g. Tversky and Kahnemann, 1973, 1974, 1980; Bell, 1979; Cohen, 1972; Kelley, 1967), draw in various ways on models of statistical or other mathematical probability. In common with psychological research, legal discussions confront questions about the appropriateness of these uses of ideas of probability. Psychologists use concepts of probability not merely to model decision processes, but also to provide criteria for correct, or 'rational' judgments – an even more doubtful use of such notions (see Lloyd-Bostock, 1983). There is no *a priori* reason to prefer a particular sort of 'scientific' solution to practical causal questions as is common in attribution research (see Nisbett and Ross, 1980), and indeed it seems rather rash to assume that a model such as analysis of variance or Bayes' theorem provides an adequate or 'correct' solution and that the subject who comes up with a different solution is biassed or in error. A model appropriate to certain kinds of enquiry may not be at all appropriate in other contexts.

In a series of publications Jonathan Cohen has challenged the whole basis of research in the psychology of deductive and probabilistic reasoning (Cohen, 1979a, 1980a, 1981), suggesting that it has 'become entangled in a web of paradox' (Cohen, 1981, p. 317): his challenges have provoked fundamental discussion amongst the researchers concerned (see, e.g. the Commentary in the issue of *Behavioral and Brain Sciences* in which Cohen, 1981, appears). Cohen has also been carrying on a debate with such lawyers as Eggleston and Glanville Williams over the use of notions of probability to describe the task of the evaluation of proof in the courts (Cohen, 1977, 1980b; Eggleston, 1978, 1980; Williams, 1979). It is agreed that the structure of forensic proof in both criminal and civil cases involves notions of probability. Cohen, Eggleston and others have debated the specific conception of probability that one should apply. Cohen distinguishes two different ways of evaluating the strength of an inference from one particular fact to another – 'Pascalian' and 'Baconian'. As Cohen indicates, many people have been educated to think of the Pascalian calculus as *the* theory of probability: psychologists are certainly no exception. However, Cohen argues that the probabilities that fall to be evaluated by juries or other triers of fact are Baconian, not Pascalian. In constructing 'proof beyond reasonable doubt', rather than establishing certainty in terms of chance, he argues, we have to eliminate legitimate reasons for doubting what we want to prove. Cohen supports his argument by pointing to absurdities and paradoxes which result from the application of Pascalian probability to certain kinds of case. For example, complex civil cases illustrate a difficulty which arises when a number of independent points have to be conjointly established. On the Pascalian interpretation, the standard of proof in civil cases (i.e. the balance of the probabilities) would seem to require a probability of 0.5 or greater. But if there are two independent issues and the plaintiff proves each with a probability of 0.7 the conjoint probability falls below the required standard, at 0.49. As the number of issues involved goes up so does the level at which each has to be proved in order that the overall case may be proved at the required level. A complex case becomes virtually impossible to prove. However, if what is required is not the balance of Pascalian probability but the balance of Baconian probability, Cohen argues that this problem is met. (Others disagree.)

This kind of discussion raises for psychologists questions about not only the appropriateness of models of decision-making, the relationship between subjective and objective probabilities, and so on, but also the relationship between the concerns of psychology and of law. In order to clarify how legal material might and might not relate to the interests of psychologists, it is necessary to look carefully at the particular purposes of the particular discussion or analysis. This varies and is generally a tricky question over which lawyers themselves probably would not agree. A constant difficulty for psychologists is that the legal literature is normative in emphasis. Though some of the more recent literature is more empirical, particular discussions often defy classification as empirical or otherwise. In the context of the discussion of probabilities, it would seem that both the legal and the psychological discussion is concerned in some way with understanding 'mental life'. As Cohen has discussed (e.g. 1979b) the problems about applying Pascalian probability to legal cases correspond to some of the problems in using such conceptions of probability in empirical research on the psychology of probability judgments. In the debate over probabilities referred to above Eggleston writes of Cohen's '. . . forcing us to think about the mental processes involved in fact-finding in the courts' (1980, p. 678). But this clearly does not mean that Cohen and Eggleston are debating the psychology of decision-making. As Cohen, in stating that the proper structure of forensic proof as the Anglo-American system now stands is

Baconian, adds in a footnote the standard analogy: 'This is not of course a claim about how juries and other tribunals of fact actually do reason in ordinary practice, just as a statement of the traffic laws is not a description of how motorists actually drive' (Cohen, 1980b, p. 103).

In other areas legal discussion seems to come closer to making claims about how people actually reason in practice. One such is when legal definitions of responsibility and liability purport to accord with commonsense, non-legal notions of cause and responsibility.

Responsibility

Legal concepts of cause and responsibility are very extensively explained, analysed, and argued over in the legal literature. While use of this literature to refine such concepts for use in psychological research must obviously be critical, there are certainly possibilities and these have to some extent been pursued by attribution researchers (e.g. Hamilton, 1978; Fincham and Jaspars, 1980). Discussion of such concepts as foreseeability, reasonableness, risk, standards of care, and duty of care suggest not simply refinements to attribution theory but the basis of a quite different approach to the psychology of attributing causes and responsibility; I have suggested that a starting point for a much more social theory of attribution can be derived from tort doctrine (Lloyd-Bostock, 1983).

It would seem that in this area both lawyers and psychologists are interested in how ordinary people attribute responsibility in ordinary everyday extra-legal settings. This would mean that legal analyses such as Hart and Honoré's analysis of commonsense notions of cause and responsibility (1956, 1959) are quite directly related to the substance of some attribution research. In addition, textbooks on tort law, justifications of legal decisions given by the courts, case books, and law reports, all appear to be potential goldmines for the attribution researcher. But even given this apparently close relationship these sources need to be used with care if they are not going to be a source more of confusion than of clarification or inspiration. Even within the body of legal material which refers explicitly to commonsense, several different kinds of reference to commonsense need to be distinguished (see Lloyd-Bostock, 1981c). The courts may appeal to commonsense as a legal standard, or as part of a legal standard, so that the test of what in law constitutes 'a cause' is, or involves, 'what common sense tells us is a cause'. In so far as commonsense is the basis of the legal test, the meaning of causation in law has to be analysed with reference to commonsense (e.g. Hart and Honoré, 1959). Compatibility with commonsense is also invoked to explain, to justify, or to set limits on legal rules and decisions without the implication that commonsense was the legal standard. Yet another context is law reform debates, where appeals have been made to commonsense, ordinary ways of thinking – even public opinion. In order to decide whether psychological research relates closely to a particular appeal to commonsense it is necessary to examine closely the particular context in which the appeal is made.

Some, for instance, can be argued to involve empirical claims about non-legal rules. Thus I have argued (Lloyd-Bostock, 1979) that discussions such as that by Hart and Honoré (1956, 1959) involve empirical claims about non-legal rules in the following way. Attributions of cause or responsibility as social acts are comparatively rare events in comparison with the very rapid and continuous process of causal inference which is carried on unseen and in general unconsciously and unreflectively. We constantly act on assumptions about causal relationships, but rarely see fit to offer any kind of commentary on what we see as causally related and why. It seems that this second kind of attribution is called for by events which are puzzling or violate some kind of norm and require explanation, excusing, justifying, or otherwise accounting for. Social, cultural, and socio-linguistic rules will govern what, in the particular context, calls for an attribution, what constitutes an adequate explanation or account, how it is made or negotiated, and what further action may be implied – such as the imposition of sanctions or rewards. It appears that what the courts and such writers as Hart and Honoré are primarily concerned with, though they do not define what they are doing in these terms, is the extra-legal rules governing attribution as a social act. Hart and Honoré's analysis of common-sense explanatory and attributive inquiries seems to focus largely on the rules for adequate explanation and accounting in a given context. Such inquiries, are, for example, prompted by something abnormal or puzzling, and form part of a sequence of event; and what constitutes an answer is related to the context in which the inquiry arose. They write that 'in ordinary life . . . a causal explanation is most often prompted by the occurrence of something unusual: we ask for the causes of accidents, catastrophes, deviations from the normal or accepted course of events' (1956, p. 335). They note that 'what is normal and what is abnormal [and hence a candidate for a cause] will of course be relevant to the context of any given inquiry' (p. 334) and that what in one context it would be correct to cite as a cause, in another would be eccentric. In discussing attributive inquiries they suggest that 'we have less non-legal material on which to draw' (than in explanatory inquiries) because 'there is no precise system of rewards, punishments, or compensation to be administered by commonsense' (1956, p. 335).

It seems clear that they are thinking of attribution of the second kind outlined above, and seen an attributive inquiry as part of a sequence which may lead to some form of reward or sanctioning. Though empirical observation of attributions actually made may help identify the rules governing them, the 'ordinary man' seen in this way is not the average, consensus, majority vote, or whatever, of actual people, but a kind of personification of prescriptive rules supposedly actually in use. In so far as both Hart and Honoré and psychologists are concerned with the rules and norms applied in explanations and attributions of this kind, they appear to have interests in common. It may be that similar empirical claims underlie some arguments over probabilities, in as far as they appeal to our intuitive recognition of certain outcomes of reasoning as absurd, out of line with legal rhetoric, or whatever.

Conclusion

A view of the relationship between psychology and law as a one-way applied enterprise underrates the importance of psychologists and lawyers developing an understanding of each others' field. The kind of practical contribution that psychologists may make to law cannot always – or even often – take the form of a ready solution to a problem, but rather will consist in helping to clarify the dimensions of a problem, or bringing a new perspective and important insights (see Lloyd-Bostock, 1981a). I have tried to suggest in this section that law can sometimes serve a similar purpose for psychology.

CHALLENGES TO PSYCHOLOGICAL MODELS AND THEORY

There can be little doubt that the challenge of tackling practical problems has sharpened, and will continue to sharpen and expand the conceptual and theoretical framework of psychological research. Psychology and law research is certainly not alone among fields of applied psychology in this respect. The benefits of applied work for cognitive psychology have repeatedly been emphasized (e.g. Baddeley, 1979; Broadbent, 1980). Broadbent, who is particularly keen on this idea, has recently set out what he calls the 'credo of an applied experimental psychologist' (1980, p. 117) in which he explicitly advocates approaching research via practical problems as against starting with a model of man and investigating those areas in which the model predicts particular results. Giving reasons why the latter approach is an inefficient strategy, he comments that 'the point of the real-life situation is that it stops you overlooking things' (p. 118), and gives three illustrations of this from his own research interests. First, psychologists failed for many years to notice that one of the most important factors in human performance is the time of day at which it is observed: the incorporation of this factor into academic thinking came, not from pure research, but from the concerns of industry. Second (and probably the best known example), it was not until psychology was applied to modern communications systems that discussion of attention was reinstated in psychological models. And third, it was psychological study of how pilots land aeroplanes which led to the incorporation into academic theorizing of the contribution of dynamic and textual cues to depth perception. Further examples are not hard to find. Baddeley (1979) for instance, similarly argues that pursuing real-world problems benefits pure psychology by drawing attention to interesting and important questions, and by ensuring that theories and concepts do not become too laboratory-bound. To Broadbent's illustrations he adds vigilance, short-term memory, and signal-detection theory, as research areas of theoretical importance which entered the laboratory via real-world problems.

Illustrations from Eyewitness Research

Feedback from research in psychology and law to the theories and concepts of cognitive and social psychology occurs continually, although the relatively small body of research in this area makes it feedback on a fairly limited scale. The closest parallels to the examples cited above are probably to be found in research on the reliability of eyewitness evidence. Research in this area has frequently fed back into theory in cognitive psychology and to a lesser extent social psychology, at both specific and general levels. At a general level, dealing with questions about the reliability of memory for real-life events (such as criminal assaults) points up the limitations of laboratory research, not only in the generalizability of findings to other settings, but also in basing inferences about practical memory on theory developed through laboratory studies (see Rabbitt, 1981). Studies using staged-event methodologies have repeatedly failed to reproduce effects found in laboratory studies, or to produce results predicted by theory developed on the basis of laboratory studies. Thus there is the general finding that visual memory for faces is far worse when measured in field studies than in the laboratory. Laboratory-based theory which cannot account for such findings is shown to be inadequate.

One direction in which eyewitness research is pushing theory is towards more integrated approaches. Eyewitness research has demonstrated that there is a great deal more to the reliability of eyewitness evidence than the inherent limitations of human perceptual and memorial abilities, and has had to confront rather than simply acknowledge the dangers of attempting to study subsystems in isolation and of ignoring the intimate interconnections between various aspects of cognitive functioning. In the first of a series of recent texts to appear on eyewitness research, Clifford and Bull (1978) not only emphasize these interconnectons, but go further, and see the mechanisms of perception and memory as at base social systems. Perceiving and remembering man, according to their view, is inseparable not only from feeling and striving man, but also from man as a social being. A full and adequate understanding of person identification in everyday life must therefore take into account a dauntingly wide range of social, situational, and individual factors. Trying to escape this by over-simplifying can produce misleading results, as this body of research repeatedly illustrates.

At present the eyewitness literature is still based to a very large extent on laboratory research, and relies heavily on theory developed in the laboratory.

Now that there is a well-established and growing body of researchers in North America, Britain, and elsewhere working in this area it seems likely that the necessity of 'ecologically valid' or 'forensically relevant' research will increasingly lead to use of extra-laboratory methodologies, and hence increasingly have this kind of impact on theory (see Lloyd-Bostock and Clifford, 1983).

Examples of feedback at a more specific level, comparable to Baddeley's and Broadbent's illustrations, are widely found: when I informally raised the possibility with some of the researchers in the eyewitness area I found that they could readily point to examples they had come across in their own work. For example, studies of composite face-recall systems (such as Identikit, Photofit) feed into theoretical controversy over the encoding of faces. Experimental studies of these systems show low accuracy of recall, and insensitivity to variables that normally influence recall performance. Laboratory studies of recall, in contrast, typically yield high levels of performance under a variety of conditions. Davies (1981) and Davies and Christie (1982) discuss possible explanations for these discrepancies and for the gap in performance between face-recall and face-recognition. For example, one hypothesis is that the procedures used in composite systems are incompatible with the way faces are stored in memory. Composite systems require subjects to synthesize a face from component features. However, faces may be perceived and stored as holistic gestalts, not perceived serially, and stored as lists of features. Baddeley's training studies (Baddeley and Woodhead, 1983) have led to the same conclusion – a feature-based approach to training to improve face recognition is not successful. At a slightly broader level, a recent development within the eyewitness field is the growing interest in the question of the response of jurors and other decison makers to eyewitness evidence. This interest is encouraging the development of theory of the 'naive', lay, psychology of memory, or 'metamemory' (see Wells and Lindsay, 1983).

The field of law and psychology is immensely diverse, and while eyewitness research can be seen to have fed back into cognitive psychology, a similar process occurs in many other areas and in other ways. Saks and Hastie (1978) for instance refer to the various courtroom and mock-courtroom settings which have been studied as providing real-world tests of theory in social psychology. The pay-off for theoretical psychology of research in these and other legal settings does not arise solely from the fact that applied research demands a measure of ecological validity. The challenge to existing theory can also arise partly from the fact that such research is generated not by existing theory and the body of previous research surrounding it, but by practical questions arising outside psychology. This can indicate questions about, and aspects of, a process, which have not been confronted within theory apparently concerned with that process. My own research on the attribution of responsibility for accidents has illustrated for me how this can happen.

Illustrations from Research on Attributions of Responsibility

The stimulus to this research was not any prior interest in attribution theory or research, but an interest in legal questions about the operation of the tort system of compensation for victims of personal injury whereby the fault of another provides the basis for a claim for damages. This system has been widely criticized, and has been the subject of a Royal Commission (Pearson, 1978). It has been wholly or partly abolished in several other countries and states of America, and may ultimately be abolished in Britain. The specific questions I was tackling therefore arose from policy considerations. They concerned the roots of legal definitions of fault and liability in commonsense, and the reasons why only a minority of accident victims who might bring a damages claim in fact do so.

Attribution theory and the associated literature has been concerned with, amongst other things, questions about how and why we attribute responsibility for accidents and the consequences of making one attribution of cause or responsibility rather than another. Attributions of cause and responsibility for accidents in legal contexts provide some of the most obvious and dramatic 'real-life' instances of attributions. Yet when I sought to draw on attribution theory in the course of this research it became apparent that it did not confront some major dimensions of this kind of attribution process. In particular, it became clear that attribution theory was insufficiently social in emphasis to cope with explanation of many attributions of cause and responsibility outside the laboratory. (This, and the theoretical implications for attribution research, are discussed in more detail in Lloyd-Bostock, 1983.)

Firstly, certain powerful influences on attributions of responsibility, which arose from the social context, were inevitably almost totally missing from laboratory experiments. Thus data from accident victims indicated that *social* factors, such as the prospect of compensation, contacts with others, and the relationship between the victim and people who might potentially be held responsible, can strongly influence the ways in which responsibility is attributed (see Lloyd-Bostock, 1979; 1984). Secondly, it seemed that attribution theory had been outgrown by the research that it had generated. In particular, questions about the perception of causes and unspoken causal inferences had become confused with questions about the much rarer social processes of explaining, accounting, accusing, and so on, which were my primary concerns in studying attributions in legal contexts. Attributions of cause or responsibility can be in varying degrees reflective, made with reference to social rules, and so on, without being communicated to others. Nonetheless, at the two extremes, attributions as social acts and attributions as unobservable causal inferences raise very different sorts of question, and need to be approached through differing methods and with differing theoretical emphases. Thus, for example, if one is concerned with the social act of explaining events to others, then a question of primary importance is 'how does the individual select *the* cause (or even *a* cause) from a network of conditions and complex causal connections?'. Indeed, this is the central question posed by causal attributions of this sort, and must be answered with reference to why, and in what context the attribution occurs. (If it is a laboratory it will reflect that context.) However, if one is concerned with the continual rapid causal inferences which are part of the process of making sense of, and getting about in the world, the question of how causes are selected is not central; and indeed may not even make sense, since such a choice may simply not be made, and not need to be made for an adequate execution of the task or tasks at hand. Moreover, explicit causal judgments may not be an appropriate measure of such attributions by virtue of the very fact that they are explicit. Using causal statements as a measure of causal inferences involves viewing the relationship between them as direct and unproblematic – a view which is highly questionable – and placing emphasis on the question of *which* cause is focused on, rather than how causal links themselves are inferred. Thus it appeared that explicit attributional judgments elicited in the laboratory (the method which gave attribution theory its *prima facie* relevance to my concerns) may sometimes have been used inappropriately as dependent variables.

'Real-world' Research and Applied Research

In all the examples cited in this section, the potential and actual theoretical implications of applied work arise from tackling problems in the 'real world'. There is no reason in principle why these developments should come as spin-offs from applied psychology rather than through theoretical interests in natural settings. Baddeley (1979) draws a distinction between 'applied cognitive psychology' and 'cognitive applied psychology' which could also be drawn in respect of social psychology. According to this distinction, 'cognitive applied' psychology is primarily concerned to provide answers to practical problems, whereas 'applied cognitive' psychology is concerned to reach a theoretical understanding of 'real-world' psychological processes in natural settings – or in other words, aims to be an ecologically valid cognitive psychology. Of course, these two are related in that cognitive applied psychology, in tackling practical problems, will generally call for applied cognitive psychology. This would suggest that the kinds of contribution from applied to theoretical psychology emphasized by Baddeley and by Broadbent arise indirectly, via the need for external validity, and occur partly because there has been so little of what Baddeley calls applied cognitive research. Neisser (1978) in his opening address to the International Conference on Practical Aspects of Memory (Grüneberg *et al.*, 1978), offers a depressing list of illustrations of what he calls 'a principle that is nearly as valid in 1978 as it was in 1878: if *X* is an interesting or socially significant aspect of memory, then psychologists have hardly ever studied X' (p. 4). Applied research provides a valuable antidote to the consequences of concentrating so overwhelmingly on laboratory-based research and theory in esoteric areas.

Looking at the feedback from psychology and law research into theoretical psychology reveals that there are several sides to the relationship between pure and applied research. Much research in the field is not clearly categorizable as either pure or applied, but is rather, to borrow Baddeley's distinction again, a hybrid between 'applied social (or cognitive) psychology' and 'social applied psychology'. Research which sets out to attempt to understand behaviour in legal contexts almost inevitably, by the nature of the topic, soon takes on the guise of applied research as potential practical applications (and perhaps sources of co-operation and funds) seem to emerge. Perhaps as interest in natural settings grows the distinction between pure and applied psychology becomes a false dichotomy and the distinction between narrowly laboratory-based research on the one hand and 'real-world' research on the other becomes more marked. Baddeley's distinction raises the possibility also that as psychologists turn their attention increasingly to natural settings for their intrinsic psychological interest, rather than in attempts to apply psychology in useful ways, the role of applied research in the development of theory could diminish, since functions it now fulfils could be fulfilled from within theoretical psychology. But other factors make this unlikely. Some of the incidental spin-offs from applied to theoretical psychology are linked to particular stages and fashions in the development of psychology and, as suggested above, might perhaps equally be brought about by more deliberate means, adapting research strategy to overcome some of the negative results of tendencies to narrowing of perspective. However, Broadbent's observations about the role of human nature in the use of theory are convincing (Broadbent, 1980). Perhaps applied researchers, because of their focus of interest on practical problems, and different reference groups, are sometimes less inclined than pure researchers to be committed to a pet theory, methodology, or paradigm.

Conclusion

It is clear that there is great scope for feedback into theory from applied research in psychology and law as there is in other fields. It seems that these opportunities arise mainly because of a tendency (often necessary) to narrowness of focus in pure research – narrowness in the conception of theory itself, in the contexts and phenomena studied, the range of experimental paradigms used, and the perspectives and horizons of researchers. Conversely, applied research *does* need theory and good laboratory research. The implication would appear to be that it is important not to ignore either the 'pure' or the 'applied' camp, a distinction which in some respects has been over-simplified. To optimize the balance and cross-fertilization of different styles and categories of research, changes in attitudes are called for as much as changes in strategy.

MULTI-METHOD AND MULTI-THEORETICAL APPROACHES

Two reasons for pay-offs for psychological theory and methods from applied work were mentioned above: (i) that applied psychology, including psychology and law, provides an antidote to some of the weaknesses of over-narrow theoretical psychology; and (ii) more specifically, that applied work means looking at extra-laboratory contexts and 'real' problems. This does not mean, however, that going outside the laboratory and shaking off preconceived ideas is all there is to it. Developments in theory from applied work may sometimes be unforeseen and unsought and therefore appear to be fortuitous; but both of the above reasons are rooted in a more general necessity for applied research to be very much concerned with external validity. This and similar concerns also mean that applied research, more than pure research, tends to employ a combination of methods and to allow an open mind on theory. A balanced combination of methods and theoretical approaches is often most fruitful, particularly where research, applied or otherwise, aims to be ecologically valid.

Multiple Methods in Law and Psychology

Psychology and law research has frequently demonstrated the value of employing several methodological approaches to a problem, and less happily, the dangers of not doing so. Perhaps the clearest and most striking instance is the series of studies by Konečni, Ebbesen and colleagues (Ebbesen and Konečni, 1975; Kone˘and Ebbesen, 1979) on bail-setting and sentencing by judges. These studies are of interest at least as much for what they reveal about research findings obtained through experiments and other methods as for what they reveal about bail-setting or sentencing. Their work on both these topics is discussed specifically from the viewpoint of external validity by Konečni and Ebbesen in a special issue of *Law and Human Behaviour* devoted to Simulation Research and the Law (Konečni and Ebbesen, 1979). In this particular article they are concerned primarily with the implications of their work for problems of external validity in psychology and law research, and the doubt their findings throw on the results of many studies in this field, especially jury studies. However, there are implications for both theory and methodology in social psychological research in many fields, applied or otherwise.

Their more ambitious work was that on sentencing, which involved six data collection methods, including interviews with Superior Court Judges; questionnaires administered to judges; rating scale responses with judges, attorneys, and college students as subjects; experimental simulation which used judges, probation officers, and students as subjects; observation and coding of actual sentencing hearings; and archival analyses, coding court files after the sentence has been passed. The results were, as might be expected, very complicated, but in brief, it became clear that a very different picture of the factors affecting sentencing decisions, their relative weights, and their causal sequence would be reached by each of the different methods. For instance, the interviews with judges would suggest that their sentencing decisions are exceedingly complex, take a great deal of time to make, and are based on a careful evaluation of a great many factors. In contrast, the analysis of court files (which the authors argue produced the most trustworthy results for this study) revealed that a single factor – the probation officer's recommendation – makes a very accurate prediction of the judges' sentence. Discussing the implications of the work, Konečni and Ebbesen point out that the method which they considered produced the most powerful and accurate model of bail-setting decison-making (namely, observation of live hearings) was different from that which produced the most powerful and accurate model of sentencing; and moreover, that this difference could not be predicted, so that 'The rule "use as many different methods as you can" still applies' (p. 66).

The field of eyewitness research again reveals the dangers in basing practical recommendations on too limited methods (see Lloyd-Bostock and Clifford, 1983). This field of research also clearly shows that, while an open mind on theoretical issues is valuable, embarking on empirical research without a theoretical framework can be rather fruitless. Broadbent's (1980) reasons for recommending that research be approached via practical problems rather than via a prior theoretical model are persuasive, but even this approach must presuppose a theoretically informed formulation of research questions, and not some kind of theory-free approach which hopes that theory will emerge in due course. At the least, a general theory is clearly necessary to enable links and syntheses between applied and pure research (or between laboratory and extra-laboratory research) to be made and recognized. Eyewitness research has developed through the use of a combination of laboratory and 'staged-event' research. As mentioned above, it is now generally accepted that quite different results may be obtained in the laboratory and in more realistic settings (see Clifford, 1978). Almost without exception, researchers are pressing for a more widespread use of 'live-event' or 'staged-event' methodology. However, very similar methods were used in the early days of psychology and law research at the turn of the century, and yielded little more than a general recognition that eyewitnesses are extraordinarily fallible, and sometimes in curious ways. In the absence of a theoretical framework within which such findings could be understood, research in this area produced a rather aimless accumulation of poorly integrated, if sometimes intriguing findings. The theoretical advances which have since occurred took place almost exclusively through laboratory research. More recent work in the field is set against a rich and elaborate framework of theory – albeit theory developed almost entirely through laboratory experiment, and which is in some ways inappropriate to the topic of eyewitness research. Not only theory in the area of memory and recognition is drawn on. For instance, Deffenbacher has recently reinterpreted conflicting findings over the influence of arousal on the accuracy of recall and recognition, with reference to the Yerkes–Dodson curves (1983). Over a long time span (the best part of a century) research in this area demonstrates the benefit of bringing alternative methods and perspectives to bear on a problem and the potential sterility of confining one's methods, for whatever reason, too narrowly. Most researchers in the eyewitness field would agree that the proportion of laboratory studies, and the dominance of laboratory-based theory, is still undesirably high. Moreover, staged-event methodology is itself only in varying degrees successful at simulating real events (cf. Konečí and Ebbesen, 1979, discussed above). One limitation is that, as Malpass and Devine (1983) point out, the public do not always take kindly to being hoodwinked too thoroughly. In most studies, for example, subjects are at least partly debriefed between observing the staged event and measures of their recall or other dependent variable being taken. The development and refinement of methods therefore continues.

A fruitful series of studies in another area of psychology and law, which has deliberately started from 'real-life' observations and moved on to experiment, is that by O'Barr and colleagues (O'Barr, 1982) on the use of language in the courtroom. Prior to carrying out their experiments on the social psychology of language in the courtroom, these researchers made an extensive study of the speech actually used in the courtroom. The research programme thus combined ethnographic with experimental methods. More than 150 hours of taped court speech were obtained, together with observations noting the legal and social contexts of the speech samples. A team of investigators trained in linguistics, anthropology, and law analysed these data. Hypotheses were developed and the recordings provided raw material to create stimulus material for use in the subsequent programme of experiments. It is worth noting that this series of studies was embarked on for its theoretical interest and was not primarily intended to have practical implications for courtroom participants. The stimulus to start with extensive and systematic observations of actual courtroom speech lay in the fact that ecological validity was theoretically paramount, which in turn led to a study which was likely to yield information potentially of practical use – and perhaps the fact that the leading researcher was an anthropologist for whom it was natural to adopt an ethnographic approach. (The multi-disciplinary nature of this project also means that it should not only – or even primarily – be labelled 'psychology and law'.)

The use of multi-method approaches is all the more valuable in pscyhology and law, applied or otherwise, because the research questions are generally highly complex and multi-dimensional in comparison with the issues researched in much human experimental psychology. As Rabbitt shows (1981), narrowly focused laboratory research may be the most appropriate and useful approach to certain kinds of research questions, but generalization to the more complex questions which concern lawyers can be quite mistaken. The difficulties of generalizing to real-life legal contexts and the high likelihood that such uses of research results will be misleading have often been emphasized (see, e.g., Lloyd-Bostock, 1981a, b). Konečni and Ebbesen (1979) go so far as to suggest that erroneous information obtained by scientific methods, and therefore having an aura of truth, is more harmful than no information at all (p. 68). However, such a view in effect rules out the possibility of advancing our knowledge at all. If the application of findings can do more harm than good, the answer is not to abandon doing research at all because it cannot meet certain demanding criteria, or immediately produce applicable results, but to be most careful about the use to which the findings might be put. Of course the practical usefulness of particular pieces of research, and also of larger bodies of research, is limited, and it is of the greatest importance that these limitations should be understood, made explicit, and not lost sight of. There has sometimes been over-enthusiastic and premature application of psychology in legal contexts, and this needs to be guarded against. But sometimes discussions of the limitations of particular approaches and methods are overly negative (cf. for example the almost religious refusal to have anything to do with surveys amongst some sociologists). Since the search for a method which can avoid all pitfalls where practical use is concerned is necessarily doomed to failure, it would perhaps be more helpful to emphasize the value, however slight, in different methods, and the value of using several methods wherever alternatives are possible.

Flexibility in Theory and Theoretical Models

To some extent, similar comments apply to theory, though one would not wish to recommend theory-hopping as a general rule. If theory is regarded, not as a statement or claim about the way things are, but as a tool which will be modified or discarded when a better one is developed, it is evident that it is not logically necessary to pin one's hopes on any single theory or theoretical model; and the conceptual basis of a particular theory or model may well obscure alternative interpretations and approaches. In that it sets out to tackle practical problems, psychology and law research may profitably be open-minded about theory, provided this is not done indiscriminately, and provided the proper use of theory is not lost in the process. Often a varied range of theories appear to be relevant to a topic in law and psychology. Confession, for example, has been discussed from several theoretical bases, from psycho-analytic to decision-making models (Hilgendorf and Irving, 1981; Inman, 1981). The field of psychology and law is so diverse that a variety of models and theories would anyway have to co-exist.

There is, however, another level at which psychology and law research may be multi-theoretical and that is in the theoretical models used to define the problem or process being studied. This will in turn inform the more specific theoretical approach taken. King (1981) elaborates this idea in relation to the magistrates' court, making the essential point that it is not enough for theory merely to be grounded in data in the sense advocated by Glaser and Strauss (1967). He shows that the function of the magistrates' court can be thought of in six different ways: (i) Justice; (ii) Punishment; (iii) Rehabilitation; (iv) Management of crime and criminals; (v) Denunciation and degradation; and (vi) Maintenance of class domination. He shows how multiple versions of what is going on can exist side by side and legitimately account for various aspects of the system's operation in different ways. The six social functions he distinguishes are not all mutually exclusive, but are based on different theoretical models and give rise to different formulations of research questions. Each would produce an explanation of what is going on in the court couched in different terms. A multi-theoretical approach, he argues, shows up the weakness of all explanations which rely on a uni-dimensional approach to the criminal justice system. In a similar vein, Miller and Boster (1977) distinguish three 'images' of the trial: (i) the trial as a rational, rule-governed event; (ii) the trial as a test of credibility; and (iii) the trial as a conflict-resolving ritual. While these three are, again, not mutually exclusive, each image suggests differing research priorities and implies certain research questions.

It is rare for psychologists to discuss explicitly this aspect of their theoretical approach. It may be that such discussion looks more like a discussion of legal, political, or sociological theory than psychological, and therefore not the psychologist's concern. But certainly when psychologists make policy recommendations they must invoke theory at this level – implicitly if not explicitly. The first section of this paper tried to show that psychologists neglect these questions at their peril, and that failure to confront them has in the past been a source of weakness in psychology and law research.

Conclusion

This section has used the terms 'theory' and 'method' quite loosely in making the general point that it is sometimes advantageous to keep an open mind on theory, use multiple approaches, be aware of alternatives at various theoretical levels, and avoid undue pessimism over limitations. Some pieces of psychology and law research illustrate this and suggest that similar strategy might be appropriate in other areas.

CONCLUSION

Underlying this paper has been a wish to move away from a model of psychology and law which sees psychologists coming in and bringing their expertise to bear on practical legal problems with a view to recommending improved, more just laws, decisions, and procedures. The reason for dissatisfaction with this model is not pessimism about the prospects of psychology contributing anything of practical use in this context, but rather that the narrowly defined one-way, one-dimensional relationship such a model invokes is ultimately sterile. An expanded model would set this directly applied relationship in the context of the many other interrelationships between psychology and law; and between this and other forms of collaboration and exchange between psychologists and lawyers. This chapter has explored some of these interrelationships and tried to suggest some ways in which they have developed fruitfully, and might develop further.

Although this paper has been hung on the 'law and psychology' peg, much of it relates to psychology more generally. A rather restricted idea of what might be meant by 'useful' research, and an unimaginative view of the forms that applied research might take, is widespread. One consequence is that discussion of applied social psychology has often seemed to place it in an uncomfortable and usually second-class limbo, struggling for respectability with no real audience. Stringer's introductory remarks to papers in *Confronting Social Issues* (Stringer, 1982) reflect this. He writes, for example, that

> The great majority of so-called applied social psychology conducted in academic settings is not applied in any overt concrete way. The label is assumed because of the researchers' superordinate concern with issues or problems. . . . The source of questions to be examined is different from the source of theoretical questions but the destination of the answers is the same. . . . Who might apply research results under what circumstances and with what outcome is not part of the agenda of applied social psychological study. (p. 1)

Later he writes:

> If [academic researchers] wish to study problems plucked from the outside world they have to justify their work in conventional academic terms. They should add to the store of knowledge, for example, and publish research results in acknowledged journals. They have to live with colleagues who do just that. One consequence is the incantation that applied need not be separated from pure research. . . . One way in which the boundary is erased is by recourse to Lewin's famous dictum about the practicality of theory. . . . But . . . [t]here is no reason to believe that theoretically founded applied research is any more likely to be useful. (p. 2)

I have tried to show that, at least where law and psychology is concerned, the 'destination of the answers' is an item which should be very high on the psychologist's agenda, and that the pressure to gear research to colleagues within psychology and to such outlets as psychology journals can lead to too little attention being paid to legal literature and dialogue with lawyers. I have also tried to suggest that statement of the close interrelationships between pure and applied research cannot be dismissed as an 'incantation' which results from this pressure; and that applied research which is not applied in an overt, concrete way is rarely best viewed as research which has fallen short of its ultimate goal, but should often be viewed as research which has fulfilled quite different, perhaps less questionable, aims, which in turn need to be made explicit. If ideas about the nature of applied research are broadened, the relationship with pure research and the role of theory need also to be reconsidered.

The discussion has necessarily been tentative and rather selective. It has only been possible to refer to small parts of the now very diverse and sprawling field of law and psychology research, and scarcely at all to the practice of psychologists as experts. Much of it relates to aspects of the psychology–law relationship which have not been developed at all fully. In particular, the relationship between legal literature and the concerns of psychologists has barely been examined from psychology's point of view. If the discussion leads to any definite conclusion, it is the general one that psychology in many areas, and particularly, psychology and law, benefits from open strategies – open in theory and methodology, and in perspectives on the issues, on the psychologist's role, and on the possible relationships between psychology and law.

ACKNOWLEDGMENTS

I would like to thank for their help those who read and commented on an earlier draft, especially Professor William Twining and Dr Graham Davies.

NOTE

1. *DPP v. Lynch* [1975] Appeal Cases 653. The case concerned a man who drove a car containing a group of the IRA in Northern Ireland on an expedition in which they shot and killed a policeman. The man was not a member of the IRA and had acted unwillingly under the orders of the leader of the group, convinced that if he disobeyed he would be shot. The trial judge held that the defence of duress was not available to him and found him guilty: the Court of Criminal Appeal in Northern Ireland upheld the conviction: the House of Lords allowed the appeal, Lord Simon of Glaisdale and Lord Kilbrandon dissenting.

REFERENCES

Baddeley, A.D. (1979). Applied cognitive and cognitive applied psychology: the case of face recognition, in *Perspectives on Memory Research*, (Lars-Göran Nilsson (ed.), New Jersey: Erlbaum.

Baddeley, A.D. and Woodhead, M. (1983). Improving face recognition ability, in *Evaluating Witness Evidence: Recent Psychological Research and New Perspectives*, S.M.A. Lloyd-Bostock and B.R. Clifford (eds.), Chichester: Wiley.

Bell, C.R. (1979). *Uncertain Outcomes*, Lancaster: MTP Press.

Bentley, D. (1979). The infant and the dream: psychology and the law', in *Psychology, Law and Legal Processes*, D.P. Farrington, K.O. Hawkins, and S.M.A. Lloyd-Bostock (eds), London: Macmillan.

Blackman, D.E. (1981). On the mental element in crime and behaviourism, in *Law and Psychology: Papers Presented at SSRC Law and Psychology Conferences 1979-1980*, S.M.A. Lloyd-Bostock (ed.) Oxford: SSRC Centre for Socio-Legal Studies.

Broadbent, D.E. (1980). The minimization of models, in *Models of Man*, A.J. Chapman and D.M. Jones (eds), Leicester: The British Psychological Society.

Clifford, B.R. (1978). A critique of eyewitness research, in *Practical Aspects of Memory*, M.M. Grüneberg, P.E. Morris, and R.R. Sykes (eds), London: Academic Press.

Clifford, B.R. and Bull, R. (1978). *The Psychology of Person Identification*, London: Routledge and Kegan Paul.

Cohen, L.J. (1972). *Psychological Probability or the Art of Doubt*, London: Allen and Unwin.

Cohen, L.J. (1977). *The Probable and the Provable*, Oxford: Oxford University Press.

Cohen, L.J. (1979a). On the psychology of prediction. Where is the fallacy?, *Cognition*, 7, 385–407.

Cohen, L.J. (1979b). Some problems about probabilities and their psychology, Paper presented at SSRC Law and Psychology Conference, March 1979, Oxford.

Cohen, L.J. (1980a). Where is the fallacy? A rejoinder to Daniel Kahneman and Amos Tversky, *Cognition*, 8, 89–92.

Cohen, L.J. (1980b). The logic of proof, *Criminal law Review*, February, 91–103.

Cohen, L.J. (1981). Can human irrationality be experimentally demonstrated?, *The Behavioural and Brain Sciences*, 4, 317–370.

Davies, G.M. (1981). Face recall systems, in *Perceiving and Remembering Faces*, G.M. Davies, H.D. Ellis, and J.W. Shepherd (eds), London: Head Press.

Davies, G.M. and Christie, D. (1982). Face recall: an examination of some factors limiting production accuracy, *Journal of Applied Psychology*, 67, 1, 103–109.

Deffenbacher, K.A. (1983). The influence of arousal on reliability of testimony, in *Evaluating Witness Evidence: Recent Psychological Research and New Perspectives*, S.M.A. Lloyd-Bostock and B.R. Clifford (eds), Chichester: Wiley.

Dingwall, R. (1984). Child protection in its social and legal context, in *Legal Decisions Concerning Children*, Sally Lloyd-Bostock (ed.), Oxford: SSRC Centre for Socio-Legal Studies.

Dingwall, R., Eekelaar, J., and Murray, T. (1983). *The Protection of Children: State Intervention in Family Life*, Oxford: Basil Blackwell.

Ebbesen, E.E. and Konečni, V.J. (1975). Decision making and integration in the court: the setting of bail, *Journal of Personality and Social Psychology*, 32, 805–82.

Eggleston, R. (1978). *Evidence, Proof and Probability*, London: Weidenfeld and Nicolson.

Eggleston, R. (1980). The probability debate, *The Criminal Law Review*, November, 678–88.

Farrington, D.P. and Hawkins, K.O. (1979). Psychological research on behaviour in legal contexts, in *Psychology, Law and Legal Processes*, D.P, Farrington, K.O. Hawkins, and S.M.A. Lloyd-Bostock (eds), London: Macmillan.

Fincham, F.P. and Jaspars, J.M. (1980). Attribution of responsibility: from man the scientist to man as lawyer, *Advances in Experimental Social Psychology*, Vol. 13, L. Berkowitz (ed.), New York: Academic Press.

Glaser, B. and Strauss, A. (1967). *The Discovery of Grounded Theory*, Chicago: Aldine.

Greer, D. (1971). Anything but the truth? The reliability of testimony in criminals trials, *British Journal of Criminology*, 131–154.

Grüneberg, M.M., Morris, P.E., and Sykes, R.R. (1978). *Practical Aspects of Memory*, London: Academic Press.

Hamilton, V.L. (1978). Who is responsible? Toward a social psychology of responsibility attribution, *Journal of Social Psychology*, 41, 316–328.

Hart, H.L.A. (1961). *The Concept of Law*, Oxford: Clarendon Press.
Hart, H.L.A. and Honoré, A.M. (1956). Causation in the law, *Law Quarterly Review*, 72 1, 58–90; reprinted in *Freedom and Responsibility*, H. Morris (ed.), Stanford: Stanford University Press, 1961.
Hart, H.L.A. and Honoré, M.M. (1959). *Causation in the Law*, Oxford: Clarendon Press.
Hilgendorf, E.L. and Irving, B. (1981). A decision making model of confession, in *Psychology in Legal Contexts: Applications and Limitations*, S.M.A. Lloyd-Bostock (ed.), London: Macmillan.
Inman, M. (1981). Police interrogation and confessions, in *Psychology in Legal Contexts: Applications and Limitations*, S.M.A. Lloyd-Bostock (ed.), London: Macmillan.
Kelley, H.H. (1967). Attribution theory in social psychology, in *Nebraska Symposium on Motivation*, D. Levine (ed.), Nebraska: University of Nebraska Press.
Kenny, A. (1978). *Free will and Responsibility*, London: Routledge and Kegan Paul.
King, M. (1981). *The Framework of Criminal Justice*, London: Croom Helm.
Konečni, V.J. and Ebbesen, E.E. (1979). External validity of research in legal psychology, *Law and Human Behaviour*, **3**, 39–70.
Lloyd-Bostock, S.M.A. (1979). The ordinary man and the psychology of attributing causes and responsibility, *Modern Law Review*, **43**, 2, 143–68.
Lloyd-Bostock, S.M.A. (1981a). Introduction: Does psychology have a practical contribution to make to law?, in *Psychology in Legal Contexts: Applications and Limitations*, S.M.A. Loyd-Bostock (ed.), London: Macmillan.
Lloyd-Bostock, S.M.A. (1981b). Psychology and the law: a critical review of research and practice, *British Journal of Law and Society*, **8**, 1–28.
Lloyd-Bostock, S.M.A. (1981c). Do lawyers references to 'commonsense' have anything to do with what ordinary people think?, *British Journal of Social Psychology*, **20**, 161–163.
Lloyd-Bostock, S.M.A. (1983). Attributions of cause and responsibility on social phenomena, in *Attribution Theory, Essays, and Experiments*, J. Jaspars, M. Hewstone, and F. Fincham (eds), New York: Academic Press.
Lloyd-Bostock, S.M.A. (1984). Fault and liability for accidents: the accident victim's perspective', in *Compensation and Support for Illness and Injury*, D.R. Harris, M. Maclean, H. Genn, S. Lloyd-Bostock, P. Fenn, Y. Brittan, and P. Corfield (eds), Oxford: Oxford University Press.
Lloyd-Bostock, S.M.A. and Clifford, B.R. (1983). Introduction, in *Evaluating Witness Evidence: Recent Psychological Research and New Perspectives*, S.M.A Lloyd-Bostock and B.R. Clifford (eds), Chichester: Wiley.
McBarnet, D. (1981). *Conviction: Law, the State and the Construction of Justice*, London: Macmillan.
Malpass, R. and Devine, P. (1983). Measuring the Fairness of Eyewitness Identification Lineups, in *Evaluating Witness Evidence: Recent Psychological Research and New Perspectives*, S.M.A. Lloyd-Bostock and B.R. Clifford (eds), Chichester: Wiley.
Miller, G.R. and Boster, F.J. (1977). Three images of the trial: their implications for psychological research, in *Psychology in the Legal Process*, B.D. Sales (ed.), New York: Spectrum.
Neisser, V. (1978). Memory: what are the important questions?, in *Practical Aspects of Memory*, M.M. Grüneberg, P.E. Morris, and R.R Sykes (eds), London: Academic Press.
Nisbett, R. and Ross, L. (1980). *Human Inference: Strategies and Shortcomings of Social Judgment*, Englewood Cliffs, NJ: Prentice-Hall.
O'Barr, W.M. (1982). *Language Strategy in the Courtroom*, London: Academic Press.
Pearson, Lord (Chairman) (1978). *Report of the Royal Commission on Civil Liability*

and Compensation for Personal Injury (3 vols), HMSO, London, Cmnd 7054.

Rabbitt, P.M.R. (1981). Applying human experimental psychology to legal questions about evidence, in *Psychology in Legal Contexts: Applications and Limitations*, S.M.A. Lloyd-Bostock (ed.), London: Macmillan.

Saks, M.J. and Hastie, R. (1978). *Social Psychology in Court*, New York: Van Nostrand Rheinhold.

Stringer, P. (1982) (ed.). *Confronting Social Issues: Applications of Social Psychology*, Vol. 1, London: Academic Press.

Tapp, J. (1976). Psychology and the law: an overture, *Annual Review of Psychology*, **27**, 359–404.

Tversky, A. and Kahneman, D. (1973). Availability: a heuristic for judging frequency and probability, *Cognitive Psychology*, **5**, 207–32.

Tversky, A. and Kahneman, D. (1974). Judgment under uncertainty. Heuristics and biases, *Science*, **125**, 1124–31.

Tversky, A. and Kahneman, D. (1980). Causal schemas in judgments under uncertainty, in *Progress in Social Psychology*, M. Fishbein (ed.), New Jersey: Erlbaum.

Twining, W.L. (1972). Law and anthropology: a case study in inter-disciplinary collaboration, *Law and Society Review*, **7**, 561–583.

Twining, W.L. (1983). Identification and misidentification in legal processes: redefining the problem, in *Evaluating Witness Evidence: Recent Psychological Research and New Perspectives*, S.M.A. Lloyd-Bostock, and B.R. Clifford (eds), Chichester: Wiley.

Twining, W.L. and Miers, D. (1982). *How to Do Things With Rules*, 2nd edn, London: Weidenfeld and Nicolson.

Wells, G.L. and Lindsay, R.C.L. (1983). How do people infer the accuracy of eyewitness memory? Studies of performance and on metamemory analysis, in *Evaluating Witness Evidence: Recent Psychological Research and New Perspectives*, S.M.A. Lloyd-Bostock, and B.R. Clifford (eds), Chichester: Wiley.

Williams, G. (1979). The mathematics of proof, *Criminal Law Review*, 297–308 and 340–354.

Progress in Applied Social Psychology, Volume 2
Edited by G.M. Stephenson and J.H. Davis
© 1984 John Wiley & Sons Ltd

10

Psychological Studies of Procedural Models

L. WALKER
School of Law
University of Virginia
and A. LIND
Department of Psychology
University of Illinois, Urbana-Champaign

INTRODUCTION

In the law of most nations, considerable attention is devoted to the procedures prescribed for the enforcement of substantive law. Procedures often are viewed as devices for enhancing the fairness and accuracy of legal decisions, and they are accorded such importance that it is not uncommon to see cases decided on procedural rather than substantive grounds. Specific legal procedures are generally chosen on the basis of their conformity with an underlying procedural model, a theory of legal behaviour. Different nations use different procedural models as the conceptual basis of their legal systems, and even within nations various adjudicative institutions may differ in the procedural model used. We have been engaged for some time, in collaboration with John Thibaut and other colleagues, in applying the methods and theories of social psychology to the study of models of legal procedure.[1] We describe below our approach to this undertaking, and we review our work on the subject.

RATIONALE AND RESEARCH STRATEGY

Our decision to focus on the application of social psychology to investigations of procedural models, rather than some other type of legal issue, was based on several features of procedures that make them attractive topics of study. First, we were aware that the law often seeks to improve and reform the institutions it governs through changes in procedures, and we believed that procedural reform required a solid base of empirical research. Second, we knew that there existed in the legal literature several different models or theories of legal behaviour, and we realized that the methods of experimental social psychology were particularly appropriate for testing such models. Third, because procedures are usually based on assumptions about individual and group social behaviour, many of the topics that have been of longstanding interest to social psychologists arise in procedural debates, and we believed that our research would benefit both our disciplines. Finally, we saw that procedures, because they must be specific to be useful, are especially amenable to experimental operationalization and to theoretical analysis. (See Davis, 1980, for an approach to jury decision-making research that is similar in spirit to that we advocate here.)

The use of procedural change to achieve social reform is common in law. Procedures are the methodology of law, and other major changes in legal procedure can have effects as profound for the legal system as major methodological innovation would have for a scientific discipline. An example of such change can be seen in the expansion during the last decade and a half in the United States of the rights of recipients of social welfare. This reform was accomplished not only through changes in substantive law that provided new programmes and expanded existing programmes; it was also accomplished through procedural changes mandated by the courts and Congress, including for instance the application of a more elaborate procedural model to benefits hearings (see, e.g. *Goldberg v. Kelly*, 397 US 254, 1970).

It is important to consider how such reform comes about in order to know how psychological research on procedures can be most useful. Examination of court decisions and legislative debate suggests that much procedural reform is based on theoretical analyses. That is, potential procedural change is evaluated by policy-makers in terms of what effects would be expected on the basis of prevailing models of legal behaviour. Consider the benefits hearing example. A major part of the reasoning that produced change in benefits termination procedures involved the consideration of what constituted 'due process', and of what results seemed likely to occur if representation were allowed at benefits hearings. This consideration was based largely on assumptions and predictions arising from acceptance of an adversary procedural model. That is, legal representation in these hearings was believed to be worthwhile because the adversary model dictates that partisan representation promotes justice.

There are two stages in this reform process at which social psychological research methods can be put to especially good use: in testing the underlying theory or in evaluating the efficacy of particular reforms generated by the theory. We have concentrated, in the research reported below, on the former, theory-testing, enterprise. Our decison was based on our conviction that we could contribute most by discovering the strengths and weaknesses of the general procedural models used in policy formation and by offering new theory to overcome the weaknesses. As will be seen below, this decision led to the use of laboratory experimental methods, because such methods are best suited for theory testing. Before we describe our methodological strategy, however, a few words about the social psychological significance of procedures are in order.

The study of procedures and procedural models is particularly appropriate for social psychology. The procedural issues of importance to legal policy-makers are essentially questions about how groups should go about collecting and considering information for social decisions. These questions involve, of course, many issues that have long been of interest to social psychologists. In the research we report below, the independent variables have been rules about some aspect of group decision-making and the dependent variables have been individual beliefs, attitudes, or behaviour that might be affected by the rule variation. Our work includes many traditional topics both from individual social psychology and from group social psychology. We have drawn on methods and concepts from the social psychology of attitudes, attribution and social cognition, group decision-making, conflict resolution, and interdependence theory. Indeed, from the very beginning of our work on procedure we have been struck with the similarity of the issues and questions that arise in social psychology and in the legal analysis of procedures.

Procedures are more easily operationalized and more amenable to theoretical analysis than are some other aspects of legal behaviour. Because procedures are intended to guide routine decision-making, they must be relatively straightforward and specific. We were able to identify quite quickly the major variables that distinguish various procedural models and we had little difficulty in operationalizing these variables. When we began to accumulate empirical findings, we found that the systematic implications of our findings were generally clear because of the specific behaviours and role relations mandated by the procedures we were studying. For example, one of our early studies showed that adversary attorneys' search for evidence depended on the extent to which the facts in the case benefited the attorney's client (Lind, 1975; Lind *et al.*, 1973). As will be shown below, this finding had some clear implications for the types of bias that can be expected to arise in the information transmitted to legal decision-makers in an adversary justice system. Because adversary procedures allow only the attorneys to present information to the decision-maker, we could immediately see the systematic implications of the effects observed on individual attorney behaviour.

Research Methods and Initial Theories

Throughout our research we have employed laboratory methods of varying levels of complexity and experimental realism. Our methods choices were largely determined by a strategic decision mentioned above: we have adopted a theory-testing and theory-development approach to the study of legal procedures. The most accurate and most efficient methods for such an approach are those which capitalize on the control available in the laboratory. As is appropriate in deductive, theory-testing research, we have placed greater emphasis on internal than on external validity concerns. (A more complete presentation of our methods philosophy can be found in Lind and Walker, 1979.)

Laboratory research was especially appropriate for the study of procedure for two reasons. Like scientific theories, the legal theories that are offered in support of various procedural models usually specify what elements of the model are relevant for each advantage hypothesized. This permits construction of a laboratory situation with all the necessary elements for occurrence of the hypothesized phenomenon. In addition, the legal theories contained in procedural models are generally intended to be applicable to a wide variety of situations. This meant that we could construct theory-testing situations in the laboratory without violating some limiting condition of the legal theory. For example, the study described in the next section tested the hypothesis that adversary presentation of evidence counteracts pre-trial expectancy bias. Because the theory was quite specific in linking the hypothesized effect with adversary (two-sided) presentation of evidence, we knew that the mode of presentation, rather than some other element of the adversary procedural model, was the crucial variable. And because the theory makes it clear that the hypothesis does not depend on the nature of the case or on the type of decision-maker involved, we could use cases and decison-makers that improved experimental control and facilitated measurement of the dependent variables.

We have already mentioned that many decisions about procedural issues in law are based on acceptance of some model of procedure. These procedural models existed, of course, well before we began our research, and their existence allowed us to bring the full theory-testing strength of the laboratory experiment to bear on our research concern from the outset of our investigation. In particular, we began our research with a series of studies designed to test several hypotheses that legal scholars had derived from the adversary model of procedure. We were interested from the outset in comparing the adversary procedural model with non-adversary procedural models. The adversary procedural model is a theory of legal behaviour that advocates placing in the hands of the parties to a legal dispute primary responsibility for the development of issues and for the presentation of evidence and arguments at trial. The adversary model is realized when procedures restrict the decision-maker to a relatively passive role with respect to the pre-judgment trial process and when procedures allow the parties and their attorneys substantial latitude in the development and presentation of evidence. Non-adversary procedural models, in contrast, advocate placing control over the development of the issues and evidence in the hands of the decision-maker and his or her agents. Procedures based on non-adversary models would include the use of a court functionary to investigate the dispute and prepare evidence, encouragement of independent and active questioning of witnesses by the decision-maker, and restrictions on the extent to which the parties to the dispute can provide the decision-maker with unsolicited information about the case.

The procedural manipulations we used in our experiments and the hypotheses we tested were based on legal theories that consider the procedural models under consideration as ideals or pure types. The use of procedural models in policy-making frequently employs arguments concerning the properties of such ideals, so we felt that we should begin our studies with experiments that addressed the basic models, rather than attempting to recreate any particular manifestation of adversary or non-adversary legal systems. Nevertheless, it is important to note here some of the uses of adversary and non-adversary legal systems. In general, the civil and criminal procedure used in the United Kingdom and in many English-speaking countries, including the United States and Canada, is based on an adversary model. In contrast, the civil and criminal procedure of West Germany, France, and, indeed, most of the other nations of the world is based on the non-adversary model (see Thibaut and Walker, 1975, Chapter 4, for further information on these differences). National differences in the use of procedural models were important to our research project. Their existence allowed us to use cross-national replications of some of our experiments to test whether the effects we found were due to intrinsic properties of the procedures or to cultural familiarity and national endorsement of some of the procedures under study.

Among the hypotheses we tested were contentions offered in support of using procedures based on the adversary, rather than the non-adversary, model: that adversary procedures reduce expectancy bias in legal decisions, that adversary attorneys are more diligent in their search for evidence, and that litigants are more satisfied by the experience of adversary trials. As will be seen below, our results supported some of these hypotheses and failed to support others. Following the accumulation of some findings, it was possible to formulate a new theory of procedure (Thibaut and Walker, 1978) and begin a new round of studies.

THE ADVERSARY MODEL AND EXPECTANCY BIAS

One of the desiderata of any system of justice is that it should decide each case on its own merits. It is clearly unfair for the result of one case to depend on the other cases that previously have been brought before the decision-maker. But it is probably naive to think that decision-makers are unaffected by experience with other cases, and if there are dependencies between current and past decisions, one would certainly like to know how they could be limited or eliminated. It has been suggested that adversary presentation of evidence lessens the likelihood that the evaluation of current information will be biased by previous experience (Fuller, 1961). Our first experiment tested the hypotheses that expectancy bias is less evident in responses to two-sided evidence presentation than in response to one-sided evidence presentation (Thibaut *et al.*, 1972).

We constructed a stimulus case that involved a stabbing during a bar-room fight. The case turned on the question of whether the defendant's violent response to an assault was justified. The case consisted of a summary, which presented the basic situation and a statement of a self-defence rule, and 50 factual statements about the situation and individuals involved. The factual statements were selected (on the basis of pre-experimental scaling) so that half favoured the position that the defendant had acted unlawfully and half favoured the position that the defendant had acted lawfully. We also constructed six shorter cases to be used in inducing an expectancy bias; in five of these the accused had clearly acted unlawfully. None of the shorter cases involved people or situations similar to those in the larger, test case, but all involved a physical assault and the issue of self-defence. We hoped that subjects exposed to these cases would come to expect that defendants in such cases had acted unlawfully. US undergraduate students served as subjects in the experiment.

Three factors were manipulated. Half of the subjects were exposed to the six biasing cases prior to being exposed to the test case, and the remaining subjects were exposed only to the test case. Half of the subjects heard the case presented in a non-adversary fashion: the facts for both sides were read by a single individual. The remaining subjects heard an adversary presentation of the same facts: the facts favouring the defendent were presented by one individual and the facts against the defendent were presented by another individual. The third factor was the order in which the facts were presented in the test case: half of the subjects heard first the facts suggesting that the defendent had acted unlawfully, then those suggesting that he had acted lawfully; the remaining subjects heard the opposite order. The major dependent variable was the subjects' final ratings of the lawfulness of the defendant's actions.

The results of the experiment are presented in the first row of Table 1, which shows the mean final judgments collapsing across the order of presentation factor. We were apparently successful in inducing an expectancy bias: the average rating was closer to the 'unlawful' end of the scale in the conditions that included exposure to the six preliminary cases than in the conditions that did not. Given successful induction of expectancy bias, we could test the hypothesis concerning the bias-reducing characteristic of adversary presentation.

A comparison of the adversary- and non-adversary-presentation conditions for those subjects exposed to the bias-inducing experience shows that Fuller's hypothesis is supported. Subjects who heard the evidence presented in an adversary format gave higher ratings, showing they were less affected by the expectancy bias than were subjects who heard the evidence presented in a non-adversary format. The effect is all the more striking when the relatively mild nature of the procedural manipulation is considered. Before we could

Table 1.   Decision-maker Judgements with Adversary and Non-adversary Evidence Presentation

Experiment	Exposed to biasing cases		Not exposed to biasing cases	
	Adversary	Non-adversary	Adversary	Non-adversary
US Experiment	3.62	2.18	4.27	3.76
French Experiment	4.18	2.64	4.85	4.60

Notes: Values are mean ratings of the lawfulness of the defendant's actions, using nine-point scales. Lower values are in the direction of the expectancy bias.
Data from Thibaut, *et al*., 1972, and Lind, *et al*., 1976.

accept the results as clearly supportive of the adversary model, however, we needed to eliminate an alternative explanation for the effect.

It could be argued that the effect we observed was not caused by some intrinsic characteristic of adversary presentation. The reduction of expectancy bias might instead have come about because the adversary presentation conditions were more likely to remind our US subjects of a court trial and because this resemblance made salient standards of fairness that prompted subjects to suppress their bias. That is, the reduction of bias might have depended on the use of adversary procedures in the courts of the subjects' country.[2] This line of reasoning predicts that subjects from countries with non-adversary justice systems would show a reduction of expectancy bias when confronted with non-adversary presentation, because for them it would be this condition that reminded them of court trials.

We tested this explanation by replicating the experiment in France, where a non-adversary model of legal procedure prevails (Lind, *et al*., 1976). Our subjects were French undergraduates, but otherwise the method, manipulations, and measures were essentially the same. The results are shown in the lower row of Table 1. The French students are more likely in all conditions to believe that the defendant had acted lawfully, but otherwise the results were the same as those found in the original study. For the French subjects, as for the US subjects, adversary presentation reduced expectancy bias.

It appears that there is something about adversary presentation of evidence that reduces expectancy bias. We have not gone beyond these two studies in search of the processes that give rise to the effect, so we can do little more than endorse Fuller's original suggestion that adversary presentation leads to a reservation of judgment until all the facts have been heard, thus permitting facts incongruent with the expectancy bias to have their full impact. Perhaps the two-sided presentation does render more salient the possibility that incongruent facts will have to be considered and lessens the assimilation of incoming information to the opinion produced by the expectancy bias. Whatever the process involved, the existence of the effect offers some support for the adversary procedural model. As we shall see in the next section, such support was not always found in our experiments.

THE ADVERSARY MODEL AND INFORMATION SEARCH

In addition to the hypothesis that the adversary model of procedure limits expectancy bias, advocates of adversary procedures had proposed that the quality of information presented to the decision-maker is higher when adversary procedures are used (e.g. Freedman, 1970). They reason that the close alignment of attorneys' interests with their clients' interests provides a strong incentive for diligent investigation of the case. If an attorney receives better outcomes when his or her client wins the case, the attorney will be strongly motivated to discover all potentially beneficial evidence, according to this reasoning. With highly motivated attorneys on both sides of the case, the additional facts discovered by this more diligent investigation will be presented to the decision-maker by one side or the other.

We tested this claimed advantage of the adversary model by constructing a task that simulated the situation that confronts an attorney during the discovery and presentation of evidence (Lind, 1975; Lind *et al.*, 1973). Our subjects, who were first-year law students, could expend resources to accumulate facts about a legal case to which they had been assigned. This expenditure of resources reduced, in proportion to the number of facts found, the subjects' payment for participating in the experiment, but they could gain additional payment if they succeeded in meeting the demands of their role. By manipulating elements of the roles to which subjects were assigned, we would create the crucial elements of adversary and non-adversary roles. We also manipulated the nature of the case and the role supposedly given to another law student participating in the same experimental session as the subject.

All of the subjects were told that their task would be to accumulate evidence about a case by purchasing sets of facts from the experimenter and then to decide which evidence should be presented to an impartial decision-maker. Half of the subjects were assigned an adversary role. These subjects were told that they had been assigned to represent one of the parties in the dispute and that their primary goal should be to win a favourable decision for their client. Subjects in the adversary role were told that they would receive a bonus payment if their client won the case. The remaining subjects were assigned a non-adversary role. These subjects were told that they were to represent the decision-maker and that their goal should be to provide the decision-maker with an accurate and complete picture of the case. Non-adversary role subjects were told that they could win a bonus payment if the decision-maker was pleased with their work. Crossing the manipulation of the subject's own role was a manipulation of the role said to have been assigned to a second law student in the session: half the subjects were told that the other law student had been assigned an adversary role and the remaining subjects were told that the other had been assigned a non-adversary role.

The manipulation of the nature of the case concerned the proportion of evidence favouring the two sides. Some of the subjects in adversary roles found 25 per cent of the facts favourable to their client, some found 50 per cent of the facts favourable, and some found 75 per cent of the facts favourable. For subjects in non-adversary roles the manipulation varied the percentage of facts favourable to the defendant.

The hypothesis under test was that adversary role subjects would invest in more facts regardless of the role of the other law student and regardless of the nature of the case. The mean number of facts accumulated by adversary and non-adversary subjects in each case condition is shown in Table 2. Only in the 25 per cent favourable column is the difference between adversary and non-adversary subjects significant; in the 50 and 75 per cent favourable columns there are no significant differences. That is, it was found that only when most of the facts were unfavourable to the attorney's client did adversary attorneys engage in more extensive search than did non-adversary attorneys. When the case was neutral or favourable, however, adversary attorneys were no more diligent in their fact search than were non-adversary attorneys.

Table 2.   Number of Facts Accumulated by Adversary and Non-adversary Attorneys

Subject's role	Percentage of Favourable Facts		
	25	50	75
Adversary	26.00	21.00	18.25
Non-adversary	20.25	22.60	23.00

Note: Values are mean number of facts accumulated.
      Data from Lind, 1975.

In addition to accumulating evidence, the subjects chose which evidence they wanted to present to the decision-maker. The effects of the differences in diligence of investigation on the transfer of information through various procedural systems could be assessed by examining the facts that pairs of attorneys chose to present. Pairs of attorneys were constituted by randomly matching two subjects whose roles were complementary. That is, subjects were paired with other subjects who had been assigned the role that matched the first subject's 'other role' condition. These dyads simulated the role relations in adversary, non-adversary, or 'mixed' (one adversary and one non-adversary attorney) procedural systems. The number and distribution of facts presented by dyads in each type of system were analysed. These analyses showed no significant differences between systems in the number of facts reaching the decision-maker. However, the systems did vary substantially in how the distribution of evidence reaching the decision-maker differed from the distribution of evidence found by the attorneys. We found that the non-adversary pairs generally presented the decision-maker with distributions of evidence that faithfully portrayed the distribution they discovered. 'Mixed' pairs generally produced a distortion in the distribution of evidence reaching the judge, and this distortion took the form of over-representation of facts favouring the party represented by the adversary attorney. Adversary pairs exhibited a more subtle distortion: the distribution reaching the decision-maker was accurate if the case was balanced, but if the case was unbalanced (i.e. if the original distribution of evidence was 75 per cent favourable to one side), the distribution was distorted in favour of the party disadvantaged by the evidence. The distortion observed in the presentation of adversary pairs was the result of the more diligent search by adversary attorneys in the 25 per cent favourable condition.

These findings do not provide much support to the adversary model hypothesis that the facts reaching the decision-maker are better under adversary than under non-adversary procedures. Overall, the evidence presented by adversary pairs was no more extensive than the evidence presented by non-adversary pairs, and the evidence presented by adversary pairs was subject to distortion when the case was unbalanced. Other research shows additional limitations on the quality of information reaching the decision-maker in adversary procedural systems. Sheppard and Vidmar (1980) studied the possibility that adversary attorneys are more likely than non-adversary attorneys to persuade witnesses to give biased testimony, and found evidence that such effects occur. It appears that at least some elements of the adversary model are incorrect. Before we describe a new model of procedure that was designed with these findings in mind, we will describe our studies of subjective appraisals of justice. These studies are crucial to the new theory, and they represent the great majority of our work on the social psychology of procedural models.

THE ADVERSARY MODEL AND FAIRNESS JUDGMENTS

The research described above shows that procedures vary in their effects on the beliefs and behaviour of decision-makers and attorneys. The third general topic we have addressed in our study of procedural models concerns the effects of procedures on the remaining major role in the legal system: the litigant or disputant. In legal writing dating back at least to the early years of this century (Pound, 1906), there has been concern about the satisfaction or dissatisfaction of those whose disputes or actions are tried by the justice systems. Our research on this topic has included studies of the preferences of uninvolved parties with respect to procedures that would be used if they were in a legal dispute, studies of the reactions of observers of trials, and studies of the reactions of disputing parties. Our experiments on the reactions of people in the disputant role are particularly striking, because they have usually shown that procedures affect satisfaction and fairness judgments independently of the outcome of the procedure.

In the first study of subjective judgments of procedures (Walker *et al*, 1974), we manipulated disputant subjects' belief in their innocence, the procedure used at trial, and the trial outcome. We measured subjects' judgments of the fairness of the procedure and the verdict, and their satisfaction with the verdict and the procedure. The experimental method used was rather elaborate: In order to construct the social situation of interest we needed to place subjects in conflict over real outcomes, and we needed to generate a question of rule-breaking that would be the basis of the trial in which we made our procedure manipulation.

We told the subjects (US undergraduate students) that they were participating in a business simulation that involved a competition between advertising companies. Several options were included to make the simulation more realistic, including an opportunity for the subject's coworker, who was actually an experimental confederate, to use 'industrial espionage' to gain an advantage in the competition. The subjects were manoeuvred into a situation in which they believed that another company had charged the subject's coworker with having used the espionage option. The rules of the simulation provided that espionage charges be resolved by a brief trial conducted by attorneys and a judge who were available in the event of such a charge being made. The rules further provided that the result of the trial would determine not only the guilt or innocence of the coworker, but also the monetary pay-off to be given to all members of the company, including the subject.

By giving the subjects a method of supposedly monitoring the use of the espionage option by their coworker, we could manipulate their belief about the validity of the charge. Some subjects were given information that showed their coworker to be innocent, others were given information that showed the coworker to be guilty, and still others were given no information about the coworker's actions. We manipulated the procedural model used to resolve the espionage dispute by varying the rules governing the trial. In the adversary procedure condition each disputant was represented by a partisan attorney; in the non-adversary condition a single attorney represented both sides. The same evidence was presented at the trial regardless of the procedure used. The outcome of the trial was manipulated by notifying some subjects that the judge had found their company guilty and reduced their earnings to nothing and by notifying other subjects that the judge had found their company innocent and left unaltered their cash payment. The subjects completed the major rating scales after they learned that they had either won or lost the monetary payment.

The disputants' average ratings on several measures are presented in Table

Table 3.   Disputant Ratings of Reactions to Trial

| | Procedure | |
Rating scale	Adversary	Non-adversary
Fairness of procedure to self	6.30	4.80
Satisfaction with procedure	5.90	4.34
Opportunity to present evidence	5.78	4.26
Satisfaction with verdict	5.70	4.93

Notes: All values are means on nine-point rating scales. Higher values are ratings in direction of scale name.
Data from Walker, *et al.*, 1974.

3. The entries in the table are means collapsed across the knowledge of guilt and trial outcome factors. The results were straightforward: across a variety of scales, including measures of satisfaction and perceived fairness, the adversary procedure produced higher ratings than did the non-adversary procedure. In most instances the effect of trial procedure did not interact with either of the other manipulations – both winners and losers responded more favourably to adversary than to non-adversary procedures. The effect appeared not only for the disputants but also for observer subjects, who were told what the trial was about and who were brought in to watch the procedure without being party to it. Because later studies have pointed to perceptions of the fairness of the procedure as the major variable driving the other evaluative reactions, this effect has come to be known as a procedural-fairness effect, in contrast to the distributive-fairness effects that had been long a concern of investigators interested in equity theory (cf. Adams, 1965). The procedural-fairness effect in the Walker *et al.* study was the first of many findings showing that procedures, as well as outcome distributions, are important determinants of satisfaction and fairness.

There have been at least three very close replications and extensions of this first study, all using the same business-simulation cover story. LaTour (1978) tested the effects of each of the components of the classic adversary procedure: the assignment of a different lawyer to present each side of the case, the alignment of the lawyer's outcome with his or her client's outcome via a contingent fee arrangement, and the provision that disputants can choose the lawyer that represents them. He found that disputants' judgments of the fairness of the procedure and the verdict were enhanced by each component. In a more recent study, we used the business-simulation procedure to test whether the enhancement of the perceived fairness of procedure and verdict by adversary procedures applied even to disputants who did not directly participate in the trial (Walker, *et al.* 1979). The situation of being affected by the outcome of litigation in which one does not actually participate has become increasingly common in the US, where many people are affected by class action law suits. We found that adversary procedures led to higher ratings of the fairness of the *procedure* by both participating and non-participating disputants, as well as by observers, whose outcomes were unaffected by the trial. However, only participating disputants showed higher ratings of the fairness of the trial *outcome* when the procedures were adversary. In a study described in greater detail below, the enhancement of procedural-fairness judgments by adversary procedures was found in both binding and non-binding hearing procedures (Lind, et al. 1983).

In addition to the experiments using the business-simulation procedure, there have been a number of other studies testing the effects of adversary and non-adversary procedures on subjective evaluations of the procedure and the outcome of trials. Quite a few studies have used the method of placing subjects in conflict by assigning them to opposite sides of a hypothetical dispute and giving them evidence on the case, then asking them to evaluate several procedures that might be used to resolve the dispute (e.g. Houlden *et al.*, 1978; LaTour *et al.*, 1976; Thibaut *et al.*, 1974; see Thibaut and Walker, 1975, for a description of much of this research). In general these studies have shown a strong preference for adversary procedures, although they have shown a lessening of the difference between adversary and non-adversary procedures under certain circumstances. For example, when disputants' outcomes are correspondent, when a standard is available for deciding the dispute, or when a disputant is advantaged by the evidence, the preference for adversary procedures is less strong.

Other studies have simply instructed subjects to imagine themselves in the role of either a defendant or a plaintiff in a dispute and then asked subjects for ratings of their preferences and fairness judgments of adversary and non-adversary procedures described in terms of the actions and roles of those involved (Kurtz and Houlden, 1981; Lind *et al.*, 1978). These studies have provided evidence that fairness is a major factor, perhaps the most important factor, in preferences for legal procedures. They have also shown that favourable reactions to adversary procedures generalize across populations. Kurtz and Houlden found that prisoners in US military stockade preferred adversary procedures and judged them more fair than non-adversary procedures. The Lind *et al.* study used a cross-national study to test whether the more favourable reactions of US subjects to adversary procedures were due to familiarity with adversary courtroom procedures, by soliciting preferences and fairness judgments from residents of nations that use non-adversary procedures and by comparing their responses to those collected in nations that use adversary procedures. We found remarkably similar preferences and fairness judgments, always favouring adversary procedures, among French, West German, British, and US university students.

With these later studies, a finer analysis of the components of procedural systems became possible. Houlden *et al*. (1978) noted that dispute resolution procedures could be distinguished in terms of who controls the pre-decision presentation of evidence, which they termed 'process control', and in terms of who controls the decision that resolves the dispute, which they termed 'decision control'. Thibaut and Walker (1975) suggested that a crucial element of the adversary procedure was its property of vesting process control in the disputants and their representatives and decision control in the third party. In all of the experimental studies of disputants' reactions to procedures, differences in ratings of control over the trial and differences in ratings of opportunity to present evidence have mirrored the fairness and satisfaction effects. As described in more detail in the next section, differences between procedural models in the distribution of control have assumed major theoretical significance.

The effect of adversary procedures on perceptions of procedural fairness is remarkable both in its simplicity and in its consistent replication in different experimental settings and with different populations. We will return to empirical studies of procedural-fairness judgments later, but first we will present a brief description of the theoretical position that has produced some of the more recent studies.

A THEORY OF PROCEDURE

We begin our discussion of the new theory by distinguishing the types of conflicts that might be addressed by dispute resolution procedures (see Thibaut and Walker, 1978, for a full presentation of the theory). The crucial distinction is between conflicts about the true state of the world and conflicts about the proper distribution of outcomes. Conflicts of the first type are resolved by the determination of truth; conflicts of the second type are properly resolved by distributions of goods or penalties that conform to norms of fairness. Truth conflicts are exemplified by disputes over scientific facts; fairness conflicts include civil and criminal law cases.

Truth disputes are generally characterized by substantial correspondence of interests (Thibaut and Kelley, 1959) that leads all parties to seek the correct answer to the question at hand. All parties will agree that what is needed to resolve the dispute is a process that maximizes the likelihood that the answer is accurate; its fairness is of lesser importance. The theory argues that truth disputes are best tried using non-adversary procedures. Recall that our study of the effects of adversary and non-adversary procedures on information search and presentation showed that non-adversary legal systems were least likely to distort the evidence, and one would certainly prefer that the procedures used to resolve truth conflicts be free of distortion. The potential loss of perceived fairness that results from forgoing adversary procedures is less serious in truth disputes, because high correspondence of outcomes between disputants has been shown to lessen disputants' preference for adversary procedures (LaTour, *et al.*, 1976).

Fairness disputes (termed 'conflict of interests' in Thibaut and Walker, 1978) differ from truth disputes in having no solution that will be accepted as true or desirable by all disputing parties. In fairness disputes the goal of the dispute-resolution process must be the allocation of outcomes in line with disputant standards for fairness. According to the Thibaut and Walker theory, the predominant standard for legal fairness is that embodied in equity theory (see Adams, 1965, and Homans, 1961, for seminal works on this topic), which states that the distribution of outcomes should be proportional to individual contributions to the situation in dispute. For equity norms to be used, however, the decision-maker charged with resolving the dispute must know what were the contributions to and outcomes from the disputed situation. Adversary procedures, by giving process control to the disputants, place responsibility for evidence presentation in the hands of those best positioned to provide evidence of contributions and outcomes, and this enhances the likelihood that the outcome of the dispute will be fair by equity standards. Because fairness is a much more subjective standard than truth, the preference of disputants for adversary procedures and the greater apparent fairness of these procedures are especially desirable in resolving conflicts of interests. Because fact-finding in these conflicts is important only in the service of equity decisions, rather than in its right, the biases that occur in information search are less troubling here than in the resolution of truth conflicts.

Another argument that suggests the propriety of adversary procedures for trying fairness disputes involves well-documented differences in attributional processes between actors and observers (Jones and Nisbett, 1971). The decision-maker in a dispute-resolution hearing is in a position that corresponds to that of an observer, in attributional terms, and he or she may err in over-estimating the causal influence of dispositional factors in the dispute. To place process control in the hands of the decision-maker would invite an under-consideration of situational factors. In contrast, when disputants are given process control they can be expected to emphasize situational causes in the disputed situation, because as the actors in the dispute situational factors are most salient to them. Disputant presentations may well contain sufficient information on situational causes to counteract some of the dispositional attribution bias to which decision-makers are subject. It might be argued that this line of reasoning suggests that both decision control and process control should be given to the disputants, through the use of a bargaining or mediation procedure. However, the theory advocates that a third party be given decision control in fairness disputes, at least when correspondence of outcomes is low, because the disputants will find it very difficult to agree on any particular decision.

Although we are most concerned here with procedural models and therefore with variations in process control, it should be noted that the theory predicts that not only process control, but any procedural variable that affects the presentation at the trial of individualized arguments and evidence, will affect procedural and distributive fairness. For example, the codification of legal principles formerly in common law, by limiting individualized argument in each separate dispute, will reduce the presentation of information needed to produce equitable outcomes and will therefore reduce the fairness of legal procedures. Even if potential litigants are allowed to exercise process or decision control in the codifying legislation, the result would not be as effective as allowing process control at trial because prior to the emergence of a particular dispute even the potential litigants cannot know exactly what factors will be relevant to a fair resolution.

Although most disputes contain elements both of the cognitive conflict that characterizes truth disputes and of the conflict of interest that characterizes fairness disputes, in most instances one element or the other predominates and the choice of procedure is clear. There are some disputes, however, in which the two elements are of approximately equal importance. When truth issues arise that are amenable to scientific or logical solution, and when these truth issues are tied to substantial outcome conflict, it is difficult to accept the trade-offs required in using one procedure or another. Examples of such disputes can be found when unresolved scientific issues affect substantial outcome interests, as has occurred in debates about the safety of nuclear power or in disputes about the fairness and validity of psychological tests. In such instances, the theory calls for a two-stage process in which non-adversary procedures are used first to resolve the truth conflict and adversary procedures are used subsequently to resolve the outcome conflict.

There are other theories that address some or all of the questions that arise in procedural-fairness research and its applications. We will not present these other theories in this chapter, but we mention them in the hope that readers will seek them out. Sheppard (1983) has developed a typology of stages of dispute resolution and types of control that is much more detailed than that employed in the Thibaut and Walker (1978) theory. His analysis has allowed him to propose new procedures that appear to combine some of the beneficial elements of both adversary and non-adversary procedures. Leventhal (1980; Leventhal, *et al*., 1980) has proposed a theory of allocation rules that includes both procedural and distributive components and that begins to examine the question of when each is most important to fairness judgments. Lerner and Whitehead (1980) offer an analysis of procedural-fairness judgments that links variation in which procedures are preferred by disputants to variation in the nature of the relationship from which the dispute arose. In addition to this encouraging level of theoretical effort, empirical studies of procedural models continue, as will be seen in the next section.

RECENT RESEARCH ON PROCEDURAL MODELS

The theory just described places most legal disputes in the general category of conflicts of interests, and it predicts that the use of procedures high in disputant process control will maximize fairness in such disputes. The research described above has shown repeatedly that disputants' perceptions of procedural fairness are in accord with this prediction in hearings that involve binding judgments. The frequent observation of the process-control effect on procedural-fairness judgments prompts one to wonder whether the effect would generalize to other, non-binding forms of conflict resolution. The question of whether the process-control enhancement of procedural fairness occurs in non-binding hearings has recently taken on additional practical importance.

Many US courts have begun to require cases to undergo non-binding dispute resolution hearings prior to trial, in the hopes of increasing voluntary settlements and reducing backlogs and delay (Adler, *et al*., 1982; Ebner, 1981; Lind and Shapard, 1981). An important question confronted by policy-makers designing such programmes is how various procedures would affect disputant satisfaction, and it would be quite useful to know whether the now substantial literature on procedural fairness can be applied to non-binding hearings. Indeed, given evidence that perceptions of procedural fairness increase disputant acceptance of trial outcomes (Lind *et al*., 1980) and given that non-binding hearings are, by definition, successful only if the decision-maker's suggestions are accepted by both sides, one could argue that procedural-fairness judgments have even greater importance in non-binding than in binding hearings.

The theory just described concentrates on binding procedures because in the most severe disputes the decision-maker must be given decision control if a resolution is to be assured. However, the logic that leads the theory to endorse adversary procedures for trials of fairness conflicts should also hold for non-binding dispute resolution hearings. If alloting process control to the disputants enhances the fairness of binding trials by promoting the consideration of individual contributions and outcomes, the same processes should cause disputant process control to enhance the fairness of mediation hearings. A recent study tested the hypothesis that disputant process control would enhance procedural-fairness judgments regardless of the bindingness of the conflict resolution forum (Lind *et al*., 1983).

The study, which was mentioned briefly above as a positive replication of the original experiment on procedural-fairness judgments, used the business-simulation method described earlier. The subjects were male and female American undergraduates. Three factors were manipulated: the procedure used in hearing evidence on the espionage charge, the extent to which subjects were required to accept the decision-maker's judgment, and the nature of that judgment. The trial procedure was either adversary, with high disputant process control, or non-adversary, with low disputant process control. The decision-maker's judgment was either binding, in which case the disputant's decision control was low, or it was non-binding, in which case the disputants' decision control was high. In the former conditions the disputants were required to accept the outcome of the conflict-resolution hearing, in the latter they could reject the outcome and attempt to negotiate a resolution of the dispute with their opponent. The decision-maker recommended either that the subject's company lose most of its earnings or that it be allowed to retain most of its earnings.

Table 4.   Disputant Reactions to Binding and Non-binding Hearings

Outcome	Binding hearings		Non-binding hearings	
	Adversary	Non-adversary	Adversary	Non-adversary
Favourable	7.15	5.87	7.07	6.06
Unfavourable	5.64	5.40	6.36	4.50

Notes: All values are means on nine point rating scale. Higher values indicate higher procedural fairness.
Data from Lind, *et al.*, 1983.

Manipulation checks showed that the subjects perceived the manipulations as intended: subjects in the non-binding conditions rated their influence over the final outcome higher than did subjects in the binding conditions, and subjects in the adversary conditions rated their control over what happened in the hearing higher than did subjects in the non-adversary conditions. The average procedural-fairness judgments of disputants in this study are shown in Table 4. As expected on the basis of the theory, high disputant process control enhanced perceived procedural fairness regardless of the bindingness of the dispute resolution and regardless of the favourability of the outcome. The decision-control manipulation had no significant effect, either alone or in interaction with other independent variables, on procedural-fairness judgments. It appears that the process-control effect on procedural-fairness judgments can indeed be generalized to conflict resolution contexts other than trial.

Other studies have shown similar effects for procedures that affect the flow of information in ways similar to those involved in the process-control manipulation. Folger (1977) found that procedures that allowed workers the opportunity to exercise 'voice', the capacity to offer complaints about disputed pay allocations, resulted in enhanced judgments of procedural fairness regardless of the success of the complaints. Tyler and Caine (1981) found that procedures used to decide disputed legislation were judged more fair when hearings were held to allow citizens to offer their views on the dispute.

CONCLUSIONS

Recent research, such as that presented in the preceding section, makes it clear that the psychology of procedural fairness has applications to non-legal, as well as legal, procedures. It remains to be seen just how far we can generalize procedural effects and processes such as those we have described in this chapter. There is good reason to push our study of procedural models to new settings. Many of the questions that are posed by competing models of trial procedure arise also in the context of legislative, administrative, and organizational procedures.

There is much still to be done in the study of legal procedures. The research that has been conducted and the theoretical development that has occurred since we began studying procedural models have led to a better understanding of legal behaviour. However, we have devoted most of our efforts to the study of a single cluster of procedural variables and there are many other independent and dependent variables to be investigated before we will have exhausted this topic. We hold to our initial belief that social psychological research can play an important part in ensuring that the theories used to develop procedural innovations have a sound empirical base. It is in the development of that base and in the initiation of the scientific process of theory testing and theory development that we have attempted to contribute to improving procedural justice.

NOTES

1. The work we report here includes as much of John Thibaut's effort, insight, and reasoning as it does of our own, of course. In addition, many others contributed to the research projects we describe here. We recognize their important contributions through citation of their published reports.
2. We never used the terms 'adversary' or 'non-adversary' in conducting this or any other experiment, but it is possible that the subjects noticed that the adversary presentation was similar to what they would see in a courtroom while the non-adversary presentation was not.

REFERENCES

Adams, J.S. (1965). Inequity in social exchange, in L. Berkowitz (ed.), *Advances in Experimental Social Psychology*, Vol. 2, New York: Academic Press.

Adler, J.W., Felstiner, W.F., Hensler, D.R., and Peterson, M.A. (1982). *The Pace of Litigation*, Santa Monica: Rand.

Davis, J.H. (1980). Group decision and procedural justice, in M. Fishbein (ed.), *Progress in Social Psychology*, New York: Erlbaum.

Ebner, P. (1981). *Court Efforts to Reduce Delay: A National Inventory*, Santa Monica: Rand.

Folger, R. (1977). Distributive and procedural justice: Combined impact of 'voice' and improvement on experienced inequity, *Journal of Personality and Social Psychology*, **35**, 108–119.

312   PROGRESS IN APPLIED SOCIAL PSYCHOLOGY

Freedman, M. (1970). Professional responsibilities of the civil practitioner, in D. Weck-
stein (ed.), *Education in the Professional Responsibilities of the Lawyer*, Charlottes-
ville: University Press of Virginia.
Fuller, L. (1961). The adversary system, in H. Berman (ed.), *Talks on American Law*,
New York: Vintage.
Goldberg v. Kelly, (1970), *U.S. Reports*, Vol. 397, 254–279.
Homans, G.C. (1961). *Social Behavior: Its Elementary Forms*, New York: Harcourt,
Brace and World.
Houlden, P., LaTour, S., Walker, L., and Thibaut, J. (1978). Preference for modes of
dispute resolution as a function of process and decision control, *Journal of Experi-
mental Social Psychology*, **14**, 13–30.
Jones, E.E. and Nisbett, R.E. (1971). *The Actor and the Observer: Divergent Percep-
tions of the Causes of Behavior*, New York: General Learning Press.
Kurtz, S. and Houlden, P. (1981). Preference for modes of conflict resolution by post
court-martial military personnel, *Basic and Applied Social Psychology*, **2**, 27–43.
LaTour, S. (1978). Determinants of participant and observer satisfaction with adversary
and inquisitorial modes of adjudication, *Journal of Personality and Social Psychology*,
36, 1531–1545.
LaTour, S., Houlden, P., Walker, L., and Thibaut, J. (1976). Some determinants of
preference for modes of conflict resolution, *Journal of Conflict Resolution*, **20**, 319–
356.
Lerner, M.J. and Whitehead, L.A. (1980). Procedural justice viewed in the context of
justice motive theory, in G. Mikula (ed.), *Justice and Social Interaction*, New York:
Springer-Verlag.
Leventhal, G.S. (1980). What should be done with equity theory? New approaches to
the study of fairness in social relationships, in K. Gergen, M. Greenberg, and R. Willis
(eds), *Social Exchange: Advances in Theory and Research*, New York: Plenum.
Leventhal, G.S., Karuza, J., and Fry, W.R. (1980). Beyond fairness: A theory of
allocation preferences, in G. Mikula (ed.), *Justice and Social Interaction*, New York:
Springer-Verlag.
Lind, E.A. (1975). The exercise of information influence in legal advocacy, *Journal of
Applied Social Psychology*, **5**, 127–143.
Lind, E.A., Erickson, B.E., Friedland, N., and Dickenberger, M. (1978). Reactions to
procedural models for adjudicative conflict resolution, *Journal of Conflict Resolution*,
22, 318–341.
Lind, E.A., Kurtz, S., Musante, L., Walker, L., and Thibaut, J. (1980). Procedure and
outcome effects on reactions to adjudicated resolution of conflicts of interest, *Journal
of Personality and Social Psychology*, **39**, 643–653.
Lind, E.A., Lissak, R.I. and Conlon, D.E. (1983). Decision control and process control
effects on procedural fairness judgments. Unpublished manuscript, University of
Illinois.
Lind, E.A. and Shapard, J.E. (1981). *Evaluation of Court-annexed Arbitration in Three
Federal District Courts*, Federal Judicial Center, Washington.
Lind, E.A., Thibaut, J., and Walker, L. (1973). Discovery and presentation of evidence
in adversary and non adversary proceedings, *Michigan Law Review*, **71**, 1129–1144.
Lind, E.A., Thibaut, J., and Walker, L. (1976). A cross-cultural comparison of the effect
of adversary and inquisitorial processes on bias in legal decisionmaking, *Virginia Law
Review*, **62**, 271–283.
Lind, E.A. and Walker L. (1979). Theory testing, theory development, and laboratory
research on legal issues, *Law and Human Behavior*, **3**, 5–19.
Pound, R. (1906). 'The causes of popular dissatisfaction with the administration of

justice.' Address presented to the annual meeting of the American Bar Association, St. Paul, Minnesota.

Sheppard, B.H. (1983). Third party conflict intervention: A procedural framework, in B. Staw and L. Cummings (eds), *Research in Organizational Behavior*, vol. 6, in press.

Sheppard, B.H. and Vidmar, N. (1980). Adversary pretrial procedures and testimonial evidence: Effects of lawyer's role and machiavellianism, *Journal of Personality and Social Psychology*, **39**, 320–332.

Thibaut, J.W. and Kelley, H.H. (1959). *Social Psychology of Groups*, New York: Wiley.

Thibaut, J. and Walker, L. (1975). *Procedural Justice: A Psychological Analysis*, New York: Erlbaum/Halstead.

Thibaut, J., and Walker, L. (1978). A theory of procedure, *California Law Review*, **66**, 541–566.

Thibaut, J., Walker, L., LaTour, S., and Houlden, P. (1974). Procedural justice as fairness, *Stanford Law Review*, **26**, 1271–1289.

Thibaut, J., Walker, L., and Lind, E.A. (1972). Adversary presentation and bias in legal decisionmaking, *Harvard Law Review*, **86**, 386–401.

Tyler, T.R. and Caine, A. (1981). The influence of outcomes and procedures on satisfaction with formal leaders, *Journal of Personality and Social Psychology*, **41**, 642–655.

Walker, L., LaTour, S., Lind, E.A. and Thibaut, J. (1974). Reactions of participants and observers to modes of adjudication, *Journal of Applied Social Psychology*, **4**, 295–310.

Walker, L., Lind, E.A. and Thibaut, J. (1979). The relation between procedural and distributive justice, *Virginia Law Review*, **65**, 1401–1420.

Author Index

Abelson, R.P., 124, 127
Abrahamson, L.Y., 154, 256
Adams, J.S., 185, 197, 204, 304, 307, 311
Adelman, L., 179, 180, 182
Adler, J.W., 309, 311
Aiken, M., 24, 26, 211, 257
Akers, R.H., 138, 139, 140, 157
Aldag, R., 261
Aldrich, H.E., 208, 209, 212, 216, 226,
    253, 256
Allegro, J.T., 223, 261
Allen, G., 54, 58
Allison, G.T., 163, 164, 180
Allport, F.H., 129, 130, 132, 139, 151,
    154, 157, 158, 215, 256
Anderson, L., 126
Anderson, N.H., 197, 204
Argyle, M., 123, 126
Arrowood, A.J., 190, 193, 204
Asch, S.G., 103, 104, 125
Ashton, P., 114, 125
Atkinson, J.W., 101, 117, 125
Averill, J.R., 258
Azuma, H., 181

Bachrach, L.L., 31, 51, 57, 58
Baddeley, A.D., 267, 277, 279, 281, 282,
    289
Bahn, A.K., 54, 58
Bakke, E.W., 6, 26
Bales, R.F., 192, 204, 246, 256
Balke, W.M., 179, 180
Bandura, A., 234, 254, 256
Ballachey, E.L., 158
Banks, M.H., 29
Bar-Tal, D., 116, 125
Bass, R.D., 61

Beales, H.L., 4, 6, 8, 11, 26
Becker, H.S., 125
Becker, S.W., 238, 257
Beez, W.V., 115, 125
Bell, C.R., 273, 289
Bekkers, F., 261
Benne, K.D., 157
Bennett, S.N., 98, 99, 101, 125
Bennis, W.G., 155, 157
Benoist, F., 259
Bentley, D., 272, 289
Berger, P.L., 20, 26, 218, 256
Bergman, J.T., 188, 205
Berlinger, D., 128
Bernstein, B., 119, 120, 125
Berrien, F.K., 213, 256
Berscheid, E., 206
Bickerman, T., 126
Bickman, L., 55, 58
Biddle, B.J., 94, 95, 126
Billig, M., 69, 90, 91
Binkhorst, D., 261
Blackburn, R., 19, 26
Blackman, D.E., 272, 273, 290
Blau, P.M., 210, 215, 256
Bonauito, G.B., 182
Boster, F.J., 287, 291
Bourdieu, P., 94, 120, 125
Bourgeois, L.J., 210, 212, 230, 256
Boutillier, R.G., 260
Boyer, E., 123, 128
Breed, W., 132, 133, 139, 157
Brehmer, B., 166, 167, 168, 169, 170,
    171, 172, 174, 175, 176, 177, 178,
    179, 180, 181, 182
Brenner, M.H., 4, 5, 13, 26
Briar, K.H., 8, 26

315

Broadbent, D.E., 277, 278, 281, 282, 284, 290
Brookover, W.B., 121, 125
Brophy, J.E., 94, 99, 100, 101, 113, 114, 115, 116, 120, 123, 125, 126
Brown, B., 126
Brown, L., 177, 181
Brown, R., 70, 71, 72, 90, 131, 157
Brunswik, E., 165, 181
Bucuvalas, M.J., 158
Bull, R., 278, 290
Bundy, R., 91
Burns, T., 209, 256
Burnstein, E., 200, 202, 204
Buss, A.H., 20, 26
Butcher, H.J., 110, 125
Butler, N.R., 127

Caine, A., 310, 313
Cantril, H., 132, 157
Carroll, J.B., 98, 125
Carroll, P., 3, 26
Carter, J., 172, 179, 183
Cartwright, D., 222, 256
Catalano, R., 4, 26, 27
Cavan, R.S., 7, 26
Chertkoff, J.M., 191, 193, 205
Child, J., 207, 212, 256, 257
Chin, R., 157
Christie, D., 279, 290
Clarke, D.E., 123, 126
Clifford, B.R., 278, 279, 284, 290
Cobb, S., 4, 5, 11, 13, 22, 23, 26, 28
Codol, J.C., 71, 91
Cohen, J., 19, 30
Cohen, L.J., 273, 274, 275, 290
Conlon, D.E., 312
Cooke, R.A., 208, 212, 213, 215, 218, 219, 220, 221, 222, 223, 230, 241, 260
Coopersmith, S., 117, 126
Coulthard, R.M., 123, 128
Cowan, J.R., 29
Cragg, A., 15, 26
Craig, J.R., 253, 258
Croll, P., 126
Crutchfield, R.S., 158
Cummings, A., 258

Daniel, W.W., 6, 22, 26
Davenport, P.R., 8, 27

Davie, R., 127
Davies, F., 125
Davies, G.M., 279, 289, 290
Davis, J.H., 219, 235, 257, 294, 311
Dawes, R.M., 165, 181
Dawson, T., 15, 26
Day, J.V., 218, 257
Day, R., 218, 257
De Cecco, J.P., 114, 126
Deffenbacher, K.A., 285, 290
De Jong, R.D., 259
Delamont, S., 123, 128
Deschamps, J.C., 70, 71, 72, 90, 91
Deutsch, M., 192, 193, 203, 204
Devine, P., 285, 291
Dickenberger, M., 312
Dill, W.R., 208, 257
DiMajo, G., 182
Dingwall, R., 268, 290
Doeringer, P.B., 19, 26
Doise, W., 69, 91
Dooley, D., 4, 26, 27
Douglas, J.W.B., 119, 126
Downey, H., 212, 216, 257
DuBick, M.A., 210, 257
Duff, E., 4, 5, 7, 8, 10, 20, 28
Duggan, J., 291
Duncan, R., 208, 212, 217, 254, 257
Dunkin, M.J., 94, 95, 126

Ebbesen, E.E., 283, 284, 285, 286, 290, 291
Ebmeier, H., 126
Ebner, P., 309, 311
Edwards, J., 108, 109, 126
Eekalaar, J., 290
Eggleston, R., 273, 274, 290
Ehrlich, H.J., 87, 91
Einhorn, H.J., 169, 172, 181
Eisenberg, P., 4, 6, 7, 10, 11, 19, 27
Elashoff, J.D., 115, 126
Eltis, K., 108, 126
Emerson, R.M., 194, 196, 204
Erickson, B.E., 312
Erickson, E.L., 125
Esser, J.K., 191, 205
Evertson, C.M., 99, 100, 101, 113, 115, 120, 123, 125, 126

Faden, V.B., 58
Fagin, L., 4, 6, 7, 17, 24, 27

Falbo, T., 255, 257
Farkas, A.J., 197, 204
Farrington, D.P., 265, 267, 290
Faucheux, C., 182, 189, 206
Feather, N.T., 8, 27
Felstiner, W.F., 311
Ferman, L.A., 26
Ferracuti, F., 135, 159
Festinger, L., 69, 91, 218–257
Fincham, F.P., 275, 290
Fiedler, F.E., 192, 204, 210, 213, 257
Fields, J.M., 133, 139, 157
Finch, S., 114, 119, 121, 127
Fineman, S., 17, 23, 24, 27
Fink, S.L., 8, 12, 27
Flament, C., 91
Flanders, N., 123, 126
Fletcher, D.J., 183
Folger, R., 310, 311
Fraser, C., 11, 18, 24, 27
Freedman, M., 300, 312
French, Jr., J.R.P., 219, 257
Frender, R., 110, 126
Friedland, N., 312
Friedlander, F., 217, 257
Frieze, I., 128
Frieze, L., 261
Frohlich, W.D., 182
Fryer, D., 11, 17, 21, 24, 27
Fry, W.R., 312
Fuller, L., 297, 298, 299, 312
Furnham, A., 25, 27
Furst, N.F., 94, 95, 127

Galton, M., 99, 126
Gamson, W.A., 190, 191, 204
Georgepoulus, B.S., 215, 260
Gergen, K.J., 20, 27, 117, 126
Giles, H., 110, 126
Gilly, M., 91
Glaser, B., 287, 290
Goffman, E., 56, 58, 137, 138, 140, 157
Goldberg, D.P., 6, 27
Goldberg, I.D., 54, 58
Golderg, L.R., 168, 182
Good, T., 94, 114, 115, 116, 125, 126
Goodacre, E.J., 126
Goodchild, J.D., 8, 11, 27
Gordon, C., 117, 126
Gore, S., 8, 27, 28
Gorwitz, K., 58

Gould, T., 4, 5, 27
Gowler, D., 15, 27
Gray, E.A., 58
Greer, D., 267, 290
Grob, G.N., 55, 58
Groot, R., 218, 261
Grouws, D., 115, 126
Gruneberg, M.M., 281, 290
Gruninger, W., 157
Gundelach, J., 214, 215, 257
Gurnee, H., 199, 204
Gurney, R.M., 1, 3, 4, 11, 24, 27
Guttman, J., 116, 125

Hagafors, R., 170, 181, 182
Hage, J., 211, 257
Haines, H., 4, 28
Hallworth, H.J., 112, 126
Hamachek, D.E., 125
Hamilton, V.L., 275, 290
Hammond, K.R., 165, 166, 168, 172,
    173, 174, 175, 176, 177, 178, 179,
    180, 181, 182
Haren, T. van, 213, 218, 261
Hargreaves, D.H., 100, 102, 103, 105,
    106, 111, 112, 126
Harnischfeger, A., 98, 126
Harre, R., 124, 127
Harrison, R., 6, 7, 8, 21, 24, 27
Hart, H.L.A., 271, 275, 276, 291
Hartley, J.F., 4, 6, 8, 12, 15, 16, 17, 21, 22,
    23, 24. 27, 28
Hastie, R., 265, 279, 292
Haupt, B.J., 43, 57, 58, 59
Hawkins, K.O., 265, 267, 290
Hayner, N.S., 157
Hayes, J., 5, 9, 10, 28
Hazewinkel, A., 210, 256, 257
Heather, N., 20, 28
Hellriegel, D., 257
Hemmer, G.J.F., 213, 214, 227, 233, 256,
    257, 259
Hensler, D.R., 311
Hepwroth, S.J., 4, 5, 6, 7, 8, 9, 23, 24, 28
Hickson, D.J., 209, 220, 223, 231, 235,
    239, 248, 252, 255, 257
Hilgendorf, E.L., 286, 291
Hinings, C.R., 210, 220, 257
Hill, J.M., 4, 6, 7, 8, 9, 12, 19, 28
Hinds, W.C., 131, 158
Hoffman, P.J., 168, 169, 172, 182, 183

Holley, B.J., 125
Homans, G.C., 187, 188, 204, 215, 257, 307, 312
Honore, M.M., 275, 276, 291
Hook, L.H., 238, 260
Horst, C. van der, 261
Horwitz, M., 213, 257
Houlden, P., 305, 306, 312
House, R.J., 230, 257
Howells, L.T., 238, 257
Huber, G.P., 210, 212, 258
Huczynski, A., 17, 24, 28
Hunt, R.G., 211, 258
Hursch, C.J., 182
Hursch, J.L., 175, 182
Husen, J., 93, 119, 127

Inman, M., 286, 291
Irving, B., 286, 291

Jackson, P.R., 29
Jackson, R., 26
Jacobson, L., 115, 127
Jahoda, M., 4, 6, 7, 8, 9, 10, 11, 13, 16, 17, 18, 28
Jaspars, J.M., 275, 290
Jennergren, L.P., 214, 258
Johansson, R., 181, 182
Jones, D., 121, 127
Jones, E.G., 307, 312
Jones, K.R., 60
Joyce, C.R.B., 182

Kahn, R.L., 213, 215, 217, 258
Kahneman, D., 165, 171, 183, 273, 292
Karuza, J., 312
Kasl, S.V., 4, 5, 6, 8, 11, 13, 22, 23, 26, 28
Katz, D., 129, 130, 132, 139, 158, 213, 215, 217, 258
Katz, S., 200, 202, 204
Kaufman, H.G., 4, 8, 22, 28
Kauffman, K., 138, 139, 140, 157, 158
Kavcic, B., 261
Keen, P., 125
Kelley, H.H., 131, 158, 188, 190, 193, 204, 206, 218, 258, 273, 291, 306, 313
Kellmer Pringle, M.L., 119, 127
Kelly, E.L., 134, 158
Kelvin, P., 9, 25, 28
Kenny, A., 272, 273, 291

Kenyon, J., 4, 5, 27
Khandwalla, P.N., 210, 358
Kiesler, C.A., 31, 32, 33, 34, 35, 37, 38, 42, 44, 49, 50, 52, 53, 55, 56, 57, 58, 59
King, M., 266, 287, 291
King, R., 120, 127
Kingsley, S., 6, 8, 12, 28
Kinn, J.M., 6, 28
Kirk, D., 257
Klee, G.D., 58
Kleinmuntz, B., 181
Kleinmuntz, D.N., 181
Klofas, J., 129, 157, 158
Komarovsky, M., 6, 7, 28
Komorita, S.S., 188, 190, 191, 193, 194, 195, 197, 198, 204, 205
Konecni, V.J., 283, 284, 285, 286, 290, 291
Korman, A.K., 210, 258
Korte, C., 134, 139, 158
Kostron, L., 177, 181
Kotinsky, R., 137, 140, 158
Kounin, J.S., 100, 127
Kramer, M., 58
Kravitz, P., 197, 205
Krech, D., 131, 132, 158
Kreveld, D. van, 246, 256, 258
Ktsanes, T., 132, 133, 139, 157
Kukla, A., 128, 261
Kurtz, S., 305, 312
Kuylenstierna, J., 170, 181, 182

Lambert, R.S., 4, 6, 8, 11, 26
Lambert, W.E., 126, 127
Langer, E.J., 235, 254, 258, 260
LaTour, S., 304, 305, 307, 312, 313
Lawrence, P.R., 207, 208, 210, 211, 212, 213, 217, 236, 237, 241, 258
Lazarsfeld, P.F., 4, 6, 7, 8, 10, 11, 19, 27, 28, 30
Lazarus, R.S., 254, 258
Leavitt, H.J., 213, 248, 258
Leavitt, N.J., 237, 258
Leblebici, H., 211, 259
Lee, C.A., 257
Legge, K., 15, 27
Leifer, R., 210, 258
Le Pere, J.M., 125
Lerner, M.J., 308, 312
Leung, A.S., 201, 205

Leventhal, G.S., 187, 188, 198, 205, 308, 312
Levine, E.L., 214, 255, 258
Lewin, K., 155, 158
Licata, J.W., 136, 158
Lichtenstein, S., 166, 168, 182
Liem, J., 6, 7, 28
Liem, R., 4, 6, 7, 28
Liljergren, J., 181
Lima, L.H., 60
Lind, E.A., 293, 295, 296, 299, 300, 301, 305, 309, 310, 312, 313
Linden, W. van der, 255, 258
Lindsay, R.C.L., 279, 292
Lissak, R.I., 312
Little, C., 24, 28
Lloyd-Bostock, S.M.A., 265, 273, 275, 276, 277, 279, 280, 284, 286, 291
Locke, E.A., 222, 258
Lord, R.G., 235, 238, 258
Lorenzi-Cioldi, F., 70, 72, 91
Lorsch, J.W., 207, 208, 210, 211, 212, 213, 217, 236, 237, 241
Lowin, A., 253, 258
Luce, R.D., 197, 205
Luckman, T., 256

McAllister, D.W., 256
Mackay, K., 4, 28
McBarnet, D., 268, 291
McClintock, C.G., 192, 205
McHuge, F., 256
McKinley, W., 256
Madigan, C., 22, 29
Malpass, R., 285, 291
Mann, M., 19, 26
March, J.G., 209, 221, 258, 259
Marsden, D., 4, 5, 7, 8, 10, 20, 28
Martin, J., 15, 28
Marvin, B.A., 168, 179, 182
Matza, D., 135, 136, 140, 154, 155, 157, 158
Mechanic, D., 55, 59
Meek, D., 195, 205
Merton, R.K., 94, 127, 150, 151, 158
Meyer, B., 91
Meyer, G.D., 180
Meyer, N.G., 59
Michaels, J.W., 187, 205
Michela, S.C., 218, 258
Michlin, M., 127

Miers, D., 271, 292
Mikula, G., 189, 191, 192, 200, 203, 205
Milazzo-Sayre, J.L., 60
Miller, C.E., 191, 205
Miller, G.R., 287, 291
Miller, M.J., 175, 176, 182
Mills, T.M., 256
Mindlin, S., 208, 256
Mitchell, T.R., 256
Mohr, L.B., 210, 211, 259
Moien, M., 59
Moore, D., 195, 205
Morgan, W.R., 187, 205
Morley, I.E., 91, 185, 205
Morley-Bunker, N., 7, 28
Morris, P.E., 291
Morton-Williams, R., 114, 119, 121, 127
Moscovici, S., 68, 69, 91, 182
Mulder, M., 210, 230, 259, 261
Mumpower, J.L., 182
Murnighan, J.K., 205
Murray, T., 290
Musante, L., 312

Nash, J.F., 196, 197, 205
Nash, R., 94, 106, 114, 127
Nebergall, R.E., 127
Neganda, A.R., 210, 259
Neisser, U., 71, 91
Neisser, V., 281, 291
Nelson, A.B., 59
Newcomb, T.M., 134, 158
Nisbett, R.E., 172, 182, 273, 291, 307, 312
Noble, M., 29
Norris, G., 22, 28
Nutman, P., 5, 9, 10, 28

O'Barr, W.M., 285, 291
O'Conell, M.J., 258
O'Gorman, H.J., 133, 134, 139, 158
Ossterbaan, H., 259
Oostrum, J. van, 207, 213, 214, 215, 219, 223, 229, 231, 241, 243, 248, 252, 259, 260
Opton, Jr., R.H., 258
Orne, M.T., 109, 127

Packard, J.S., 136, 137, 140, 158
Palmonari, A., 63, 64, 65, 66, 91
Passeron, J.C., 94, 120, 125

Payne, R., 6, 7, 11, 17, 18, 23, 24, 27, 28, 30
Pearson, Lord, 280, 291
Pennings, J., 208, 210, 211, 214, 215, 216, 257, 259
Pepitone, A., 18, 28
Perrow, C., 208, 210, 211, 219, 223, 259
Peterson, M.A., 311
Petrullo, L., 104, 128
Pfeffer, J., 208, 209, 211, 212, 215, 216, 220, 253, 256, 259
Phares, E.J., 254, 259
Paichaud, D., 18, 29
Piche, G., 108, 127
Pickle, H., 257
Piedmont, E.B., 5, 6, 7, 29
Piore, M.J., 19, 26
Pombeni, M.L., 63, 91
Poole, M.E., 121, 127
Popper, K.R., 96, 127
Pound, R., 302, 312
Powell, D.H., 6, 29
Powesland, P., 110, 216
Pruitt, D.G., 189, 205
Pym, D.M., 15, 29

Quarnström, G., 168, 181

Rabbie, J.M., 207, 210, 212, 213, 214, 215, 218, 219, 223, 229, 230, 231, 236, 241, 248, 252, 257, 258, 259, 260
Rabbitt, P.M.R., 278, 285, 292
Raiffa, H., 196, 197, 205
Ranke, K.H., 7, 26
Ranofsky, A.L., 59, 60
Rapoport, A., 194, 197, 205
Raven, B.H., 219, 257
Rayman, P., 28
Redick, R.W., 60
Reed, L., 128, 261
Reid, I., 110, 127
Reimann, B.C., 210, 259, 260
Rest, S., 128, 261
Rice, A.K., 217, 260
Rist, R., 122, 127, 128
Ritsema van Eck, J.R., 259, 261
Roberts, C., 15, 28
Roberts, K., 3, 29
Robinson, W.P., 93, 110, 113, 119, 120, 121, 127

Rodin, J., 254, 260
Rohrbaugh, J., 182
Rorer, L.G., 182
Rosch, G., 106, 127
Roseborough, M.E., 256
Rosenbaum, R.M., 128, 261
Rosenshine, B., 94, 95, 127
Rosenstein, M.J., 60
Rosenthal, R., 115, 127
Rosner, M., 261
Ross, L., 273, 291
Roth, A.E., 205
Rotter, J.B., 254, 260
Rubin, D., 127
Rubin, J., 55, 60
Rush, H., 4, 10, 16, 17, 28

Saks, M.J., 265, 279, 292
Salancik, G.R., 208, 220, 259
Saltzer, E.B., 254, 260
Sarason, S.B., 101, 127
Sawyer, J., 187, 205
Schanck, R.L., 130, 131, 132, 135, 139, 154, 158
Schank, R., 124, 127
Schneck, R.E., 257
Schreyögg, G., 360
Schuman, H., 133, 139, 157
Schweiger, D.H., 222, 260
Schwinger, T., 189, 200, 205
Seabrook, J., 4, 5, 29
Secord, P., 124, 127
Seeman, M., 141, 158
Seligman, C.R., 107, 108, 109, 110, 127
Seligman, M.E.P., 235, 254, 256, 260
Shank, E.L., 60
Shanthamani, V.S., 4, 29
Shaphard, J.E., 309, 312
Shapley, L.S., 196, 205, 206
Shaw, M.E., 200, 206, 240, 260
Sheppard, B.H., 302, 308, 313
Shepherd, G., 6, 29
Sheppard, H.L., 26
Sherif, C.W., 109, 127
Sherif, M., 90, 91, 127
Shubik, M., 196, 206
Silbulkin, A.E., 31, 32, 33, 34, 35, 37, 38, 42, 44, 49, 50, 52, 53, 56, 57, 58, 59
Simon, A., 123, 128
Simon, B., 126
Simon, H.A., 165, 182, 259, 260

Sinclair, J. McH., 123, 218
Sinfield, A., 18, 19, 29
Sirrocco, A., 57, 60
Slater, R.S., 8, 17, 23, 24, 29
Slocum, J., 257
Slovic, P., 166, 168, 172, 182, 183
Smeenk, G., 261
Smith, E.E., 8, 11
Smith, M.B., 136, 158
Sneath, F., 21, 30
Snow, R.E., 115, 126
Sofer, C., 9, 29
Sorrentino, C., 14, 29
Sorrentino, R.M., 260
Stafford, E.M., 3, 6, 9, 12, 23, 29
Stalker, G.M., 209, 256
Stallings, J., 101, 115, 128
Stanfield, G.C., 211, 260
Steers, R.M., 220, 260
Steiner, I.D., 199, 200, 206
Steinmann, D.O., 182
Stemerding, A., 210, 230, 259
Stephenson, G.M., 185, 205
Stern, J., 25, 29
Stewart, T.R., 172, 179, 183
Stewart, T.T., 180
Stokes, G., 6, 29
Storey, R., 261
Strahan, G.W., 60
Strauss, A., 287, 290
Streufert, S., 222, 260
Stringer, P., 228, 292
Strodtbeck, F.L., 238, 256, 260
Stubbs, M., 123, 128
Sullivan, A., 127
Sullivan, D.B., 210, 260
Summers, D.A., 172, 183
Sutton, J.F., 60
Swinburne, P., 4, 6, 12, 29
Sykes, R.R., 290

Tagiuri, R., 104, 128
Tajfel, H., 69, 70, 74, 87, 89, 90, 91, 117, 128
Taliaferro, D.J., 183
Tannenbaum, A.S., 208, 212, 213, 214, 215, 216, 218, 219, 220, 221, 222, 223, 230, 233, 235, 240, 241, 250, 251, 253, 255, 260, 261
Tapp, J., 265, 292
Taube, C.A., 58, 59, 60

Tausky, C., 5, 6, 7, 29
Taylor, K., 4, 11, 24, 27
Taylor, L., 15, 29
Tesdale, J.D., 256
Tetzschner, H., 214, 255, 257
Thibaut, J., 4, 131, 158, 188, 189, 206, 293, 297, 298, 299, 305, 306, 307, 308, 311, 312, 313
Thomas, B., 22, 29
Thomas, S., 125
Thomas, W.I., 94, 128
Thompson, J.D., 217, 261
Tiffany, D.W., 6, 29
Tiffany, P.M., 29
Tikunoff, W., 115, 128
Toch, H., 129, 157, 158
Tosi, H., 212, 216, 261
Tracy, P.K., 256
Tucker, G.R., 127
Tucker, L.R., 175, 183
Tuerk, I., 58
Tumonis, T., 190, 205
Turner, J., 70, 71, 91, 117, 128
Tversky, A., 165, 171, 183, 273, 292
Twining, W.L., 267, 268, 269, 270, 271, 289, 292
Tyler, T.F., 310, 313

Varonos, D.D., 181
Veen, P., 211, 213, 218, 220, 261
Vernooy, L., 259
Vianello, M., 261
Vidmar, N., 302, 313
Vischi, T.R., 33, 48, 49, 60
Visser, L., 218, 231, 252, 259, 260, 261
Vreugdenhil, G.C., 213, 214, 241, 243, 248, 256, 260, 261

Walker, A., 18
Walker, L., 293, 296, 297, 303, 304, 305, 306, 307, 308, 312, 313
Walster, E., 187, 188, 206
Walster, G.W., 206
Warr, P.B., 4, 5, 6, 7, 9, 12, 21, 23, 28, 29, 30
Webster, Jr., M., 246, 261
Wedderburn, D., 6, 30
Weick, K.E., 223, 253, 261
Weinberger, M., 69, 91
Weiner, B., 101, 116, 117, 124, 128, 254, 261

Wieser, G., 261
Weiss, D.H., 156, 157, 158
Wells, G.L., 279, 292
Wheeler, S., 138, 139, 140, 154, 158
White, R.W., 234, 261
Whitehead, L.A., 308, 312
Wiggins, N., 169, 183
Wiley, D.G., 98, 126
Wilkens, G., 210, 214, 230, 259
Williams, F., 108, 109, 110, 111, 128
Williams, G., 273, 292
Williams, R., 21, 30
Willower, D.J., 136, 137, 140, 158

Wilson, T.D., 182
Witkin, M.J., 61
Witmer, H.L., 137, 140, 158
Wolfgang, M.E., 135, 159
Wood, S., 19, 20, 30
Woodhead, M., 279, 289

Zander, A., 222, 256
Zani, B., 66, 91
Zavalloni, M., 92
Zawadski, B., 4, 8, 30
Zeisel, H., 28

Subject Index

Decision-making in the classroom
and criterion-reference, 112
and expectation, 113
and instructional activities, 112
and intergroup relations, 122
and personality, 105, 106
and person perception, 102, 104
and progress-reference, 112
and social identity, 105, 106
and speech and accent, 109, 110
teachers' theories, 125

Efficient teaching, 99
and active learning time, 98
and Attribution Theory, 101
and classroom interaction, 94
and management, 100
and norm-reference, 98
and process–product relationships, 101
and process variables, 99
and socio-economic status, 99
and teaching styles, 101
theories of learning and development, 101
Environmental uncertainty and organizations
experimental hypotheses, 216–223, 236–241
experimental results, 223–234, 243–252

Hospitals, 31–57
general, 42–44
private mental, 47–48
psychiatric unit, 33, 42–44
state mental, 44–46
Veterans Administration, 37–42

Law and psychology methodology, 266, 283–287, 289
multimethod approaches, 283–287
staged event methods, 278, 279
Law and psychology relationships
academic law, 266, 270
behaviourism, 272–273
courts, 267, 268, 269, 279, 283–286, 287
ecological validity (see 'real world' research and settings)
eyewitness research, 267, 268, 269, 270, 278–279, 284
goals of applied research, 288–289
juries, 267, 268, 269, 283
legal literature, 266, 269, 271–277
legal models and standpoints, 267, 268–271
mens rea, 271, 272–273
probabilities, 273–275
problem-oriented research, 266, 277–278
problems, definitions of, 266–271
'real world' research and settings, 265, 277, 278, 279, 281–282, 283, 284–286
relationship between pure and applied research, 277–283, 288–289
responsibility, 271, 272, 275–277, 280–281
rules, 271
Law and psychology theory
development of, 266, 267, 277–283
feedback into from applied research, 266, 267, 277–283
use of in applied research, 286–287, 289

323

Length of hospital stay
  American Hospital Association
    (AHA), 34, 36, 44–45
  average, 31–57
  Community Mental Health Centres
    (CMHCs), 48–49
  deinstitutionalization, 31–33, 52
  median, 39, 42–46, 48
  mental disorders, 31–57
  mental health policy, 31, 51, 55
  mental hospitalization, 31–57
  National Center for Health Statistics
    (NCHS), 34, 36, 42, 45–46
  National Institute of Mental Health
    (NIMH), 32, 34–35, 42–46, 48
  National Hospital Discharge Survey
    (NHDS), 36, 42
  National Master Facility Inventory
    (NMFI), 45–47
  nursing homes, 32, 36, 52
  Veterans Administration (VA), 36–42,
    45

Organizations
  and laboratory groups, 212–214
  contingency theory approaches,
    207–214, 254–256
  effectiveness and uncertainty, 220–223
  environmental uncertainty and
    perceived power, 214–218
  hierarchization, 218–220, 252–254
  hypotheses, 216–223

Pluralistic ignorance, 129–159
  and alienation, 146–147
  and anxiety, 135–136
  and assimilation, 133, 138, 143
  and change implications, 130, 154–155
  and conflict, 138, 140, 153
  and conformity, 130–132, 153
  and conservatism, 133
  and consistency, 144
  and corrections officers, 138–154
  and custodial subcultures, 136–139
  and cynicism, 134–136
  and delinquency, 135–136
  and disaggregation, 140–152
  and ethnic discrimination, 129–130,
    132–134
  and extreme, 149–150
  and feedback of data, 143, 155

  and group norms, 131, 155
  and index, 145–146
  and inmate subculture, 136–139
  and intensity of opinion, 134, 149
  and J-curve, 130–131
  and minority and majority, 150–151
  and resistance to change, 132
  and risk taking, 131–132
  and student radicalism, 134
  and teachers, 135
  and term origin, 130
  typology of, 147–148
Procedural models
  and Canada, 297
  and cognitive conflict, 308
  and complaints, 310
  and conflict of interests, 307
  and equity norms, 307
  and expectancy bias, 297–300
  and fairness judgments, 302–306
  and France, 297, 299
  and information search, 300–302
  and legislation, 310
  and mediation, 309
  and reform process, 294
  and research methods, 295–297
  and theory of procedure, 306–308
  and theory testing, 295–296
  and truth disputes, 306
  and United Kingdom, 297
  and United States, 297
  and West Germany, 297
Professional orientations
  and category differentiation, 69, 70
  and comparisons, 69, 70, 71, 72, 74, 76,
    78, 82, 87
  and group membership, 69, 70, 78, 84
  and ingroups, 63, 68, 70, 72, 76, 84, 85,
    87, 88
  and intergroup categorization, 70
  and intergroup relationships, 69, 70,
    88, 89
  and intragroup identification, 70, 72
  and outgroups, 63, 68, 72, 76, 82, 84,
    87
  and process of social categorization, 69,
    70
  and professional category, 63, 68, 71,
    72
  and professional role, 66, 82
  and professionalization, 64, 74, 87

and psychologists, 63, 64, 65, 71, 73, 76, 80, 82, 84, 87, 88, 89, 90
and self, 63, 70, 72, 82, 84, 85, 87, 88
and self-evaluation, 70
and similarity/differentiation, 71, 72, 74, 78, 80, 82, 84, 85, 87, 88, 89
and social and medical services, 63, 65, 71
and social groups, 69, 70, 71
and social identity, 64, 65, 68, 69, 70, 71, 72, 78, 80, 84, 88, 89
and social representations, 63, 64, 65, 68, 69, 72, 88, 89, 90
and typical structures, 78, 79, 80, 81, 88
Psychiatric care, impatient, 31–37
    alternative, 31–32, 55–56
    discharges, 34–37
    discharge days, 35–36
    episodes, 33–34, 49–55
    readmissions, 54–55
    residents, 33–34, 45
    revolving door, 54

Rational actor paradigm, 163–164, 178–179
Reward allocation, 187, 196, 198, 201, 202, 203, 204
    and arbitration, 197, 203, 204
    and bargaining, 185, 188, 192, 196, 197, 203
    and bargaining strength (see power)
    and coalition (coalition theories), 190, 191, 193, 194, 195, 196
    and comparison level for alternatives, 188, 189, 194, 195, 197
    and conflict (conflict resolution), 189, 192, 193, 203
    and dependence (see interdependence)
    and distributive justice (see equity)
    and equality norm, 192, 193, 198, 200, 201, 202, 203
    and equity (equity theory), 187, 188, 191, 192, 193, 196, 197, 198, 199, 200, 202, 203, 204

and group performance, 187, 192, 196, 197, 198, 199, 200, 201, 203, 204
and inputs, 188, 192, 193, 196, 197, 198, 199, 200, 201, 202, 203
and interdependence, 194, 196, 197, 199, 200, 201, 202
and justice (see equity)
and power, 188, 191, 192, 194, 195, 196, 197, 198, 200, 203, 204
and social policy, 185, 193, 202, 203, 204
and task performance (see group performance)

Self-fulfilling prophecy, 99
    and categorization, 117
    and comparisons, 117–118
    and self-esteem, 117
Social Judgment Theory (SJT), 165–180
    in applied settings, 179–180
    computer graphics system, 179
    conflict reduction, 176–178
    findings, 168–173
    in interpersonal conflict (IPC), 174–176, 178
    lens model equation (LME), 175–176
    linear model, 167
    multiple-cue probability learning (MPL) paradigm, 174
    quasi-rational processes, 172

Unemployment
    concept of, 14
    moderator variables, 8, 18, 19, 23
    poverty, 18
    problems of methodology, 3, 11, 14
    psychological deprivation, 9, 16, 18, 20, 23
    psychopathology, 4
    self-esteem, 6, 12, 13
    social isolation, 6, 8
    stages of response to, 7, 8, 24

DATE DUE

DEMCO 38-297